MOVING OUT OF POVERTY, VOLUME 3

The Promise of Empowerment and Democracy in India

About the Series

The Moving Out of Poverty series presents the results of new comparative research across more than 500 communities in 15 countries on how and why poor people move out of poverty. The findings lay the foundations for new policies that will promote inclusive growth and just societies, and move millions out of poverty.

The series was launched in 2007 under the editorial direction of Deepa Narayan, former senior adviser in the World Bank. She earlier directed the pathbreaking Voices of the Poor project.

Titles in the Moving Out of Poverty series:

Moving
Out of
Poverty

VOLUME 3

The Promise of Empowerment and Democracy in India

Deepa Narayan, Editor

A COPUBLICATION OF PALGRAVE MACMILLAN
AND THE WORLD BANK

©2009 The International Bank for Reconstruction and Development / The World Bank
1818 H Street NW
Washington DC 20433
Telephone: 202-473-1000
Internet: www.worldbank.org
E-mail: feedback@worldbank.org

A copublication of The World Bank and Palgrave Macmillan.

PALGRAVE MACMILLAN
Palgrave Macmillan in the UK is an imprint of Macmillan Publishers Limited, registered in England, company number 785998, of Houndmills, Basingstoke, Hampshire, RG21 6XS.

Palgrave Macmillan in the US is a division of St Martin's Press LLC, 175 Fifth Avenue, New York, NY 10010.

Palgrave Macmillan is the global academic imprint of the above companies and has companies and representatives throughout the world.

Palgrave® and Macmillan® are registered trademarks in the United States, the United Kingdom, Europe, and other countries.

This volume is a product of the staff of the International Bank for Reconstruction and Development / The World Bank. The findings, interpretations, and conclusions expressed in this volume do not necessarily reflect the views of the Executive Directors of The World Bank or the governments they represent.

The World Bank does not guarantee the accuracy of the data included in this work. The boundaries, colors, denominations, and other information shown on any map in this work do not imply any judgement on the part of The World Bank concerning the legal status of any territory or the endorsement or acceptance of such boundaries.

ISBN: 978-0-8213-7217-3 *(softcover)*   eISBN: 978-0-8213-7218-0 *(softcover)*
ISBN: 978-0-8213-7838-0 *(hardcover)*   DOI: 10.1596/978-0-8213-7217-3
ISSN: None

Library of Congress Cataloging-in-Publication Data has been applied for.

Cover design: Drew Fasick
Cover photograph: Brice Richard

Printed in the United States

Dedication

To the thousands of women, men, and youth who took the time
to share with us their experiences, their hopes, and their dreams

Contents

Tables

Figures

Boxes

Book ti: *y20*

Preface

au nxt pg.

India is the rising star of the world. It has achieved unprecedented growth in the past several years, 7–9 percent annually. It has some of the world's richest billionaires. And it has millions and millions of people still living in poverty, especially in the rural areas, where 60 percent of the population lives. The number of poor people living on less than $1 a day declined from 296 million in 1981 to 267 million in 2005. The global dollar-a-day standard has recently been revised to $1.25 a day. By this measure, the number of poor people in India has actually increased during the same period, from 421 million to 456 million. Regardless of the measure, India still faces a huge poverty problem.

Growth is good. But consistently uneven growth creates unequal worlds. Average income in the richest states of India is five times the average in the poorer states, a gap greater than in any other democracy. Growing economic inequality has many social and political implications. The spread of the Naxalite (communist) movement, often accompanied by violence, overlaps almost perfectly with the map of poverty and marginality. The movement now affects 170 of India's 602 districts. The prime minister of India, Dr. Manmohan Singh, declared in 2006, "It would not be an exaggeration to say that the problem of Naxalism is the single biggest internal security challenge ever faced by our country." Hence understanding and eliminating poverty is not only a moral issue but also is essential to India's national security.

There are thousands of studies on poverty in India—why one more? This study was motivated by three broad concerns. If 30 to 40 percent of the population of our country is still poor six decades after independence, it is hard to avoid the conclusion that some new approaches must be tried. Second, there has been no large study that attempts to understand *how to escape poverty* from the perspectives of poor people themselves who have recently managed to exit poverty. Finally, the existing studies are largely based on the same assumptions that underlie existing poverty reduction strategies.

Our study, Moving Out of Poverty, also is not perfect, but we do four things differently. First, we focus on understanding realities from the bottom up, learning from individuals and communities about their efforts to move out of poverty or avoid falling into poverty—and about how and why they sometimes succeed. Second, we focus on understanding the dynamics of social, political, and economic institutions at the local level and how they facilitate or hinder poor people's attempts to climb the well-being ladder. Third, we focus on the complex processes that are hidden beneath net poverty rates: specifically, we disentangle the two distinct dynamics of upward and downward mobility. And fourth, we let people tell their own stories, including those who have moved out of poverty, those stuck in poverty, those who have fallen into poverty, and those who were never poor. In the process we glean findings, some unexpected, that can contribute to more effective poverty reduction efforts.

We found, for example, that poor people are not lazy—they take as many initiatives as the rich, and yet they remain poor. Why? They are constrained by inadequate capital, lack of connections to markets, and lack of business skills. Local markets all too often are captured by the rich. Local-level democracy makes a difference to a lucky few, helping them move out of poverty, but often this gain comes at the expense of the rest of the community. In other words, local democracy works as a zero-sum game. Access to local economic opportunities matters tremendously for moving up and out of poverty, but health care is perhaps the most critical factor in preventing falls back into poverty. The formal private sector rarely features in people's accounts of how they accumulated assets; civil society is mentioned but plays a surprisingly small role in asset accumulation. Finally, in the state of Assam, which has had low-intensity conflict for decades, we find no difference between peaceful and high-conflict communities in their rates of poverty mobility. Central government transfers make a difference, and this has important implications for areas of violent insurgencies in high-poverty contexts.

We hope this study will provoke thought, generate debate, and lead to changes and refinements in India's poverty reduction strategies.

Deepa Narayan
Editor and Project Director
Moving Out of Poverty

NA

Acknowledgments

This book draws on the contributions of many people who supported the global Moving Out of Poverty research project, of which the India study is one part. The project was led and managed by Deepa Narayan, who served from 2002 through 2008 as senior adviser in the Poverty Reduction and Economic Management (PREM) Network of the World Bank, first in the Poverty Reduction Group and subsequently in the vice president's office within PREM.

The project would never have started if not for the insistence of John Page, then director of the Poverty Reduction Group, and Gobind Nankani, then vice president of PREM. Successors to both continued their support, including Luca Barbone and Ana Revenga, directors of the Poverty Reduction Group; Louise Cord and Sudhir Shetty, sector managers in the Poverty Reduction Group; and Danny Leipziger, vice president of PREM. We also gratefully acknowledge Lyn Squire and his successor, Gobind Nankani, of the Global Development Network for their support throughout the project, particularly with respect to the studies of conflict-affected communities, including Assam.

The global project was supported by a loose network of advisers who provided valuable guidance and encouragement at different stages of the project. They included Stefan Dercon, Alan Gelb, Ashraf Ghani, Naila Kabeer, Ravi Kanbur, Steen Jorgensen, Praful Patel, Amartya Sen, Rehman Sobhan, Eva Tobisson, and Ashutosh Varshney. Charles Tilly was an invaluable adviser in so many ways. He was brave enough to join us in a technical workshop held in St. Petersburg, Russia, in January 2006 that guided our analyses. His death in April 2008 remains a loss to us all.

The India study was led by Deepa Narayan in close collaboration with Binayak Sen and Soumya Kapoor. The team was supported successively by Kaushik Barua, Divya Nambiar, Mohini Datt, and Emcet Tas. Administrative assistance was provided by Sunila Andrews, who held us all together.

We are grateful to Michael Carter, without whose support the large India study would not have been possible, and to his successor Isabel Guerrero for continued support. A number of people provided invaluable technical guidance and feedback on the India study and on chapters in this book. They include Bina Agarwal, Nilufar Ahmad, Ahmad Ahsan, Christine Allison, Sanjib Baruah, Rachid Benmessaoud, John Blaxall, Robert Chase, Louise Cord, Maitreyi Das, Dipak Dasgupta, Stephan Dercon, Nora Dudwick, S. Galab, Elena Glinskaya, Syed Hashemi, Stephen Howes, Kapil Kapoor, Aasmeen Khan, Rajni Khanna, Valerie Kozel, Rajiv Kumar, Pratap Bhanu Mehta, Caroline Moser, Rinku Murgai, Ijaz Nabi, Ashish Narain, Ambar Narayan, Philip O'Keefe, Fayez Omar, Seeta Prabhu, Giovanna Prennushi, K. Raju, V. J. Ravishankar, E. Revathi, Abhijit Sen, Arjun Sengupta, Rehman Sobhan, Tara Vishwanath, and Michael Woolcock. In addition, review workshops for the state chapters were held in Lucknow, Delhi, Gwahati, Hyderabad, and Calcutta. We are grateful to the workshop participants for their very valuable feedback and to Rajiv Kumar and his staff for facilitating these workshops.

ACNielsen India managed the data collection, fieldwork, data cleaning, and data coding. Managers Sandeep Ghosh and Bharat M. Shah were supported by a team of field supervisors that included Mukund Kumar Chandan, Gopalakrishnan Kamath, Ruchika Kapoor, Saveena Khan, Arijit Mukhopadhyay, Sarfaraz Nasir, Vishnu Shankar Tiwari, and Devendra Tyagi.

There were four state teams for data collection. *Andhra Pradesh:* Mukund Kumar Chandan, Ghouse, Gopalakrishnan Kamath, Niranjan, Rajender, Santhosh, and Devendra Tyagi. *Assam:* Maqbul Ali, Rahul Barman, Rama Kanta Barman, Debnath Bhadra, Hiren Bhattacharjee, Rupjyoti Borah, Chandan Das, Sanjay Das, Pankaj Deka, Deuti Hazarika, Prasanna Hazarika, Tilak Kalita, Kamal Lodh, Arijit Mukherjee, Arijit Mukhopadhyay, Rapjuyoti Ratna, Utpal Saibia, Chandan Sarma, Bidya Sinha, and Shankar Thakuria. *Uttar Pradesh:* Jaiprakash Bajpai, Saveena Khan, Minoti Mitra, Anand Kumar Mourya, Ram Singh Mourya, Bhawana Nainwal, Ruby Nainwal, Narendra Pandey, Sher Bahadur Prajapati, Arvind Kumar Singh, Devendra Pratap Singh, Rajesh Singh, Pankaj Srivastav, Vishnu Shankar Tiwari, Pankaj Kumar Verma, and Raj Kumar Yadav. *West Bengal:* Bratin Banerjee, Debashish Basu, Ujjala Biswas, Arnab Bose, Mukund Kumar Chandan, Amit Chowdhury, Bismita Das, Pranab Das, Atanu Dey, Saptarshi Guha, Sujay Majumder, Jaya Mandal, Arijit Mukhopadhyay, and Paramita Sasmal.

Data analysis was a huge task. The qualitative data analyses were led by Deepa Narayan and the quantitative analyses by Lant Pritchett and Deepa Narayan. These datasets involved several researchers over time. The quantitative analysis was conducted primarily by Nina Badgaiyan, Kalpana Mehra, and Denis Nikitin with support from Rahul Shaikh and Sunita Varada. The chapter authors applied the quantitative models developed for the global data analyses, with some modifications, to the four Indian states.

The enormous qualitative dataset was analyzed by two groups. The ACN-ielsen team in India was trained by Soumya Kapoor in the use of Nudist software and coded the data. The coding tree was developed with the support of several people, including Kaushik Barua, Chris Gibson, Soumya Kapoor, Molly Kinder, and Divya Nambiar. Manzoor Ali prepared printed packages for analysis. Training in other qualitative analyses was provided by Deepa Narayan and coordinated by Mohini Datt. Researchers included Huma Kidwai and Mahima Mitra, who stayed the longest. Other team members who provided valuable support included Chester Chua, Reema Govil, Divya Nambiar, Yukti Pahwa, Brice Richard, Niti Saxena, and Gitima Sharma.

Several governments and donors provided financing for the study. We especially wish to thank the government of Sweden, whose funds were untied. We also gratefully acknowledge support from the governments of Denmark, Finland, the Netherlands, Norway, Sweden, and the United Kingdom, and from the World Bank. In addition to the support through PREM, the World Bank provided financing for the study through its South Asia Region and through a grant from the Post-Conflict Fund to the Global Development Network.

We thank the team at the World Bank Office of the Publisher, including Mary Fisk, Pat Katayama, and Nancy Lammers, who managed publication of the Moving Out of Poverty series. We deeply appreciate Cathy Sunshine's meticulous editorial work and eye for detail that helped us through successive drafts and resulted in this book.

Contributors

Nina Badgaiyan is a consultant to the World Bank. She previously worked in the Economics Department at Princeton University with Professor Cecilia Rouse, and she has also consulted with UNICEF and the government of India. Trained as an economist with specialization in statistics and econometrics, she has extensive data analysis and operational work experience in the education, health, and poverty sectors in developing countries. Her current research interests include livelihoods, education, and poverty assessments.

Klaus Deininger is a lead economist in the rural development group of the Development Economics Group at the World Bank. His research interests include income and asset inequality and its relationship to poverty reduction and growth; access to land, land markets, and land reform and their impact on household welfare and agricultural productivity; land tenure and its impact on investment, including environmental sustainability; and capacity building (including the use of quantitative and qualitative methods) for policy analysis and evaluation, mainly in Africa, Central America, and East Asia. Trained in applied economics and agricultural economics, he also holds a degree in theology.

Katy Hull is a consultant to the Poverty Reduction Group in the Poverty Reduction and Economic Management (PREM) Network of the World Bank. Her interests include human rights, democratization, and political institutions. She is a co-author of "Democracy and Poverty Reduction: Explorations on the Sen Conjecture" (with L. Barbone, L. Cord, and J. Sandefur, in *Political Institutions and Development: Failed Expectations and Renewed Hopes*, Edwin Elgar, 2007).

Soumya Kapoor is a consultant to the Social Development Unit of the World Bank in India. She was a member of the Moving Out of Poverty study team between 2003 and 2008 and is a co-author of *Moving Out of Poverty: Success from the Bottom Up* (with D. Narayan and L. Pritchett, World Bank, 2009). Other recent publications include "Beyond Sectoral Traps: Creating Wealth for the Poor" (with D. Narayan, in *Assets, Livelihoods, and Social Policy*, World Bank, 2008). Before joining the World Bank, she worked as a corporate banker with a leading bank in India and as a credit analyst with an arm of Moody's. Her research interests include social exclusion and participatory development and how private enterprise can help reduce poverty while increasing profits.

Deepa Narayan is project director of the 15-country World Bank study titled Moving Out of Poverty: Understanding Freedom, Democracy, and Growth from the Bottom Up. From 2002 through 2008 she served as senior adviser in the Poverty Reduction and Economic Management (PREM) Network of the World Bank, first in the Poverty Reduction Group and subsequently in the vice president's office within PREM. Her areas of expertise include participatory development, community-driven development, and social capital, as well as use of these concepts to create wealth for poor people. Recent publications include *Moving Out of Poverty: Cross-Disciplinary Perspectives on Mobility* (with P. Petesch, World Bank, 2007); *Moving Out of Poverty: Success from the Bottom Up* (with S. Kapoor and L. Pritchett, World Bank, 2009); *Ending Poverty in South Asia: Ideas that Work* (with E. Glinskaya, World Bank, 2007); *Measuring Empowerment: Cross-Disciplinary Perspectives* (World Bank, 2005); *Empowerment and Poverty Reduction: A Sourcebook* (World Bank, 2002); and the three-volume *Voices of the Poor* series (Oxford University Press, 2000-02).

Denis Nikitin has worked as a consultant to the World Bank for eight years. His research focuses on poverty analysis and public sector governance. He has contributed to poverty assessments in Romania, Malawi, India, and Kazakhstan, as well as to gender assessment in Bangladesh. He is currently working on a study documenting the exclusion faced by India's scheduled tribes.

Saumik Paul is a consultant to the World Bank. He previously worked for Sentia Group, Claremont University, and the Indian Statistical Institute, and has taught economics, statistics, and finance at the graduate and undergraduate levels. His research addresses issues in international economics, labor, and political economy of development. Recent publications include "Opening the Pandora's Box? Trade Openness and Informal Sector Growth" (with A. Ghosh, in *Applied Economics*, 2008); and "Running the Numbers: A Comparative Perspective" (with Y. Feng, in *Worst of the Worst: Dealing with Repressive and Rogue Nations*, Brookings Institution Press, 2007).

Patti Petesch is an independent researcher with expertise in qualitative inquiry into the causes of poverty and poverty escapes and the roles of institutions and poor people's agency in these processes. Her most recent work focuses on mobility in conflict contexts, including recovery among displaced populations in Colombia. She served as study coordinator for the Voices of the Poor and Moving Out of Poverty research and is a co-author of two volumes in the *Voice of the Poor* series and *Moving Out of Poverty: Cross-Disciplinary Perspectives on Mobility* (with D. Narayan, World Bank, 2007). Other publications include "Evaluating Empowerment: A Framework with Cases from Latin America" (with C. Smulovitz and M. Walton, in *Measuring Empowerment: Cross-Disciplinary Perspectives*, World Bank, 2005) and *Voices of the Poor from Colombia: Strengthening Livelihoods, Families, and Communities* (with J. Arboleda and J. Blackburn, World Bank, 2004).

Giovanna Prennushi is an economic adviser in the New Delhi office of the World Bank. Since joining the World Bank in 1993, she has worked on poverty analysis, monitoring, and evaluation and on poverty reduction strategies, particularly in Africa and South Asia. She worked with the team that produced *World Development Report 2006: Equity and Development* (Oxford University Press, 2007).

Brice Richard is a consultant to the International Finance Corporation (IFC), a part of the World Bank Group. After conducting research on Chinese diplomacy at Tsinghua University in Beijing, he worked with the Moving Out of Poverty project, first in New Delhi and then in Washington, DC, focusing on social mobility and local democracy issues in India. He has also worked for the International Monetary Fund and is currently undertaking private sector development analyses for the IFC in India and Pakistan.

Binayak Sen is a senior economist in the South Asia region of the World Bank. He has worked extensively on Bangladesh development issues and on the problems of lagging regions, pro-poor growth, labor markets, and poverty dynamics, especially in the context of South Asia. He is a co-editor of *Chronic Poverty in Bangladesh: Tales of Ascent, Descent, Marginality and Persistence* (with D. Hulme, Bangladesh Institute of Development Studies/Chronic Poverty Research Centre, 2006). Other recent publications include contributions on human capital and earnings inequality for World Bank studies on India and Sri Lanka. His current research focuses on changes in the poverty and labor market situation in Pakistan.

Ashutosh Varshney is professor of political science at Brown University. He previously taught at Harvard University and the University of Michigan. In

2008 he won the Guggenheim and Carnegie awards for his research. His books include *Ethnic Conflict and Civic Life: Hindus and Muslims in India* (Yale University Press, 2002), which won the Luebbert award of the American Political Science Association, and *Democracy, Development and the Country-side: Urban-Rural Struggles in India* (Cambridge University Press, 1995), which won the Daniel Lerner prize. He was a member of UN Secretary General Kofi Annan's Task Force on Millennium Development Goals between 2002 and 2005.

Abbreviations

AP	Andhra Pradesh
BJP	Bhartiya Janta Party
BSP	Bahujan Samaj Party
CMIE	Centre for Monitoring Indian Economy
CPI(M)	Community Party of India (Marxist)
CPL	community poverty line
DPIP	District Poverty Initiative Project
DPIP MTA	Midterm appraisal of the District Poverty Initiative Project
FGD	focus group discussion
HH	households
HYV	high-yielding varieties
KI	key informant
LF	Left Front
LIC	Life Insurance Corporation of India
LOM	leave-out mean
NFHS	National Family Health Survey
NGO	nongovernmental organization
NSS	National Sample Survey
OBCs	other backward classes/other backward castes
OLS	ordinary least squares
OPL	official poverty line
PCA	principal components analysis
PEP	percentage ending poor
PSP	percentage starting poor
Rs	rupees
SC	scheduled caste
SHG	self-help group
ST	scheduled tribe
ULFA	United Liberation Front of Assam
UNDP	United Nations Development Programme
UP	Uttar Pradesh
VO	village organization

Note: All dollar amounts are U.S. dollars.

Indexes

MOP   Moving out of poverty index
Measures extent of upward mobility by the poor across the CPL in a community.
MOP = initially poor who move above CPL ÷ initially poor.

MPI   Mobility of the poor index
Measures extent of upward mobility by those who were initially poor.
MPI = initially poor who move up ÷ initially poor.

MRI   Mobility of the rich index
Measures extent of upward mobility by those who were initially above the CPL (nonpoor or "rich" by the study's definition).
MRI = initially rich who move up ÷ initially rich.

FI   Falling index
Measures extent of all downward mobility in a community.
FI = all households that move down ÷ total number of households.

FPI   Falling of the poor index
Measures extent of downward mobility of the initially poor.
FPI = initially poor who move down ÷ initially poor.

FRI   Falling of the rich index
Measures extent of downward mobility of the rich.
FRI = initially rich who move down ÷ initially rich.

FRIP   Falling of the rich into poverty index
Measures extent of downward mobility of the rich across the CPL.
FRI = initially rich who move below CPL ÷ initially rich.

NPR   Net poverty reduction
Measures changes in the share of poor over study period.
NPR = % ending poor – % initially poor.

NPI   Net prosperity index
Measures extent of net upward mobility (upward less downward) in a community.
NPI = (all households that move up – all households that move down) ÷ total number of households.

NPP   Net prosperity of the poor index
Measures extent of net upward mobility (upward less downward) of the initially poor.
NPP = (initially poor who move up – initially poor who move down) ÷ initially poor.

PI   Prosperity index
          Measures extent of all upward mobility in a community.
          PI = all households that move up ÷ total number of households.

Variable Prefixes and Suffixes

h   household questionnaire
c   community questionnaire
a   current (at time of study, about 2005)
b   initial (approximately 10 years ago, about 1995)
r   variable was recoded
T   total number of groups
m   male focus group discussion
f   female focus group discussion

Glossary

aman rice   Wet-season (summer) rice.
barga land   Land redistributed to sharecroppers, giving them security
                    of tenure.
bigha   Unit of land. Its precise size varies by state, but it is usually
                    one-third of an acre, or about 0.13 hectare.
boro rice   Dry-season (winter) rice.
gram panchayat   Village-level local government body.
gram sabha   Assembly of all adult residents of a village.
katha   Unit of land. A fraction of a bigha: In some places one-
                    twentieth, elsewhere one-sixteenth.
kuccha   Ramshackle, roughly built.
mandal   Administrative unit below district.
patta land   Land redistributed to poor farmers or landless workers under
                    legislation that sets a ceiling on individual landholdings.
pradhan   Elected village head.
pucca   Proper, well built.
tea garden   Tea plantation.

490
1/20 (mistrubed by Doll)

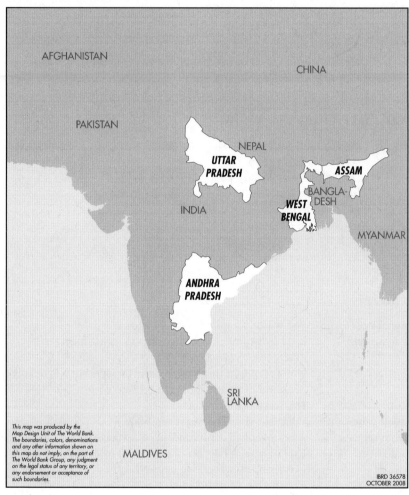

ti: Map of India

MOVING OUT OF POVERTY, VOLUME 3

The Promise of Empowerment and Democracy in India

Moving Out of Poverty in India: An Overview

Deepa Narayan, Binayak Sen, and Katy Hull

Poverty is a curse. Freedom from it brings power.

—WOMEN'S DISCUSSION GROUP,
Thengal Gaon, Assam

Freedom for the poor is like a pot full of curd that hangs up by a string. One can see it, but one cannot get it.

—DISCUSSION WITH YOUNG GIRLS,
Katmati, Uttar Pradesh

In our place, all powerful men are rich. A powerful man without money is like a sunless sky.

—MEN'S DISCUSSION GROUP,
Assam

CHAPTER 1

India
015 018 138
132 017
013 D73

W hy is it that in one village many poor people manage to escape poverty, while in another nearby village hardly anyone escapes poverty? Why is it that one household moves out of poverty while the household next door remains poor? What are the factors and processes at the community, institutional, and household levels that enable some people to move out of poverty while others remain stuck there?

Much is already known about poverty in India through the work of statisticians, economists, political scientists, sociologists, journalists, and practitioners in civil society. Their contributions are invaluable. Despite this vast knowledge, something is missing: the voices of poor people themselves and of those who were recently poor. There is a great deal to learn from them about how and why some people manage to escape poverty and others do not.

This study focuses on people who moved out of poverty during the decade from 1995 to 2005 in rural areas of four Indian states: Andhra Pradesh, Assam, Uttar Pradesh, and West Bengal. It also considers people who have fallen into poverty, those who have remained poor, and some who have never been poor but who live alongside poor people in the same communities. We started by setting aside official and expert opinions, ideologies of the right and left, and—to the extent possible—the beliefs and assumptions of the rich and the middle class, including our own preconceived notions. We let poor people speak.

The study is unique in four ways. First, it examines changes in poverty status of the same households over time. Most poverty studies are snapshots of the poor taken at a particular point in time, with extrapolations made by comparing them with the rich at that same point in time. In our study, we focus on understanding the dynamics of change by asking individuals to recall their life stories, particularly what happened to them over the past decade.

Second, most poverty studies are conducted at the national, state, or district level. We focus on local communities, mainly villages, as the unit within which individuals and households are embedded. There is much variation between villages, even within a district, and our sampling strategy enables us to examine these community-level differences. Third, we rely primarily on nonstandardized data collection methods, including life stories and discussion groups. We complement these with data we gather using household and community-level questionnaires. Finally, since we deliberately adopted an open-ended approach, we use inductive methods to systematically aggregate data from life stories and individual discussions over 50,000 pages of notes. We started with broad questions rather than a particular conceptual framework, but we did impose a framework after six months of inductive data analyses, before starting the quantitative data analyses.

Policy makers often dismiss subjective data collection methods and individual life stories as anecdotal and "not scientific."[1] In this study, we deliberately give primacy to people's own experiences while accepting that these data collection methods, like all methods, are prone to error. We cross-check data by asking the same questions at different times of the same people and of different people. Usually studies that employ subjective methods are done on a small scale, using informal sampling methods. By contrast, we bring together the life experiences of more than 30,000 women and men from 300 rural villages across Andhra Pradesh, Assam, Uttar Pradesh, and West Bengal.[2] Individuals were carefully selected through stratified random sampling methods.

The book is based on people's own definitions of poverty and their own poverty thresholds, and it examines a broad range of factors—economic, psychological, social, political, institutional, and community-level—that people tell us are important for escaping poverty. It belongs to a line of cross-disciplinary literature that aims to give voice to those whom Fuller (2004) provocatively describes as "nobodies"—those who are all too often trapped in a voiceless existence and perceived as the faceless poor.

India in the first decade of the new millennium is in the enviable position of maintaining high levels of economic growth. Yet it continues to be home to millions and millions of poor people—women, men, youth, and children—who suffer high levels of malnutrition and hunger. In the political arena, the 73rd amendment to the Constitution introduced local government at the village level, bringing democracy to Indian villages in the 1990s. We seek to understand how these economic and political changes over the past decade have affected poor people's lives. We hope that insights from this study will help policy makers refine policies and will inspire new ways of reducing poverty to lift up the millions who still live in dehumanizing conditions.

We begin by describing two communities with contrasting poverty trajectories. This is followed by a presentation of the conceptual framework and a summary of our 10 major findings. The next two chapters explore cross-cutting themes across the four states: chapter 2 focuses on learning from life stories, and chapter 3 on processes and factors that affect community-level prosperity. Each of the remaining chapters in the volume looks in depth at one of the four study states: Uttar Pradesh, Andhra Pradesh, West Bengal, and Assam.

A Tale of Two Villages

Bidrohipar and Gobhali in Assam are two of the 300 Indian villages visited by the Moving Out of Poverty study teams. Each of these 300 villages is, of course, unique. Yet a closer look at these two suggests the many factors that can either help or hinder economic mobility across villages. These factors relate to economic opportunities, individual and collective empowerment and agency, and local political, social, and economic institutions.

Bidrohipar, in Cachar district, lies in a region of great natural beauty, surrounded by the northeastern states of Mizoram and Manipur on two sides and the nation of Myanmar on the third. Agriculture is the primary livelihood, with rice the principal crop. But even those farmers who employ a "modern" system of cultivation, using fertilizers, high-yield seed varieties, and pesticides, are held back by a lack of irrigation facilities. According to a discussion group member, Fokhrul Islam, 500 bighas (approximately 167 acres) of land remain unused because of the dryness of the soil.[3] This problem, together with repeated flooding, makes farming an unappealing prospect for the village's young people, who increasingly look for alternative sources of livelihood in the nearby town of Silchar or farther afield, in Guwahati and Mumbai. "By their jobs, they are feeding their families," observed another man.

The village government, or panchayat, has helped promote prosperity in Bidrohipar. It set up and supervises a daily market called the *swadhin bazar*. Discussants note that starting a new business is easy: licenses are issued by the panchayat and vendors pay a fee of Rs 20–30 a month. Basic infrastructure has also improved over the course of a decade. Electricity has been available since 1997, and 90 percent of houses now receive power, although the majority of these are "illegal" or nonpaying customers. A male discussant noted,

"Electric facilities have affected the working life of people. Now shops are open until 7 p.m." As a result of the central government's sanitation program, a quarter of the village now has concrete latrines. Link roads were repaired in 2000, and a principal road connecting the village to neighboring towns was constructed in 2001. As a result, villagers commute to town for work on a daily basis, and students can reach the college easily. The improved roads have also helped local businesses develop.

Bidrohipar has also experienced remarkable growth in its education services and now has seven primary schools, two middle schools, and one higher secondary school, in addition to the three private schools run by the panchayat. The college is located 7 kilometers from the village and the closest university is 30 kilometers away. A health center and family planning center offer basic services, while a number of private doctors operate from the marketplace. Government-sponsored child care services distribute food and provide some health care. But discussants still consider the health system to be in "very bad condition."

People's collectives form an integral part of community life, supporting agricultural activities, disseminating information on government schemes, promoting health and sanitation, and offering loans and flood relief. Satana Sangh is just one of the many social welfare groups operating in the village. Among its numerous activities, it has distributed high-yield seeds, fertilizers, and pesticides, disbursed loans through the Kisan credit card scheme, and supported students' education. Iqbal, a college student, said, "My dream of getting a master's degree and then becoming a college lecturer is more or less associated with the willingness of our Satana Sangh. They help me from every angle."

The collectives foster a spirit of cooperation. "In our society, unity is the biggest strength," reflected a female member of a local group, the Purbanchal Demand Committee. "We can, by our joint efforts, solve all our problems." In a region marked by conflict, Bidrohipar is peaceful: neither the army nor separatist forces menace the community.

Villagers believe that local democracy has positively affected community prosperity over the past 10 years, as the local government has paid greater attention to people's needs. A men's discussion group said, "Nowadays the local government has gradually become close to ordinary people. People also feel its importance. . . . Now they freely go there and make complaints. And the local government helps people as far as possible." Participation is active in the gram sabha, the village-wide meeting. Some of the women attribute increased participation levels over the decade to improvements in education.

"The people of our society did not participate in these meetings 10 years ago because they were not so educated. Ten years ago they were not so conscious, they had no knowledge about their own life. But at present day they know everything about their own life because now they are educated so they also participate in this institution."

Corruption is nonetheless rampant. The women's discussion group observed, "One lakh [100,000] rupees, which is sent by the government to our society, becomes 50,000 when it reaches the block and becomes 25,000 at the panchayat office. As a result we can't help the people." The police are also routinely corrupt, demanding bribes from both parties in most disputes, according to male discussants. "People generally try to avoid the police," noted one man.

Yet the residents of Bidrohipar believe that democracy exists in more than just name. Effective governance is possible because of the increased awareness of people and their desire for a prosperous future. In the words of Maneruddin Laskar, "Self-confidence of people becomes high. So they can freely speak out and present their views before public meetings." Two young men summed up: "We must speak out against injustice. . . . If we do not demand the good maintenance of our roads from our contractors, why would they not be corrupt? . . . Freedom of speech is most important. . . . We should speak out against such corruptions that it will reduce the number."

The second village, Gobhali in the Kamrup district of Assam, sits on the banks of the Brahmaputra River, 18 kilometers from Guwahati city. The principal livelihoods include farming and daily wage work. Few people own businesses, and still fewer are public employees.

This community has experienced major setbacks over the decade. Landslides between 1997 and 2004 destroyed 1,000 bighas (more than 300 acres) of land, forcing people to abandon their traditional livelihoods of growing rice and vegetables. "This erosion has snatched away the food of the people," reflected one villager. Major private sector employers have also disappeared following the closure of a power plant and the subsequent folding of the National Textile Corporation. Bubul, a 41-year-old woman, said that economic opportunities have decreased over the decade "because there was a cotton mill and a power house in our village before. But both are closed now and the former workers have no advantage of any work." A male discussant noted, "About 1,000 workers have become jobless. . . . Now labor of all kinds of job has dropped." Even daily wage laborers have trouble finding work, as they used to depend on the employees of the power house and spinning mill to hire them.

The panchayat has done little to stem the tide of misfortune. It is "unwilling to transfer the benefits provided by government to society," observed members of the male discussion group. "The economic support for repairing roads or development is wasted by the leaders," said another. In the face of landslides, "petitions were made to the government to stop the erosion," explained Tilok, one of the few government schoolteachers in the village. In 2004 at least Rs 600,000 was designated to deal with the problem, but "the contractors only built a few bamboo post barriers and digested the rest of the money."

There is only one self-help group in the community, with 13 members, and it is burdened by debt. A nongovernmental organization (NGO) taught the group to make candles, but discussants noted that because of "lack of money, this group cannot go forward. If the government gives loans or training, they can do business." Youth organizations have been rendered inactive by the mass migration of young people in search of better work opportunities outside the village.

In the absence of a strong collective tradition, social divisions persist. Though the village is shielded from the separatist conflict in Assam, local land disputes divide rich from poor. Land that is theoretically set aside for members of scheduled tribes has been captured by more powerful members of society. "Height is right" in Gobhali, reflected a female discussant.

The male discussion group said that Gobhali is a democracy only "in its name . . . in its activities there are no characteristics of democracy. . . . Leaders give more importance to self without giving any importance to people's social problems." Only "those who have money can win the elections," as candidates buy votes by feeding villagers with "fish and meat and giving them a party of rice and wine." Once candidates are elected, their promises to provide drinking water or repair roads come to naught, while a handful of cronies benefit from food cards and free electricity. People's perceived ability to contact local government has only decreased over the decade. "The public of the village cannot influence the decisions of panchayat members. They do not give any importance to the common people," noted one man.

Bidrohipar and Gobhali share much in common. Each is a predominantly agricultural community, exposed to the vagaries of nature. In a state that is no stranger to conflict, each is generally peaceful. And in a system of decentralized democracy, residents of each village have struggled with the consequences of corrupt local governance.

Yet the two villages are even more noteworthy for their differences. Thanks to a relatively effective local government, Bidrohipar has experienced remarkable improvements in the quality of its basic infrastructure and education over the course of a decade, although much remains to be done in the areas of health and sanitation. By working together in groups, residents have overcome internal divisions and reinforced their mutual prosperity. Villagers testify to feelings of empowerment, even in the face of persistent corruption. By contrast, the local government in Gobhali has done little to reverse negative shocks to livelihoods, and residents seem to be locked in a low equilibrium of poor economic opportunity and weak organizational power. Far from feeling like empowered participants in their local democracy, ordinary people feel increasingly distant from the institutions of power and unable to affect their own fates.

These contrasts are reflected in the two villages' different rates of economic mobility. While more than 20 percent of villagers are perceived to have moved out of poverty in Bidrohipar, only 6 percent have crossed the poverty line in Gobhali. Location is not destiny, however. Even in relatively prosperous Bidrohipar, some people remain trapped in poverty, while in Gobhali, generally marked by low economic mobility, a few households have managed to prosper.

Conceptual Framework

The Moving Out of Poverty study is concerned with the dynamics of poverty reduction, as opposed to trying to measure poverty incidence alone. This is because net poverty rates are the product of two contrasting phenomena: movement out of poverty and falling into poverty, processes that may have very different dynamics.

The men and women who participated in the study testify that the local economic and political environment, individual attributes, and collective characteristics all matter for movement out of poverty. Reflecting their observations, we employ an opportunity-agency structure as our basic conceptual framework. The framework indicates that movement out of poverty will depend both on changes in the *opportunities* offered by local economic conditions and political institutions and on changes in the capabilities of poor individuals or groups to take purposeful actions, that is, to exercise *agency* (Narayan 2006).[4]

Economic opportunity in a community is one important factor that favors mobility for the poor; a responsive and effective local democracy is another. But even when these are present, it cannot be assumed that all residents of a community will have equal access to them. Social stratification and discrimination—based on caste, tribal, or gender distinctions, for instance—

will constrain the extent to which individuals and groups are able to advance their interests. And equal access to fair prices, credit, and justice will largely determine whether opportunities are available to the many or the few.

A combination of individual and collective agency can be critical to overcoming institutional inequalities that lead to economic, social, and political exclusion. Agency at the individual level is measured by a sense of self-confidence, power, and a capacity to aspire. At the collective level, it is measured by community members' willingness to assist one another and solve common problems, as well as by the strength of local organizations and networks.

Figure 1.1 provides an overview of this conceptual framework. While we recognize that national-level policies are important, our study focuses on the local level and our methods are best suited to understanding local realities.

FIGURE 1.1

Initiative and opportunity interact to produce upward movement

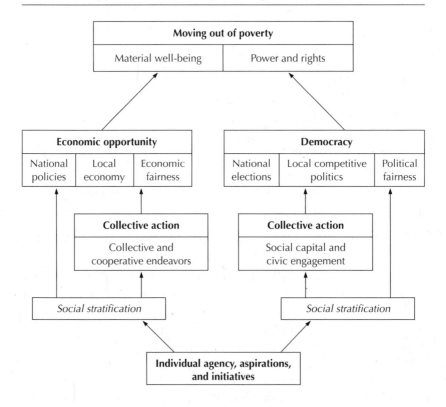

While the core objective of the study is to explore from the bottom up how and why people move out of poverty, each of the individual state chapters also addresses an issue of particular relevance to local economic mobility in that state. The Andhra Pradesh chapter focuses on the role of self-help groups in movement out of poverty. The chapter on Uttar Pradesh considers the role of caste in facilitating or hindering people's mobility, and the West Bengal chapter focuses on the role of local governance, particularly with respect to land reform. The Assam chapter explores the links between conflict and economic mobility.

Methodology: Moving and Falling on the Ladder of Life

What is poverty? Who is poor? In contrast to most studies, which use as their starting point an objective definition of poverty often based on income or consumption data, the Moving Out of Poverty study set out without any definition of poverty at all. Instead, the study teams asked local people participating in the research to define what it means to be poor in the context of their own communities.

The "ladder of life" is the main tool by which village-level discussion groups defined poverty in their communities.[5] The principal questions addressed in the ladder of life exercise include the following:

- What are the various levels of well-being in your community?
- What are the characteristics of households at each of these steps?
- What factors enable upward movement or cause downward movement from each step?
- On which step does a given household stand today (in 2005), and on which step was this same household approximately 10 years ago (around 1995)?
- At which step are households no longer considered poor in this community?
- Where would the official poverty line fall on this community's ladder of life?

As a first step in the exercise, discussion groups were asked to describe the levels of well-being in their community, from the poorest to the most affluent. Researchers prescribed neither the number of levels nor the content of the descriptions, leaving groups free to explain the full spectrum of conditions in their village along both economic and noneconomic lines.

Table 1.1 provides an example of a ladder constructed by a focus group in Kamalapur village in Andhra Pradesh. Although the details are unique to Kamalapur, the descriptions of the various levels are common to many of the ladder of life exercises conducted throughout the four states. For instance, employment status and assets feature in most groups' descriptions of the various steps. In the case of Kamalapur, the lowest step is occupied by landless laborers, while the middle steps consist of farmers with incrementally larger plots, who in some cases combine land ownership with government jobs. Step 6, the highest step, is reserved for two landowning families in the village who can afford to employ others to cultivate their land. In this drought-prone region, irrigation assets are an important mark of status within the community: farm households at step 3, for instance, are entirely dependent on rainfall, while farmers at steps 4 and above have access to borehole wells.

TABLE 1.1
The ladder of life in Kamalapur, Andhra Pradesh

Step 6	Landlords: Employ servants to cultivate their lands; own huge buildings; command high respect in the village. Only 2 families in the village are at this step.
Step 5	Big farmers: Own 15–25 acres of ancestral property and 4–5 houses, plus motorbikes, fans, and cattle. Cultivate crops like cotton, chilies, soybeans; land gives good yields. Banks provide loans. Educate their children and can live without working.
Step 4	Medium farmers: Own 5 acres of land. Some have government jobs. Own houses with cement walls, cattle, borehole wells, televisions, fans, and cots. Eat fine rice. Women wear gold ornaments, and children study in good schools. Banks provide loans.
Step 3	Small farmers: Own 3–5 acres of land. Own houses and cattle but do not have wells. Their lives depend on rainfall. During periods of drought, they migrate to towns or work as agricultural labor. They are a little bit educated.
Step 2	Laborers with small landholdings: Own 1–2 acres of land. Land is rarely fertile, and they have to do wage labor; some serve as bonded labor. Don't have proper houses. They are illiterate and belong to backward and scheduled castes. Every day is a struggle.
Step 1	Landless laborers: Lack proper food, proper clothes, and proper houses. Don't find work regularly and are able to work only 12–15 days a month. They are usually illiterate, and their children cannot attend school because they have to work.

Source: Male ladder of life discussion group, Kamalapur, Andhra Pradesh.

Note: Bold line indicates the community poverty line.

Participants across communities also refer to noneconomic criteria when defining steps on the ladder of life. Kamalapur is no different in this regard: social identities play an important role in the village hierarchy, with households on step 2 belonging to scheduled and backward castes and those on step 6 commanding "high respect in the village."

Once the ladder of life was created, groups identified the factors that were instrumental in moving up or down from each step. The discussion group in Kamalapur identified hard work, savings, and investment, together with government assistance (in the form of land and housing programs or irrigation and marketing facilities) as preconditions for upward mobility. Weather-induced crop failure and sickness of a family member were cited as reasons for falling down.

Discussion groups were next asked to identify the step at which households were no longer considered poor. The line between this step and the ones below was designated the community poverty line (CPL). In this way, each community arrived at a definition of poverty that was specific to local circumstances and that integrated both objective and subjective measures of well-being. In the case of Kamalapur, the CPL was set just above step 2 on the ladder of life. At step 3, where people typically owned 3 to 5 acres of land, a house, and some cattle, and had some education, households were no longer considered poor, although they remained exposed to significant economic insecurity due to their reliance on rainfed agriculture.

Only once the CPL had been established did the interviewer inform discussants of the government of India's official poverty line (OPL) and ask them to identify the step on the ladder where a person with this income would fall. The OPL could then be compared to the CPL on the community's ladder. In other words, focus groups determined whether income at the official poverty line would be sufficient for a household to be no longer considered poor by local standards. In Kamalapur's case, discussants placed the OPL below the CPL, at step 1 of the ladder. Villagers at this lowest step, described as landless laborers, were typically employed in daily wage work and were considered to lack proper food, clothing, and shelter. In the great majority of the communities in the study, as in Kamalapur, focus groups placed the OPL below the CPL.

As a final stage in the ladder of life exercise, focus groups ranked all households in their village according to their position on the ladder in the year of the study, 2005, and about a decade earlier, around 1995.[6] This exercise generated a community mobility matrix consisting of four mobility groups:

- *Movers:* households that were poor in 1995 but moved out of poverty by 2005
- *Chronic poor:* households that were poor in 1995 and remained poor in 2005
- *Fallers:* households that were not poor in 1995 but fell into poverty by 2005
- *Never poor:* households that were not poor in 1995 and remained not poor in 2005 (also called the "chronic rich")

Figure 1.2 reproduces a community mobility matrix for the village of Pathari in Uttar Pradesh. In this community, focus group participants identified five steps on the ladder of life and placed the CPL at step 2. Of the 22 households above the CPL in 1995, 20 remained there in 2005, gaining the status of never poor (bottom right quadrant), while two dropped below the poverty line and became fallers (bottom left quadrant). Of the 128 households that were below the poverty line in 1995, 96 stagnated at the same step in 2005, gaining the unfortunate title of chronic poor (top left quadrant), while 32 succeeded in crossing the community poverty line to become movers (top right quadrant).

In the course of formulating the rankings, discussion groups stated causes for individual households' upward or downward movement or stagnation. For instance, in Pathari, upward mobility from the lower steps was seen to be the result of hard work in agriculture and outward migration for relatively high-paying work opportunities, such as masonry. At the middle and higher steps, investments—whether in modern agricultural equipment, higher education of children, or an additional business—enabled further upward mobility. Falling at the lower steps was perceived to be the result of large family size, irregular work opportunities, and cycles of illness and indebtedness, while at the higher levels discussants cited family divisions and sale of land because of marriage expenses as reasons for falling.

Across the 300 villages, the ladder of life exercises and community mobility matrixes provided rich insights into the nature of poverty and the factors that helped and hindered household and community mobility. They also offered an important source of data on economic mobility in each village during the study period and a means of comparing trends across communities. Table 1.2 summarizes the indexes that could be derived from the community mobility matrix. Many of these indexes will be discussed in the state-level chapters.

FIGURE 1.2

Community mobility matrix for Pathari, Uttar Pradesh, shows household mobility over a decade

		Now				
Steps	1	2	3	4	5	Total
10 years ago 1	13, 23, 57, 58, 59, 60, 67, 68, 74, 85, 86, 87, 88, 95, 96, 97, 98, 108, 109, 116, 127, 128, 129, 133, 143, 144, 146	11, 12, 19, 20, 48, 49, 61, 103, 104, 105, 107, 113, 114, 115, 118, 120, 121, 125, 126, 135, 136, 139, 141, 142, 145	82	*Movers*		53
2	21, 22, 33, 37, 38, 41, 132	14, 15, 16, 17, 18, 24, 25, 26, 27, 29, 32, 36, 39, 40, 42, 43, 44, 47, 50, 53, 54, 56, 64, 66, 77, 78, 79, 80, 91, 94, 112, 119, 122, 123, 124, 131, 134	5, 6, 7, 28, 34, 35, 45, 46, 51, 52, 55, 75, 76, 92, 93, 99, 100, 101, 102, 106, 110, 111, 117, 140, 147, 148	3, 4	1, 30, 31	75
3	69, 149	*Fallers*	8, 9, 10, 72 *Never poor*	62, 65, 70, 71, 137, 138, 150	130	14
4				2, 83, 89, 90	81	5
5					63, 73, 84	3
Total	36	62	31	13	8	150

Chronic poor (label within row 1/2, column 1)

Source: Male ladder of life discussion group, Pathari, Uttar Pradesh.

Note: Bold lines indicate the community poverty line.

TABLE 1.2
Summary indicators of mobility

MOP	Moving out of poverty index	
	Measures extent of upward mobility by the poor across the CPL in a community. MOP = initially poor who move above CPL ÷ initially poor.	
MPI	Mobility of the poor index	
	Measures extent of upward mobility by those who were initially poor. MPI = initially poor who move up ÷ initially poor.	
MRI	Mobility of the rich index	
	Measures extent of upward mobility by those who were initially above the CPL (nonpoor or "rich" by the study's definition). MRI = initially rich who move up ÷ initially rich.	
FI	Falling index	
	Measures extent of all downward mobility in a community. FI = all households that move down ÷ total number of households.	
FPI	Falling of the poor index	
	Measures extent of downward mobility of the initially poor. FPI = initially poor who move down ÷ initially poor.	
FRI	Falling of the rich index	
	Measures extent of downward mobility of the rich. FRI = initially rich who move down ÷ initially rich.	
FRIP	Falling of the rich into poverty index	
	Measures extent of downward mobility of the rich across the CPL. FRI = initially rich who move below CPL ÷ initially rich.	
NPR	Net poverty reduction	
	Measures changes in the share of poor over study period. NPR = % ending poor – % initially poor.	
NPI	Net prosperity index	
	Measures extent of net upward mobility (upward less downward) in a community. NPI = (all households that move up – all households that move down) ÷ total number of households.	
NPP	Net prosperity of the poor index	
	Measures extent of net upward mobility (upward less downward) of the initially poor. NPP = (initially poor who move up – initially poor who move down) ÷ initially poor.	
PI	Prosperity index	
	Measures extent of all upward mobility in a community. PI = all households that move up ÷ total number of households.	

Finally, each community mobility matrix provided a basis for stratified random sampling of households for further quantitative and qualitative investigation, first through detailed household questionnaires and then through individual life story interviews. All households within each mobility group were randomly selected. Since the primary objective of the study was to explore how and why households moved out of poverty, the sampling for household questionnaires favored movers, followed by the never poor, chronic poor, and fallers.[7] The questionnaires collected information on respondents' subjective perceptions of freedom, democracy, social capital, insecurity, and personal aspirations, as well as more objective measures of assets, expenditure, and education.

A subset of households was then randomly selected from within each mobility group for open-ended individual life story interviews, which aimed to identify the web of social, economic, institutional, and psychological factors that helped or hindered individual mobility—details and dynamics that could not be gleaned from the household questionnaire alone. Each life story interview covered five themes: migration history; occupational history; financial history; social, cultural, and psychological history; and educational history. Trend lines were created for each thematic area and then consolidated to provide an overall record of individual well-being over the course of the decade. Chapter 2 discusses in detail results from the analyses of life stories.

In addition to the ladder of life discussions, household questionnaires, and individual life stories, seven additional data collection tools were employed to gain a rich understanding of poverty mobility at the household and community levels (see volume appendix 2).

Three Caveats

Before highlighting some of the key findings across states, it is important to note several ways in which the strengths of the Moving Out of Poverty study—its most innovative elements—also entail certain limitations.

Use of subjective measures

First, the poverty numbers generated by the study tools are based on perceptions rather than on objective measures. While the use of group rather than individual interviews in the ladder of life helps overcome the well-known problems associated with recall data, it remains true that any household's position on the ladder of life reflects subjective perceptions and the fallibility of memory. However, a comparison between measures of well-being established through the ladder of life exercise and more objective measures—for instance, expenditure—demonstrates that subjective and objective measures tend to align with one another and move in the same direction.

We tested the extent to which subjective measures of household well-being determined by focus groups meshed with more objective measures of income poverty. The results are reassuring (table 1.3). Movers and the never poor reported higher levels of mean expenditure and asset accumulation than both fallers and the chronic poor. With respect to levels of food adequacy, households ranked as movers by focus groups also reported the greatest improvement in ability to meet their food needs over the decade: the percentage with adequate food increased by 42 percentage points, from 52 to 94 percent. Households ranked as fallers reported the greatest decline in food adequacy, decreasing by 55 percentage points (76 to 21 percent). The never poor and chronic poor both tended to experience stagnant levels of food consumption, as might be expected of groups that experienced little upward or downward mobility. The level of food adequacy for never-poor households changed by only 5 percentage points (90 to 95 percent), and that of the chronic poor by only 3 percentage points (from 20 to 17 percent).

Use of the community poverty line

Second, researchers prescribed neither the number of steps on the ladder of life nor the position of the community poverty line, each community profile is unique. This raises some questions about the extent to which comparisons can be made across communities, although there are plausible arguments to be made in defense of the CPL (box 1.1).

TABLE 1.3
Objective measures of well-being largely align with subjective perceptions

Mobility group	Expenditure (mean, rupees/year)	Difference in assets[a]	Adequate food (%) 1995	Adequate food (%) 2005
Movers	45,146	0.333	52	94
Chronic poor	31,392	−0.482	20	17
Fallers	25,818	−0.797	76	21
Never poor	58,202	0.399	90	95

a. To see the change in asset distribution, we took the principal components analysis (PCA) of the difference in assets between 1995 and 2005 and then the given means for each mobility group. A negative result implies that improvements in assets were below the mean, and a positive result indicates that improvements in assets were above the mean. Data are from all four Indian states in the sample.

BOX 1.1
In defense of the community poverty line

There are several reasons why we think that a poverty comparison based on each community's own definition of poverty is valid and useful. First, and most fundamentally, it is important that a poverty measurement make sense in the local context and be "owned" by the community itself. Thus, we took a deliberate decision to stick with people's own definitions of poverty rather than imposing the researchers' definition or the official definition in a given country.

Second, the focus of the study is on subjective and multidimensional poverty rather than on monetary and unidimensional poverty. This also requires us to allow each community to self-define poverty, and we were prepared to accept whatever multidimensional aspects might appear. In the context of this study, the multidimensional factors considered by communities include consumption adequacy, asset ownership, educational status, housing conditions, and occupational categories. Also included are nonquantifiable class/status characteristics such as being "respected" or having "good social links" or, conversely, being a member of an excluded caste, religious, or social group. Since there is no satisfactory way of privileging one dimension over another or objectively combining them into a synthetic multidimensional poverty line, we take the community's definition of poverty, and of which local households are considered poor and nonpoor, at face value.

Third, when we use "subjective and multidimensional poverty" as a yardstick necessarily defined by the community, problems may arise in operationalizing the idea through the ladder of life approach. For instance, the number of steps on the ladder differs across communities (some use four steps, some six, some eight, and so on), and this difference can create problems in making poverty comparisons across communities. However, we found that the "churning index," which measures step-down or step-up mobility, is quite uniform across communities for a given state in the Indian sample irrespective of the number of steps on each ladder. We do not see more churning in communities where the ladder of life has a larger number of steps.[8]

Finally, a community-defined subjective and multidimensional poverty line is a relative poverty line. Any index constructed for movement out of poverty is subject to the placement of a threshold line that can vary across communities and contexts. Placement of such relative thresholds can affect reporting of changes in overall well-being. Given problems that relative lines like the CPL can pose, a broader index of upward movement of the poor (MPI) is also used alongside the moving out of poverty (MOP) index; the MOP is defined in relation to the CPL, but the MPI is not. In the actual empirical analysis of factors influencing movement out of poverty, the study uses both the MOP and MPI indexes for all states in the India sample.

Local specificity

Third, the India study produced 300 community-specific investigations of what it means to be poor and of the processes—individual, collective, and institutional—that enable movement out of poverty. Due to their highly localized nature, the statistical findings should not be interpreted as representative of economic realities in each state as a whole. So while the study presents data from, say, West Bengal, the findings hold true only for the particular communities sampled in West Bengal, although they may also be indicative of certain statewide trends. Where the findings are most valuable is in helping us see poverty through the eyes of local people and understand the processes involving individual and collective agency and the local-level political, social, and economic institutions that help or hinder economic mobility.

Ten Findings

Many insights emerged from this study. In this overview, we highlight 10 of the most important. While we draw attention to some differences in findings across states, it is impossible to do justice here to all the nuances, which are detailed in chapters 4 through 7.

One: Official poverty lines systematically underestimate poverty

> *What can a person do with such a poor income [income at the official poverty line]? He would die of starvation.*
> —Discussion with men, Tihuliya, Uttar Pradesh

The study found that local people's definitions of what it means to be poor differ substantially from the definitions used by government officials. The income levels underlying official poverty lines tend to underestimate poverty as it is perceived at the community level.

When ladder of life discussion groups in the villages were informed of the official poverty line in their state, many participants jeered and said that it was impossible to live on such a small income. Many expressed anger that the better-off people expected them, the poor, to live such a meager existence. In three of the four states—Assam, Uttar Pradesh, and West Bengal—more than three-quarters of communities placed the community poverty line above the official poverty line, meaning that more people face poverty than would be indicated by the OPL (figure 1.3). In other words, poverty rates are higher than official statistics would imply.

FIGURE 1.3

Majority of villages across states place the community poverty line above the official poverty line

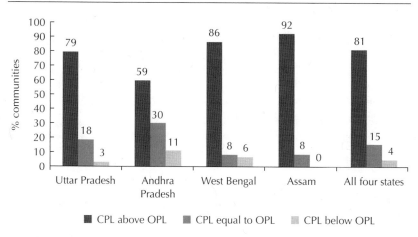

This finding should not be interpreted as an indictment of official poverty lines. OPLs are extremely useful as a basis for intrastate and interstate analysis and as a factor in determining the distribution of public resources. However, the finding does underscore the importance of listening to the voices of poor people who are calling for adjustments to official poverty lines. When community and official definitions of poverty do not mesh, policy responses based on the OPL alone may violate local notions of fairness and justice and may fail to reach the majority of poor people. This is particularly true during periods of rising aspirations.

In the India study, poor people said, quite clearly and repeatedly, that the income deemed sufficient according to official lines is inadequate to meet their basic needs or preserve their dignity. By contrast, community poverty lines usually tend to represent a dividing line between those who have adequate income, land, and housing to live with dignity—although they may still be vulnerable—and those who do not.

Ladder of life descriptions of households just below the community poverty line attest to dire situations. In Patnapur village, Andhra Pradesh, men in a discussion group said, "At this step people don't have houses. . . . They don't have lands. . . . These people are illiterate and never send their children to school. They work in the summer season as agricultural laborers, but in the rainy season they do not have work. These people cannot afford minor expenses that occur suddenly. . . . To go to higher steps, they have to work hard. Only some miracle can do this because they don't have even one decimal of land." Similar descriptions of households just below the CPL were offered in other communities as well.

Descriptions of households just above the CPL, on the other hand, often make clear the importance of acquiring permanent assets. In Niddam village, Andhra Pradesh, women described families at this step as follows: "We have farmers with 5 acres of land who also migrate seasonally to other places for work. These people live in good houses and have no problems for basic amenities. They have modern electronic durables in their home. They get their children educated in the nearby villages and towns." Such descriptions suggest that concerted policy interventions are required to support the livelihoods and asset base of poor households so as to enable them to move up. One key event seems to be the acquisition of a permanent house, often through a government program that builds houses for the poor. Acquisition of a home often marks the beginning of the process of accumulating assets and slowly moving out of poverty.

Two: Net poverty figures hide two distinct phenomena: moving out of poverty and falling into poverty

> *The reason for my progress has been my hard work. I worked very hard and educated my son, as a result of which he got a government job. Hence, the condition of my family improved considerably. Previously, I didn't have enough to eat, whereas today I have surplus.*
>
> —A scheduled caste mover, Uttar Pradesh

> *Everything was going on happily. But in 1994, it seemed as if all grief attacked my life, when my eldest son died of brain tumor and my husband after hearing this news died of heart attack within 15 days. I was then continuously struck by thunder and lightening. I hadn't come out of my sorrow, but after two years my eldest daughter died in 1996 while delivering a child. . . . My happiness has gotten eclipsed. My economic and mental condition deteriorated day by day as I fell into the ocean of disappointment.*
>
> —Manjawa, a 52-year-old faller, Uttar Pradesh

The almost exclusive focus on net poverty reduction rates in many studies obscures two crucial and contrasting phenomena: moving up and out of poverty, and falling down into poverty. Each has a different set of associated processes. This focus on aggregate rates is partially a result of the poverty methodology that has been adopted as the standard approach, based on one-time national household surveys that by definition cannot reveal dynamics over time. Our study finds that just reducing the numbers of people falling into poverty has quite dramatic effects on overall poverty rates. And the underlying reasons for falling are different from the reasons for upward movement.

In Uttar Pradesh, poverty was reduced by 7.3 percentage points during the decade covered by the study. But the overall poverty reduction rate tells only part of the story. Ant Sant village has experienced relatively high rates of both movement out of poverty and falling into poverty. Almost 20 percent of the village inhabitants moved out of poverty and almost 5 percent fell into poverty, which meant a net reduction in the percentage of poor from 76.3 percent to 61.2 percent. Accordingly, the overall poverty reduction rate in this particular community was 15.1 percent, which is more than twice as high as the average poverty reduction rate in the communities studied in Uttar Pradesh. But it would have been almost 20 percent if no one had fallen into poverty.

Prem, a 34-year-old man, is one of Ant Sant's movers. He was born into a poor family of low caste. He remembers, "My father used to work hard as a laborer for others. Only then were we able to get one meal for the day. This is because right from the beginning the village *zamindars* [landlords] had an upper hand and they kept us in servitude." In spite of the family's poverty, Prem's father took great pains to ensure his son's education. "Time passed and I cleared the high school exam in 1989. I was very happy because this was my first aim in life." Unable to find a job in the private sector, he took "land on lease and started working." Six years later, in 1995, "I learnt how to make taps with the India Mark II [a brand of hand pump] and this has enabled me to earn more today." Prem's fortunes began to turn around: "The government helped us, and in 1996 I got a house in the Indira Awas [residential] colony. Today I have proper house to live in and two meals in a day." Meanwhile, the village's caste system, once so rigid, has begun to ease, enabling Prem to pursue his aspirations. He reflects, "Gradually the time started changing and the influence of the [upper-caste] Thakurs also reduced. In this case the government played a substantial role."

Jagdev, age 37, is one of Ant Sant's fallers. He remembered, "Ten years ago, we had a substantial amount of land. At that time my father and my brothers— all of us used to live jointly." But an argument between Jagdev and his father prompted the older man to apportion the land between Jagdev's two brothers. Jagdev was also saddled with a Rs 50,000 loan that he had taken with his father's support. "When we were together, everyone was ready to help in paying back the loan, but when I got separated, nobody was ready to help and I had to repay it," he said. His household slipped into poverty. "In 2002, a proposal came to the village to appoint a *shiksha mitra*," a government-appointed primary school teacher. Jagdev got the job but he said, "we have not progressed, because I am not paid even once in two years and the situation of farming is such that the condition is really bad." He is "unable to repay the interest itself" on the loan. "With great difficulty we are able to eat twice a day."

Prem and Jagdev represent two faces of mobility in Ant Sant, rising and falling—a reality that is obscured by the focus on net poverty reduction figures alone.

This core finding of the Moving Out of Poverty study, that rising and falling are both important and should be considered separately, is borne out by statistics across the communities. Results from the four states affirm a net decline in poverty over the 10-year period, ranging from 11.1 percentage points in the sampled villages of West Bengal to 7.4 percentage points in Andhra Pradesh, 7.3 percentage points in Uttar Pradesh, and 1.5 percentage points in Assam (table 1.4). Although the sampling is not meant to be representative of each state as a whole, these results are consistent with what we know about statewide performance.[9] But more importantly, the statewide statistics on movers and fallers confirm that communities that are superior in generating opportunities for upward mobility may not be equally successful in preventing slippage into poverty.

For instance, in West Bengal the research finds that 18.8 percent of households moved up and out of poverty between 1995 and 2005. But 7.7 percent of households—a higher percentage than in any other state sample—fell into poverty, resulting in the net poverty reduction rate of 11.1 percent. Without the falling, West Bengal would have had almost 19 percent poverty reduction. In Assam, a falling rate of 5.5 percent almost entirely negated the moving rate of 7.0 percent to produce the lowest net poverty reduction rate across the

TABLE 1.4

Moving out of poverty and falling into poverty both affect net poverty reduction rates

State	% initially poor	% movers	% fallers	% change in poverty
Uttar Pradesh	66.7	12.8	5.5	−7.3
Andhra Pradesh	63.8	10.6	3.2	−7.4
West Bengal	63.3	18.8	7.7	−11.1
Assam	71.5	7.0	5.5	−1.5

four states, 1.5 percent. While the falling rate in the sampled communities of Uttar Pradesh was identical to Assam's (5.5 percent), a higher moving rate (12.8 percent) resulted in greater net poverty reduction. Finally, communities in Andhra Pradesh recorded a lower movement out of poverty than those in Uttar Pradesh (10.6 percent versus 12.8 percent), yet the two states scored about the same on overall poverty reduction because of the lower number of fallers in Andhra Pradesh (3.2 percent versus 5.5 percent).

These findings show that when we focus on net poverty reduction numbers alone, we lose sight of the different phenomena that together contribute to the net poverty numbers. This can lead to policy missteps. Movers and fallers face very different opportunity sets and different challenges in their pathways out of and into poverty. If we hope to accelerate poverty reduction, these phenomena have to be disaggregated and correctly understood.

Three: While moving up is primarily a story of initiative, the chronic poor are not lazy—they undertake as many initiatives as the well-off, but they still remain poor

> *A rat who is caught in a rat trap tries everything to escape. In the same way, a poor person does everything he possibly can to escape poverty, but he is so deeply surrounded by it that his wish is just left a wish.*
>
> —Women's discussion group, Uttar Pradesh

One of the most important findings of the study, and one that should fundamentally reframe the public policy debate on poverty in India, is that poor people are constantly taking initiatives to escape poverty. In an effort to understand how people accumulate assets and move up, the study carried out systematic analysis of 2,700 life stories and over 35,000 events and shocks in people's lives. This analysis revealed three important patterns. First, when we asked movers how they had managed to move up and escape poverty, the reason they mentioned most frequently was their own initiative. Second, the most important reason for upward movement across *all* mobility groups, including the chronic poor, is individual initiative.

Third, the kind of initiative the chronic poor are able to undertake differs from the initiatives taken by movers and the rich, and this helps explain why their upward movement is not enough to lift them out of poverty. Lacking capital to buy equipment and assets, and with few social connections to networks of the well-off, poor people face extremely limited choices. They try to make up for lack of capital and connections with sheer hard work, most often backbreaking physical labor, but this is seldom enough. There is no evidence that most poor people are lazy, drunk, or sitting idle. The problem is lack of opportunity and lack of the supports that poor people need to take advantage of new opportunities. Particularly crucial is the ability to connect to markets on fairer terms.

Life story data also provide insights into the channels through which people accumulate assets that enable them to move up. These data show that initiative is the most frequent channel: in a discussion of triggers for asset accumulation, initiative was mentioned 53 percent of the time and institutions 42 percent of the time, while inheritance and infrastructure were barely mentioned at all (table 1.5). The results by mobility group are more telling still. Initiative was the single most frequent reason for asset accumulation by the chronic poor (54 percent). This was slightly higher than the corresponding figure for the never poor (52 percent) and only slightly lower than the figure for movers (56 percent).[10] This finding alone should lay to rest any lingering perceptions of the poor as lazy or unmotivated.

The study found that while the chronic poor take a similar number of initiatives as movers and the never poor, the initiatives they are able to take are critically constrained, hampering their ability to move out of poverty. Life story after life story revealed poor people who attempted many different economic activities and worked hard yet remained poor (box 1.2).

The detailed quantitative data on the kinds of initiatives undertaken by the different mobility groups provide some answers as to why the chronic poor remain in poverty (table 1.6). First, in their main activity, agricultural production, poor people rely disproportionately on hard work. This undoubtedly reflects their inability to make complementary investments in assets and

TABLE 1.5

Across mobility groups, initiative is most important reason for upward movement

	% of asset accumulation events				
Trigger for asset accumulation	Movers	Chronic poor	Fallers	Never poor	Total
Initiative	56	54	46	52	53
Institutions	41	43	46	42	42
Inheritance	3	3	8	6	5
Infrastructure	0	0	0	0	0

Source: Narayan, Nikitin, and Richard (2009), chapter 2 in the present volume.

BOX 1.2
The chronic poor work hard to escape poverty

Prafulla is a 43-year-old man from Bilpar village in Assam. "At the time of my birth, our family economic condition was not good. My father used to do farming as well as work on daily wage. With much hardship, I read up to class 10, and in the year 1979, I appeared for matriculation examination but failed to get through the examination. After failure in matriculation, I went to Silchar in search of work."

Prafulla tried his hand at multiple jobs as he strived to improve his household's income. He first worked in a paper mill in Silchar. "I didn't like to continue there at such a low salary. So I returned to my village in 1983 and started farming. But by farming, I could sustain my family up to six months only and for the remaining six months I had to work on daily wage basis. In 1998, I went to Rani to work under a mason as a helper." In mid-1998, he returned to Bilpar, his birthplace, and started working as a daily wage laborer. The following year, he purchased two plowing bulls, and his family's condition improved as a result. "The worry about rice has decreased. But in the same year, my beloved mother expired."

Prafulla now relies primarily on his income as a daily wage laborer. "Farming could not sustain, and there was scarcity everywhere because of bad rains." In 2002, his daughter graduated from high school. "It was a remarkable event in my life because there was not a single matriculate in our whole family." But "there was no money to admit my daughter into a college. I am not getting work regularly."

TABLE 1.6

In agriculture, movers benefit from new assets and technology while chronic poor rely on hard work

Trigger for asset accumulation	% of asset accumulation events			
	Movers	Chronic poor	Fallers	Never poor
New business	27	32	39	23
Purchase of asset or new technology	28	7	15	31
Hard work	11	23	15	10

Source: Narayan, Nikitin, and Richard (2009).

new technology for farming. Movers, by contrast, cited hard work as a trigger for asset accumulation only half as often as the chronic poor, and they were four times as likely as the chronic poor to say that purchase of assets or new technology had played a role. This purchasing power enables movers to invest in the kinds of initiatives that remain out of reach for poor people.

The chronic poor do not *choose* to take less effective initiatives. Rather, weak social and familial networks limit the extent to which they can mobilize external support to make the kinds of investments necessary for escaping poverty. In Hathina, Uttar Pradesh, Suresh said, "Nobody has helped me in any way in my life," while in Bidrohipar, Assam, Ziauddin observed that he has many good friends "but they cannot help me because they are also poor." In fact, the chronic poor are half as likely as movers to rely on family support in their business ventures.[11]

Like fallers, the chronic poor are also disproportionately subject to shocks (see finding four below). But, in contrast to fallers, the chronic poor experience these shocks from a very low initial asset base and thus have even fewer prospects of recovery. All too often, the poorest are forced to sell the few assets they own in a desperate attempt to ensure their family's survival. In West Bengal, discussants who had received small parcels of land under the state land reform program spoke of how they had to sell the land parcels to meet unexpected expenses, ranging from medical treatments to food during poor harvests. In Halapara, West Bengal, Ranjan, a 45-year-old chronic poor man, said, "I got 8 katha patta land [about 0.7 acre of redistributed land] in 1982. Due to ill health, I had to sell off the land in 1983 for 8,000 rupees." And in Gutri, Amol described how he was forced to sell the 5 katha of land that he had received from the government in 1980. "In 1998, I lost everything as I sold my land that year. For cultivation, our main source of water was our nearby canal. But in 1996, water of the canal dried up. So cultivators faced difficulty, and their condition became worse. So to return money that I had borrowed earlier, I had to sell my land." Thus, while shocks can drive those once wealthy into poverty, they also ensure that a large number of the poor are confined to years of hard work at the margins.

Four: Falling is primarily a story of health and social shocks

Malaria first took my youngest child, then my husband. I was forced to become a maidservant. Without husband there's no life. Then my eldest got malaria too. I sold my jewelry to save him from the jaws of death.

—A faller, Uttar Pradesh

The study found that most fallers are plunged into poverty by unexpected events and expenses related to ill health or death, family and social obligations, and family breakdown.

Mohiroop, a 30-year-old man from Dostpur, Uttar Pradesh, told the story of his family's descent into poverty. "My financial condition was very good earlier. Farming was inherited from our forefathers. . . . We never faced any shortages of life. . . . When I started doing this work, my elder brother was not keeping good health. A lot of money was spent on his treatment and in a way our family was ruined since then. In the year 1996, I had to sell 2 bighas of land for the purpose of meeting expenses on the treatment of my elder brother. But we could not save our elder brother still. In the year 2002, I sold another 2 bighas of land in order to meet expenses on the marriage of my younger sister. I felt very sad about this, but it was the marriage of my sister after all so I had to do that."

Biren, a man from Leteku Gaon village in Assam, recounted how his household fell into poverty. "At one point in time our family condition was good. My father had four sons. He had also cultivable land to maintain us all. In 1990, we divided our father's property among the brothers. I used to do cultivation before 1991. From 1991, I started doing daily wage work. In 1995, my father died and after four months my mother was also dead. From 1997, my wife has been suffering from mental disease. I did all possible means to give her a good treatment but she was not cured. . . . At times I faced problems even to get enough food for my family. In 1999 I had to mortgage out a piece of my land for 3,000 rupees. In 2002, I sold my wife's golden ring for 1,800 rupees. I had to maintain my family through these resources."

Various shocks related to death, ill health, social obligations, or other factors can bring about or hasten a downward spiral of asset depletion and poverty. With each expensive family event—first illness, then a wedding—Mohiroop was forced to sell more land, his most important asset. Biren mortgaged his land and sold his wife's jewelry in an attempt to meet unforeseen costs.

The psychological impact of shocks can be as damaging as the financial effects. Losing land and other valuable assets and barely able to feed their families, fallers like Mohiroop and Biren struggle to maintain their dignity. Some fallers give up hope that they will ever rise on the ladder of life once more. A villager in Assam spoke of his exhaustion in facing a series of illnesses in his family—his own illness, his parent's illness, and the mental illness of his brother resulting from the conflict. As a final blow, in 2005, floods destroyed all his land. "I don't think my life is dynamic. It has become static," he said. "I feel demoralized."

Mohiroop's and Biren's stories are typical of the broader experiences of fallers throughout the 300 Indian communities in this study. When we coded life story data to explore the triggers for asset depletion among people who have fallen into poverty, we found that death and health shocks together play the largest role (34 percent). They are closely followed by social shocks, including family divisions and the expenses incurred for marriages of children (27 percent). Financial shocks such as business or crop failures, destruction of property, or theft account for a further 18 percent of descents (table 1.7).

Differences do, however, emerge across the state samples. Death- and health-related shocks dominate the accounts of fallers in Assam. Fifty percent of all fallers interviewed for the life story exercise in that conflict-affected state cited illness or death as the main trigger for their asset depletion, the highest among the four sampled states. In Uttar Pradesh, a state with a falling rate similar to Assam's (table 1.4), the significance of death and health shocks is lower: together they account for only 31 percent of all asset depletion events. Social shocks, including family divisions and expenses for ceremonies like marriages, explained another 31 percent of descents in Uttar Pradesh, more than in any other state in the study. Poor people interviewed in Uttar Pradesh lamented the ever-increasing expenditures on the marriage of their daughters, among other social obligations. One woman spoke of saving money for her daughter's dowry since the day of the child's birth:

TABLE 1.7

Death and health shocks are leading reason for asset depletion among fallers

	% of asset depletion events among fallers				
Shock	Uttar Pradesh	Andhra Pradesh	West Bengal	Assam	Total
Death	20	22	15	28	20
Health	11	10	15	22	14
Social	31	16	30	16	27
Financial	17	19	23	14	18
Education	10	15	9	11	10
Other	11	18	8	9	11
Total	100	100	100	100	100

Source: Narayan, Nikitin, and Richard (2009).

"I was happy on her birth because she was my first child. But I was also sad because the birth of a girl in a poor family is equivalent to death." Social shocks are also high in West Bengal, explaining 30 percent of downward movements.

In contrast, social shocks receive less mention in Andhra Pradesh: they were cited only 16 percent of the time as a trigger for falling. And while shocks related to death figure prominently in explanations (22 percent), those related to health (10 percent) are mentioned less frequently than in any other state. The low explanatory power of social and health shocks in Andhra Pradesh hints at the valuable role played by women's self-help groups, which provide loans at favorable rates to help members cope with just such family crises and obligations. Women in Malkapur reflected on the role of numerous self-help groups organized under the state government program known as Velugu (literally "light"): "These groups have helped us in many ways by giving us loans for the marriages of our daughters. At the time of our daughter's marriage many of us borrowed 15,000 rupees. . . . The rate of interest is very much less [than for other loans]." In Appilepalle, members of a self-help group recalled, "One member utilized her loan amount for her treatment in the hospital, and now she is all right. One member took loan to perform her daughter's marriage."

A range of factors contribute to falls into poverty, including household, community, and institutional circumstances.[12] A quantitative exercise based on survey data reveals several correlates of descent among the vulnerable (annex 1.2). Households that experience difficulties finding work or accessing medical treatment in time of sickness, or are burdened with debt, have higher risks of falling. Household-specific factors such as an adverse change in the composition of the household—the addition of dependent members or the departure of wage earners, for instance—are also associated with greater risks of falling down. Conversely, access to regular employment and responsive local government can help reduce the risk of falling.[13]

Most accounts of fallers in the India study place the onset of decline much earlier than 1995, the benchmark year selected for mapping movements in and out of poverty. In fact, the life story analyses reveal that people typically start on their path toward poverty or affluence *as early as 15 years of age*. This points to the need to study long-term dynamics. Descent and ascent alike are often the product of long-term processes—a frequently overlooked point in conventional income poverty dynamics involving short panels. And this divergence happens very early, in the teenage years, in rural villages. While the demographic bulge has been celebrated, strategies to create economic opportunities for young teenagers are critical in breaking poverty traps.

Five: Aspirations are a powerful force for moving out of poverty

> *I am dreaming to see my children as doctors and engineers. That is my desire.*
>
> —A woman who recently moved out of poverty, Chennampalle,
> Andhra Pradesh

> *I want to start a dairy farm in the next 10 years to supply pure milk to the villagers. I also want to be an honest social worker, because social service is our duty. I am ready to invest my profit in social service. My parents' blessing is the most important. Don't you think that this blessing is the most important?*
>
> —A male youth who moved out of poverty, Assam

Few large poverty studies to date have sought to integrate the psychological dimensions of human and social capabilities. In the Moving Out of Poverty study, individuals and groups consistently spoke of the importance of psychological characteristics—motivation, determination to succeed, and belief in oneself, one's community, and one's country. Poor people attest that, despite the great difficulties they face, they have high aspirations for themselves and for their children.[14] And we find strong evidence to suggest that these aspirations against all odds do contribute to upward mobility.

We see this in the life of Urmila. She has blazed a trail, not only in her family but also in her village of Booti in Uttar Pradesh. Her aspirations have been a powerful force for her own education and a source of inspiration for others. She said, "I am doing BA and I want to be IAS [Indian Administrative Service]. Therefore, I am doing preparation. I am making notes and studying seriously. . . . I faced difficulty because my family members were not allowing me to study after fifth but I insisted. I was beaten in the home also, but still I did not change my mind. I escaped from the home and went on to sit on one branch of the tree. Then people find me, and my uncle and father agreed for my further study."

Sandhya, another young woman in Booti, believes that Urmila's aspirations have helped expand the realm of the possible for others. "I want to be a teacher after completing study. Therefore, I am doing study with heart. I will study after marriage also. The helping factor in this is Urmila of the village who is the first to study after class 5 after fighting with her family members. We are also studying further since then."

Overall, 77 percent of households expect that their children will be better off in the future, another 17 percent say they will be in a similar situation, and only 6 percent believe they will be worse off (table 1.8). Moreover, 65 percent of the chronic poor hold an optimistic view of their children's future. In short, the majority of poor people do not lack what Appadurai (2004) describes as a "capacity to aspire," that is, to imagine a different future. And aspirations serve as a motivation to action that can lead to better futures.[15]

It is not surprising, however, that movers have a higher level of aspiration for their children than the chronic poor (table 1.8). Running linear regressions, we also find that aspirations for a better future are highly significantly associated with mobility in Uttar Pradesh, West Bengal, and Assam (table 1.10). Interestingly, in Andhra Pradesh, most probably because of the self-help group movement, even the chronic poor have high aspirations and hence there is little association between aspirations and mobility.

Success is likely to reinforce belief in oneself, and so as people move out of poverty, their aspirations also grow. But aspirations are far from entirely state-dependent. Among young people discussing their future goals in West Bengal, for example, 35 percent favored an occupational choice similar to that of their parents, such as farming, while 65 percent aspired to a different career path, such as nonfarm occupations. Bringing the voices of other young people and their parents to the fore, box 1.3 indicates that there is little intergenerational transfer of low aspirations.

TABLE 1.8

In all mobility groups, a majority of parents have high aspirations for their children

| Expectation for children's future | % of households | | | | |
	Movers	Chronic poor	Fallers	Never poor	Total
Better	87	65	54	86	77
Same	10	26	29	10	17
Worse	3	9	17	4	6
Total	100	100	100	100	100

BOX 1.3
Shaping pathways out of poverty

The occupational aspirations of young men and women serve as their inspiration—their driving force for the future. And youth tend to hope for different occupations than those practiced by their parents, especially in mover and chronic poor households. In Bhotpara, West Bengal, Ashok's father is a farmer while his mother works in the home and sells puffed rice. But Ashok has different plans: "I want to run a business of my own in the future. My plans are to start my own stationery shop with my savings or by taking a loan, if I am allowed one." Sibu from Biruha, West Bengal, is determined to relieve his parents from the drudgery of agricultural labor and paper packet making: "At present, I am doing vegetable business after passing Madhyamik [secondary school exam]. . . . I will provide two meals a day to my parents by earning myself and will bring my brother in this business after getting him educated up till Madhyamik."

Parents, too, are determined to provide their own children with a brighter future. Pampa from Amdahara, West Bengal, recalled that her father toiled on 2 bighas of land and couldn't afford to educate her beyond the sixth grade. She does not want to limit her own children's dreams because of poverty. "I have a son and three daughters. I'm trying to educate them and make them government [civil] servants."

Six: Poor people's self-confidence and empowerment matters

Courage, ability, and power to assist oneself gives empowerment, which in turn helps to come out of poverty.
—Men's discussion group, Virupapuram, Andhra Pradesh

Now that I am old, I have seen too many things and worked a lot, but there is no freedom from poverty. Poverty is a daily friend of mine. It will not leave me until I die.
—Dhruba, a 51-year-old chronic poor woman, Saturia, West Bengal

A belief in oneself, a sense of one's own power and rights, and a feeling of control over decision making are all important for moving up. This emerged from both the qualitative and the quantitative survey data.

When poor people experience upward mobility, it reinforces their self-belief and also earns them respect from their families and peers. This boosts their confidence further. Netai from Gutri village in West Bengal was once a day laborer. He now runs a successful tea stall in the local marketplace. Netai alludes to a virtuous cycle of self-belief, respect from others, and economic mobility: "Today I am standing in a good position and have confidence in myself. I get respect from my family as well as from society." Men in a village in Uttar Pradesh said, "People feel more powerful after coming out of poverty because their relations with other people start improving. There is a common saying that a hungry man only invites further drought and is not welcome anywhere. A rich man however is welcome everywhere." Young women from the youth group of Hathina village in Uttar Pradesh insist that hard work and confidence go hand in hand in determining mobility. "When a poor person has got confidence that he can earn some money by doing hard work, he works extra hard and becomes self-dependent. This work automatically gives him power."

By contrast, those trapped in extreme poverty sometimes describe a cycle of low self-confidence, low social respect, and few prospects for upward mobility, in many cases going back to childhood. Banshiram from Bamrana village, Uttar Pradesh, said, "I spent my childhood in extreme poverty. I used to walk naked at the age of four or five. I could not go to the school because of poverty. Gradually, I grew old and started doing labor. . . . As a whole, my condition is the same. Neither do I have prestige in society nor have I got confidence."

In addition to evidence from life stories and discussion groups, the study uses two quantitative measures of empowerment: self-ratings on extent of power and rights and on extent of control over everyday decisions. In all states except Andhra Pradesh, people who moved out of poverty between 1995 and 2005 identified themselves as higher on a ladder of power and rights at the beginning of that period than those who had remained poor (figure 1.4).

FIGURE 1.4

In three states, movers rate themselves higher than chronic poor on power and rights 10 years ago

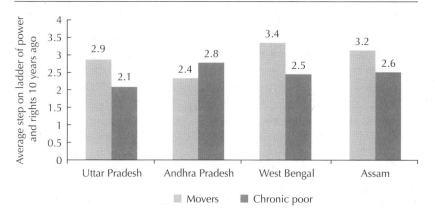

These findings suggest that starting off with a sense of "I can do it" may matter for economic mobility. Our regression results confirm a strong positive association between the two empowerment measures and movement out of poverty, even within a multivariate framework that controls for many other factors (table 1.10). The association between initial empowerment ranking and subsequent mobility is statistically significant in Uttar Pradesh and West Bengal, and the association between control over everyday decision making and mobility is significant in West Bengal and Assam.[16] The only exception to the pattern is Andhra Pradesh.

What explains the outlying results for Andhra Pradesh, where the chronic poor place themselves even higher on the ladder of power and rights 10 years ago than movers? As seen in the aspiration ratings as well, participation in self-help groups has helped build poor people's self-confidence in Andhra Pradesh, although it has not, as yet, translated into mobility out of poverty for all. This is explored in greater detail in chapter 5. Arika, a chronic poor woman from the village of Seedhi, notes that in spite of her continued poverty her social status has improved since she joined a collective. "In 2000 I joined the self-help group. My life changed after joining the group . . . Both in my house as well as in my village, I was respected by all the people. The group helped me to come up in my life." For now, Arika remains poor. But our findings suggest that her membership in a self-help group, which promotes its members' dignity, social standing and sense of "I can do it," could be an important first step to helping her escape poverty.

These findings corroborate a body of psychological evidence showing that self-belief affects people's "aspirations, level of effort and perseverance, resilience to adversity, and vulnerability to stress and depression" (Bandura 1998).[17]

Seven: Among institutions, family matters most

> *My wife gave me the inspiration and strength to progress in life. It was very difficult to run the family when I worked as a laborer. But my wife never complained. I was unable to fulfill the needs and dreams of my children and it made me feel sad. But she always encouraged and consoled me . . . Only because of her have I been able to progress in life and we have been able to see light at the end of the day.*
> —Uttam, a daily laborer, Ranigar, West Bengal

Life stories shed light on the roles of different local-level institutions in asset accumulation. In this study, four kinds of institutions—family, public institutions, civil society, and the private sector—mattered for moving out of poverty. Of these, family was by far the most important (table 1.9). When people discussed the institutions that helped them accumulate assets, about 83 percent of all references were to the family. Another 10 percent were to public institutions, while private sector and civil society accounted for only small fractions. Family becomes, if anything, more important to people who are facing economic difficulty: it is mentioned in 88 and 84 percent of cases by fallers and chronic poor respectively, versus 82 and 81 percent of cases by movers and the never poor.

This is not to say that public institutions, the private sector, and civil society do not matter for economic mobility. For one thing, the quantitative findings measure only the frequency with which various institutions played a role in asset accumulation; they say nothing about the relative importance of each event. It is plausible that even occasional interventions by government, civil society, or the private sector may contribute more to household well-being than regular support from family. For instance, Shymapada of Barwa village, West Bengal, moved out of poverty between 1995 and 2005. But his process of upward mobility began earlier, when his father received land under the state's land reform program. "In 1980 my father got land on barga [surplus land redistribution], which I am cultivating now."

When the testimonies of our participants are combined with the quantitative results, however, the overall picture suggests that family is indeed the first and most frequent recourse in good times and bad. The contributions of families are enhanced by family unity and diminished by family divisions. Mustafa, a 54-year-old man who has managed to move out of poverty in Nachni Ghat, Uttar Pradesh, reflected that "the main reason for my

TABLE 1.9

Across mobility groups, family is the most important institution in asset accumulation

Institution that helped in asset accumulation	% of asset accumulation events				
	Movers	Chronic poor	Fallers	Never poor	Total
Family	82	84	88	81	83
Public	10	7	7	13	10
Civil society	5	7	4	5	5
Private	3	2	1	1	2
Total	100	100	100	100	100

Source: Narayan, Nikitin, and Richard (2009).

upward movement is unity of family." Others have not been so lucky. Life story interviews resonate with the voices of chronic poor and fallers beset by family divisions.[18] One such person is Parvati, who was unable to continue in school beyond eighth grade because of a family dispute. "We had to pay for admission to school and my father went there to pay the fees. But my elder brother obstructed him from making the payment. That's why I had to leave my studies." Her father died the following year and the family's land was divided. Upon receiving 3 bighas, her brother distanced himself from the family. "He went away after father's funeral. He became our enemy after that," Parvati said. Heavy rainfall destroyed the family home in 2000. Parvati remembered, "I along with my mother passed our days in the temple, the villagers guarded us, my brother didn't even come to see us. Then I sold 11/2 katha out of 3 katha and I constructed my house newly with that money. After that my condition deteriorated further. I used to pass my days with half meal and after that I passed my days without taking any food." Parvati continues to eke out a living on her remaining land, under constant threat that her brother will snatch it away.

Families are, of course, not only important from a financial point of view. For Nurbibi, a woman from South 24 Parganas district, West Bengal, who has fallen into poverty, family represents a pillar in an unstable world. "My relation with my husband is the most important . . . Today he is bedridden, but for many years he brought up our children, arranged for our daughter's marriage. After his accident our land and other assets were sold. My family respect has remained the same; it has become neither more, nor less. We have good relation with everyone in the society." Nurbibi considers her husband to be a crucial source of relational and emotional support, even though he is unable to provide her with financial support.

The younger generation is also a source of solace and hope. Poor men and women in the study express pride in having provided their children with a higher level of education than they themselves received. Biren, a faller from Assam, sees his eldest son's scholarship to attend a lower primary school as "the only good news" in a decade. Prafulla, also from Assam, considers his daughter's graduation from high school to be "a remarkable event in my life because there was not a single matriculate in our whole family." Their pride reflects the expectation that their children will benefit from greater social esteem and income-earning opportunities thanks to their higher level of education. In close-knit families, parents will also be direct beneficiaries of their children's success. Nuruzan, of Baintala, West Bengal, remains in chronic poverty, and his son represents his principal source of hope. "The most important event in my life is my son's passing in BA examination. In the beginning we took the pain in getting him educated but after passing Madhyamik he went to Kolkata and passed the BA examination on his own expenses. Maybe he will get a good job and this will bring an end to our sufferings."

Eight: Poor people value democracy even when it does not help them

Those who pay more can get their work done faster; since the poor don't have money to give bribes, their work is never done.
—Women's discussion group speaking about obtaining licenses,
Doola Mau, Uttar Pradesh

If a man fails in intermediate college he becomes a doctor [quack], and if he fails in high school he becomes a political leader.
—Discussion with men, Hathnasa, Uttar Pradesh

The easiest way to be powerful is to grasp the hand of the party. Only then will you have many privileges.
—Women's discussion group, Kantipur, West Bengal

In all states, poor women and men value democracy as an ideal even when the practice of it is less than perfect. While local democratic structures are instrumental in promoting economic mobility, not everyone benefits equally. Contrary to the skeptics' view, local democracy has helped at least some poor people move out of poverty; it is not always captured by the elite. But the gains of the movers from local democracy do not come without costs. Using the statistical tool of leave-out means (LOM), we establish that movers often achieve their gains at the expense of nonmovers, especially in West Bengal and Assam. This seems to be related in part to the party, political, factional, and other clientelist links that the movers are more successful in forging. And while movers benefit more than the chronic poor, the rich benefit most of all from local democracy—a comment on pervasive inequality and corruption. Finally, the two most important factors across states associated with responsive local democracy are availability of information about local government and individual empowerment.[19]

Democracy is not an abstract notion for the people in our discussion groups. For many, it is akin to freedom and equality: in the words of female discussants in Kantipur, West Bengal, "Democracy means equal rights for men and women. Men will not get more freedom and women will not get less freedom." Participation is frequently mentioned as an essential element. "Democracy means to join with people to rule ourselves," said a men's group from Mechiri village in Andhra Pradesh. And empowerment and fairness are cited as two key principles of democracy. Men from Shekh Dahir in Uttar Pradesh said democracy exists "where more importance is paid to the voice of the people." Those in Pakhimora Gaon, Assam, said that "in democracy, all are equal. A poor person can reject or select an MP [member of Parliament] or a minister [of government]. There are no religious differences." However, as we will see, the participants in our study also recognize that their local governments are imperfect vehicles for realizing freedom, equality, participation, empowerment, and fairness.

The context for local democracy is different in each of the four states. In many parts of Andhra Pradesh, a strong self-help group movement acts as a complement to local democratic structures by demanding accountability from officials and amplifying the voices of poor people in local politics. In Assam, local governments face the challenge of operating in a conflict environment. In Uttar Pradesh, caste divisions have historically shaped local democratic structures. And finally, West Bengal's local democracy is unique due to three decades of Left Front rule and the implementation of extensive land reforms from the late 1970s onward.

Villagers across these states testify to democracy's potential to contribute to their economic prosperity. They suggest that local governments can facilitate mobility when they transfer funds from the state to the district or village level and help implement programs providing access to land, housing, and credit. Sankata, a 38-year-old man in Gautamman Khera, Uttar Pradesh, attributes his ability to move out of poverty to a government land redistribution program: "I moved upward only because the government had given me 1.5 bigha of land in 1996. This brought happiness in my family and the living standard also became good because earlier I was landless." Rajamma, a mover from Kondittangi, Andhra Pradesh, said, "We got financial help from government to construct our house, which increased our status in society." Niranjan of Paila, Assam, attributes his upward mobility to the Prime Minister's Rojgar Yojana (PMRY) program to promote self-employment. "After taking PMRY loan in the year 2001, I developed the shop. Presently it is my main source of livelihood."

Our quantitative findings confirm the positive association between local democracy and movement out of poverty. In all states except Assam, the majority of movers report being very or somewhat satisfied with their local government. Moreover, in all states, among those who were poor 10 years ago, a higher proportion of movers than chronic poor report being very or somewhat satisfied with their local government. That is, those who moved out of poverty were more satisfied with local democracy than those who remained poor over the study period (figure 1.5).

We constructed a composite measure of local democracy using four variables: perceptions of responsiveness, ability to influence action of local government, trust, and satisfaction. In three of the four states—Assam, Uttar Pradesh, and West Bengal—there are strong positive and significant associations between responsive local government and moving out of poverty, even after controlling for an array of other community- and household-level variables (table 1.10).[20] However, the association is not statistically significant for Andhra Pradesh.

These positive findings about the links between responsive local democracy and movement out of poverty support the optimists' view on the promise of local democracy, even though, as we will see, much remains to be improved.[21]

Notwithstanding this generally positive association between local democracy and movement out of poverty, participants in the study—especially the

FIGURE 1.5
More movers than chronic poor are satisfied with local democracy

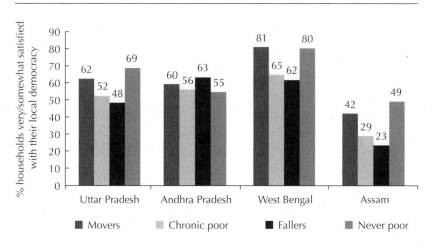

TABLE 1.10

Correlates of escape from poverty: Summary results from state-level household regressions for movers

Correlates of moving out of poverty	Uttar Pradesh	Andhra Pradesh	West Bengal	Assam
Responsiveness of local democracy	+***	+	+*	+**
LOM of responsiveness of local democracy	–	+	–***	–**
Corruption	–	+	+*	+
Fairness index	+**	+	+	+*
Empowerment (initial)	+***	n.a.	+***	+
LOM of empowerment (initial)	–**	n.a.	–***	+**
Control over everyday decisions	..	–	+***	+***
LOM of control over everyday decisions	–	–*	–*	–
Household aspirations	+***	+	+***	+***
LOM of household aspirations	–***	–	–***	–
Index of collective action	–**	–*	+	+
Violence against women	+	+*	–	+***
LOM of violence against women	–	n.a.	+	–***
Health shocks	–	–**	–	–*
Initial assets (land/asset index)	–	+*	+***	+
Education of household head	+***	+	+	+***
State-level context				
Scheduled caste dummy (Uttar Pradesh)	–***	n.a.	n.a.	n.a.
Membership in groups (Andhra Pradesh)	n.a.	+**	n.a.	n.a.
Diversification dummy (West Bengal)	n.a.	n.a.	+***	n.a.
Conflict trajectory (Assam)	n.a.	n.a.	n.a.	+*
Observations	969	531	648	452
R^2	0.32	0.18	0.47	0.31

Note: For illustrative purposes, only the signs and the level of significance of the partial correlates of upward mobility are reported. The actual regression results underlying this table are provided in annex 1.1 along with a brief discussion of regression analysis in the state chapters.

***   statistical significance at 1% level

**   statistical significance at 5% level

*   statistical significance at 10% level

..   zero coefficient

n.a. not applicable (variables not included in model)

chronic poor—emphasize the unequal advantages provided by public institutions. Who benefits and who loses depends largely on the local context. As we will see in the state chapters, supporters of the ruling coalition have tended to enjoy privileged access in Assam and West Bengal, while other backward castes (OBCs) have often gained an advantage over scheduled castes (SCs) in Uttar Pradesh.

But whatever the precise configuration of benefits, the chronic poor everywhere describe a similar phenomenon: a local institutional structure that works to the advantage of the few rather than the many. In Bidrohipar and Gobhali, the two Assamese communities featured at the beginning of this chapter, villagers allude to deep corruption in the distribution of government resources and in the administration of justice. According to men in Raja Pukhuri, Assam, "Democracy is like a pond. The pond has not only fish but also other animals like frogs and snakes. The snakes catch the frogs while the big fish eat the small fish. Democracy too is a pond where man eats man." Women in Kantipur, West Bengal, testified that "the easiest way to be powerful is to grasp the hand of the party. Only then will you have many privileges." And members of a female youth group from Sheopura in Uttar Pradesh noted that the village leaders can only be reached by those "who are of the same caste or flatter them a lot."

Movers and the never poor often corroborate these observations, noting that access to employment, business licenses, or support during emergencies stems from having privileged access to local government. Sukatan, a 30-year-old male mover from Nanagar, West Bengal, stated, "Since 1996 I am attached with the party and the involvement with the party brought me the peace of mind. At the initiative or effort of the party I was allotted a space in the market wherein I could give an opening of my business."

The notion that local democracy helps some but not others is also reflected in the quantitative data. As shown in table 1.9, the never poor are twice as likely as the chronic poor to say that public institutions helped them accumulate assets. Data on corruption also indicate that local government is more open to those with financial means. Bribe taking is perceived to have increased everywhere, more than doubling (from 24 to 57 percent) over the 10-year period across all communities. The starkest rise is in Uttar Pradesh, where the percentage of local village officials perceived as corrupt has risen from 35 percent in 1995 to 88 percent in 2005 (figure 1.6). So pervasive is the culture of bribery that a youth in a discussion group exclaimed, "I think even God would ask for a bribe to come and help us."

FIGURE 1.6
Bribe taking more than doubled across communities during the decade

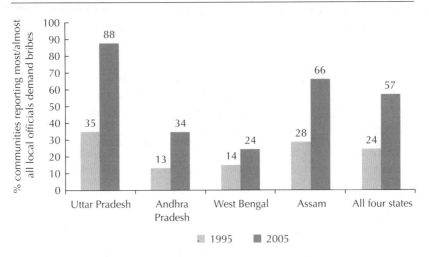

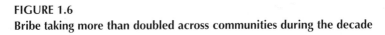

Regression analysis reinforces these findings (table 1.10 and annex 1.3).
We employed leave-out means to gauge the unevenness of households' experiences of local democracy. This technique averages all households' perceptions
of the responsiveness of local government in a community, excluding an individual household ("Household A"). The LOM for Household A is the average
of all household responses less A's own response. The technique enables us
to discern the extent to which A benefited from local democracy by excluding
or "crowding out" others. A negative coefficient in the states of Uttar Pradesh,
West Bengal, and Assam (statistically significant in West Bengal and Assam) is
indicative of considerable crowding out among households in their fight over
the very limited goods distributed by their local governments. Statistically, it
suggests that distribution of benefits through the channel of local democracy
benefits movers at the expense of the rest of the community.

In Andhra Pradesh, however, the correlation between the LOM of government responsiveness and moving out of poverty is positive, though statistically not significant. Qualitative evidence suggests that self-help groups
may perhaps have been instrumental in causing some positive spillovers for
the rest of the community. Local people cite greater accountability of local
government as one of the collective benefits accruing to communities as a
result of self-help groups (see chapter 5). In Korrapadu village, for instance,
a confederation of self-help groups now works alongside the panchayat to

solve problems related to water supply and agriculture. Male discussants commented, "The representatives are [now] working in fear of the people. They realized that the people respond to their mistakes." These communities in Andhra Pradesh are an exception to the broader observation that for many people in the study, local democracy remains a zero-sum game in which some win and others lose.

Given the spread of conflict in poor communities across India, it is important to explore the nature of the positive association between local democracy and movement out of poverty in Assam. Counterintuitively, we find a positive association between conflict in many communities and movement out of poverty. This appears to be linked to larger development transfers to Assam from the central government; these transfers are channeled directly to or supervised by local governments. Thus, despite suspicion of the state, and despite the fact that not all poor people benefit from these transfers, people do see positive associations between local democracy and mobility. These findings suggest a two-pronged approach to conflict-affected communities, comprising, one on hand, steps to strengthen law and order, and on the other hand, investment of resources to improve infrastructure (particularly roads), support people's livelihoods, and increase economic opportunity, particularly for young men and women.

Finally, responsive local democracy not only helps poor people move up, it also can help keep the well-off from descending into poverty. The quantitative results suggest a considerable role for responsive social and political institutions in reducing the chances of slippage into poverty. Communities that are rated as highly corrupt have less capability to reduce the chances of downfall; the coefficient is statistically highly significant and positive. In contrast, in communities with more responsive local government structures, the likelihood of falling into poverty is much less. Again, the matched coefficient on the index of local democracy is statistically highly significant with a positive sign (table 1.10).

Nine: The private sector and civil society are undertapped resources

I was running madly looking for a job.
>—Gonesh, a 30-year-old man, Raipur, West Bengal

People have developed well with the help of women's groups. They have more knowledge. They are becoming partners in politics. They want to know about government programs and form good, bad opinions on parties.
>—Discussion with men, Bestharapalle, Andhra Pradesh

Although they are potentially highly effective pathways out of poverty, the private sector and civil society rarely featured in people's accounts of economic mobility in their households and communities. Jobs, where they exist, are greatly valued and feature centrally in people's accounts of mobility. Gonesh, a 30-year-old man from Raipur, West Bengal, saw his life turn around when he finally found work in the nearby industrial town of Durgapur, two years after graduating from college. "I was running madly looking for a job. I used to send applications to different places but did not get any job. In the year 1997 my luck struck me. I got a job in Tara private company. All wants of my life were settled." But more often than not, poor people lament the lack of private sector opportunities in their villages. We are prompted to remember the fate of the villagers in Gobhali, the low-mobility village described at the beginning of this chapter, where the closure of a power house and mill left a vacuum in economic opportunity.

Overall, among the thousands of interviews conducted, we find little evidence that the formal private sector has contributed to movement out of poverty. As shown in table 1.9, movers cite the private sector only 3 percent of the time as a trigger for their asset accumulation. Moreover, those private sector opportunities that exist are not equally accessible to all. Nepotism and corruption place poor people, who lack the appropriate social networks or financial capital, at a distinct disadvantage. In the words of female youth group members in Langpuria, Assam, "To get a job, money is necessary. Nowadays one has to give bribe to get a job . . . It is even necessary for the highly educated guys to give bribe."

The wealthy also dominate access to loans for businesses. Male focus group discussants in Lakshmanpalle, Andhra Pradesh, commented that "it is difficult to do business by taking individual loans—those who don't have contacts and land holdings [cannot access them]." Gourikanta, a chronically poor construction worker in Raipara, Assam, related how his efforts to pull his family out of poverty were thwarted. "In 2002, thinking about doing business, I had applied in the Block Office for a loan of 10,000 rupees. But the people in the Block Office had not given any importance to my application. Actually they want bribes." Gourikanta was not able to pay the bribe. He continued to eke out a living through underpaid construction work, and his family remained trapped in poverty.

Denied access to more competitive sources of credit, poor people like Guru, from Ant Sant, Uttar Pradesh, often turn to informal moneylenders. Guru used an initial loan to buy two oxen. Two years later the oxen died in an epidemic and he was left with a huge debt. "I found it impossible to do farming when there were no oxen. The interest on the loan that I had taken from the moneylender kept on increasing. After this I leased out all my land and started working as a laborer," he said.

These experiences from life stories are backed up by other quantitative data from the household questionnaires. Table 1.11 indicates that better-off people have been able to capture many of the more competitive sources of credit for business. Among those who obtained credit, government banks were the source in 67 percent of cases for the never poor compared to only 23 percent of cases for the chronic poor. Meanwhile, the chronic poor and fallers are much more dependent on moneylenders (who provided credit in 23 and 20 percent of cases, respectively) than either movers or the never poor. It is telling that commercial banks are mentioned as a source of business loans across all mobility groups in only 5 percent of cases.

Civil society, comprising NGOs, self-help groups, community-based organizations, and youth groups, among others, seems largely absent from people's explanations of the most important factors that helped them move out of poverty. As demonstrated in table 1.9, civil society is deemed instrumental in only 5 percent of asset accumulation events. And, as shown in

TABLE 1.11
Well-off people get business loans from government banks, while poor people rely on moneylenders

	% of households that received a loan				
Credit source	Movers	Chronic poor	Fallers	Never poor	Total
Government bank	46	23	50	67	51
Moneylender	9	23	20	5	10
Friend	10	14	10	7	10
Relative	11	13	0	7	9
Community credit group/NGO	10	7	0	1	6
Commercial bank	4	2	5	7	5
Trader/store	1	11	5	4	4
Landlord	4	5	5	1	3
Other	4	0	5	1	2
Employer	0	2	0	0	0

table 1.11, community credit groups and NGOs are relatively unimportant sources of credit for business, used in only 6 percent of cases across mobility groups.

When it comes to credit for consumption purposes, however, civil society organizations play a more important role across the mobility groups (table 1.12). In Korrapadu, Andhra Pradesh, discussants described the situation before and after the Velugu program, which federates various self-help groups, came to the village. Before Velugu, villagers faced a number of problems, including land scarcity and drought, and "the landlords and the loan sharks took it as an advantage and gave loans to us. As people were in desperate situations they took loans at any interest that was quoted. . . . Those who could not pay had even worse situations to face. . . . They sold their cattle and sheep, they sold gold articles too. People were worried about loss of the land, property, money, and houses. . . . At that juncture Velugu scheme came as a blessing." Saraswathi, a local woman, added that thanks to Velugu they are able to "seek loans for weddings, constructing houses, treatment. . . . [I]t is saving us from the difficult situations."

Since civil society is concentrated in highly deprived areas, such as Korrapadu, it should be no surprise that its primary role has been to provide coping mechanisms to smooth consumption and meet emergency expenditures in times of crisis. Loans from civil society thus help prevent slippage into

TABLE 1.12

Civil society organizations are among the sources of credit for consumption

Credit source	% of households that received a loan			
	Movers	Chronic poor	Fallers	Never poor
Relative	27	22	21	17
Friend	16	17	16	12
Moneylender	19	26	31	22
Trader/store	10	10	14	16
Employer	0	4	0	0
Landlord	6	6	7	14
Community credit group/NGO	13	12	9	16
Government bank	8	2	2	3
Other	1	1	0	1

poverty. But these loans have been less useful for building assets and moving up, in part because they are typically small and have short repayment periods. Unfortunately, since poor people have limited access to larger government and commercial loans, they have few options for embarking on profitable off-farm activities and commercially oriented agriculture. The frustration of male discussants from Vellamaddi in Andhra Pradesh echoes throughout our sample villages: "Somebody has to help us with money. When we go to banks, the banks refuse to give big loans. The banks answer us by saying that big loans are not given by the bank. . . . New businesses are not possible for us."

Ten: Caste barriers are falling, but not everywhere

> *There is a lot of feeling of untouchability in this village. If you are a rich person, then everyone will pamper you. They try to crush us poor people under their feet.*
>
> —Rani, a poor, low-caste woman, Gautamman Khera,
> Uttar Pradesh

One of the most heartening findings of the Moving Out of Poverty study is that caste has become less of an issue in the surveyed communities of Andhra Pradesh, a state that has historically been associated with rigid caste hierarchies. This is not to imply that caste has disappeared from the equation. Indeed, as we see in the ladder of life for Kamalapur (table 1.1), and as discussed in greater detail in chapter 5, caste remains a powerful influence on perceptions of status. But villagers in the sampled communities generally point to a significant easing of social divides. For instance, male discussants in Malkapur reported, "In the past 10 years, inequality on the basis of caste has decreased to a great extent. Ten years back inequalities of caste and religion were predominant in our society. Due to these differences, people belonging to scheduled caste and scheduled tribe communities were not allowed to enter the temple. Now there are no such differences, and even SC and ST people are coming to the temple along with us. They are coming to our houses and sitting beside us."

Self-help groups have been instrumental in the process of breaking down age-old caste barriers. Across the statewide sample, villages where self-help groups have had a prominent role report more rapid decline in inequalities than villages where such groups have been marginal. In Govindapalle, Andhra Pradesh, a member of a self-help group observed, "There are no concessions, and there are no considerations to the issues of people's richness or high caste in our group. We are all equal. Though our members are of different occupations, it makes no difference. The members of our group do not belong to the same income group. There are people who are more financially backward than us, and there are those who are better off than us financially."

In Uttar Pradesh, conversely, while there has been some narrowing of the gap for other backward castes, caste remains a major barrier to mobility for members of scheduled castes. More than any other group, SC people remained trapped in chronic poverty. While they do not lack aspirations, their limited initial assets along with discriminatory local institutions and customs conspire to hold them back. In Imiliya, Uttar Pradesh, discussants acknowledge that theoretically, access to water should not be a problem—there are both wells and hand pumps in the village. But as one villager noted, "People of high castes like Brahmin and Thakurs didn't allow us to collect water from public pumps. Then we have to bring it from other villages."

Turning to the quantitative data on social stratification, we see that the number of communities reporting "no divisions" based on ethnicity, caste, or other social distinctions has increased across the entire sample over the course of the decade (figure 1.7). Assam, which has not historically faced significant caste divides, and West Bengal, which may have benefited from

FIGURE 1.7

Across states, number of communities reporting no social divisions increased between 1995 and 2005

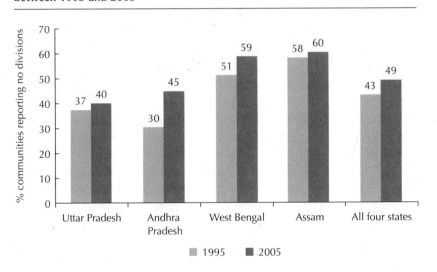

the caste-equalizing effects of decades of Left Front rule, report the lowest levels of division in 1995, with 58 and 51 percent of communities respectively described as division-free. Communities in Assam have seen little change in levels of social stratification over the course of the decade, while those in West Bengal have experienced further easing of divisions. In contrast, villages in both Andhra Pradesh and Uttar Pradesh reported a high level of division in 1995, with only 30 percent and 37 percent of communities respectively describing themselves as free of divisions in that period. While villages in Uttar Pradesh have experienced only marginal improvements over the decade, those in Andhra Pradesh have made great strides: an additional 15 percent of communities describe themselves as having no divisions in 2005.

The regression data corroborate these findings. Across the four states, caste has a strong and significant negative association with movement out of poverty only in Uttar Pradesh. In West Bengal, an insignificant caste association shows that a strong ideology of equality can play a significant role in changing social norms, while in Andhra Pradesh an insignificant correlation suggests that self-help groups have indeed played an important role in weakening the impact of caste on mobility prospects. In Assam, the caste factor has historically been unimportant in shaping social divides.

Conclusion: Some Policy Insights

The government gave me some bighas of land under land redistribution but the big farmers in the village took away that land forcibly and started tilling that land while the title deed was in my name. Till today I have not got the possession of the land. This is the main reason for my poverty.
—A chronic poor man, Teriya, Uttar Pradesh

The main purpose of the Moving Out of Poverty study in India is to generate insights with policy implications that can help expand movement out of poverty and prevent slippage into it. It is important to understand the local contexts in order to generate fine-tuned responses to the specific challenges that individual villages are facing. But the key findings across communities also help us draw some broader implications for the antipoverty agenda in India and even beyond.

First and foremost, the study underscores the importance of bottom-up approaches in which we listen to poor people and put them at the center of development policy. The life experiences related by 30,000 people across four states of India show that poor people take innumerable initiatives to move out of poverty. This finding refutes widespread stereotypes about poor people as unmotivated. It also validates the importance of maintaining, expanding, and scaling up support to poor people's initiatives. Support can take various forms (education, credit, migration, help coping with crisis) and come from various sources (state, private sector, NGO, local community, family).

Second, people in villages often see poverty as more pervasive than official data would indicate. When there are big differences between official poverty counts and people's own poverty counts, discontent with government policies will be high. This can result in electoral losses, even when programs have been expanded for the poor.

Third, the findings confirm the importance of looking beyond net poverty reduction to examine the dynamics of poverty. Reasons for moving up and for falling down are different, and to achieve the highest possible poverty reduction rates, policies must be designed to both expand upward mobility and contain falling.

To expand upward mobility, policy makers must focus on the quality of available economic opportunities as much as on the quantity. Since hard work alone is not enough to promote economic mobility, the challenge is to link poor people to markets, improve their market know-how, and provide access to sufficient credit that goes beyond immediate consumption needs. It is important to foster community-driven development programs that provide credit and skills training to members of people's organizations and federations and connect them to markets. The *organized* private sector—at present virtually absent from rural areas—can also play an important role in expanding economic opportunities and skills along with government and nongovernment actors.

Private philanthropy must refocus its attention on the inclusion of poor people in business processes. This can be done along several lines, for example, through employees sharing in equity or through creation of poor people's corporations as part of the supply chains of large enterprises. Rather than remaining at the bottom of the supply chain, poor producers need help in moving up the value chain to capture higher returns to their labor. Poor people also need access to the same financial instruments available to the well-off, including larger loans and ownership of large assets; this is essential to eliminate poverty in market-based economies. In essence, business models and practices have to change to emphasize greater profit sharing with poor people.

To prevent falling, health systems that are affordable and function well must be available to poor people. Health shocks are the single most common factor leading to the downward slide into poverty. Health insurance and other safety net schemes, as well as favorable terms of credit, can help interrupt downward spirals of asset depletion, debt, and loss of dignity and hope.

Fourth, the study demonstrates the importance of psychological factors such as aspirations, belief in self, personal agency, and empowerment, both for understanding movement out of poverty and for explaining why so many people remain trapped in poverty. While a driving sense of "I can do it" enables some poor people to move out of poverty, the chronic poor are often profoundly disheartened by the realization that the "system"—whether job opportunities, credit facilities, public goods, or social interactions—is rigged against them. Civil society, and in particular local collective organizations, can help empower poor people to connect to markets and hold corrupt local institutions to account.

Fifth, our research shows that local democracy, with all its imperfections, is already beginning to play positive roles in at least some poor people's lives. But two changes will be required if many more are to benefit. First, greater civil society presence in local communities is needed to improve the responsiveness and accountability of local democracy. Strategies include supporting organizations of poor people and increasing access to information about government activities at the local level. For example, schoolchildren can become involved in monitoring whether teachers and health care workers are present at their posts; this will prepare children for citizenship and problem solving and also help address a countrywide problem in which government programs targeted to poor people perform poorly. Second, with greater institutional accountability and increased political competition, it may become possible to change the mindsets of local politicians so that they shift from acting primarily as redistributors of state and central government subsidy programs and become facilitators of inclusive local economic development and markets.

Finally, the study highlights the importance of asset accumulation in escaping poverty. The initial level of assets, in multiple dimensions, matters: higher aggregate asset scores of households in West Bengal and Andhra Pradesh, and access to housing in Uttar Pradesh, are statistically significant correlates of subsequent escape from poverty. Qualitative datasets also confirm the importance of initial assets. Life stories collected for the study illustrate the critical importance of addressing the initial asset gap and the role a responsive local democracy can play in this. For the very poor, such asset transfer is often cited as the prime trigger for upward mobility, acting something like the "big push" in aid theory. This is true for access to land and also for access to permanent housing across all four states (not only in West Bengal, with its history of land reform). There are many ways of transferring assets to poor people. The broad policy point is that the question of poor people's access to assets—above and beyond the issue of improving the quality of their labor power—cannot be ignored if we are serious about poverty reduction.

Minimum access to assets such as housing is not just important for moving out of poverty. It also provides entry to community and citizenship. Having decent shelter, while clearly important to raising living standards, is also a bottom-line requirement for earning "citizenship in the village," living with dignity, and accessing all other benefits.

Annex 1.1 Correlates of Moving Out of Poverty

The regressions were conducted on the subsample of those who escaped poverty and rose above the community poverty line (called movers in the study). The reference category is the initial poor set, made up of movers plus the chronic poor. Overall assessment of the directionality of partial correlates of upward mobility, as presented here, is based on the results of the particular model specification and other considerations in the case of each state, as narrated in each state chapter. The chapters on West Bengal, Assam, and Uttar Pradesh present both unweighted and weighted regressions with broadly similar results; in the case of Andhra Pradesh, only weighted regression results are reported. The robustness of the results was checked under different statistical methods of estimation: ordinary least squares (OLS) versus probit in the case of West Bengal, Uttar Pradesh, and Assam, and OLS versus logit in the case of Andhra Pradesh. Those findings also suggest qualitatively similar results for the key variables of empowerment, aspirations, and democracy.

Correlates of moving out of poverty	Uttar Pradesh	Andhra Pradesh	West Bengal	Assam
Responsiveness of local democracy	0.043	0.021	0.023	0.036
	[3.87]***	[1.28]	[1.68]*	[2.02]**
LOM of responsiveness of local democracy	−0.033	0.031	−0.097	−0.088
	[1.57]	[0.89]	[2.68]***	[2.09]**
Corruption	−0.024	0.022	0.013	0.042
	[1.64]	[0.86]	[1.77]*	[1.62]
Fairness index	0.027	0.037	0.007	0.036
	[2.17]**	[0.84]	[0.39]	[1.97]*
Empowerment (initial)	0.046	—	0.074	0.016
	[3.52]***		[4.73]***	[0.77]
LOM of empowerment (initial)	−0.069	—	−0.081	0.126
	[2.43]**		[4.08]***	[2.08]**
Control over everyday decisions	0	−0.037	0.171	0.137
	[0.01]	[1.60]	[5.37]***	[3.48]***
LOM of control over everyday decisions	−0.023	−0.12	−0.124	−0.138
	[0.29]	[1.78]*	[1.88]*	[0.91]

continued

Correlates of moving out of poverty	Uttar Pradesh	Andhra Pradesh	West Bengal	Assam
Household aspirations	0.14	0.013	0.202	0.088
	[11.29]***	[1.11]	[9.53]***	[5.10]***
LOM of household aspirations	−0.173	−0.03	−0.175	−0.079
	[5.75]***	[0.93]	[5.43]***	[1.34]
Index of collective action	−0.029	−0.079	0.039	0.009
	[2.18]**	[1.98]*	[1.35]	[0.43]
Violence against women	0.029	0.046	−0.028	0.093
	[1.28]	[1.89]*	[0.67]	[3.45]***
LOM of violence against women	−0.065	—	0.074	−0.156
	[1.32]		[1.48]	[3.07]***
Health shocks	−0.015	−0.088	−0.019	−0.079
	[0.44]	[2.97]**	[0.45]	[1.75]*
Initial assets (land/asset index)	−0.018	0.061	0.038	0.056
	[0.52]	[1.98]*	[2.76]***	[1.19]
Education of household head	0.032	0.024	0.004	0.043
	[5.11]***	[0.86]	[0.58]	[3.16]***
State-level context				
Scheduled caste dummy (Uttar Pradesh)	−0.102	—	—	—
	[2.94]***			
Membership in groups (Andhra Pradesh)	—	0.068	—	—
		[2.02]**		
Diversification dummy (West Bengal)	—	—	0.146	—
			[3.11]***	
Conflict trajectory (Assam)	—	—	—	0.035
				[1.67]*
Observations	969	531	648	452
R^2	0.32	0.18	0.47	0.31

Note: Cluster-robust *t*-statistics in brackets.

*p < .10   **p < .05   ***p < .01

Annex 1.2 Correlates of Falling into Poverty for the Initially Nonpoor

The regressions were conducted on the subsample of those who have fallen into poverty, that is, who fell below the community poverty line (called fallers in the study). The reference category is the initial nonpoor set, made up of fallers plus the never poor.

Correlates of falling into poverty for the initially nonpoor	
Structural	
Unable to find work (yes=1, no=0)	0.046
	[1.72]*
Easier or harder to find work (easier=1, harder=0)	0.066
	[3.15]***
Source of income, regular employment	–0.089
	[3.00]***
Source of income, temporary employment	0.171
	[5.10]***
Initial assets	–0.048
	[4.76]***
Life cycle	
Dependency	0.062
	[3.29]***
Shocks	
Borrow credit for major household event	0.143
	[4.88]***
Dependency	0.062
	[3.29]***
Health condition (deteriorated=3, improved=1)	0.023
	[1.21]
Difficulty in getting treatment	0.157
	[4.86]***
Flood	–0.005
	[0.15]
Drought	0.034
	[1.12]

continued

Correlates of falling into poverty for the initially nonpoor	
Institutional	
Household trust: most people willing to help (no=0, yes=1)	0.036
	[1.93]*
Responsiveness of local democracy	−0.024
	[2.36]**
Local government run by a few	−0.005
	[0.18]
Corruption (high=5, none=1)	0.066
	[3.99]***
Social divisiveness	−0.008
	[0.69]
Inequality (3)	−0.004
	[0.39]
Constant	−0.303
	[2.85]***
Observations	953
R^2	0.27

Note: Cluster-robust *t*-statistics in brackets.

*p < .10 **p < .05 ***p < .01

Annex 1.3 OLS Regression Results with Responsiveness of Local Democracy as Dependent Variable

The regressions were conducted on the subsample of those who escaped poverty, that is, who rose above the community poverty line (called movers in the study). The reference category is the initial poor set, made up of movers plus the chronic poor. The results indicate that there is a significant positive association between responsiveness of local democracy on the one hand and access to information and individual empowerment on the other hand. This finding is strongly significant in all four Indian states.

Variable	Uttar Pradesh	Andhra Pradesh	West Bengal	Assam
Voting in elections (rh508)	0.094	0.019	0.174	0.043
	[3.56]**	[0.33]	[3.16]**	[1.42]
Distance to main center (c202bi)	0.001	−0.001	−0.004	0.005
	[0.16]	[0.28]	[0.56]	[1.01]
Household newspaper readership (h518)	0.012	0.008	0.009	0.009
	[3.45]**	[0.87]	[2.06]*	[2.42]*
Access to information about local government (rh515b)	1.08	0.567	1.098	0.823
	[20.47]**	[5.08]**	[7.62]**	[12.85]**
Participation in community decision making (rc916)	0.057	0.006	0.046	0.106
	[0.90]	[0.04]	[0.45]	[1.75]
Collective action (PCA rc412b, rc413b, with current weights)	0.009	0.011	0.007	0.108
	[0.18]	[0.11]	[0.11]	[2.91]**
Social capital (h406Tb)	0.025	0.001	0.081	0.01
	[0.44]	[0.03]	[1.52]	[0.24]
Individual empowerment (PCA rh501b, h708)	0.156	0.18	−0.234	0.294
	[4.81]**	2.87]**	5.75]**	[5.98]**
Violence against women in community (LOM h609b)	−0.407	−0.303	−0.084	−0.184
	[3.30]**	[0.96]	[0.35]	[1.45]
Education of household head (h106)	0.002	−0.015	0.022	−0.006
	[0.45]	[0.54]	[1.18]	[1.30]
Extent of social divisions (c414b)	0.007	0.15	−0.004	0.01
	[0.17]	[1.44]	[0.04]	[0.17]
Constant	−2.286	−1.268	−2.496	−1.689
	[7.26]**	[3.28]**	[5.40]**	[5.99]**
Observations	1,635	839	1,192	746
R^2	0.32	0.15	0.34	0.37

Note: Cluster-robust *t*-statistics in brackets.

*p < .10   **p < .05   ***p < .01

References

Alsop, R., M. F. Bertelsen, and J. Holland. 2006. Empowerment in Practice: From Analysis to Implementation. Washington, DC: World Bank.

Bandura, A. 1995. "Comments on the Crusade against the Causal Efficacy of Human Thought." *Journal of Behavior Therapy and Experimental Psychiatry* 26: 179–90.

———. 1998. "Personal and Collective Efficacy in Human Adaptation and Change." In *Advances in Psychological Science*, vol. 1, *Social, Personal, and Cultural Aspects*, ed. J. G. Adair, D. Belanger, and K. L. Dion, 51–71. Hove, UK: Psychology Press.

Bardhan, P., and D. Mookherjee. 2006. "Pro-Poor Targeting and Accountability of Local Governments in West Bengal." *Journal of Development Economics* 79 (2): 303–27.

Besley, T., R. Pande, and V. Rao. 2005. "Participatory Democracy in Action: Survey Evidence from South India." *Journal of the European Economic Association* 3 (2/3): 648–57.

Crook, R., and J. Manor. 1998. *Democracy and Decentralisation in South Asia and West Africa: Participation, Accountability and Performance*. New York: Cambridge University Press.

Dercon, S., and J. S. Shapiro. 2007. "Moving On, Staying Behind, Getting Lost: Lessons on Poverty Mobility from Longitudinal Data." In Narayan and Petesch 2007, 77–126.

Foster, A., and M. Rosenzweig. 2004. "Democratization and the Distribution of Local Public Goods in a Poor Rural Economy." Working Paper. adfdell.pstc.brown.edu/papers/democ.pdf.

Fuller, R. W. 2004. *Somebodies and Nobodies: Overcoming the Abuse of Rank*. British Colombia, Canada: New Society Publishers.

Kohli, A. 1990. *Democracy and Discontent: India's Growing Crisis of Governability*. New York: Cambridge University Press.

Krishna, A. 2004. "Escaping Poverty and Becoming Poor: Who Gains, Who Loses, and Why?" *World Development* 32 (1): 121–36.

Lewis, O. 1959. *Five Families: Mexican Case Studies in the Culture of Poverty*. New York: Basic Books.

Narayan, D. 2006. "Moving Out of Poverty: Conceptual Framework." Available on the Moving Out of Poverty Web site, http://go.worldbank.org/8K2Q8RYZ10.

Narayan D., S. Kapoor, and L. Pritchett. 2008. "Moving Up and Out of Poverty: Countries, Communities, and Individuals." Available on the Moving Out of Poverty Web site, http://go.worldbank.org/8K2Q8RYZ10.

Narayan, D., and P. Petesch, eds. 2007. *Moving Out of Poverty: Cross-Disciplinary Perspectives on Mobility*. New York: Palgrave Macmillan; Washington, DC: World Bank.

Narayan D., L. Pritchett, and S. Kapoor. 2009. *Moving Out of Poverty: Success from the Bottom Up*. New York: Palgrave Macmillan; Washington, DC: World Bank.

Petesch, P., C. Smulovitz, and M. Walton. 2005. "Evaluating Empowerment: A Framework with Cases from Latin America." In *Measuring Empowerment: Cross-Disciplinary Perspectives*, ed. D. Narayan, 39–67. Washington, DC: World Bank.

Rao, V., and M. Walton, eds. 2004. *Culture and Public Action*. Palo Alto, CA: Stanford University Press.

Sen, B. 2003. "Drivers of Escape and Descent: Changing Household Fortunes in Rural Bangladesh." *World Development* 31 (3): 513–34.

World Bank. 2005. *World Development Report 2006: Equity and Development.* New York: Oxford University Press.

Notes

1. For a brief review of the vast literature on subjective methods, see volume 1 in the Moving Out of Poverty series, *Cross-Disciplinary Perspectives on Mobility* (Narayan and Petesch 2007) and chapter 1 in volume 2, *Success from the Bottom Up* (Narayan, Pritchett, and Kapoor 2009).

2. To protect the privacy of participants, all villages in the study are identified by pseudonyms in this book. Higher-level entities (blocks, districts, states) are identified by their real names. Individual participants are identified only by their first (given) names.

3. The land units *bigha* and *katha* can have slightly different meanings in the different states of India and in different parts of a state. In this volume we assume that 1 bigha equals roughly one-third of an acre, the standard used in West Bengal (Bardhan and Mookherjee 2006). A katha is a fraction of a bigha. In some places 20 kathas equal 1 bigha, while in others 16 kathas make a bigha.

4. The framework is reflected in work by, among others, Rao and Walton (2004), World Bank (2005), Petesch, Smulovitz, and Walton (2007), Alsop, Bertelsen, and Holland (2006), and Narayan and Petesch (2007).

5. Separate focus groups were usually held for men and women.

6. If the village was too large, information was completed for at least 100 to 150 randomly selected households in that community.

7. In each village, household questionnaires were conducted with 15 individuals, 10 of whom were also interviewed for an open-ended life story. The respondents for these interviews were selected from the mobility matrix in a predefined proportion of 4:3:2:1 favoring movers, followed by never poor, chronic poor, and fallers respectively.

8. Some communities had as many as 10 steps on their ladder of life—by virtue of the diligent categorization work of the focus group—while others had fewer than five. We expected that villages with more steps might present a picture of greater economic mobility, as even small movements up or down would take a household from one step to the next. In villages with fewer steps, corresponding to broader well-being categories, we expected to see less movement from step to step. However, this does not appear to be the case when we compare summary statistics for mobility across villages. Specifically, churning (combined upward and downward movement) of households does not seem to be systematically higher in villages with 10 steps than in villages with five. Further details of the findings regarding the impact of number of ladder steps on measured indexes can be found in Narayan, Kapoor, and Pritchett (2008, 23, table 6).

9. This is in spite of a heavy bias toward poor communities in the sampled districts of Andhra Pradesh.

10. The only significant difference emerges among fallers, but even in their case, initiative is cited in 46 percent of all instances of asset accumulation.

11. According to the coding of individual life stories, family support contributes to businesses in 9 percent of cases for movers, 13 percent of cases for the never poor, 4 percent of cases for the chronic poor, and 11 percent of cases for fallers.

12. These factors can be broadly divided into four groups: structural (lack of growth and employment; level of initial assets); life-cycle factors (increase in dependency, property division among members of the same family); shocks (expenses associated with ill health, natural disaster, social obligations surrounding family weddings and funerals); and institutional (quality of local government, social capital, etc.). Information on a limited number of these indicators is available from the survey data, which has conditioned the choice of precise variables. On these aspects see Dercon and Shapiro (2007), Krishna (2004), and Sen (2003).

13. It is interesting to note that propensity to collective action—the indicator of "willingness to help each other in crisis"—is associated with higher chances of falling. This apparently perverse finding actually shows the possibility of reverse causality: falling households aspire to get together to collectively cope with their crises, but in most cases such initiatives meet with failure. Collective social action can partially mitigate but cannot prevent falling in the presence of credit market failures and in the absence of other risk-mitigating institutional interventions that remain outside poor people's control.

14. Expectations about one's future (and about children's futures) were considered as a close proxy for aspiration in the framing of the questionnaire. These measures were subsequently found to be positively correlated with the likelihood of movement out of poverty (table 1.10). More needs to be done methodologically to operationalize the concept of aspiration in the context of household surveys—a subject matter for future research.

15. Our findings further shatter the notion of a "culture of poverty" (Lewis 1959), in which children of the poor are socialized into believing that they deserve to be poor.

16. The movers' sense of empowerment does not appear to be the result of a pure "halo effect," whereby movers would retrospectively attribute a higher level of power to themselves because of their economic mobility, since we run the regressions on community-assigned rather than self-designated measures of mobility (table 1.10). In other words, our results for West Bengal and Uttar Pradesh demonstrate a strong positive correlation between those who self-identify as having been higher on the ladder of power and rights 10 years ago and movement out of poverty since then. Alternative indicators of empowerment also tell the same story.

17. Bandura (1995) demonstrated experimentally that when beliefs about self-efficacy are manipulated *independent* of performance or external conditions, they affect future performance.

18. While the life story evidence assembled here shows a cohesive and supportive family to be an important institutional correlate of upward mobility, we do not claim a causative "strong family leads to better upward mobility" nexus. This is because family cohesiveness is also influenced by the prior experience of enrich-

ment or impoverishment and should not be treated as a given, unchanging institution or essence. This is also an issue for further empirical research.

19. See annex 1.2 for correlates of democracy in the four Indian states studied in this volume. For the correlates of local democracy for all other MOP study regions, see chapter 6 in volume 2 of the Moving Out of Poverty series (Narayan, Pritchett, and Kapoor 2009).

20. The basic specification includes variables on economic opportunity, local democracy, collective action, agency, aspirations, violence against women, and social inequality/divisions. Also included are household characteristics (assets, livestock, house ownership, education level, health shocks), with some minor variation across the four state chapters. All regressions are OLS cluster-corrected and tested for robustness under different estimation methods. Note that the regression framework for "movers" in the Andhra Pradesh state chapter is based on different specification, given the nonrandom nature of sampling and the data.

21. The Indian debate has fluctuated between pessimism and optimism regarding the degree to which local democracy can play a positive role in helping poor people move out of poverty. Among more skeptical analysts, Kohli (1990) asserts that after independence, politicians ignore "mobilized but unorganized" groups that have served their political purpose and now add considerable volatility to the polity. By implication, the introduction of a three-tier local government system in the 1990s would only lead to further factionalization and social unrest. Among the optimists, Besley, Pande, and Rao (2005) show that where local village heads are from lower castes, allocations are more favorable to the poor, while Foster and Rosenzweig (2004) find that villages with democratic governance are more likely than those with nondemocratic governance to invest public resources in public infrastructure that benefits all community members.

Assets Gained and Lost: Understanding Mobility through Life Stories

Deepa Narayan, Denis Nikitin, and Brice Richard

When I can do everything myself, why would I consider myself poor?

—DILIP, A YOUNG MOVER,
Tapaioli, Assam

With the power of hard work, I send poverty packing.

—LALLU, A DAILY WAGE LABORER WHO MOVED
OUT OF POVERTY,
Darogapur, Uttar Pradesh

I have never felt secure in my life, as I own nothing. This struggling as a laborer over a lifetime makes a man miserable.

—A CHRONIC POOR MAN,
Andhra Pradesh

S torytelling is an ancient human art. People's stories about their own experiences and those of their families and communities provide vivid insights into their lives. Of particular interest to us, their narratives track in detail their upward and downward trajectories, the rising and falling that has brought them to their present position in life. The Moving Out of Poverty Study systematically collected and analyzed life stories from approximately 2,700 people in 300 villages in India. We begin with the stories of three of these people: Atanu who moved out of poverty, Kironmoy who stayed poor, and Chander who fell into poverty but climbed out again.

Atanu is 34 years old and lives in the village of Tola, in the Burdwan district of West Bengal. He spoke about the ups and downs in his life as he struggled to accumulate assets and finally moved out of poverty. "There is change in my life. My father has 1 bigha [approximately a third of an acre] of land from which income is obtained by cultivation, but there is no sufficiency in money. I started in the rice business first in 1995. I am eager to do business, so I started business by getting Rs 2,000 from my father. First, I watched how people buy rice and sell it, at what price, by roaming in the market. Next, I started buying rice in little amounts from the Kalna market. . . . I thought of increasing the business and also thought of supplying rice in Kolkata [the capital city]. Then in 1996, I supplied rice to a shopkeeper in Park Circus at Kolkata. The business was done in cash. Then, they started taking it on credit, that credit amount increased, and slowly they blocked my capital and did not pay Rs 15,000. I believed in them. I have no known person there, so I cannot get back the money, and I have to stop the business.

"I sat in my house after losing the business. I was not mentally peaceful. But instead of sitting, it is better to do something, so I started working with my father in the field. By this, I didn't get any income myself, but my father got help. From the small field, our income was monthly Rs 1,200 on average, not enough for food. I had no interest in this cultivation work. So I tried every time to do business. . . . Only thinking will do nothing; I have to learn a business well, know how to run it.

"I started the business of cable television in 2001. In Baddipur, my father-in-law had this business. I first saw the cable line and dish antenna in my father-in-law's house. He taught me about this business and helped with money, Rs 20,000, to start the business. I watched first in the locality to see how much profit I could make. Yes, I can do it. I set up a dish antenna on the roof and supplied connections to 10–12 neighbors. From this business, I can get an income of Rs 3,000 monthly. I am well-to-do in my family, and I am living happily with my family. Today, the reins of the family are in my hand. . . . In 2003, I opened an account in the State Bank of Kalna and saved for the first time. In 2004, I opened an LIC [life insurance policy]. This is my last saving for the time being. I will not have to beg anyone if I am in hunger; I am protected with my saved money.

"The first and main relation in my life is my father and mother. I am their only son, so I got much love and affection from them. And I respect them. They educated me; I graduated from Kalna College. Another important relation of my life is my wife. I got married in 1995. She is my important company in life. For every up and down, she stays behind me. There is a good relation with my parents-in-law since 1995. The help that I got from my father-in-law, I can never return in my life.

"The year 2001 was the turning point in my life. In this year, there is a change in my life after starting the business of cable. I improved in my life and was established, and respect for me increased in the society."

Kironmoy, 35 years old, lives in the village of Chatrakhali in District 24 Parganas, West Bengal. He told a very different kind of life story. Still poor despite his many efforts to rise, he wistfully concluded, "Every dream does not come true."

"I am very poor, and I do not have any strong relationship with anyone in my life. The saddest thing is that my present state is the same as it was in the past. Sometimes we eat; sometimes we starve. I am still a daily laborer. The biggest obstacle in my life is that I do not have any land to cultivate. Thus, during the time of farming, I have to cultivate other people's land. I have not obtained land from my father. He has only 1 bigha of land. What can he give me anyway?"

Kironmoy dropped out of school after standard 5. He left his family at age 17 for a job in Haldia, a port city, but eventually left the job behind to reunite with his family in his village. "I started to earn for the first time in

Haldia, where I stayed for two years. My uncle took me there and got me the job of weight measuring in a grocery store. My salary, aside from food and clothes, was Rs 100. We were seven such guys. I did not like my job and missed my parents. After two years, when my mother became very sick, I left the shop. . . . When I came back to the village at the age of 19, I was jobless again. Whatever money I had was spent for my mother's treatment. My situation became worse. Whatever I learned was useless because there is no big market here. Then I started to do the work of sowing, harvesting, and thrashing of paddy for others. I also took the job of digging land in Sonarpur or Bongaon. Until today I am doing the same job.

"I think about it, and I cannot find any solution. There is no opportunity of work is this community. The little amount of jobs in the land has to be shared with everyone. Everyone has his family to look after. There are no earning members in my family other than myself. There is no opportunity of any kind of profession either. My children are very young. I cannot leave them for long and stay in some other place for the sake of some job. I do not have any savings. Whatever I earn is spent immediately. We hardly manage to eat once a day. I have never bought anything in my life except for food and child's food.

"I do not have any important relationship that can bring some change into my life. . . . I am not connected to any party or group. I have a very nice relationship with my wife and children. I have taken the responsibility to raise them. My marriage and the births of my children have brought peace in my mind. The birth of my eldest son brought ecstasy to my life. They remind me that I must earn. I am held with high esteem in my family. Even in my neighborhood, people respect me, and no one speaks foul about me. I have no harmful addictions. I think my confidence level has remained same; there is no increase or decrease in that. I get my food in exchange for physical labor."

Chander is a 55-year-old woman from Dostpur village in the Sitapur district of Uttar Pradesh. She was born into a well-off family but plunged into poverty after marriage and a family split; finally, she managed to climb out of poverty once again. Her life story demonstrates how a woman's prosperity is interconnected with that of her husband. It also shows how self-confidence and respect from others create a virtuous cycle, leading to further asset accumulation.

"When I was born, the financial condition of my family was very sound because my father was among the big farmers of the village. We were three sisters and one brother. When I was five years old, I lost my mother. However, my father did not lose heart at that loss, and he brought us up with good care. We were properly sent for education. . . . After studying up to the fifth level, I discontinued my studies and started helping my elder sister in the household chores. After my elder sister was married, all the household responsibilities fell on my shoulders. . . . The love and affection of my father used to inspire me to do all the household work.

"When I was 13, my father's friend came to see him, from a faraway distance. When he glanced at me, he immediately liked me and chose me to marry his son. Instantly, my marriage was arranged. After some time, I got married. Thereafter, I came to stay with my in-laws.

"After a few months, my father-in-law met with a sudden death. One year after the death of my father-in-law, we had to face a lot of misery. My husband's elder brother decided to split the family. My husband and I could not understand what to do because my husband was still studying and he was unable to make any earnings independently. Then, my father came to our help, and he was instrumental in the continuation of my husband's studies. I came back to stay with my father, who also gave my husband some spending money.

"What can I tell you about my economic condition? When I was a small child, I had a piggy bank that I bought at the fair. I used to collect all the money I received, and I kept it very carefully. When I got married, I brought the piggy bank with me. When I broke it, I found I had collected Rs 200 in it. With this money, I purchased one wristwatch and presented it to my husband. I was very happy at that time because this was the costliest thing that I had bought for someone dear to me. My husband has kept this watch safely till now.

"I was blessed with my first child in 1966. Six years later, I was blessed with a second son. One year after the birth of my second child, there was a happy turning point in my life: my husband got a government job. I consider the job of my husband as my own success. We returned to my in-laws' village to resettle and claim the land that was our share. But until such time as I could earn something of my own, how could I consider myself being in any occupation?

"The happiest moment of my life came when in 1995, for the first time, I won the election for the position of the pradhan of the village. I consider this as the highest point in my life. My prestige increased in the entire village, and people started respecting me also. In the same year, I had got my youngest son married. As such, the year 1995 was a golden year of my life. Now, the circumstances had changed. We got our house renovated, because earlier it was all *kuccha* [ramshackle]. . . . My husband used to give his salary to me, and I used to save some money from it. I invested this money in making the house. I did this because now I was the pradhan, and my social status had also increased. Therefore this renovation was necessary.

"Five years later, I was reelected as the pradhan of the village. All my children grew up, and I got them all married. Now the size of my family has increased. The family into which I came as a daughter-in-law is the family that I am heading today. At the same time, I have the feeling of being the head of the entire village, and that does not give less pleasure. That is why I always thank the Lord."

Life stories allow participants to provide insights into the pivotal events in their lives, unencumbered by fixed questions and detailed question-naires. For this reason, they are commonly used as a data collection tool by anthropologists and psychologists.[1] In this chapter, we highlight some of the insights that emerge from systematic analysis of over 2,700 life stories randomly selected from four mobility groups: 919 movers, 728 chronic poor, 231 fallers, and 840 never poor. All these participants also completed tradi-tional questionnaires, but the focus of this chapter is primarily on findings that did not emerge from the survey data using questionnaires.

The chapter first explains key concepts and methods, centering on an assets-based approach to analyzing the life stories. It then highlights find-ings with respect to the portfolio of assets and the overall processes of accumulation and depletion. We focus in particular on processes that help people accumulate intangible assets and on the processes that lead to deple-tion. Finally, the chapter explores the impact of life cycle forces and the macro policy context on mobility outcomes and offers reflections on policy implications.

Assets-Based Approaches to Poverty Reduction

I am confident upon myself because I have savings in my name with which I could challenge all danger and remove all obstacles in my life.
—Runa, a 33-year-old well-off woman, Bhaturia, West Bengal

Recent conceptual and empirical work on assets provides a useful founda-tion to inform the analysis of life stories. Assets-based analytic frameworks grew out of the sustainable livelihoods approach of the 1990s (Sherraden 1991; Chambers and Conway 1992; Carney 1998; Moser 1998; DFID 2000). This approach entails two innovations. First, it expands the range of assets to include social and natural assets alongside physical, human, and financial assets. Second, it examines how local institutions influence people's ability to put these assets to productive use (Carney 1998, 1999). The increasing focus on assets was accompanied by greater recognition of the need to address the vulnerability of poor people through social protection programs (World Bank 2000; Narayan et al. 2000).

Recently, a number of scholars and practitioners have renewed the call to focus on assets-based rather than income-based approaches to poverty reduction (Carter and May 1999; Boshara and Sherraden 2004; Ford Foundation 2004; Moser 2007; Carter 2007). The current emphasis on asset accumulation strategies has two new twists. First, some authors favor expanding the definition of assets to include political assets such as citizenship rights (Moser and Norton 2001) and psychological dimensions such as personal and collective agency (Narayan 2002). Second, the focus on assets implies policies and programs that directly help poor people accumulate assets, particularly housing and savings, both of which can reduce their vulnerability and help them move to livelihood activities with greater returns. Based on the extent of asset accumulation among different categories of poor people, Michael Carter characterizes the "poverty threshold" as the level at which poor people have accumulated enough assets to move up but still risk falling backward because of vulnerability. These households, he argues, will benefit from a safety net policy to protect them from slippage, while those much below this level need further asset accumulation, a "cargo net," before they can reach the poverty threshold and be in a position to move out of poverty. Thus, focusing on assets can allow for more differentiated social policies.

We adopt an assets-based approach to analyzing the life stories because the income-focused approach proves totally inadequate to the task. Working inductively, we developed a coding tree to analyze all life events, processes, and shocks reported during the telling of the life stories. The coding methodology was developed in two phases: 200 life stories were coded to capture most of the information, and then the coding approach was applied to the entire sample. We did not predefine assets, but we let the categories of assets emerge. The coding categories were different for asset accumulation and asset depletion, as the processes described were very different.[2]

Life stories, like all data collection tools, are subject to recall error (Ritchie 1995; Slim and Thompson 1993; Thompson 1998). In addition to cross-checking with household data, we attempt to minimize errors by anchoring the recall period to 10 years, with the life span providing the overall context. We focus on five thematic areas: (a) migration history; (b) occupational history; (c) economic history; (d) social, cultural, and psychological history; and

(e) education. As key events emerged in each of these areas, the interviewees were asked to rate each event in terms of its impact on their individual well-being, from a –5 (representing a large decline in well-being) to a +5 (a large increase). At the end of the discussion, people summarized by identifying the main turning points, both high points and low points, in their lives.

Early in the coding process, two broad findings jumped out. The first is that a wide range of assets are important, not only tangible assets like housing but also intangible assets such as social respect. We examine the intangible category in some detail. The second is that processes of accumulation and depletion occur simultaneously among both movers and fallers. These findings were later supported by our detailed analysis.

The Importance of Intangible Assets

I returned to this place of my in-laws after increasing our self-pride.
My husband completed his studies with my father's help.
    —Chander, a 55-year-old mover, Dostpur, Uttar Pradesh

Our three opening life stories suggest that the range of assets that people consider important is even wider than that conceptualized in the livelihoods or assets-based framework. People consistently emphasize the importance of tangible assets such as jobs, housing, livestock, and furniture. However, they also extensively discuss a range of intangible assets such as family and community relationships, respect, happiness, self-confidence, and ability to plan for the future. These intangible assets figure in roughly 40 percent of all events where gain or loss of an asset is mentioned (table 2.1). But they have been largely missed in the asset-accounting frameworks because standard surveys, considering intangible assets to be unimportant, ask no questions about them. Indeed, intangible assets are dismissed as irrelevant.

TABLE 2.1
Life stories show the importance of intangible as well as tangible assets

Type of asset	% of asset accumulation or depletion events			
	Movers	Chronic poor	Fallers	Never poor
Intangible	39	44	39	42
Tangible	61	56	61	58
Total	100	100	100	100
N	15,986	13,674	3,805	15,087

The life stories gathered for the study are full of emotional content as people looked back on the signal events in their lives. Relationships and emotions, both positive and negative, are seen to affect opportunities and decisions, and in this way they can have major impacts on people's assets. In this regard, the life story accounts resonate with other studies that find that emotional states and relationships can stimulate or discourage trust, initiative, risk taking, and entrepreneurship, thereby influencing economic behaviors and outcomes (Takahashi 2005; Goette and Huffman 2005; Graham and Fitzpatrick 2002).

In the three life stories that opened this chapter, relationships and the emotional connections between individuals changed people's lives. Atanu's relationship to his father-in-law gave him a business opportunity, providing cable television to neighbors, and led to a substantial loan to start the business when his own father, who only had 1 bigha of land, could not help him financially. Atanu moved out of poverty and feels that today he is the provider for his family. Kironmoy, on the other hand, gave up his small salaried job in town that he obtained through an uncle. He returned to his village, where there was little economic opportunity, because he was unhappy, missed his parents, and needed to take care of his sick mother. He has remained poor.

Types of intangible assets

Today I am standing in a good position and have confidence in myself. I get respect from my family as well as from society. Because I do not behave badly with anyone, so all love and respect me.

—Netai, a male mover, Gutri, West Bengal

An important relation of my life is with my teacher Kishor Mohan Mukherjee. It was possible for me to have education because I got my books from him. He taught me without any money. He also helped me economically at times of necessity. His importance is much in my life, and I respect him as same as my parents.

—Dinabandhu, a male mover, Tola, West Bengal

To better explore the different types and roles of intangible assets, we first distinguish between emotional and relational assets. Emotional assets relate to states of mind, such as happiness or peace of mind, and relational assets refer to intangible social relations. While individual events may have both emotional and relational aspects—for example, positive family relationships increase one's happiness—we distinguish between the two. Relational assets involve others: they join individuals to social networks and allow them draw on others' resources to access jobs, money, support, formal and informal safety nets, and further social connections. Emotional states, on the other hand, are limited to the individual who experiences them and are resources proper to that individual. They can provide powerful motivations—many movers, for instance, cherish the memories of their initial success and draw strength to persevere from them. As demonstrated in the flourishing literature on the economics of happiness, such positive emotions foster self-confidence, which in turn can lead to entrepreneurship and future income.

Each mobility group accumulates different shares of the various intangible assets. All four groups refer to emotional assets more often than they do to relational assets. However, the chronic poor place an even higher emphasis on emotional assets than other groups because they have fewer relational assets to fall back on (table 2.2). Poverty is clearly marked by isolation from others in terms of social relations as well as exclusion from ownership of tangible assets.

TABLE 2.2

All groups emphasize emotional over relational assets, but the chronic poor rely on emotional assets most of all

	% of events where an intangible asset was mentioned			
Type of intangible asset	Movers	Chronic poor	Fallers	Never poor
Emotional assets				
Happiness	55	74	53	57
Harmony	2	1	2	2
Overall well-being	2	1	1	2
Peace of mind	8	4	6	6
Total emotional assets	67	80	62	67
Relational assets				
Family condition	16	9	23	17
Old-age security	4	3	4	3
Psychological support	2	1	2	1
Respect	4	2	2	3
Social standing	9	4	6	10
Total relational assets	35	19	37	34
N	6,281	6,037	1,503	6,298

Of all the intangible assets, rising happiness is the most frequently mentioned by all four groups. It is associated with greater self-confidence and motivates further action. People hold especially strong memories of their first successes in life and the joy they felt on these occasions. Gundala, a woman stuck in chronic poverty in Penta, Andhra Pradesh, described the elation of buying herself a sari for the first time: "This is the happiest moment in my life since I bought it from my own earnings. I consider myself at a plus four [the second highest rating on the life story trend lines]. I got lot of confidence in knowing that I am earning on my own and I am moving ahead along with my kith and kin." For Padma, a mover from Dudhma, Uttar Pradesh, her education remains a source of happiness to this day: "I started going to school at the age of five in 1968. I liked going to school so I would like to place myself at plus two. In 1979 when I passed graduation, I was extremely happy because I was the first woman in the family to pass graduation. I rate my happiness then at plus five." Breaking gender-based barriers in her youth encouraged Padma to become a risk taker and innovator later in life.

First encounters with love and marriage are also common sources of deep happiness. Shanti, a never-poor woman in Tola, West Bengal, recalled, "The first thing I obtained in the year 1990 is a golden chain from my husband, which is more than an asset for it is a token of his affection. It keeps an importance in my life because it gives me happiness. I can rate it at plus three." Shanti recounted the despair she felt when she had to sell this gold chain so the family could survive, followed by joy when she was able to buy a chain again in later years.

Fulfilling family obligations is a source of great happiness as it reaffirms people's sense of belonging to a family and community. The marriage of a woman is often cited as bringing peace of mind for the woman's family members. Ganesh, a man in chronic poverty in Sadhupur, West Bengal, said that 1995 was the happiest year of his life: "In this year, I arranged the marriage ceremony of my sister. It was the fulfillment of my greatest responsibility in life." Similarly, Latif, a chronic poor man from Bilpar village in Assam, testified, "In 1993, I held my first daughter's marriage with a lot of pomp and fanfare. It upheld my prestige in the society. Mentally, I was well off and put my position at a plus three."

Family unity is also an important source of mental peace. Cheniram, a never-poor man in Langpuria, Assam, was in the armed services all his life and stayed away from home for 24 years until he finally retired and reunited with his family. He described his contentment: "I retired from the services in 1995. Since then, I have been living in this village. I shall give a plus four for the period subsequent to my arrival home. This is because I could live a happy and peaceful life together with my family after coming back home. I have been engaged in agriculture ever since."

Although increases in social standing are often linked to economic mobility, discussants frequently focus on the nonmonetary rewards that accompany their newfound status. Padmaamma, a chronic poor woman from Penta, Andhra Pradesh, earned the respect of her neighbors because of her ability to educate her children in spite of her poverty. "I felt very unhappy because of my inability to feed my children. But later, we earned money and raised our social status in the village. We earned respect in the society as we are educating our son even though we are working as laborers." Gita, a mover from Gautamman Khera, Uttar Pradesh, basks in the glory of her husband's successful entrepreneurship, which brought the family wealth and social standing. "When my husband opened a shop in 1995, then I was very happy because he had a source of income. In 1998 we made a *pucca* [well-built] house, and I was very happy. We were earlier considered as laborers, but now we are counted as one of the good families in the village and have gained respect in the society."

Social networks of family and friends can help directly in accumulating assets. They also provide both financial and psychological support that is critical when shocks strike or retirement age comes. These assets constitute an invisible but very real safety net that people rely on to take risks and weather bad times. For instance, Vishunath, a mover from Shekhapur, Uttar Pradesh, owes much to the help and support of his relatives and his main "servant." When Vishunath's father died, other family members took care of the farming, and when his mother died, a "loyal servant of my father called Ram Kumar Harijan took care of the family and started looking after everything." He got Vishunath admitted to school and helped till the land. "That servant was a very loyal person who helped us through a tough time where no other was ready to help us. As long as he was alive, we faced no problems."[3]

Among movers and the never poor, each economic success begets an incremental improvement in social standing that in turn opens opportunities to further consolidate both relational and financial assets. Praneswar, a mover from Kandulimari, Assam, owes much of his increased social standing to his son, who was hired in 1996 as a clerk in a government department. To mark the achievement, his son threw a banquet for 50 people and gave Rs 500 to the temple. A few years later, the son installed electricity and a latrine in the family house, built a shop for his father, and bought saris and gold necklaces for his mother, signaling to all that his was now one of the rich families in the village. In 2004, Praneswar gave two fans to the local temple, demonstrating his dedication to the community. He was later selected to be the treasurer of the temple committee: "Through the blessings of God, I rose to a higher position."

Acquiring intangible assets

> *People live in this community with unity. We do every work here by the help of each other. In every good and bad situation, everybody stands with each other.*
>
> —Women's discussion group, Suchi, Raibareli district,
> Uttar Pradesh

Given the importance of intangible assets in people's lives, it is not surprising that both rich and poor people strive to acquire them, but they do so in different ways. The movers and never poor more often say that they acquire peace of mind and social standing through public employment and the purchase of assets. In Gautamman Khera, Uttar Pradesh, Urmila, a mover, notes that her husband's job in Dubai enabled the family to purchase status-enhancing assets: "We made a pucca house, and we increased the number of rooms. Our status in society went up. Then when more money came, we bought a TV. This increased our status even more in the village and nearby areas."

By contrast, the chronic poor have limited access to government jobs and little purchasing power. For them, badges of community recognition, such as being named to a village post, play key roles in acquiring prestige. Manchuk, a poor mason from Thengal Gaon, Assam, gained respect when he became the chief prayer of the village church. Social events such as the marriage of a daughter or the birth of a son also increase social standing and lead to new relationships. Marrying off a sister or a daughter may be an expensive affair, but it is a source of immense happiness in the family and a boost to self-confidence, respect, and belonging to a community. In the absence of professional success or wealth-related prestige, poor people thus give much importance to family bonds, traditions, and social belonging in enabling them to feel safe, augment their status, and call for help when needed.

Simultaneous Processes: Accumulation and Depletion

The classification of people into different mobility groups in this volume parallels the divisions used in the extensive literature on poverty dynamics. Based on mobility history, people are classified as movers, chronic poor, fallers, or never poor (the latter sometimes called chronic rich). Then each group is compared with the others to show its contrasting trajectories and asymmetric reasons for moving out of poverty or falling into poverty, the experiences of movers and fallers being of particular interest (Dercon and Shapiro 2007; Krishna 2007). What is missed in this telling of the story is that the people in each mobility group, including movers and fallers, are *simultaneously experiencing processes that lead to accumulation and processes that lead to depletion.* The mobility outcome depends on the interaction between these two processes and the ratio of accumulative to depleting events in a person's life. In particular, it reflects the assets that people have at their disposal to cope with the depleting events, mostly shocks of different kinds.

The life stories of movers and fallers typically do not depict an uninterrupted process of asset accumulation or depletion. Rather, like Chander, people tend to experience asset accumulation and depletion events alongside one another. All mobility groups on balance experience more instances of asset accumulation than depletion. Not surprisingly, movers and the never poor report a greater share of events leading to accumulation than others. The accumulation to depletion ratio is roughly 80:20 for movers and the never poor, and 60:40 for chronic poor and fallers (table 2.3).

As tragedies intermingle with successes, mobility seems to be the result of an elaborate alchemy of events, of complex interactions and sequencings that determine individual mobility paths. The following two life stories, one of a mover and one of a faller, demonstrate how the interaction between the accumulation and depletion of assets determines mobility outcomes.

Bakul is a 40-year-old man from Thengal Gaon village in the Jorhat district of Assam. Poor in 1995, he moved out of poverty by 2005. But he also experienced poverty during much of the decade, along with family divisions, expenses for marriages, and illness. These depleting events took place even as he was simultaneously accumulating resources through farming.

"I was born in 1965 in this village. At the time of birth, the condition of my home was not good. Mother and father expired in my childhood, and

TABLE 2.3
Accumulation and depletion are simultaneous across mobility groups

Type of event	% of all asset events			
	Movers	Chronic poor	Fallers	Never poor
Accumulation	77	64	59	78
Depletion	23	36	41	22
Total	100	100	100	100
N	13,674	15,986	3,804	15,092

I grew up by working with my brothers. From 12 years of age onwards, I started plowing by going to the fields. My brother showed me every agricultural work.

"From 1995, I started agriculture on my own. Then we three brothers got separated. Brothers get separated one day; it does not matter now much love they have among themselves. This is the rule of the society, and we also follow it. Without much argument, we got separated.

"In 1996, I got married according to my choice. . . . For my marriage, I had to take some credit. I had to take it from my friend, who is not present right now. In the name of the bride, I spent Rs 10,000. It was spent in the name of clothes and gold ornaments. Through marriage, I got my partner [he rated his happiness at +3]. My relation with my friends and relatives is good. Until now, there is no ill feeling. I have a good sense of togetherness with everyone.

"I didn't have bullocks for plowing. And so I saved money, and in 1997, I bought a pair of bullocks. At that time, I had expense of Rs 11,000, but still I was happy because the primary thing in agriculture is that bullocks are required for plowing. There is a saying, *halat goru salat kumura* [bullock in plow, gourds on roof].

"In 2002, my brother was married. At the time of marriage, I was very happy because I took all the responsibility for arranging the marriage. The money was mostly my brother's, though Rs 5,000 of my money was also spent. I was very happy about my brother's marriage in the village.

"In 2004, I bought 2 bighas of land, on which Rs 8,000 was spent. I bought the lands at a very low price. A poor person sold his land for medical treatment. The land will stay as my property on which farming will be done. I am happy with the lands because land is not a perishable commodity. I can sell it in time of trouble. [In the same year] I opened an LIC [savings plan] of Rs 40,000. I am giving Rs 321 quarterly.

"[Also in 2004] my wife's tumor operation was conducted. . . . Around Rs 20,000 was spent in the name of disease. After it, when she was becoming well, I was happy. Saved money was spent, but no property was sold.

"In 2005, with the help of Kisan credit card, I took a loan of Rs 10,000 for farming. At present, I am using it. The condition of farming will be known after harvest. This time, rain has not occurred. The weather is still drought. If high-quality seeds and fertilizers can be used, it will be good. If irrigation facility can be introduced in the fields, it will be even better."

Radhe, a 50-year-old man from Chakmanmohan Das village in Sitapur district, Uttar Pradesh, related the interaction between accumulation and depletion of assets that led him to fall below the community poverty line. He started not in poverty but with substantial land. Gradual expansion of the family through marriage and births was followed by family division, however, and this depleted his resources, eventually leaving him poor.

"I was born in 1955. My father was a farmer. He had 12 bighas of land, and he used to support the whole family in that way. At that time, our family was small so there were no problems of food and clothes. [In 1964] my father was finding it difficult to cope with all the farming on his own because we had a lot of land. So I left my studies and started farming with my father, and the farming started going well; the yield also increased. I had wanted to study more and do a government job. But my wishes didn't come true.

"I got married in 1968. My responsibilities increased, and I felt like earning more money. I started growing sugarcane in 1969, and my earnings increased. All the needs of my family were satisfied with that.

"As time passed I had two children, and our expenses kept rising. . . . I had my third child in 1982, but he died in a year because someone had done black magic on my child, and I couldn't get medicines for him. He just got ill in an hour and died, and I couldn't do anything for him. . . . In 1985 I got my [first] son married, and my daughter-in-law came home. As my family kept growing, my father moved away from us in 2001. We were three brothers so the land and the house got divided into three portions. I got 4 bighas of land and one room, which was a thatched roof and a kuccha house, where I started living with my family. In 2001, my daughter-in-law and my son started living in her parents' house. There was no one to support me, and my situation started deteriorating.

"Somehow I did farming and labor work, and I got my second son married. With my daughter-in-law also in the house, our expenses increased even more. . . . I used to feel that my elder son had gone to stay with his in-laws and didn't care about us anymore, and the younger one didn't do any work."

We now turn to life stories to tease out salient patterns in the underlying processes of accumulation and depletion.

Accumulation Processes

Family members helped me a lot to move ahead. Earlier, I was a day laborer. When I started cultivation farming, I got advice from my relatives, friends, and family. They inspired me, so without their help I could not reach the position I am in right now.

—Jonab, a 50-year-old male mover,
Brindakhali, West Bengal

To discern patterns across hundreds of life stories, we traced sequences of events over time and the interactions between them. We asked "how" and "why" questions to shed light on the underlying processes that lead to asset accumulation. Life stories are particularly suited to understanding processes that are difficult to capture adequately in questionnaires. Proceeding inductively, we categorized all accumulation events and processes into four broad categories by their underlying cause or trigger: initiative, institutions, inheritance, and infrastructure. We also constructed detailed subcategories within each category.

Initiative

> At my early age, I went outside my house in Burnpur. I used to do work like clearance of garden and herding of animals like cattle, goats, etc. Besides this, I used to work as laborer for a carpenter and as the helper of a mason. They gave me Rs 20 per day. Yet I began to continue work on that small payment. I worked with them in order to learn the work.
> —Tarapada, a 40-year-old chronic poor man, Khalsi, West Bengal

The single most frequently mentioned reason for accumulation of assets across all mobility groups is people's own initiative (table 2.4). Initiative is the trigger that accounts for between 46 and 56 percent of all accumulation events among movers, chronic poor, fallers, and never poor. This is followed closely by institutions, with 41 to 46 percent. Inheritance and infrastructure play much smaller roles.

It is of course conceivable that respondents, being human, would attribute success to their own efforts and blame failure on others. If this were true, we would expect to see the chronic poor and fallers—who have not been as successful—reporting much lower levels of initiative than movers or the never

TABLE 2.4
Poor people take as much initiative as movers and the never poor

Trigger for accumulation	% of asset accumulation events			
	Movers	Chronic poor	Fallers	Never poor
Initiative	56	54	46	52
Institutions	41	43	46	42
Inheritance	3	3	8	6
Infrastructure[a]	0	0	0	0
Total	100	100	100	100
N	12,280	8,723	2,266	11,807

a. Infrastructure accounted for 0.1–0.3% of accumulation events, here rounded to 0.

poor. But we do not see this. Just to make sure, we looked more closely at the numbers on different types of initiative and entrepreneurship among the different mobility groups and how they led to accumulation of assets, including land, jobs, money, and agricultural products. In all, we find that the chronic poor take *more* initiatives than the rich and at least as many as the movers.

Poor people in the communities visited in rural India do not seem to be caught in a "culture of poverty" characterized by laziness, low aspiration, and lack of initiative.[4] They take initiatives at a rate equal to or greater than the more successful groups, but there are severe constraints on the kinds of initiatives that they are able to take. Their limited resources and assets tie them to low-end jobs and other economic activities with low return, a cycle from which it is difficult to escape. In agriculture, the core activity for most rural households, the chronic poor try to make up for lack of access to new technology and other assets by working hard (table 2.5). But hard labor does not increase their agricultural production enough to lift them out of poverty.

Access to new technologies and farming methods increases the profitability of agricultural activities and reduces vulnerability to farm losses due to floods and droughts. Mridul, a mover from the village of Upper Deuri in Assam, explained, "In 1994, after getting some training, I used modern scientific methods to grow crops. I would irrigate my field with a power pump,

TABLE 2.5

In agriculture, the chronic poor rely more than other groups on hard work, less on new technology and assets

	% of asset accumulation events in agriculture attributed to initiative taking			
Type of initiative	Movers	Chronic poor	Fallers	Never poor
Additional economic activities	7	11	10	7
Crop diversification	7	8	6	7
New business	27	32	38	23
New technology	12	5	10	16
Other	0	4	0	1
Hard work	11	23	15	10
Purchase of asset	16	2	6	15
Subtotal	80	85	85	79
N	370	123	52	344

Note: Only major categories are reported.

spray pesticides on the plants, and harvest with a tractor. I got good results. In 2001, I did the same thing with cabbages. Although I invested Rs 10,000 that year, I made Rs 30,000 in profit."

The chronic poor, by comparison, have little to invest in new technologies and assets. They often try to diversify by starting a myriad small business ventures (73 percent of all economic initiatives) to improve their income. They sell milk, drive rickshaws, sew clothes, take in washing, and breed small herds of goats. These new activities, far less profitable than market-oriented agriculture, cannot provide that necessary push upward. Despite a strong sense of entrepreneurship, Kartik from Betuabati, West Bengal, never crossed the poverty line. "In 1993, I learned tailoring and got a sewing machine. I did tailoring for five years but couldn't reap any profits, so I quit. Then I worked in Paradip for six months, Durgapur for three months, and Haldia for three months, but I would get the same pay everywhere. . . . I finally started my own shop, which I've been running for the past three years."

In terms of jobs, many more of the never poor (18 percent) and movers (10 percent) have public sector employment, compared to only 2 percent of the chronic poor. Such employment, with its regular income stream, is a reliable way to move out of poverty and vulnerability.

Upward mobility is thus not just a matter of initiative and hard work but of being able to diversify and invest in *profitable* activities. Poor people, however many initiatives they undertake, are often trapped in situations where they must choose between poor options with poor returns.

Institutions

I worked very hard and educated my son, as a result of which he got a government job. Hence, the condition of my family improved considerably. Previously I didn't have enough to eat, whereas today I have a surplus.
    —A scheduled caste mover, Uttar Pradesh

People have developed well with the help of women's groups. They have more knowledge. They are becoming partners in politics. They want to know about government programs and to form good or bad opinions on parties.
    —Discussion with men, Bestharapalle, Andhra Pradesh

Here there are no companies that provide jobs. The beedi industry [hand-rolled cigarettes] is only a cottage industry. Hence, it cannot offer any job potential.
    —Men's discussion group, Andhra Pradesh

Beliefs about the most important institutions for poverty reduction are deeply entrenched in the beliefs and ideologies of development practitioners and theorists. Depending on one's perspective, the most important institutions for poverty reduction may be the state, the private sector, civil society, or some combination thereof. In the Indian life stories, across mobility groups, 45 percent of asset accumulation events are related to institutions—the second-highest percentage after initiative. Surprisingly, though, none of the classic trio of state, markets, and civil society features prominently in the accounts told by our participants. Rather, the family emerges as the most frequently mentioned institution, figuring in a remarkable 85 percent of all asset accumulation events involving institutions (table 2.6). Government, civil society, and the private sector play a much more limited role in asset accumulation across mobility groups. Annex 2.1 presents a detailed breakdown of the institutional channels of accumulation.

Family. Families, with all their problems, are still the foundation of most people's well-being, both emotionally and financially. Family members typically provide the love, support, and respect without which happiness cannot be complete. The birth of a child is the most frequently cited source of increased individual well-being in the India life stories. Every birth—but especially the birth of a son—fills parents with joy and inspires hope that their child will take care of them when they grow old. Good marriages also increase a family's comfort and prestige. Rupeswar, a well-to-do cattle breeder from Huttar, Assam, said, "In 2003, we married our son with a girl from Nagan. When this beautiful, educated daughter-in-law entered our house, our lives changed. Her mere presence turned our house into gold."

TABLE 2.6
Family is the most important institution in asset accumulation

Type of institution	% of asset accumulation events involving institutions			
	Movers	*Chronic poor*	*Fallers*	*Never poor*
Family	82	84	88	81
Public	10	8	7	13
Civil society	5	6	4	5
Private	3	2	1	1
Total	100	100	100	100
N	5,038	3,791	1,050	4,911

Families are also important sources of financial support and proxy professional achievement. By contributing land, money, or jewelry, relatives can complement a household's income and sometimes even finance life-changing projects. With an uncle's support, Ramkhiladi, a mover from Lalpur, Uttar Pradesh, was able to get ahead. "My life changed in 1997 when my uncle helped me buy an engine with which I increased my production. In 1999, my uncle gave me 7 bighas of land and in 2001 another 6 bighas of land. I could increase my production even more. I was very happy." Arun Kalita, a mover from Gobordia, Assam, attributes his own success to his son's professional achievements. "After his BA, my son applied to many government jobs, in vain. But at last, God saw him, and he was hired as a clerk for the railway company. Our days of sadness were over. He had a high salary and bought many things for us. He installed electricity in my house, purchased a fan and a TV, and bought 9 bighas of land."

Public institutions. In comparison with families, public institutions play an infrequent role in asset accumulation, being cited in only 7 to 13 percent of asset accumulation events (table 2.6). However, when they are involved, public institutions may be disproportionately important as the conveyers of substantial assets: jobs, houses, and land. Among the different public sector mechanisms, government jobs and public subsidies are the most important mechanisms for accumulating assets, but there is significant variation across the mobility groups in this respect.

Government employment and job promotions are important for asset accumulation among the never poor and movers. They are mentioned much less frequently by fallers and the chronic poor. Public positions—as a village development officer, panchayat official, or teacher in a government school, for example—are highly vulnerable to elite capture, since entrance may require substantial bribes as well as completion of public exams. When well-educated poor individuals can secure them, however, such jobs often represent a one-way ticket out of poverty. Ram Kali, a male mover from Thana, Uttar Pradesh, had that chance. His wife said, "In 2003, my husband got a job in the forest department, and my second son also got married this year. Our economic and social standard became higher after that. There was a change in my life, and my life became safe."

When the chronic poor benefit from public institutions, it tends to be as recipients of public subsidies or assistance. This is reflected in the life stories: 65 percent of the chronic poor who mention public institutions mention these subsidies, as do 30 percent of movers, who were recently poor. Public subsidies thus seem to be well targeted to the needy. The most frequently mentioned programs are those that distribute houses or land. Even these, however, can be subject to elite capture. Krishan, a 38-year-old chronic poor man in Boodanpur, Uttar Pradesh, recalled, "My entire life, I have been work-ing to death and have not even been able to make a hut. Last year, I was supposed to get a house in the colony allotted by the government, but I did not get it because the pradhan got it allotted to his hamlet. He got houses for many Chamars who did not even need it. I was left with nothing."

Civil society. Despite the growing attention to civil society in development literature, it receives relatively little mention in the life stories, figuring in about 5 percent of all asset accumulation events involving institutions (table 2.6). Civil society is slightly more important among the chronic poor. Within civil society, informal social networks and self-help groups (particularly in Andhra Pradesh) are the most prominent. A range of other local institutions, including religious, political, and economic associations, also appear in the life stories. Local nongovernmental organizations (NGOs) receive relatively little direct notice, accounting for about 3 percent of the civil society institu-tions mentioned by the chronic poor.

Social networks of patrons and acquaintances who have contacts or financial resources can make the difference between a life in poverty and the chance to escape poverty. Tiwari, a male mover from Dasarathpur, Uttar Pradesh, attributes his ability to move out of poverty to help from a wealthy contact. "The owner of the mill lent me some rupees that I used to invest in a tubewell. Now, I can irrigate my field on time, and I get a good production." Nurjahan, a faller from Narenga, West Bengal, implies that her slide into poverty would have been even worse were it not for the support of a local preacher. "The most important relation in my life is with the imam. He has been beside us when days were bad. He gave me a job. Since I am not able to do any other job, it is only with his help that I can live today."

Self-help groups have helped some women escape poverty. Shivamma, a chronic poor woman from Govindapalle, Andhra Pradesh, said, "In 2001, I joined the DWACRA [Development of Woman and Children in Rural Areas] group. Before that, I was spending all my time in the house. But after I joined, I began to know everything and to talk about many things in detail. I took a loan from DWACRA and bought two buffaloes. With the help of the buffaloes, I made some money and am now living well socially and economically."

References to civil society become prominent in discussion of savings among the chronic poor. Even though few poor people have savings, 30 percent of those who said they had been able to accumulate savings attributed this to support from civil society, especially women's self-help groups. However, these savings are not enough to enable people to meet all their needs. Poor people still turn to moneylenders or personal relations like family and friends for loans.

Private sector institutions. The formal private sector is strikingly absent from the lives of villagers in this study, figuring in a mere 2 percent of asset accumulation events. There is, nonetheless, little doubt that employment in shops, firms, and factories, where such businesses are present, can stimulate prosperity and individual mobility. Private jobs, a rare commodity in rural areas, can provide a way out of poverty. Sagar's life changed completely after he became a permanent employee of a tea garden (tea plantation) in Bangram, Assam. He said, "After becoming permanent, the happy days of our family came back." Working in companies can also provide employees with valuable business experience that they can later use for their own profit, as exemplified by Swapan, a mover from Batagram, West Bengal. His early career as a dishwasher in a hotel taught him about business and helped him start his own stationery store years later.

Our sample also suggests that movers and the never poor have better access than others to opportunities in the formal and organized private sector, including well-established firms and factories. The chronic poor and, to a lesser extent, fallers tend to have access only to small, informal businesses, particularly those run by traders and shopkeepers. A private sector job for poor people, moreover, can mean work in dangerous conditions without any protection by law. Bhoopendra, a chronic poor man in Jamalnagar Bhains, Uttar Pradesh, spent years destroying his health in the toxic vapors of a glass factory, only to see his salary embezzled by the manager.

Inheritance

> *The reason of remaining rich for me is that I was parental rich. My fore-fathers had good agriculture. We have always done hard labor and never did any wrong work. We always had the grace of God.*
> —Arshad, a 35-year-old rich man, Nachni Ghat, Uttar Pradesh

Compared to initiative and institutions, inheritance and infrastructure play minor roles in asset accumulation, but they should not be completely disregarded. Their infrequent mention may be a result of the life story methodology, as individuals may consider these two factors as merely the *context* within which they have to act.

Respondents report inheritance accumulation at two moments in life: at birth, when they become part of a family with a particular store of assets, and later in life, when they may inherit the assets of a relative who has passed away.

The events that contribute to asset accumulation early in life can play an important role in mobility prospects, as will be shown below in the section on the timing of accumulation and depletion events. This finding corroborates other mobility studies on the intergenerational transmission of wealth, which also find that initial conditions matter a lot. In our Indian life stories, most asset accumulation events related to inheritance occur early in life (70 to 87 percent). This provides a propitious start for the never poor and fallers, who command land, wealth, and respect (at least for a while), and a difficult start for movers and the chronic poor, who begin with little money and few physical assets.

Nevertheless, inheritances later in life can sometimes usher in positive change. Suddenly bequeathed an inheritance, Kutubuddin from Baintala, West Bengal, was able to move out of poverty. He recalled, "In 1995, I received 2 kathas of land from my grandfather. I thus became self-sufficient, could cultivate my own land, and managed to earn enough to secure two meals a day for the entire family. My condition definitely improved."

Infrastructure

You call these roads? They are used by the cattle.
—Biswajit, a participant in a men's discussion group, Bhuinadi,
West Bengal

During focus group discussions about factors affecting the prosperity of their communities, villagers repeatedly stress the importance of roads, hospitals, and schools in fostering local business development and increasing overall well-being of community members. But when sharing life stories about the factors shaping their own prosperity, people rarely identify infrastructure as an underlying cause of their accumulation. Rather, they perceive it as a backdrop against which accumulation and depletion take place. Only when the construction of a school, bridge, or hospital brings dramatic changes to their individual well-being do respondents mention it in their life stories. "In 1999, I had to stay in Silchar with my family because the road from Montinagar was very bad," explained Tapas, a never-poor man from Sibpur, Assam. "But by 2004, the quality of the road had improved, so I was able to come back to my house in Montinagar."

Depletion Processes

My hotel burned in 1993: all became ashes in front of my eyes. It completely broke my backbone, and I have never recovered. In 1996, my younger son became handicapped in a cycle accident. I sold my Bajaj scooter for Rs 5,000 for food. My family condition is going down and even more down. In the year 2000, I got a BPL [Below Poverty Line] card after bribing, and then, in 2002, I had to sell two pieces of my wife's jewelry. I cannot manage daily meals. Now I feel very ashamed in front of our villagers. My joyful days are gone; God is really heartless. My sons can't find a job even after enough qualification. Sometimes I think of suicide.

—Abhoy, a faller, Raipat, Assam

For individuals, moving up or staying up depends both on accumulating assets and on protecting assets from depletion. As demonstrated earlier, both movers and the never poor experience many fewer depletion events. Like accumulation events, depletion events have their own interactions and ripple effects. Alongside the direct costs associated with a specific shock comes the loss of opportunities. When a member of the family falls ill, there are immediate expenses for medical treatment, but the illness also affects the person's capacity to earn income or pursue an education and may erode savings that were set aside for a productive investment. Depending on the depth of the shock and the extent of preexisting assets, families may find themselves trapped at lower levels of well-being.

Raish, a 40-year-old man from Bagnera Bagneri, Uttar Pradesh, fell into poverty between 1995 and 2005. "When I was born [in 1965], the condition in my family was very good. There was no lacking of food and clothes. . . . I got married in 1984. After getting married, there was a new conflict daily. There was fighting every day among the family members. Therefore, in 1986, there was separation among my brothers. Everything was divided among us. Tractor was sold, and its cost was distributed among us. . . . Due to separation the condition of the family swung wildly. I have finally decided that I will go outside to earn some money. . . . I got a job in a mill in Nepal. But the mill was running only for eight months a year and remained closed for the next four months. When the mill closed, then I returned back to home.

"Suddenly in 1995, my elder son fell ill, so we took him to the doctor. After some days of treatment, [the doctor] said, 'It is beyond my control and get him to some other doctor.' A lot of my money was wasted. I [lost] 2 bighas of land after selling them for my son's treatment. We were nowhere: so much money was spent, and in spite of all this, my son was also not getting well still. I asked God, how merciless are you that you are showing so much cruelty to the poor? The God listened to my wish, and my son got well. Now we have got some happiness finally because my child is feeling well now. It does not matter that my land has been sold because we can buy the land again. . . . Had the child left the world, then it is not possible to get him back. A man can buy everything by his money but not a son. . . .

"I had not recovered from my child's disease yet when my wife fell ill. She had stomach pain often. . . . Ultimately, I thought there is no way except selling the land. I had an ultrasound done of my wife. After seeing the report, the doctor said that she has a stone in her stomach. If the operation is not done, then her life will be in danger. A heap of trouble fell upon me. I was not sure of what to do, what not to do. If I had not gotten the operation done for my wife, then the children would have become orphans. Therefore, I sold my 2 bighas of land again. It was at this time when it was difficult to get even bread to eat. Now I had lost everything. . . . I started doing labor in 2002. . . . I do wherever and whatever work I get because I have to maintain the livelihood of my children anyhow. Today my situation is worst."

To what extent are Raish's experiences typical of the kinds of shocks faced by countless others? Once again, we inductively developed a coding system to catch most of the descriptions in the life stories. In the piloting, it became clear that most downward movement was caused by events that became shocks. Following the extensive social protection literature, we classified all shocks first as either idiosyncratic or covariant and then developed a detailed subclassification within each of these two categories.

Across all mobility groups, idiosyncratic, or personal, shocks account for the vast majority of depletion events, 96 percent, while covariant or community-wide shocks account for only 4 percent (table 2.7). Although many communities experience covariant shocks such as floods or drought, these become part of the context, and individuals telling life stories often do not mention them unless the shock is particularly harsh.

TABLE 2.7
Idiosyncratic shocks are the most important in causing asset depletion

Type of shock	% of asset depletion events			
	Movers	Chronic poor	Fallers	Never poor
Idiosyncratic	97	96	95	96
Covariant	3	4	5	4
Total	100	100	100	100
N	3,692	4,955	1,536	3,287

Idiosyncratic shocks

My condition deteriorated at my husband's death. We had to spend almost everything we had in order to pay for his treatment and funeral. At that time, I was so worried I couldn't sleep at night.

— Chabi, a faller, Detya, West Bengal

Somehow I did farming and labor work and got my second son married. With a daughter-in-law, my expenses increased further. The marriage expenses wiped us out and I became thin, and now where should I go to get food to eat?

— Radhe, a 50-year-old faller, Shekhapur, Sitapur, Uttar Pradesh

Death and health shocks are the most frequently mentioned form of idiosyncratic shock across all mobility groups, ranging from 30 to 40 percent (table 2.8). In this sense, Raish's experience is typical. Social shocks such as births, marriages, and the breakup of family (also experienced by Raish) account for a further 22 to 31 percent of idiosyncratic shocks. Problems pursuing education rank third in importance for all groups except fallers, who mention financial losses more frequently. Together, these four types of shocks represent about 90 percent of idiosyncratic shocks resulting in asset depletion. For a detailed breakdown of all idiosyncratic shocks, see annex 2.2.

TABLE 2.8
Death, health, and social stresses are most important idiosyncratic shocks

| Type of shock | *% of idiosyncratic shocks leading to asset depletion* | | | |
	Movers	*Chronic poor*	*Fallers*	*Never poor*
Death/health	36	30	34	41
Social	31	29	27	22
Education	18	15	10	20
Financial	6	14	18	7
Occupation	6	9	7	7
Migration	2	2	2	2
Judicial/legal	1	1	2	1
Political	0	0	0	0
Total	100	100	100	100
N	3,575	4,783	1,465	3,146

Death and health shocks hit the chronic poor and fallers the hardest. Mahadev, a 45-year-old chronic poor man from Tikariya, recalled, "In 1989, a mountain of sorrow descended upon the family due to the death of my mother. Expenses were mounting, and we had to cope with this expense also by taking a loan. And now the entire family was drowned under debt. Once you take a loan from a *mahajan* [moneylender], it is difficult to come out of it."

There are two reasons that death and health shocks have a greater impact on the chronic poor and fallers. First, fatalities and illnesses affect the main income earner in the family more often among the chronic poor (21 percent) and fallers (31 percent) than among movers (15 percent) and the never poor (16 percent). When other family members get sick or die, it is an obvious strain on family resources, but income still flows from the main earner, even if interrupted briefly. Loss of a key breadwinner by contrast depletes tangible assets and affects family morale, cohesion, and social standing. Second, the chronic poor are worse affected because they have fewer resources to cope with health shocks. The fallers may have initially greater resources, but they suffer greater financial distress, which reduces their ability to cope with health shocks.

Marriage obligations and family divisions drain resources. Social tensions and shocks affect the chronic poor and movers more than fallers or the never poor. When we examine the nature of social shocks, we find that the chronic poor, the never poor, and fallers are most affected by marriage, that is, by the expenses incurred in their own marriage or that of a family member. The rituals surrounding weddings are expensive, and expectations keep rising. As marriage rituals are considered to be crucial markers of social standing in a village, most parents make immense financial sacrifices to ensure an appropriate celebration for a child who marries, even if this means falling or remaining trapped in poverty. "In 2003, my economic condition worsened a lot because my daughter got married. To pay for the ceremony, I spent huge sums of money, which resulted in the ruin of my trade," explained Ram Sunder, a chronic poor man from Bhubankhal, Assam.

After marriage, family division is the social shock mentioned most often. As Raish's life story indicates, family breakup can result in a redistribution of assets, including land, housing, and agricultural equipment, along with reduced economic cooperation and risk sharing. Once a family separates, individual members become more vulnerable to shocks. For Bhal, a faller from Khetoosa, Uttar Pradesh, family division was especially ruinous. He lamented, "In 1996, our family split, and things went from bad to worse. I received only a small share of land, which, because of its location right beside the river, is often flooded. Because the waters flush away whatever I cultivate during the rainy season, I can grow only one crop a year. In 2000, my eldest son left the family. This was a huge blow for my finances: I had been counting on my son to help me repay the loan I took for his marriage. He doesn't even talk to us now. How can I reimburse the entire amount?"

Among fallers, "draining habits" including drinking account for a larger portion of social shocks (10 percent) than among other groups (1 to 2 percent). Many of the alcohol habits among fallers appear to be a consequence of their downward slide rather than the initial reason for falling. Men, in particular, are more likely to start drinking to cope with their failures than to fail because of drinking. Udal of Garhima, Uttar Pradesh, rated his well-being at –5 in 1995. He explained that he started drinking wine because of his sorrow and shame at having to close his dairy business, sell his buffalo, and rely on daily farm jobs in order to cover his debts from his sister's wedding. Mitun from Kantipur, West Bengal, said he started drinking to cope with the anguish of his eldest son leaving the family, a wound he will carry to his death. It is notable that the chronic poor rarely mention depletion through bad habits.

All groups also suffer educational shocks that limit their long-term earning potential; these usually occur when a person is forced to leave school for financial or other reasons. Finally, it is no surprise that depleting shocks also include financial shocks (debt, crop failure, and so on) that constrain ability to cope further.

Coping is especially difficult for the chronic poor and fallers. When a crisis occurs, individuals who have a stable livelihood, substantial savings, and a strong network of relations may spend money to cushion the blow, but they often retain their capacity to reaccumulate lost savings once the crisis has passed. Those who have neither stable earnings nor savings are forced to sell important productive assets and resort to high-interest debt to surmount a shock. Deprived of their earning capability and burdened by debt, these individuals frequently find it almost impossible to amass wealth again. They remain stuck in poverty. Table 2.8 demonstrates that the chronic poor and fallers record more financial depletion events and incur more debt as a percentage of idiosyncratic shocks than do movers and the never poor.

The life of Budh Sen, a faller from Nachni Ghat, Uttar Pradesh, illustrates the seemingly irreversible impact of shocks on the highly vulnerable. "In 1982, my brother left the family, taking some land with him. I had less land, and my income decreased, so I started working on other people's farms. In 1997, to pay for my daughter's wedding, I had to sell 1 acre of land, and my income decreased further. To marry off my son, in 1998, I had to borrow money at high interest rates from a moneylender, and he held me in his grip. I became very worried. In 2000, I fell sick and had to borrow money again to pay for the treatment. As repayment, the moneylender took all my land, and he won't give it back unless I give him back his money."

Loss of land is a heavy blow. As Budh Sen's story suggests, loss of land can be a particularly severe and lasting shock. Land is a key asset used to feed one's family and generate profits, and it can be used as collateral for loans. Thus, the cost of losing one's plot goes far beyond the land's market value. Landowners who fail to diversify their activities and depend entirely on farming can see their way of life wiped out overnight by a sudden shock. But while the never poor and movers can use their savings and income to minimize the amount of land they have to sell, fallers often have to give up their entire parcel, losing their only source of income. Many become landless laborers.

Land can be lost in many ways, but the role of social shocks is especially important (table 2.9). People in all groups see the size of their plots shrink following family division, and they also frequently sell land to pay for wedding ceremonies. Udal, a farmer and milk seller from Garhima, Uttar Pradesh, had just started making some profits from his dairy business when he had to pay for the marriage of his sister. The wedding, he says, "ruined me. I took a Rs 50,000 loan from the bank and had to sell my land and buffaloes

TABLE 2.9
Social and financial shocks are the main reasons for land depletion

| Type of shock | % of shocks leading to land depletion | | | |
	Movers	Chronic poor	Fallers	Never poor
Social overall	57	45	37	58
Family/family division	35	23	14	37
Financial overall	15	26	33	14
Debt	1	5	16	2
Financial hardship/ poverty	10	20	16	11
Death and health	14	18	21	14
Judicial/legal overall	6	6	4	2
Environment overall	6	0	4	11
N	79	112	132	57

Note: Only major categories are reported.

to pay back the debt. After I sold my land, I started working as a daily wage laborer. This was very painful for me because I used to have my own field, and I am now obliged to work on other people's plots. But I had no choice."

Fallers also lose large amounts of land due to health and death shocks. To pay for treatments and funerals, they either sell their plot or borrow money using land as collateral. Moneylenders will then seize the land if the loan is not repaid on time, explaining why debt is such an important land depletion channel for fallers (almost 16 percent) compared to other groups (1–5 percent).

Covariant shocks

> My father was a farmer, but flood caused havoc in our lives and destroyed our fields. We faced a lot of difficulties in our studies and had to work as daily laborers.
>
> —A chronic poor youth, Kardohola, Assam

> There was a drought in 2003. Then the crops were badly affected because the rainwater could not reach the fields. Irrigation from the canal was costly as diesel was costly, and we could not even get the drought relief fund. However, the big farmers got the money from the drought relief fund. This was my low point.
>
> —Hardas, a man from a well-off family,
> Dhan Bilgaon, Uttar Pradesh

The bulk of covariant shocks or community-wide shocks consist of environmental hazards and lack of basic services (table 2.10). Covariant shocks account for a relatively small portion of events that lead to depletion of assets, just 4 percent (table 2.7). This may give a misleading picture, however, as these events are very much a part of rural people's everyday reality. Indeed, drought, flood, or fire struck 90 percent of the study villages at some point between 1995 and 2005. It seems that people accept adverse weather conditions or poor services as a fact of life and therefore tend not to refer to them explicitly when explaining the depletion of their assets.

The whims of Mother Nature stand out as the most critical form of covariant shocks for all mobility groups. In a matter of days, droughts and floods can obliterate years of work. Shanti, a faller from Thana, Uttar Pradesh, said, "In 2003, heavy rains destroyed my crops. All crops of peanuts, ginger, and sesame were destroyed. That was a great economic loss: all our income depended on these crops. In 2004, a drought destroyed our crops again, and I lost a lot of money. I got disturbed mentally."

TABLE 2.10
Most covariant shocks relate to environmental hazards or lack of basic services

| Type of shock | % of covariant shocks leading to asset depletion | | | |
	Movers	Chronic poor	Fallers	Never poor
Environment	56	45	52	55
Basic services	32	42	30	34
Social tensions	9	2	0	3
Economic	1	5	14	6
Migration	1	5	0	0
Policies/political shocks	1	0	4	1
Judicial/legal	0	1	0	1
Total	100	100	100	100
N	117	172	71	141

The chronic poor are more vulnerable to hardships due to lack of public services than other mobility groups. They seldom have the resources to pay for transportation to a distant hospital or school. Sharifuddin from Sundari, Assam, recalled, "In primary school, I had to go all the way to Pathsala. I passed all my classes, but as our high school was even further, I had to drop out of school and start working."

Timing of Accumulation and Depletion

In exploring the differences among mobility groups in their asset portfolios and in the factors affecting asset accumulation and depletion, we have so far omitted a crucial variable: time. How do the timing and sequencing of events influence individuals' mobility? To help answer this question, we examine key events in the life stories of our Indian participants in the context of India's economic liberalization policies of the 1990s.

Life stages

From birth until death, individuals pass through distinctive life stages. Because our study focused on a rural economy in which children start working at a very young age, we classify childhood as up to 10 years old, adolescence as 10–16 years old, young adulthood as 17–26 years old, and adulthood as 27 years old onwards. Childhood is a time during which natural development and parental nurturing lay the groundwork for the adult to come. The teenage years are a period of learning and often of work; this is also a very vulnerable time. The early twenties often bring the first formal work experiences that will shape future careers and standards of living. The first 26 years of life hence constitute a decisive period during which individuals develop the human and financial capital necessary to earn a livelihood and handle the responsibilities of adult life. *World Development Report 2007* emphasizes the critical importance of these early years, when key experiences set the stage for a lifetime of loss, stagnation, or achievement (World Bank 2007).

We look at the effect of accumulation and depletion events that occur at different stages of a person's life, beginning with what they inherit at birth (0 years of age). Instead of reporting accumulation and depletion events separately, we construct a ratio of depletion events to total events, called the incidence of depletion. We report the incidence of depletion for all assets, tangible and intangible, in figure 2.1, and for tangible assets only in figure 2.2.

The figures reveal three important results. First, the chronic poor start life with fewer tangible assets than the movers, who also start poor but are clearly not as depleted.

Second, though they start at different points, the four mobility groups even out in terms of depletion events or shocks over the first decade of life.

FIGURE 2.1

Incidence of depletion of tangible and intangible assets shows paths diverging in the middle teen years

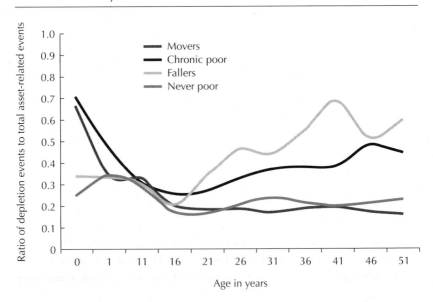

FIGURE 2.2

Incidence of depletion of tangible assets shows paths diverging in the middle teen years

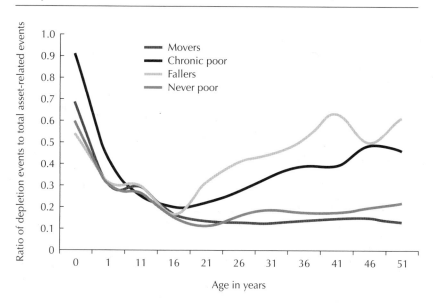

Up to age 10 or 11, most children remain relatively protected and usually get at least some primary education.

Third, there is a dramatic divergence of paths around age 16, which seems to set up divergent trajectories for life. Movers and the never poor maintain a solid path of accumulation as they complete secondary and perhaps tertiary education, obtain stable jobs, and start profitable businesses. This provides them greater capacity to weather all kinds of shocks. For fallers and the chronic poor, the proportion of depletion events, for both tangible and intangible assets, starts to rise steeply in the middle teen years.

Consider the diverging paths of two men, Prasanda and Debranda. Their lives illustrate how the different timing of similar shocks—in this case, the father's death—can contribute to very different mobility outcomes.

Debandra and Prasanta, both in their mid-30s, live in Bhotpara, a struggling village with low poverty mobility in West Bengal. Each managed to break out of daily wage labor and currently earns around Rs 1,800–2,000 a month. Each man saw his father die of a stroke, and each had a sister to marry. Although they have much in common, their lives have taken markedly different turns. Debandra moved above the poverty line, from step 1 to step 4 on the community's ladder of life, while Prasanta remained stuck below the poverty line, moving only from step 1 to step 2.

Debandra, the mover, told us, "I was born in 1970. My father worked as a daily laborer and was the only earner of the family. We could barely earn a square meal a day, and sometimes only had *muri* [fried rice] at night. As income from daily labor is quite small, it was impossible for our father to support our family properly.

"In 1975, my parents put me in school, but because we had no money, I had to drop school after class 3. I immediately started working as a cow boy, earning 1 rupee a day and some food. Then, eight years later, I started working as a daily laborer, earning Rs 25 and two meals per day. In 1994, my father received half a bigha of land through barga [the state's land distribution program], but we didn't have enough money to plow it.

"In 1990, my sister got married; in 1993, my brother got married and left us; and in 1995, I got married. I received Rs 5,000 for my dowry and some land from my father. I started to plow this land he gave me, but only once a year because water was scarce. In 1997, I started cultivating vegetables as I couldn't make enough income from paddy cultivation only. But a flood destroyed my crops in 1998. My father and my friends then advised me to start cultivating potatoes, which I did in 2000. Now I can earn Rs 2,000 per month from cultivation. I couldn't grow groundnuts because I didn't have enough money.

"In 1998, I had a son and opened an insurance policy of Rs 960 per year for my son. That same year I opened an account in a mini-bank and started making some deposits. In the past, I didn't have enough money to make deposits. In 1999, I bought a bicycle for transportation.

"My father died in 2001, and I was shocked. After the death of my father, my mother fell ill. Now we are living peacefully with my mother. I put my son in primary school, and I have money, people respect me."

Prasanta, the chronic poor man, told us: "I was born in 1969. I lived with my father, a daily laborer, my mother, and my sister. My father had to work very hard to make a living and would earn only Rs 1,200 a month. I studied until class 8, but as our father wasn't able to support the house by himself, I started working with him as a daily laborer and would earn Rs 1,400 per month. Together, we would earn Rs 2,600 and could deposit Rs 400 of our earnings every month in Uttarbanga Kshetriya.

"In 1983, my father died of a stroke, which put me in great trouble since his death left me in charge of the entire family. In 1985, I got married and didn't receive anything. In 1986, my son was born. In 1987, my sister got married, and I managed to get the money by selling my mother's bangles. My mother died in 1989.

"With my savings, I bought a van in 1992, which made me happy because thanks to the van, I started making more money: Rs 1,800 a month. Still, there were already many vans out there, and the fares were fixed. Today, I still make Rs 1,800 a month as more and more people drive vans for a living. All our money is spent on daily expenditures, so I cannot save anything."

Both Debandra and Prasanta are hardworking and managed to save some money to diversify their incomes. But the timing of a negative event, in each case the death of the father, made the difference between Debandra's ascent and Prasanta's downfall. Prasanta's father died when he was just 14. The teenager was left in charge of his entire household, facing steep expenses for weddings, births, and deaths. Today, though he works hard, he can barely make ends meet. Debandra, on the other hand, lost his father much later in life, when he was 31. This allowed the household to enjoy two incomes and save for much longer, which, in turn, eased the costs of Debandra's sister's marriage.

Impact of broad economic policies

A significant body of academic literature has examined India's economic liberalization of the 1990s and its impact on growth, poverty, and inequality. Although there is little debate around the notion that liberalization has boosted the profitability of export-oriented industries, some writers argue that it has had an adverse impact on rural economies and poverty reduction (see, for example, Topalova 2005). Using the life stories data, we can chart incidences of depletion along a political-economic timeline.[5] This enables us to consider whether the period of economic liberalization coincided with the period in which the asset depletion paths of the chronic poor diverged from those of the movers, and the paths of the never poor diverged from those of the fallers.

In figures 2.3 and 2.4, we see that the depletion paths of the never poor and fallers diverge from each other in the 1980s, long before India's economic opening. In the early 1980s, the fallers' incidence of depletion started increasing and never stopped, whereas depletion among the never poor remained low and steady. Although the chronic poor and movers do exhibit diverging paths in the 1990s, their respective trajectories took root much earlier: even as early as 1942 to 1969, movers depleted fewer assets than the chronic poor (and far fewer *tangible* assets, as shown in figure 2.4). Inequalities in exposure to shocks between the chronic poor and movers were thus noticeable many years before the gap between them increased in the 1990s.

FIGURE 2.3
Incidence of depletion of tangible and intangible assets shows paths diverging in the 1980s

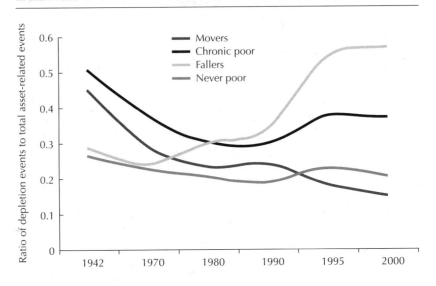

FIGURE 2.4
Incidence of depletion of tangible assets shows paths diverging in the 1980s

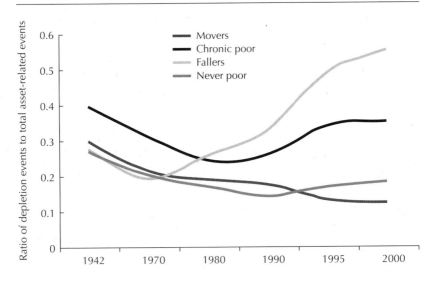

Therefore, it seems unlikely that liberalization policies created the differences between movers and the chronic poor, and surely not between fallers and the never poor. However, the impacts of the policies may have exacerbated the differences. The 1990s saw an even greater divergence between movers and the chronic poor, as well as between the never poor and fallers.

When we examine the types of shocks, our analysis confirms earlier findings. Fallers experience more trauma—death of the main earner, debt, and social trauma—than those who stay above the poverty line. The chronic poor report considerably more death/health issues affecting their main earner, financial shocks (especially debt), social shocks, and occupational shocks, especially exploitation and a bad working environment.

Long-term effects of depleting events

Life stories, as well as the trajectories of depletion highlighted in the previous sections, show that mobility is the outcome of a succession of depletion and accumulation events. Shocks, whether positive or negative, often have an influence that persists long after the event. For instance, the death of an important family member can have economic repercussions on a household that may still be visible decades after the tragedy.

To further explore the temporal impact of negative events on mobility, we ran the regression analyses presented in table 2.11. We regressed mobility outcome (chronic poor versus movers, fallers versus never poor) on a selection of seven important negative events including environmental, educational, financial, occupational, death, health, and social shocks. In addition, we include five control variables: initial levels of key assets in 1942–69, age of respondent, age of respondent at time of the event, gender, and state. Each regression is run for each of the six historical time periods shown in figures 2.3 and 2.4.

Regression coefficients in table 2.11 express the change in probability of being a mover (versus remaining poor) or faller (versus remaining nonpoor) associated with a 1-unit increase in the number of shocks of a given type in a given period. Thus, we see to what extent experiencing certain depletion events earlier in life is associated with subsequent upward and downward mobility.

Our regression clearly shows that, of the seven depleting shocks we have identified, financial shocks have the largest and most lasting effect on mobility, whether comparing chronic poor to movers or fallers to never poor. Financial shocks in almost all periods have a significant negative effect on upward mobility and wealth. Experiencing a financial shock between 1942

TABLE 2.11

Financial shocks have the largest and longest impact on mobility

Type of depletion event	Dependent variable: chronic poor vs. movers						Dependent variable: fallers vs. never poor					
	1942	1970	1980	1990	1995	2000	1942	1970	1980	1990	1995	2000
Environment	0.200	0.191	0.097	−0.076	−0.291	0.370***			0.715	−0.315	0.627***	0.152*
Education	−0.142	0.084	−0.056	−0.515***	−0.255	0.173	0.037	0.023	0.060	−0.087	0.165	0.184
Death	0.035	−0.035	0.125*	0.052	0.180***	0.119**	0.006	0.048	0.005	0.008	0.188**	0.158*
Financial	0.773***	0.283**	0.433***	0.150	0.235**	0.699***	−0.550	−0.012	0.471***	0.715***	0.928***	0.536***
Health	0.122	−0.133	0.189	0.245**	0.157*	0.236***		−0.158	−0.016	0.470***	0.298***	0.292***
Social	0.065	0.101	0.144*	0.189***	0.269***	0.224***	0.090	0.211*	0.106	0.398***	0.434***	0.419***
Occupation	−0.115	0.340**	0.198**	0.098	0.106	0.221		0.187	0.084	0.135	0.440**	0.496***

Note: Regression shows type of depletion event and movement in and out of poverty, using probit, with initial assets. The following additional controls have been included in the regressions, but their coefficients are not reported: initial levels of key assets in 1942–69, age of respondent, age of respondent at time of the event, gender, state. Dependent variables: chronic poor dummy (1=chronic poor, 0=mover) and faller dummy (1=faller, 0=never poor).

*p < .10 **p < .05 ***p < .01

and 1969 increases the probability of staying below the poverty line by about 77 percent.

We also find that shocks due to ill health or death, while having an undeniable impact on one's chance of moving up or down, do not have as lasting an impact as financial shocks. Effects of fatalities and illnesses, it seems, tend to be short- or medium-term. This does not mean that death and health issues have no lasting effects, but rather that their impact on mobility is usually channeled through financial shocks. Indeed, medical treatment, funerals, and death of an earner directly affect households' finances and ability to earn an income, with potentially long-term consequences. When people talk about what hindered their mobility, however, they often emphasize health shocks. This may be because health shocks are not only financially draining but also emotionally and socially damaging, as death of the breadwinner changes life opportunities and status for everyone in the household.

It is surprising that educational shocks do not appear as significant predictors of mobility. Only from 1990 to 1994 for chronic poor versus movers do events mainly associated with withdrawal from school seem to hamper upward mobility. This is probably linked to the demand for workers with higher levels of education.

Conclusions and Policy Recommendations

The life stories from India illustrate time and again that poor people are not lazy, stupid, or crippled by addictions. They work extremely hard in an effort to substitute for lack of assets, technology, and savings. But hard labor alone is not sufficient to lift them out of poverty. Nor are poor people lacking in initiative; indeed, *they sometimes take more entrepreneurial initiatives than the rich.* But the kinds of initiatives they can attempt are severely constrained by their meager material resources and lack of influential contacts. They take risks, but often, they fail.

Poverty policies do not yet reflect the fact that the main problem of poverty is not poor people themselves but their circumstances. In rural areas, at least, they tend to live in impoverished villages with few economic opportunities or connections to modern markets. They have low assets, low financial capital, low education, and often low skills as well. Drawing on the life story findings, we make six recommendations for enabling poor people in rural areas to move out of poverty in the next five to ten years.

First, poor people are entrepreneurial, but they require additional support for their efforts to turn profits. Life stories are full of cases in which too many people in a given community produce the same goods for local markets, which are quickly saturated. Poor people often have little knowledge of modern markets and the products that will sell well in them. They need access to financial capital that will help them start businesses, and these loans need to be large enough to go beyond daily consumption needs. Access to financial capital together with support to improve poor people's entrepreneurial knowledge and skills can help lift poor people out of poverty.

Second, it is clear that having basic assets such as housing and land early in life is critical and gives a person a head start toward consolidating wealth. Where government schemes have reached poor people and provided them with permanent houses, this gives the recipients a tremendous psychological boost, increasing their dignity in their own eyes and the eyes of the community. In addition, these houses often serve as an essential basis for production. Distribution of land to very poor people is helpful, but it needs to be coupled with other resources to enable the recipients to put the newly acquired land to productive use. In short, poor people need generous transfers that can give them a boost out of poverty, not just small transfers that help them cope but leave them trapped.

Third, in addition to policies that support accumulation, policies to halt the depletion of assets are crucial. Particularly needed are measures to cushion the impact of health and social shocks. Affordable, timely, high-quality health care and health insurance are critical for everyone and particularly for poor people. Social shocks, from which families typically recover even more slowly, require a different type of action, one that seeks to change social norms. In particular, expectations about appropriate wedding expenditures must change. Poor people try to emulate the rich, and with lavish wedding ceremonies on display in the cities and in Bollywood movies, expectations of a "proper" wedding in rural areas have also escalated, driving people into destitution. The middle class, the rich, and civil society, including the mass media, have important roles to play in changing social norms about wedding expenses.

Fourth, social networks, particularly families, are often pivotal in successful mobility processes, sustaining individual initiative and providing mechanisms for coping with shocks. It is rational for villagers to invest heavily in their families in an environment in which formal safety nets are scarce or nonexistent. But not all families work as harmonious wholes, and the life stories repeatedly show how family division or dysfunction impedes well-being and mobility. Self-help groups are also worthy of increased support, since they strengthen women's positions and forge cooperative ventures across family lines. Given the importance of psychological factors and relationships in asset accumulation, it is important to explore culturally appropriate community-level counseling services that can be provided by trained laypersons.[6]

Fifth, to break the cycle of poverty, policies are needed that directly help poor youth to accumulate assets. The early years of life lay the basis for later periods of asset accumulation and maintenance. Scholarships that help youth stay in school are important, but they are not enough. Youth also need formal and informal opportunities for training and mentoring to gain employment and entrepreneurial skills. And they need help finding jobs and accessing credit so they can put these new skills to good use. Youth who face traumatic events, such as the loss of the family's main earner due to illness or death, need targeted mentoring and support to ensure that these events do not cut their own life opportunities short.

Finally, an important conclusion from this study is that it matters greatly *how* development policies are implemented. Mobility processes have both intangible and tangible dimensions, and policy interventions should be designed in ways that enhance relational and emotional assets as well as the more conventional tangible assets. Do programs and services foster and build on individual aspirations, initiative, and community ties? Or do they undermine self-confidence, respect, and cohesion? This important aspect of all development programs is often overlooked.

Annex 2.1 Channels of Accumulation

ANNEX TABLE 2.A

Composition of accumulation through four types of institutions

Channel of accumulation	% of asset accumulation events involving each type of institution			
	Movers	Chronic poor	Fallers	Never poor
Family help	63	62	55	57
Spouse/marriage of self	24	23	33	30
Family marriage	13	14	13	14
Change in family structure	0	0	0	0
Public				
Central/state government	69	78	65	70
Local government	13	15	19	16
Military forces	6	1	1	4
Political institutions	4	4	4	3
Financial sector	4	2	7	4
Police	2	0	4	2
Legal/judicial	1	1	0	1
Public services	1	0	0	0
Civil society				
Social network	48	44	59	38
Self-help groups	15	31	17	24
Religious organizations	10	4	10	7
Political associations	8	4	5	4
Economic associations	5	9	5	10
Cultural organizations	4	0	2	5
Youth organizations	4	0	2	1
Gender associations	2	3	0	3
Self-defense groups	2	1	0	5
Ethnic organizations	1	1	0	1
NGOs (local)	1	3	0	1
Educational organizations	0	0	0	1
Private				
Firms	64	28	70	71
Factories	31	30	10	21
Traders and buyers	3	39	20	4
Financial sector	2	2	0	0
Market behavior	1	1	0	4

ANNEX TABLE 2.B
Composition of accumulation through central/state government

Channel of accumulation	% of asset accumulation events involving central/state government			
	Movers	Chronic poor	Fallers	Never poor
Employment/promotion	60	21	30	75
Subsidy	30	65	49	6
Financial support/gifts	3	9	2	3
Transfers	3	0	0	8
Service delivery	1	1	0	0
Loans	1	1	9	2
Pricing policies	1	1	2	1
Behavior positive	0.5	2	0	1
Connections/associations	0.5	0	0	1
Corruption	0	0	0	0
Retirement	0	0	6	3
Education (informal)	0	0	0	0
Law and order	0	0	2	0
Total	100	100	100	100

Annex 2.2 Channels of Depletion

ANNEX TABLE 2.C

Composition of idiosyncratic depletion of all tangible and intangible assets

Type of event	% of idiosyncratic asset depletion events involving each main type of shock			
	Movers	Chronic poor	Fallers	Never poor
Death				
Family/unspecified cause	67	61	55	67
Earner	14	15	13	11
Family/illness	10	11	18	11
Health				
Family/major illness	43	38	32	40
Self/major illness	22	26	31	20
Family/major accident	6	5	7	10
Earner/major illness	4	0	12	1
Social				
Family/birth circumstances	48	34	16	25
Family/marriage of self	8	16	6	17
Family/family division	18	13	25	18
Family/marriage of child	5	13	15	12
Family/birth	6	11	9	12
Draining habits/family alcohol or drugs	1	2	10	1
Family/problems and tensions	3	2	5	4
Family/marriage of family	2	2	4	3
Education				
Financial constraints	39	37	21	14
Family obligations or problems	18	19	21	23
Unspecified cause	9	11	7	12
Loss of interest	8	8	20	15
Social discrimination	5	7	7	10
Failure on exam	13	6	17	13
Poor quality education	2	4	3	3

Type of event	% of idiosyncratic asset depletion events involving each main type of shock			
	Movers	Chronic poor	Fallers	Never poor
Financial				
Financial hardship/poverty	43	42	40	32
Debt	27	44	42	38
Crop failure	7	4	2	8
Death of livestock	6	4	6	3
Occupation				
Exploitation	25	47	13	23
Job loss	16	8	12	15
Lack of interest	14	10	10	14
Dissatisfaction	13	8	11	8
Business failure	11	6	32	13
Bad working environment	9	14	10	11

References

Boshara, R., and M. Sherraden. 2004. *Status of Asset Building Worldwide*. Washington, DC: New America Foundation.

Carney, D. 1998. *Sustainable Rural Livelihoods: What Contribution Can We Make?* London: Department for International Development.

———. 1999. "Approaches to Sustainable Livelihoods for the Rural Poor." ODI Poverty Briefing 2, Overseas Development Institute, London.

Carter, M. 2007. "Learning from Asset-based Approaches to Poverty." In Moser 2007, 51–61.

Carter, M., and J. May. 1999. "Poverty, Livelihood and Class in Rural South Africa." *World Development* 27: 1–20.

Chambers, R., and G. Conway. 1992. "Sustainable Rural Livelihoods: Practical Concepts for the 21st Century." Discussion Paper 296, Institute of Development Studies, University of Sussex, Brighton, UK.

Dercon, S., and J. S. Shapiro. 2007. "Moving On, Staying Behind, Getting Lost: Lessons on Poverty Mobility from Longitudinal Data." In *Moving Out of Poverty: Cross-Disciplinary Perspectives on Mobility*, ed. D. Narayan and P. Petesch, 77–126. New York: Palgrave Macmillan; Washington, DC: World Bank.

DFID (Department for International Development). 2000. "Sustainable Livelihoods—Current Thinking and Practice." Department for International Development, London.

Ford Foundation. 2004. *Building Assets to Reduce Poverty and Injustice*. New York: Ford Foundation.

Goette, L., and D. Huffman. 2005. "Do Emotions Improve Labor Market Outcomes?" IZA Discussion Paper 1895, Institute for the Study of Labor (IZA), Bonn.

Graham, C., and M. Fitzpatrick. 2002. "Does Happiness Pay? An Exploration Based on Panel Data from Russia." Working Paper 23, Brookings Institution, Washington, DC.

Krishna, A. 2007. "Escaping Poverty and Becoming Poor in Three States of India, with Additional Evidence from Kenya, Uganda, and Peru." In *Moving Out of Poverty: Cross-Disciplinary Perspectives on Mobility*, ed. D. Narayan and P. Petesch, 165–97. New York: Palgrave Macmillan; Washington, DC: World Bank.

Lewis, O. 1959. *Five Families: Mexican Case Studies in the Culture of Poverty*. New York: Basic Books.

Moser, C. 1998. *The Asset Vulnerability Framework: Reassessing Urban Poverty Reduction Strategies*. World Development 26 (1): 1–19.

———. ed. 2007. *Reducing Global Poverty: The Case for Asset Accumulation*. Washington, DC: Brookings Institution Press.

Moser, C., and A. Norton, 2001. "To Claim Our Rights: Livelihood Security, Human Rights and Sustainable Development." Overseas Development Institute, London.

Narayan, D., ed. 2002. *Empowerment and Poverty Reduction: A Sourcebook*. Washington, DC: World Bank.

Narayan, D., R. Patel, K. Schafft, A. Rademacher, and S. Koch-Schulte. 2000. *Voices of the Poor: Can Anyone Hear Us?* New York: Oxford University Press for the World Bank.

Ojermark, A. 2007. "Presenting Life Histories: A Literature Review and Annotated Bibliography." Working Paper 101, Chronic Poverty Research Centre, Manchester, UK.

Ritchie, D. 1995. *Doing Oral History.* New York: Twayne.

Sherraden, M. 1991. *Assets and the Poor: A New American Welfare Policy.* Armonk, NY: M. E. Sharpe.

Slim, H., and P. Thompson. 1993. *Listening for a Change: Oral Testimony and Development.* London: Panos.

Takahashi, T. 2005. "Social Memory, Social Stress, and Economic Behaviors." *Brain Research Bulletin* 67 (5): 398–402.

Thompson, P. 1998. "The Voice of the Past: Oral History." In *The Oral History Reader,* ed. R. Perks and A. Thompson, 21–28. New York: Routledge.

Topalova, P. 2005. "Trade Liberalization, Poverty, and Inequality: Evidence from Indian Districts." NBER Working Paper 11614, National Bureau of Economic Research, Cambridge, MA.

World Bank. 2000. *World Development Report 2000/2001: Attacking Poverty.* New York: Oxford University Press.

———. 2007. *World Development Report 2007: Development and the Next Generation.* New York: Oxford University Press.

Notes

1. For literature reviews on life stories, see Ojermark (2007) and Thompson (1998).
2. The details of our methodology, including the coding process, can be found on the Moving Out of Poverty study Web site at http://go.worldbank.org/ 8K2Q8RYZ10.
3. The name of the servant discloses that he is an untouchable (or Dalit) and works with "complete loyalty" to his master. He is expected to sacrifice his own interests and not attempt to seize opportunity or even receive fair monetary returns for his labor. This mindset is currently being questioned in India through the Dalit social movements that encourage formerly oppressed people to see a wider set of choices for themselves and their children.
4. Anthropologist Oscar Lewis (1959) first used the term "culture of poverty" and associated it with these characteristics, among others.
5. Repeating the exercise accounting for the size of events does not significantly change the results. The trajectories of accumulation/depletion of assets remain largely the same, and all the period effects are observed.
6. Professor Vikram Patel is currently piloting such an effort in southern India under the auspices of the London School of Hygiene & Tropical Medicine.

Communities Where Poor People Prosper

Deepa Narayan, Patti Petesch, and Saumik Paul

Democracy is the leader elected by the people. When people of all castes can work together and the rich and poor get similar justice, it is democracy.

—MEN'S DISCUSSION GROUP,
Uttar Pradesh

The worst time in my life was the flood in the year 2000. At this flood, our land was submerged for so long that the entire crop was damaged. We had taken a loan and plunged into poverty; eating one meal a day was difficult. In 2001, we took more loans with the hope of production, but bad luck does not come alone. The entire crops were destroyed in an attack of insects.

—A MALE FALLER, KANTIPUR,
West Bengal

Matka and Ashikabad, two potato farming villages, are located a few kilometers apart in the Salon block of Raibarelli district in Uttar Pradesh. Matka prospered over the study period of 1995 to 2005. Ashikabad did not.

The Indian government subsidized the introduction of tube wells for irrigation in Matka in the early 1990s, and cheap and reliable water became available to large and small farmers alike. The Yadavs and Brahmins, traditionally the largest landholders in the village, have reaped the biggest profits from irrigation. But poor farmers and farm laborers have gained, too. No one goes hungry anymore, and most children of the village attend the primary school.

With their savings, many of Matka's villagers have branched into new ventures such as setting up fertilizer and grocery shops, and a few have found government jobs. A main highway bisects the village, aiding economic diversification. The availability of credit has eased villagers' access to new opportunities, and people express particular appreciation for the Kisan (farmers') credit card and for the village cooperative society. But Matka also has faced hardships, and 2004 was a particularly bad year. Hailstorms hit the region and ruined crops. Adding to the losses, the cooperative's secretary absconded with Rs 2.5 million that year, leaving 60 families without their deposits. Nor do people feel that local government helps them much. Their pradhan initially did good works for the entire village, such as opening a school and helping to bring in new boring facilities for water. But in recent years, he has worked only for those from his own area.

Nevertheless, villagers say the gap between the richest and poorest in Matka has decreased over the past decade as many of Matka's poor have moved up. And because so many poor families have been able to prosper, "The poor can easily approach the rich and are no longer afraid of them."

113

In the nearby village of Ashikabad, by contrast, only a few families have been able to escape poverty. The village irrigation system is not functioning, and this has greatly constrained farm productivity. Although they were installed only in the mid-1990s, the tube wells have sat in disrepair since 2000 despite repeated requests for help from the irrigation department.

As in Matka, caste differences divide and exclude. "A person belonging to the Harijan [lower-caste] community cannot be allowed to mix with the caste of the pandits," said a poor villager. Until recently, the landowners of Ashikabad paid farm wages in grain; they now offer rates of just Rs 20–30 per day, even though triple that amount can be earned elsewhere. Moreover, the work is only seasonal. Many families send one or more members out of the village to earn income elsewhere, but villagers report that even poor families with migrant workers cannot afford to eat two meals a day or send their children to school.

Drought struck in 2003, but without irrigation, little could be done. Crops withered, and debts went unpaid. When hailstorms ruined the 2004 crop in Ashikabad, as they had in nearby Matka, farm debts mounted further. But mechanisms for coping seem less accessible than in Matka. In Ashikabad, both men and women said the only credit to be found is through a women's cooperative formed by the Anganwadi (the government child development center).

Unlike Matka, Ashikabad sits a kilometer off the main highway, and this seems to add to its difficulties. Until 2000, muddy roads made walking around the village treacherous during the rainy season, and water pooling in the potholes carried disease. Buses and vans stayed away. Farmers endured losses because they were forced to take whatever price they could get for their crops from the few traders who made their way to the village. The installation of drainage ditches and hand pumps for drinking water at the turn of the century greatly eased transportation and health problems.

Residents give a lot of credit to their pradhan for the new infrastructure. Yet like Matka's villagers, they voice intense dissatisfaction with local politics and detail practices involving favoritism, bribery, and misuse of funds that have derailed local projects. While they participate actively in community decision making, this has little effect on government performance. As a male villager explained, the corruption and bribery means that "proper information is not made available to the common man." And local women say that it is growing worse. "The officials demand bribery openly and fearlessly. The job is done only after the payment is made."

Matka saw 60 percent of its poor families escape poverty between 1995 and 2005. In Ashikabad, just 5 percent did so. How could this be? How could opportunities for poor people vary so greatly between two apparently similar villages two kilometers apart in the same district of the same state? Was it the fact that Ashikabad is farther from the main road? Was it the success of Matka's irrigation, or its more accessible credit? And do other villages feature such tremendous differences in the chances for poor people's mobility?

Community-level variation in performance on reducing poverty has been noted before and has prompted the design of community-level targeting approaches for poverty reduction programs (Galasso and Ravallion 2000; Ravallion 1993; Bardhan and Mookherjee 2004, 2006).[1] Our study adds to this literature by focusing on community-level differences and on factors and dynamics *within* communities that seem to lead to dramatic differences in poverty outcomes.

This chapter first presents the study sample and the outcomes for community-level poverty escapes and for other types of transitions experienced by the villages. It then briefly reviews the study's conceptual framework for analyzing poor people's mobility and explores, with qualitative data and descriptive statistics, how mobility outcomes are shaped by economic opportunities, local democracy, collective action, and inequalities in access to opportunities. Findings are presented from regression analysis of village-level correlates of movements out of poverty and of other upward and downward poverty transitions. The chapter concludes with policy reflections.

Variation in Mobility Outcomes among Study Communities

Upward movement is a bit difficult for poor people. If people start saving their earnings, then they can easily move a step upwards. Availability of work and government assistance is very important for upward movement.
    —Men's discussion group, Jambugumpala, Andhra Pradesh

Loss of crops, bad monsoons, poor irrigation facilities, and nonavailability of loans from government, and wasting their money on alcohol, will hinder movement upwards. In addition to this, illiteracy or poor education also affects the chances of upward movement.
    —Women's discussion group, Appilepalle, Andhra Pradesh

Variation is the defining feature of the Indian villages visited for this study. Not only are there many historical and cultural differences, but the mobility patterns also show tremendous diversity. Of the 296 villages in the sample for which we have village-level data, just 62 were founded less than 100 years ago. Seventy-one are a century old, 42 villages date back 200 years, and 56 are between 300 and 600 years old. Nearly all report Hinduism as the primary religion practiced; in 12 villages, 4 percent of the total, Islam is the primary religion. In all regions, complicated and deeply embedded caste, religious, and ethnic structures still determine much of the economic, social, and political life of the villages.[2] Numerous languages are also spoken as one moves across the villages in the four states.[3]

The study villages experienced important demographic growth during the study period. In 1995, the median population was 1,750. By 2005, the smallest village had a population of 400 and the largest had 16,000, and the median population of the sample had risen to 2,450.

The Moving Out of Poverty study developed its own methodology for assessing mobility patterns in the sample villages (see chapter 1 for details of this process). Focus groups in each study community created a "ladder of life" to graphically depict the different levels of well-being among households in their village. After discussing how and why residents of the village might move up or fall down the steps of the ladder, focus group members identified the step that a household in their village had to reach to be considered no longer poor. This is referred to as the community poverty line (CPL). Finally, the group sorted 150–60 households in the village according to their positions on their ladder of life both 10 years ago and presently. Based on these data, the study teams were able to calculate for each village the number of households that had moved up and across the CPL over the 10 years (the movers), remained below the CPL (the chronic poor), remained above the CPL (the never poor), or slid below the CPL into poverty (the fallers).

Seven summary indicators or indexes are used in this chapter to describe different types of transitions experienced by the communities during the study period. The statistics are derived from the household sorting exercise based on the communities' individual ladders of life (see chapter 1, table 1.2). They are designed to enable rough comparisons of upward and downward transitions across communities.

- *MOP:* Moving out of poverty index. Measures extent of upward mobility by the poor across the CPL in a community.
- *MPI:* Mobility of the poor index. Measures extent of upward mobility by those who were initially poor, irrespective of whether or not they crossed the CPL.

- *MRI:* Mobility of the rich index. Measures extent of upward mobility by those who were initially above the CPL (nonpoor or "rich" by the study's definition).
- *FPI:* Falling of the poor index. Measures extent of downward mobility of the initially poor.
- *FRI:* Falling of the rich index. Measures extent of downward mobility of the rich.
- *FRIP:* Falling of the rich into poverty index. Measures extent of downward mobility of the rich across the CPL.
- *NPR:* Net poverty reduction. Measures changes in the share of poor over study period.

Summary mobility outcomes

Table 3.1 presents average statistics for the seven different types of mobility outcomes experienced by the study communities. Taken together, the findings illustrate that beneath India's extensive rural poverty is a very dynamic story of significant accomplishment *and* vulnerability. Across the sample, more than a fifth of those who were poor in 1995 crossed the CPL and escaped poverty by 2005 (MOP). And more than a third of the initially poor made gains of at least one ladder step (MPI). By comparison, only 17 percent of the households that were already above the poverty line in 1995 (MRI) experienced further upward movement. Reversing directions, the slides down the ladder were much more modest for the poor than for the rich. Only 7 percent of the initially poor in the sample fell further down. However, 25 percent of the initially nonpoor households fell down at least one step (FRI), and 19 percent fell all the way below the CPL and into poverty (FRIP).

Overall, the study finds a net decline in poverty of 7 percent (NPR). High rates of poverty escapes were to a large extent offset by descents into poverty among the better-off. Because of the small size of the initially nonpoor population, however, the declines among this group did not totally wipe out the

TABLE 3.1

Summary mobility outcomes for total village sample show simultaneous movements up and down

MOP	MPI	MRI	FPI	FRI	FRIP	NPR
0.22	0.34	0.17	0.07	0.25	0.19	0.07

sizable gains made by the larger group of initially poor. These disaggregated mobility statistics reveal how average poverty rates hide important up-and-down dynamics: some people are rising while others are falling.

Variance in mobility by geographic level

Aggregate poverty statistics, which hide the contrasting movements of risers and fallers, also conceal striking variations in mobility outcomes between communities. Table 3.2 shows the standard deviation of the six key indexes across different geographic levels. As we move downward from the state level to the district level and from there to the block and community levels, the variation in this index goes up. It is not surprising to get a lower standard deviation at a higher geographic level following the concept of central tendency, but we find that the variation across different levels is very high. For the MOP index, the variation at the community level is more than double the variation at the state level.

Figures 3.1 and 3.2 show the average variation in key indexes across different geographic levels. As we move from the state to the community level, there is higher average variation, evident for all key indexes. These results are consistent with other empirical works that find important gains from targeting poverty interventions at lower geographic levels.

Variance in mobility by rate of MOP

To draw out sharper patterns in this very large dataset, we report the results for the communities that are in the top third and bottom third in MOP outcomes. We refer to these subsets as the high-MOP and low-MOP communities, respectively. The rate of poverty escapes (MOP) averaged 6.5 times higher in the top third of villages (39 percent) than in the

TABLE 3.2
Standard deviation of key indexes is lowest at state level, highest at community level

Level	MOP	MPI	MRI	FPI	FRI	FRIP
State	0.08	0.10	0.08	0.01	0.03	0.03
District	0.09	0.13	0.09	0.03	0.06	0.05
Block	0.14	0.17	0.12	0.06	0.12	0.11
Community	0.18	0.21	0.15	0.08	0.17	0.15

FIGURE 3.1
Standard deviation for upward mobility indexes rises as geographic levels decline

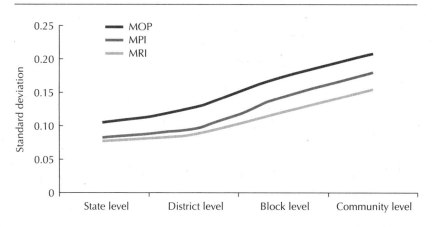

FIGURE 3.2
Standard deviation for downward mobility indexes rises as geographic levels decline

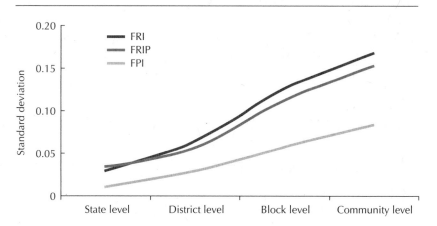

bottom third (6 percent). Moreover, half of the poor in the top villages moved ahead at least one step (MPI), while just 17 percent did so in the bottom villages. Perhaps most significantly, net poverty reduction in the top third (11 percent) was more than double the rate in the bottom third

TABLE 3.3

Summary mobility statistics show contrasts between top, middle, and bottom thirds of study villages

Portion of sample by rate of MOP	MOP	MPI	MRI	FP	FRI	FRIP	NPR
Top 33%	0.39	0.51	0.23	0.06	0.28	0.19	0.11
Middle 33%	0.16	0.29	0.13	0.08	0.27	0.21	0.06
Bottom 33%	0.06	0.17	0.08	0.08	0.21	0.17	0.05
Total	0.21	0.33	0.15	0.07	0.26	0.19	0.07

(5 percent), despite higher rates of falling among the rich in the top villages (table 3.3).

The importance of access and exclusion

Given the stark inequalities that have long marked India's countryside, the analysis draws attention to the influences on mobility outcomes of hierarchical social and political structures, of dominant values and norms that disadvantage poor groups, and of inequalities in individual and collective assets (also see Narayan and Petesch 2007). Therefore, we look not only at presence or absence of facilities and services but also at who has access to them and who is excluded.

The analysis below weaves together quantitative and qualitative data. The descriptive statistics derive from the study's community profile survey.[4] The qualitative accounts emerge from systematic content analysis of the researchers' field reports of focus group discussions and interviews conducted in the sample villages.

Rising Economic Opportunities

If we have a good job, we can get our monthly salary, and we can demand respect. If we have some property and land, all the people in the village treat us with respect.

—A male youth, Appilepalle, Andhra Pradesh

India attained spectacular macroeconomic growth in the decade covered by this study, rising from 6.4 percent in 1995 to 8 and 9 percent between 2003 and 2005. Yet the fruits of this growth were disproportionately enjoyed by the country's better-off households, those closely tied to urban centers and modern sectors of the economy (Chaudhuri and Ravallion 2006). The benefits of growth were far more meager in the countryside, where this study was conducted and where 75 percent of India's poor still resided as of 2006 (61st round, National Sample Survey).

Nevertheless, with a net poverty reduction rate of 7 percent across the sample over the decade, as indicated above, this study does uncover progress on rural poverty. As in the cases of Matka and Ashikabad, however, this progress was marked by very large variations from one village to the next. Why and how do some villages create so much more economic opportunity for their poor residents than others? We examine key factors below.

Strength of local economies

Local economies became stronger across the sample during the decade under study. This growth, moreover, was even greater in the high-MOP villages. By 2005 just 9 percent of the high-MOP villages reported a weak local economy, compared with 25 percent of the low-MOP villages (figure 3.3). This marks a

FIGURE 3.3
Growth of local economies was greatest in high-MOP villages

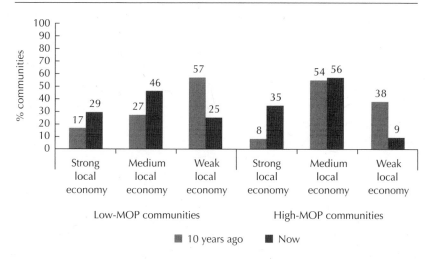

Note: The t-statistics for the difference in mean strength of local economy between now and 10 years ago are 6.41 for low-MOP communities and 7.01 for high-MOP communities, indicating that changes in strength of local economy in the past decade were significant in both contexts.

statistically significant improvement from 1995 for both high- and low-MOP contexts.

A combination of factors seem to contribute to prospering local economies. These include market outlets within the community, presence of large markets nearby, and presence of roads and transportation that allows easy movement from and to the village. For poor workers, thriving markets offer jobs in local shops, construction, and transport, as well as opportunities to engage in petty trades. Indeed, such diversification into nonfarm activities is often a defining feature of households that were able to cross the community poverty line. But large markets also help poor rural families by improving farming opportunities: those with access to land are able to market their produce more easily, and landless laborers can find farm work.

In Alipur in West Bengal, where MOP is extremely high, local people attribute the village's prosperity to their successful new market. The panchayat took the initiative to build numerous shops, stalls, and a bus terminal. Men in the village said almost everyone has been able to benefit from the investments: "The farmers need not go outside to sell paddy; on the contrary, the wholesale sellers visit the village and purchase paddy from the farmers directly. So business has flourished. More or less everybody is trading. Previously, such opportunity was not there."

Similarly, discussion groups in high-MOP Mahoa in Uttar Pradesh said their local market has ushered in diverse development gains. Farmers are getting better prices for their harvest, and in addition to potatoes and food grains they now cultivate tomatoes, cabbage, green chilies, and pumpkins. Others have gone into dairy production and poultry farming. According to key informants, farmers save time and pay less to transport their produce, and "when the prices of produce rise, they sell out their produce easily." The improved market facilities also offer local consumers a wider selection and better prices. According to one man in Mahoa, "Earlier there were very few shops, and one could get only small items. But now there are groceries, PCOs [telephone kiosks], medical stores, sweet shops, vegetable shops, etc."

Private employment opportunities

The role of private employers is not clearcut. Unexpectedly, private jobs were reported to be more present in the low-MOP communities at the outset of the study (figures 3.4 and 3.5).[5] However, by 2005, private employment opportunities had significantly deteriorated in the bottom MOP villages, while both

FIGURE 3.4
Presence of private employers has increased in high-MOP villages

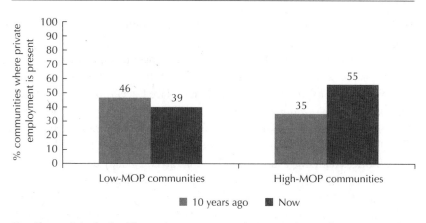

Note: The *t*-statistics for the difference in mean presence of private employment between now and 10 years ago are –3.48 for low-MOP communities and 3.00 for high-MOP communities (both significant at 5%). This indicates that private employment fell significantly in low-MOP communities and increased significantly in high-MOP communities.

FIGURE 3.5
Ease of finding private employment has improved in high-MOP villages

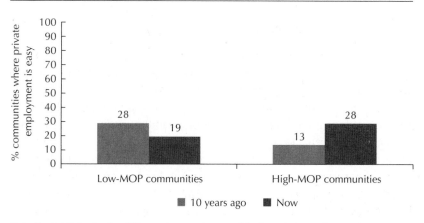

Note: The *t*-statistics for the difference in mean in ease of finding private employment between now and 10 years ago is 4.38 for high-MOP communities (significant at 5%) and is insignificant for low-MOP communities. It has increased significantly from initial low levels in high-MOP communities and declined somewhat in low-MOP communities.

the presence of private employers and the ease of finding private employment improved significantly in the top MOP villages.

The qualitative accounts from low-MOP villages emphasize the difficulties that poor people encounter when they try to find decent work or otherwise diversify their incomes. They speak as well of population growth and increased competition for work and of the technological changes that are disadvantaging numerous job seekers. In Bhaturia, a low-MOP village in West Bengal, many workers in the local handloom industry have faced declining income or job losses due to the introduction of power looms, the rising cost of thread, and increasing consumer preference for saris made of synthetic fabrics. "Nowadays," according to a woman of the village, "some of the laborers of this industry are doing work as daily wage laborers or pulling carts on a daily rent basis."

In low-MOP Bhubankhal, Assam, villagers rely heavily on work in the local tea estates, but the available jobs and earnings are not enough to help the village's growing number of families make ends meet. Villagers speak of violent labor disputes, falling wages, extensive delays in payment of wages, and a shrinking labor force on the tea estates. Of those who lack adequate food, shelter, and clothes, a villager says, "They just try to forget their tragic condition by drinking alcohol or [taking] other drugs."

If private employers alone are inadequate to ensure high MOP, what then are the complementary factors that support and facilitate the dynamism and inclusiveness of rural economies in the high-MOP villages?

Farming's limited contribution

Agriculture provides an important income source for nearly all of the study communities, but the sector's contribution to the country's growth and poverty reduction has been disappointing for decades.[6]

More than a third of the workers in both low- and high-MOP villages engage in agricultural wage labor. Yet for the landless rural poor, daily wage work on farms seems to be a dead end. This is the livelihood that routinely defines the bottom rungs of the ladder. While farm wages rose over the study period, these wages are rarely enough by themselves for poor families to make ends meet, let alone get ahead. Furthermore, the jobs are heavily seasonal, so households dependent on farm labor may go hungry during the off-season. Households in 24 percent of the low-MOP communities and 18 percent of the top tier experienced food shortages.

Panel studies on India's farm sector indicate that improvements in agricultural technologies increased inequality where they occurred (Foster and

FIGURE 3.6

Improvements in irrigation and technical support for farmers are greater in high-MOP villages

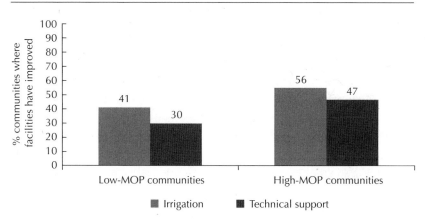

Note: The *t*-statistics for the difference in mean improvements between high- and low-MOP communities are 3.11 for irrigation and 3.07 for technical support (both significant at 5%).This indicates that both types of improvements were higher in the top MOP communities.

Rosenzweig 2004), and this is confirmed by in-depth longitudinal case studies (see, for instance, Epstein, Suryanarayana, and Thimmegowda 1998). The data from the Moving Out of Poverty study, however, suggest that improvements in irrigation and technical assistance are more prevalent in the high-MOP communities, suggesting that poor people also benefit (figure 3.6). Several of the communities with the very highest MOP indexes featured well-functioning irrigation systems (or otherwise reliable water sources due to a good climate or a nearby river) combined with use of modern farming methods such as threshing machines, tractors, high-yield seed varieties, fertilizers, and so forth.

Local Democracy's Expanding Reach

The distributions of lands to the landless and of [benefits] cards to the other people are not being done properly. They are not allowing us to even question them in this regard. Even if we ask them, they try to snub us and give us evasive replies. They are corrupt and they do anything they like as there is no one to question them.

—A youth, Bestharapalle, Andhra Pradesh

Over the course of the study decade, satisfaction with local democratic functioning rose as local political institutions, basic infrastructure, public services, and poverty-targeted schemes expanded across a large share of the study communities. But along with better local capacities for governments to be democratic and to provide services and infrastructure came rising corruption and cronyism.

With the important exception of roads, the level of public services and infrastructure varied little across high- and low-MOP contexts. Like private employers and prospering farms, these basics of development seem insufficient by themselves to ensure broad-based transitions out of poverty.

Spread of local democratic institutions

Village leaders were elected in 90 percent of the study communities, and about the same share of communities indicated their local elections to be fair. Village councils were present in 81 percent of the high-MOP communities compared to 64 percent of the low-MOP communities in 2005; these rates are significantly higher in both the high- and low-MOP communities than they were 10 years earlier (figure 3.7). The participation of women on coun-

FIGURE 3.7
Democratic institutions improved in both low- and high-MOP villages

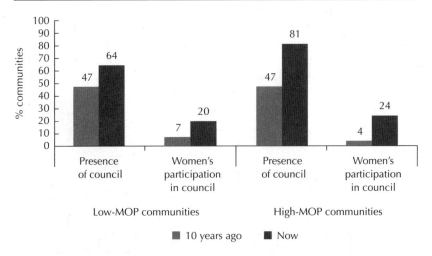

Note: The *t*-statistics for the difference in mean presence of village councils between now and 10 years ago are 4.35 and 7.28 for low- and high-MOP communities, respectively. The *t*-statistics for the difference in mean participation of women in councils during the same time period are 8.73 for low-MOP councils and 6.27 for high-MOP communities (all significant at 5%).

cils also increased significantly in both high- and low-MOP communities because of laws requiring women's membership on village councils. Along with these advances in democratic structures, villagers perceived generally improving trends in the functioning of local democracy in both high- and low-MOP villages (figure 3.8). However, while the *change* in mean perceptions is positive, mean perceptions of local democratic functioning are not significantly different across low- and high-MOP communities.

High-MOP Detya in West Bengal illustrates the multitude of benefits that people across the study communities associate with increasing government responsiveness. In the past, Detya's villagers avoided their panchayat office, but now they find it can be very helpful and they visit frequently. Villagers also said they can speak freely at village meetings, and the "panchayat gives importance to what we say." They especially credit the panchayat with undertaking projects that have "increased our work opportunities as well as our wages." People no longer live hand to mouth, village residents report.

Indeed, in the communities that report rising satisfaction with local democracy, study participants often express deep appreciation for having more voice. They frequently associate the increased government responsiveness with the numerous community development programs that are now

FIGURE 3.8

Villagers perceived general improvement in functioning of local democracy in high- and low-MOP villages

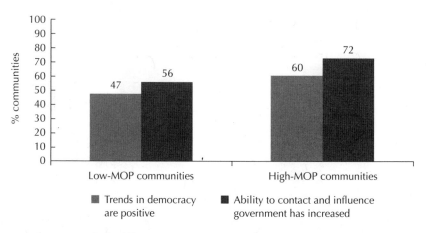

Note: The *t*-statistics for the difference in mean perception of democratic functioning across high- and low-MOP communities are 0.89 for positive democratic trends and 0.38 for better ability to influence the government (both insignificant).

administered by the panchayats. In Jugsana, Uttar Pradesh, villagers say that compared to the past, there is "more attention being paid to the problems of the people" because now their pradhan has funds and is able to do good works for the village. And in Lingatla, Andhra Pradesh, a man explained that the local development programs brought the government closer to the people," and now the people are able to influence the government's policies." In Surjana, Uttar Pradesh, villagers said their pradhan has to be attentive when they press for new facilities or he will be thrown out in the next election.

Elite capture and corruption

Coinciding with these encouraging trends in local democracy, however, are indications of rising and widespread corruption. The majority of both high- and low-MOP villages in the study regions report that most or almost all local government officials take bribes (figure 3.9). In communities that receive low ratings for government responsiveness, focus groups very often report corruption involving community development schemes. Moreover, both quantitative and qualitative accounts indicate that the levels of corruption have gotten much worse over the study period.

In both high- and low-MOP villages, people seeking to access opportunities need good connections with patrons who can provide political backing. Such connections open doors to jobs, land, businesses, loans, government

FIGURE 3.9

A majority of low- and high-MOP villages report that most officials take bribes

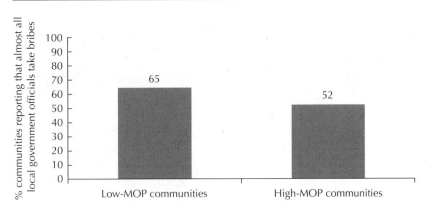

Note: The *t*-statistic for the difference in mean corruption ratings is 1.62 (insignificant), indicating that the degree of corruption is about the same across high- and low-MOP communities.

entitlements, licenses, technical support, and other resources. Belonging to a community's most advantaged caste gives a person a head start in cultivating such helpful ties. Other ways of doing so, mentioned by participants in a large share of localities, include paying a cash bribe and forging links to the political party in power (which may also be associated with an upper caste). The need to secure the support of powerful patrons is seen as a more formidable barrier to accessing opportunities in the low-MOP villages.

In the high-MOP fishing village of Sipta in West Bengal, for instance, various people spoke of the benefits of having a political patron. Kajal, a woman from the village, insisted that local businessmen need political connections "because now nothing can be done without joining the Union [the leading political party], without its help." Another woman explained that people in different occupations require different kinds of cooperation from officialdom: for instance, traders cooperate with the authorities on market development and communication, and farmers receive help with improving soil fertility. The men's group discussed the case of a rich businessman who organized 10 workers to apply for a loan for a fishing trawler while he "greased the hands" of the Samabai Samity (Cooperative Society). When asked what brings freedom, Gour Hari opined that "the most important of all is the patronage of political leaders wielding power."

Patronage systems can and sometimes do offer rewards that go beyond narrow private interests. For instance, an uncommon but, nevertheless, very powerful factor that unleashes prosperity in a community is to have a native son rise in the ranks of the local administration. This was the case in the high-MOP village of Mahoa, Uttar Pradesh. At the time the study team visited, a man from the village was the agriculture minister for Uttar Pradesh, and his son was a minister in the legislative council. The agriculture minister had brought in a cement road to his native village, which Mahoa villagers named as the biggest reason for their community's prosperity.

In the low-MOP communities, by contrast, focus groups are less likely to speak about the benefits of political connections than about the hardships for those who are excluded from such insider relationships. There are also more reports in these villages that local governments are associated with caste-based political parties and overtly favor certain caste groups. In low-MOP Khiria Khurd in Uttar Pradesh, for instance, a women's focus group complained that the local government head listens only to those from his own caste, and jobs in public works go to the government's "own people only." Both the men's and women's groups also describe severe problems in caste relations: the upper-caste Thakurs make threats, refuse to pay wages due or settle debts owed, and start fights, and it is not "safe to do business here for Harijans" (the lower-caste untouchables). "The meaning of power is that the Thakurs of the village can beat anybody whenever they want," the men said. A woman in a focus group concluded, "Therefore the local government is an obstacle for getting economic opportunities."

In low-MOP Jambugumpala, Andhra Pradesh, a village man explained why access to credit is very limited: "Those who get loan facilities from the government will have rapport with government officials." Similarly, a woman participating in a focus group in low-MOP Appilepalle, also in Andhra Pradesh, reported that people who want to start a big business need to get a loan from the government but "they have to spend a lot of money to get the loan."

Prasana, a member of a women's focus group in Jambugumpala, asserted, "The economically empowered have a linkage with the politically empowered. Only with money can one get into politics. Hence, the politicians take the financial support from the financiers, and thus they are subject to the influence of the moneyed. The politicians by their political power safeguard the interests of the rich. Thus, there is a relation of give and take or mutual exchange of support between the two."

In low-MOP Nayabans in Uttar Pradesh, the community leader is said to listen to and help only those from his own caste. In Lakhan Gaon, also in Uttar Pradesh, local people said the government has policies to support new businesses, but the prevalence of bribery and corruption makes them ineffective: "If anyone wants to start some new work, then the Lakhapal [auditor] and the block officers trouble him or her a lot." In this village, too, local people said that laborers in the fields "live in fear of the higher castes." In Assam, the axis of exclusion falls along ethnic rather than caste lines. In low-MOP Kadonga, for instance, the wealthier and more powerful Bodos are seen to be depriving the Assamese of "getting jobs or other chances like loans." Kadonga villagers also report that their youths are not getting work even though they have advanced university degrees because "they have no money to give bribes" for jobs or loans.

Infrastructure and services: Issues of access and quality

Despite extensive problems of patronage and corruption, the communities nevertheless experienced a significant expansion of public investments and services over the study decade (figures 3.10 through 3.13). But surprisingly, there is little variation by high- and low-MOP contexts in the availability of

FIGURE 3.10
Infrastructure has improved in both low- and high-MOP villages

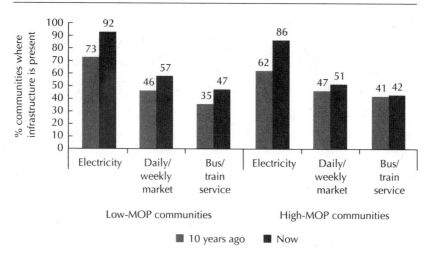

Note: The t-statistics for the difference in mean availability of electricity between now and 10 years ago are 4.15 in low-MOP villages and 5.58 for high-MOP villages (both significant at 5%). For the difference in mean availability of daily/weekly market, the corresponding t-statistics for low- and high-MOP communities are 3.32 (significant at 5%) and 1.91 (insignificant); and for the difference in mean availability of bus/train service, they are 3.37 (significant at 5%) and 0.37 (insignificant).

FIGURE 3.11
All-weather roads are more common in high-MOP villages

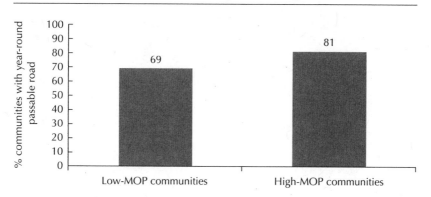

Note: The t-statistic for the difference in mean passable roads between high- and low-MOP communities is 1.98, indicating there are significantly more passable roads in high-MOP communities.

FIGURE 3.12
Presence of private health clinics improved in both low- and high-MOP villages

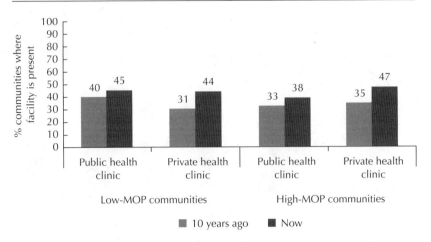

Note: The *t*-statistic for the difference in mean public health provision between now and 10 years ago is 1.92 (insignificant) for both low- and high-MOP communities. The corresponding statistics for the difference in mean private health clinics are 3.85 and 3.37 (both significant at 5%) for low- and high-MOP communities, respectively.

FIGURE 3.13
Presence of schools improved in both low- and high-MOP villages

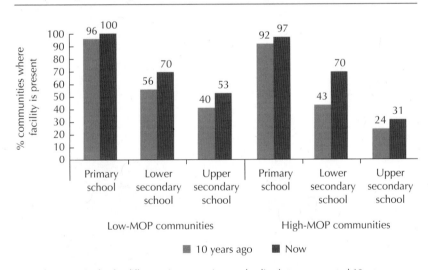

Note: The *t*-statistics for the difference in mean primary schooling between now and 10 years ago are 2.03 for low-MOP communities (significant at 5%) and 1.91 for high-MOP communities (insignificant). The corresponding *t*-statistics for the difference in mean lower secondary schooling are 4.06 and 6.19, and for the difference in mean advances in upper secondary schooling they are 3.68 and 2.73 (all significant at 5%).

these facilities. For example, both low- and high-MOP communities saw significant improvements over the 10 years in electricity, secondary schooling, and private health clinics, though public health services did not improve in either group of communities.[7] However, there are a few important exceptions to the general pattern of little variation. In particular, high-MOP villages are more likely to have all-weather roads that are passable year-round (figure 3.11 and box 3.1), while there are more upper secondary schools in the low-MOP localities. In addition, improvements in primary education, markets, and transportation services in the past 10 years are found to be statistically significant only in the low-MOP villages.

These findings force us to examine more carefully issues of access and quality and of interaction between services. The qualitative accounts indicate that restrictions on access to available services as well as the poor quality of these services continue to challenge many poor families. In many villages, for instance, people acknowledged the presence of a primary health center, but they explained that they could not rely on it because it lacked adequate staffing and medical supplies. In such cases, getting treatment for anything more than a minor problem will require leaving the village, but this is made difficult by poor roads serving isolated communities. In Langpuria, Uttar Pradesh, two or three people died because they could not travel out of the village to seek emergency medical care. In many cases, private doctors and "quacks" fill the gaps, but life stories reveal that the expenses incurred for their services can then lead to great hardship and protracted indebtedness for the poor.

Access to education is also uneven. Many life stories detail great sacrifices by parents and children for the sake of education, which is an important means of landing government and other jobs and moving a family out of poverty. But circumstances often demand that a person's education be cut short—for instance, because the secondary school is too far away or because the household urgently needs another income earner. In such cases, the sense of loss is immense and is often perceived as irreversible.

In every community, villagers were asked to identify and then rank the most important factors that have helped and hindered the prosperity of their community over the past decade. Tables 3.4 and 3.5 present the villages' combined ratings for the top two positive and top two negative factors. Public sector schemes—especially those that are poverty targeted—featured the most prominently as helping communities prosper, followed by roads and education. The government programs at the top of the list include housing assistance, land reform, farm credit, and safety net programs that offer food and jobs.

BOX 3.1
Going mobile

The field reports are packed with accounts of how profoundly transforming roads can be. Where villages report new access to good road networks, diversification of livelihoods takes off, markets grow and expand their offerings, and dependence on agriculture declines. Roads and transport that open up links to urban or semiurban centers bring especially rapid change.

Roads usher in new opportunities for farmers, entrepreneurs, job seekers, and traders, and ease access to services not available locally. In the high-MOP village of Nababpur, in West Bengal, people were nearly trapped during the rainy season without an all-weather road. When such a road arrived in 2001, their lives were transformed, as they could come and go easily to a nearby town to work. "Considering the previous 10 years, [the road] is our biggest development," a Nababpur villager declared.

In Bichhuti, another West Bengal village, upgrading of the railway from a single to a double line in 2003 is credited with helping "all class of people" there, from daily wage workers all the way to civil servants who commute back and forth to Kolkata. Many people in the village work in construction, and getting to their jobs in the city is now vastly easier. The improved rail service is also luring people from Kolkata and surrounding villages to Bichhuti to buy land and build homes to live in or rent. The local market is expanding to accommodate the growing population, and focus groups say local people who have set up businesses are doing well. New local jobs can also be found in the public and private schools, at the post office, and in private health care.

Remoteness due to lack of roads or transport is crippling, and poor people who have scarce productive assets are particularly constrained from overcoming their isolation and seizing new opportunities. Like Ashikabad, the stagnant community that began the chapter, a great many of the poorest communities in the sample lack both roads and reliable irrigation—and the combination presents a formidable poverty trap. Road conditions in some of the low-MOP villages visited in Assam were worsening, creating great hardships for local people. Three of the four buses that used to service the remote village of Kadonga have stopped coming because the road is falling apart. So people who need to get to the nearby town are left with the costly and exhausting options of hiring tractors and rickshaws to carry them half the way and walking the rest. The village youth, educated but jobless, "pay no attention to work." And in Bhubankhal, Assam, the women's focus group acknowledged many difficulties in starting a business, but "the most important among these is the road." Harmonhan of Kadonga wanted to know, "How will the society change if the roads are not developed?"

TABLE 3.4
Government programs and roads are leading factors in economic prosperity

Factor contributing to prosperity	Frequency	%
Government programs	106	19
Road	80	15
Education	69	13
Agriculture improvement	61	11
Water	55	10
Self-help groups	51	9
Electricity	33	6

Note: Only findings at 6% or above are reported. Government programs include housing assistance (Indira Awas Yojana), land reform (e.g., distribution of barren land to the poor), construction of dams (*baandh* in Hindi), Kisan credit cards for farmers, rural employment and food security scheme (Sampoorna Grameen Rozgar Yojana), targeted public distribution system for the poorest of the poor (Antyodaya Anna Yojana), and additional gainful employment for the unemployed and underemployed in rural areas (Jawahar Rozgar Yojana).

TABLE 3.5
Agricultural problems and natural disasters hinder economic prosperity

Factor hindering prosperity	Frequency	%
Agriculture	121	23
Natural disaster	99	19
Water	94	18
Family	49	9
Health	41	8
Road and transportation	36	7

Note: Only findings at 6% or above are reported. Family refers to family separations due to clashes in Andhra Pradesh, the only state that raised this family-related issue. Health includes lack of health centers (4.9%) and health shocks (2.8%).

In very high-MOP Kondittangi in Andhra Pradesh, where almost all poor households escaped poverty over the decade, people credit the numerous public programs with contributing to widespread prosperity. Government schemes provided new roads, latrines, irrigation dams, financial services, housing, land distribution, and compensation for crop failures. In many villages, in fact, it was common for key informants to report several such public investments and programs over the study period.

Housing programs are particularly valued. In the high-MOP village of Mahoa, Uttar Pradesh, housing assistance and pensions for widows are mentioned as among the important factors that help poor people save and climb up the ladder. And in low-MOP Appilepalle in Andhra Pradesh, villagers said they "used to experience hell" in their thatched houses when it stormed; they enthusiastically praised their minister, Lakshmi Dvamma, for making 80 houses available and completely resolving the problem of poor housing in the village. "Now they are not afraid of the sun and rain," a villager said.

When people were asked what most hinders community prosperity, problems with maintaining irrigation and other agricultural investments topped the list, followed by weather shocks. The government plays a strong role in irrigation and also runs programs specifically designed to help villagers recover from weather disasters and crop failures. The reach of these supports, however, appears mixed at best.

Widespread Covariant Shocks

The incidence of shocks varied little among the communities (figure 3.14). Four out of five study villages endured droughts or floods (and sometimes both), or fires, often with devastating and long-lasting consequences. Major conflicts and health disasters affected a small fraction of study villages; these were present to a slightly greater extent in the low-MOP contexts.

In the village of Pulagampalle in Andhra Pradesh, eight years of drought forced many people to sell their lands and homes. One villager described the

FIGURE 3.14

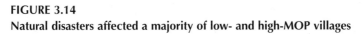

Natural disasters affected a majority of low- and high-MOP villages

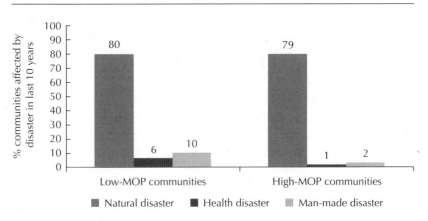

chain of misfortunes: "Because of the drought, we had to take loans. However hard we work, we were unable to repay the loans. Due to financial difficulties, we had to discontinue our children's education. Even if we became sick, we cannot afford to go to a doctor. Our lives became miserable because of the drought."

In Lalpur, Uttar Pradesh, a drought in 2003 caused massive crop loss, damaging food supplies for families and livestock. As in Pulagampalle, many farmers could not repay their loans and were forced to sell off fields and perform wage labor in order to cope with the calamity. In another Uttar Pradesh village, Katmati, daughters from poor households could no longer be married because their parents became heavily indebted during the drought. The rich of this village avoided speaking to the poor for fear they might be asked for money. In the Andhra Pradesh village of Chedulla, the drought led to widespread famine and the suicides of two farmers who were unable to repay debts. "With a feeling of fear about the future, and shame, they have ended their lives," explained a woman of Chedulla.

The tyranny of floods in the study sample is no less. In Bhotpara, West Bengal, flood waters left behind a thick layer of sand, "forcing most of the people to sell off their lands at a low price or give their lands on lease at a much lower rate. This is why the condition of the farmers is deteriorating day by day." In Dwarshini, West Bengal, a chronic poor farmer lamented that in 2005 he was still repaying his loans to the cooperative after the massive flood of 2000.

The hardship caused by weather shocks is especially crushing in low-MOP villages without irrigation. Recovery is painfully slow, if it comes at all. Vellamaddi, a low-MOP village in Andhra Pradesh, was deeply scarred by seven years of drought. Different government programs have been available but have not been sufficient for recovery to take hold. Vellamaddi received housing assistance, drought relief funds, and other safety net programs for its poorest, but these schemes are reported to have been mismanaged by the *sarpanch* (the panchayat head) in collusion with contractors and government officials. "Like dogs at burial grounds they [government officials] look for money for every work," said the villagers.

In 2001–02, under a food-for-work program, the government successfully laid a tarmac road connecting Vellamaddi to adjacent villages and the block town. The construction provided greatly needed temporary jobs, and the road brought in traders and enabled self-help groups to launch dairy farming and other ventures. It also became much easier for villagers to reach Kerala, where many of the poorest families now go to beg for money. Yet despite all of these government schemes, mobility has been very low in Vellamaddi, suggesting that additional interventions beyond safety nets will be needed to turn this village around.

In the more favorable high-MOP contexts, drought and flood relief sometimes work effectively. For instance, high-MOP Nakkapeta endured three years of drought, but a farmer reported that the government provided recovery assistance to cover lost investments, which "encouraged farmers to go for further cultivation in the common monsoon"—a "morale booster." In 2004 the government also responded with a food-for-work scheme in which one member of every family was eligible to earn wages for cleaning local canals and ponds.

Among the non-weather-related shocks that struck study communities, conflict and violence had a particularly severe impact on villages in Assam. Villagers described fearful periods when small bands of militants invaded their homes in search of food and shelter. The army sometimes countered these incursions with brutal attacks, destroying property and livestock and causing mass displacement.

Village-wide health disasters also caused loss of life and well-being in a small set of study communities. For example, in the low-MOP village of Leteku Gaon in Assam, a malaria epidemic in 2004 led to mass deaths, and lack of clean water poses a continuing threat of diarrhea and cholera. In Chintada and surrounding villages of Andhra Pradesh, a mix of typhoid, cholera, and malaria in 2005 inflicted many deaths and immense economic losses. Participants said they received very little help from the government, though many people visited to console them.

The Role of Collective Action

Freedom of a person increases when he is friendly and cooperates with the community members sharing their problems. Such a person easily mingles with anyone in the society. Entire community supports his deeds and offers timely help in his endeavors.

—Female youth discussion group, Chintada, Andhra Pradesh

Social capital refers to the norms and networks that enable collective action. When poor people mobilize into formal and informal groups, they begin to be recognized on their own terms. Worldwide, grassroots organizations have been critical in giving the poor a voice with which to claim their rights and entitlements. The links between poor people's social capital and mobility out of poverty, however, are not well understood.

Proliferation of local groups

This study finds a very significant expansion of organized groups in the villages between 1995 and 2005. But one of the more unexpected results is that local people's tendency to form and join groups has been greater in low-MOP villages than in high-MOP ones, even though both types of communities experienced significant increases over this period.

As shown in figure 3.15, in 1995 the average number of groups ranged from four to six in low- and high-MOP communities respectively. By 10 years later, the averages had skyrocketed and the prevalence reversed. Low-MOP communities now averaged 20 groups per village compared with 11 groups in the high-MOP set.

In addition, public participation in village political affairs is higher in low-MOP villages (table 3.6). An exception to this pattern is that women are

FIGURE 3.15

Expansion of self-help groups has been greatest in low-MOP villages

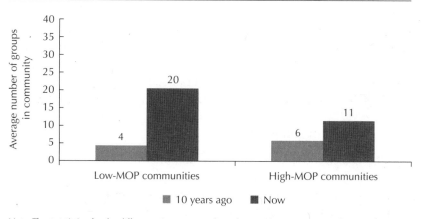

Note: The *t*-statistics for the difference in mean number of groups between now and 10 years ago are 8.69 and 4.61 (both significant at 5%) for low- and high-MOP communities, respectively.

TABLE 3.6

Public participation in community affairs is higher in low-MOP villages

Response	Bottom 33% MOP communities (%)	Top 33% MOP communities (%)
Many (rather than few) participate in decisions on important community affairs	51	41
The most important groups in the community are open to many (rather than few)	67	48

about twice as likely to attend a public meeting in a high-MOP village as in a low-MOP one, although their overall participation rates of 6 and 3 percent respectively remain very low despite their increased representation on village councils.

Finance and credit groups emerge as the most common type of group in both high- and low-MOP villages in 2005. This no doubt reflects the major expansion of self-help groups (SHGs) since the late 1990s. The self-help groups spark entrepreneurship, serve as invaluable coping mechanisms, and raise awareness and self-confidence. But there is no evidence yet that the increase in this form of bonding social capital is contributing to widespread poverty escapes.

This is consistent with the social capital literature, which stresses the importance of heterogeneous networks that can help poor people form ties with those who are unlike themselves. Referred to as "bridging" or "linking" networks, these confer advantages because they put poor people in touch with influential contacts, additional resources, new ideas, and technical advice, including from beyond their village (Narayan 2002; Narayan and Cassidy 2001; Woolcock 1998). These are precisely the types of associations, however, from which poor rural villagers are typically excluded. High-MOP Hogalduri in West Bengal, for instance, boasts a successful local agricultural cooperative that helps farmers access paddy seeds and loans through the minibank. But only cultivators who own their land can be members, a requirement that excludes those on the bottom steps of the ladder.

Limited impact of groups

Taken together, the study data suggest that the context as well as the type of collective action matter. Such activism seems to be less important where local economies are stronger and governments are more responsive, as found in many high-MOP contexts. In high-MOP Kondittangi, where 97 percent of poor villagers escaped poverty over the study period, a focus group of men acknowledged that "we leave decisions to our member of the legislative assembly. He makes decisions that are useful for our community. We all adore him for the good things he has done for us." But villagers of Kondittangi also report that nothing happens without giving bribes, and since the poor have no money for bribes, "their work is never done." Similarly, in high-MOP Hogalduri, villagers acknowledge that perhaps 40 percent of their officials take bribes, often "through agents." They say people are "only spectators" of local decision making, which is monopolized by "a few political leaders and rich people." Yet they nevertheless are grateful for the development schemes brought into the village, which include better roads and a new high school. Recent work by Roy (2008) on local health groups in two contiguous regions of rural Uttar Pradesh similarly found evidence of stronger organizations in the poorer of the two regions. These groups, however, had very limited success in improving services, local decision making, or economic activities affecting their members' lives—a pattern also seen in the villages in our study.

But if the links are weak between social capital, political participation, and movement out of poverty, it may also reflect a case of successful targeting. SHG investments are taking hold in communities with larger poor populations, and so their impacts may take longer to be felt. Despite small gains to date, villagers express great optimism that their collective action is sowing the seeds for more rapid socioeconomic changes in the years ahead. A self-help group member from the low-MOP village of Konteluru in Andhra Pradesh recounted: "We were scared of boarding a bus, and we were very ignorant. We used to give our daily wages to our husbands. We were ignorant about spending money. . . . Caste and religious-based discriminations were higher. But once the groups were formed, *maa bathukulaku velugu nichchayi* [our lives became brightened]. Now all of us have formed into a group together. All of us are sitting together in the groups. We are listening to everybody's problems. Everyone's problems and difficulties are the same. Because of the groups, we realized that we can lead a better life if all of us live together. Further, our intelligence has increased. We got the courage to go and talk at the police station, mandal, or panchayat office. Our children are studying. We are saving from our daily wages for ourselves and for our children's sake. We benefited because of this help from the government."

Inequalities Reinforcing Each Other

> *In our village, we see inequality among the people. The villagers are divided into rich and poor, literate and illiterate, high and low.*
> —A villager, Raja Pukhuri, Assam

In his seminal work *Durable Inequality*, Charles Tilly explains why inequality is so difficult to dislodge. Importantly, the explanation centers not on individuals but on social groups. It is the inequalities in advantage and disadvantage between groups that "do crucial organizational work, producing marked, durable differences in access to valued resources" (1999, 8).[8] And it is these social group differences that are also most difficult to dislodge.

In India, the principal divide is along caste lines. And power in an Indian village very often coalesces around the intersecting political and economic advantages of the upper castes. You cannot be politically powerful without being rich, and you cannot get rich without having political connections and backing. One villager in Rahamat in Uttar Pradesh offered that politics is really "like another business" for the rich; if a poor man tried to go into politics, his family would go hungry. According to Narasimhappa in low-MOP Appilepalle, Andhra Pradesh, "Whoever may be in power, whether a person of lower caste or higher caste, the decision taking is only by the higher-caste people. If the poor man commits any mistake, that would be made public."

Norms of powerlessness and exclusion have important context-specific dimensions, but nonetheless some broad patterns among the four states can be discerned. In Uttar Pradesh, caste differences form the axis for potent inequalities. In West Bengal, party affiliation is often paramount, and electoral victories if not bureaucratic posts frequently go to wealthy landed groups. In Assam, key social differences relate to ethnicity and whether one is a Bodo tribal, Assamese, or Naga. In Andhra Pradesh, caste divides are weakening; many villages show little evidence that factors other than poverty and low occupational status foster exclusion, although some differentiation among the poor also seems to be emerging on the basis of whether one is or is not a member of a self-help group.

Inequalities in power and access to resources are often reinforced in villages where opportunities are scarce. These are the places where hardships seem to intertwine: the economy is weak, the local government is overtly corrupt, and social inequalities remain severe. Impoverished farmworkers are scared to ask for wages owed, and hungry families do not dare claim public entitlements. The overlap between the politically and economically powerful keeps the poor disempowered, disenfranchised, and frightened.

In low-MOP Saraspur in Assam, for instance, relief and seeds promised in the wake of a terrible flood never made it to the village farmers. Despite urgent need, all the goods went to a relative of a member of the gram panchayat. People in Saraspur also say they need to pay bribes to obtain almost anything, including the Kisan credit card for farm loans. Should someone risk publicly denouncing the ruling party for such practices, villagers say, that person would then be denied all types of government help: "Here it is a crime to speak against the party."

Similarly, in the low-MOP village of Leteku Gaon, Assam, many obstacles come together to leave poor people with scant options for getting ahead. Local people say that transport is poor, they have no major market close by, and bribes are needed to obtain any credit or jobs. According to a villager named Mahendra, "There are lots of educated youths, but they have not got a job. Nowadays, to get a job, people should have a good relationship with politicians. But in our village, there are no such people, so it's very hard to get a job."

In describing inequality in her village, a female youth in low-MOP Chincholi in Andhra Pradesh reported that everything is easier for the rich, from acquiring food to getting things done at a government office to dealing with the police. In countless community reports, villagers emphasize that the rich are treated with respect and courtesy; the poor are not. In Rassimata, Andhra Pradesh, where not a single villager escaped poverty over the study period, a female villager argued that the rich have much more freedom than the poor because "everyone trusts a person who is rich. . . . No one trusts a poor man." Poor people know all too well the practices and norms that perpetuate their powerlessness and poverty.

The villages that rely solely on farming, which are often dominated by a small group of powerful landlords and politicians, provide especially limited pathways for poverty escapes. Though expanding markets are widely seen to play an important role in giving poor men and women more options, some of the key underlying mechanisms that should help markets contribute to broad-based mobility do not seem to function as expected (also see Drèze, Lanjouw, and Sharma 1998). A major puzzle is that private employers by themselves are negatively associated with poverty exits unless they are located in communities where villagers say their access to economic opportunities is rising. What, then, does "rising access" mean and look like on the ground?

Overcoming exclusion: Importance of credit and roads

Breaking through entrenched inequality is very difficult. Here we look at communities where villagers report that access to local opportunities is expanding, and we examine the conditions under which this contributes to mobility. It seems that access to diverse sources of credit, especially when combined with road access that increases options, helps poor people overcome their exclusion from opportunities and exercise initiative.

The focus groups were asked to reflect on different aspects of economic, social, and political inequalities and trends in these inequalities over the study period. At relevant points in those discussions, the groups were also asked to rate whether there was more, the same, or less access for local people to (a) new economic opportunities, (b) the most important associations and networks in the village, and (c) arenas of decision making on important community affairs.

Nearly a third of the study communities reported rising access on all three fronts. Yet many of these "rising-access" communities that seemingly had so much going for them still had low levels of MOP.

To better understand the role of access and what distinguishes the MOP performers in contexts where access is rising, a systematic review was conducted of the qualitative data from 10 villages that reported favorable economic, social, and political access conditions. Five of the 10 rising-access villages were purposely selected for their very low MOP and five for their very high MOP.

As in the earlier findings on factors that were not strongly associated with MOP differences, we find that the 10 rising-access communities demonstrate little variation on infrastructure or public services. These were widely available and seemed to provide a necessary foundation for reducing inequalities in access to opportunities. But if services and infrastructure are not enough to ensure high MOP, what else matters?

We find that credit opportunities when combined with road access make a major difference. The five high-MOP villages all reported access to credit from government banks or self-help groups, allowing poor villagers to take business loans and purchase productive assets such as buffaloes, rickshaws, fishing boats, and agricultural land. In some cases, like high-MOP Laskarpur in West Bengal, agricultural cooperatives have relationships with rural banks, so that a Rs 10 deposit purchases a share that can be redeemed in the rural bank for a Rs 100 loan. Such schemes are reported to directly benefit those small farmers just below the community poverty line, giving them the opportunity to cross over. And in the high-access communities where bank loans may not be available to the poorest, credit via well-functioning SHGs helps fill the gap.

In stark contrast, the five low-MOP communities in the sample, such as Purani in Uttar Pradesh, report continued dependence on moneylenders who charge interest as high as 3 percent per month (versus, for example, the central government's Kisan credit card scheme, which charges 9 percent per year). Moneylenders are traditionally a village's big farmers who occupy the top steps of the ladder of life. In Purani they are said to have grown fat on the land and on gold that poor villagers were forced to pawn and then lost when they fell behind on debt payments. Some poor men and women in the study remarked openly that they were "fools" to use moneylenders. But the reality is that in very many villages, poor families have no other way to put food on the table in the inevitable periods when wage work is inadequate or unavailable, shocks strike, or expenses must be met for a wedding or other family obligation.

When we asked people about credit sources, moneylenders emerged as the most important for both high- and low-MOP villages at the beginning of the study period (figure 3.16). By 2005, however, government banks and relatives had overtaken moneylenders in importance—but *only* in the high-MOP villages. SHGs may be present in many low-MOP villages, but there are also many reports of SHG inactivity, delays in villagers getting promised funds, corruption, and other difficulties with these poverty-targeted schemes. As discussed earlier, focus groups in low-MOP villages also called more attention than those in high-MOP villages to the need to pay bribes and make political connections in order to access government programs.

FIGURE 3.16

Government banks have become most important credit source in high-MOP villages

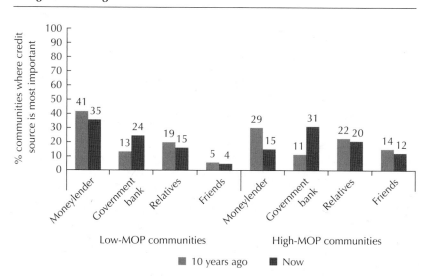

Note: The *t*-statistics for the difference in mean presence of moneylenders between now and 10 years ago are –1.58 for low-MOP communities (insignificant) and –2.84 for high-MOP communities (significant at 5%). The corresponding *t*-statistics are 3.47 and 4.21 for the difference in mean presence of government banks (both significant at 5%); –1.81 and –0.58 for the difference in mean presence of relatives (both insignificant); and –2.10 (significant at 5%) and 0 (insignificant) for the difference in mean presence of friends in low- and high-MOP communities, respectively.

The role of social divisions

There is a growing literature that conceives of local-level development processes as inherently conflict-laden, involving "multiple, uneven, and contested
transitions in social structures, rules systems, and power relations" (Barron,
Diprose, and Woolcock 2007; also see Bates 2000). We thus wanted to examine whether social divisions in communities affect access and also mobility
prospects. We indeed find a strong association between social division and
access. And as recent theories would predict, we also find more incidences of
overt social strife in communities with higher mobility.

A question in the community profile asks: "To what extent do factors
like religion, ethnicity, social status or wealth divide people in the village
from one another today? And 10 years ago?" We first identified two sets of
communities: (a) those that reported *no* social division 10 years ago, and (b)
those that reported that social divisions were *great or very great* 10 years ago.
We then looked at how these initial conditions were associated with the set
of rising-access communities (figure 3.17).

More than 70 percent of the communities with no social division in
1995 reported higher access to new economic opportunities, compared to 49

FIGURE 3.17

**Access has increased more in communities with no social division 10 years ago
than in communities with great social division**

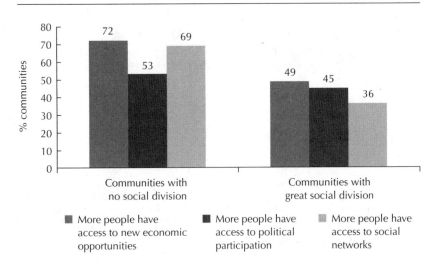

- More people have
  access to new economic
  opportunities
- More people have
  access to political
  participation
- More people have
  access to social
  networks

percent of the communities with great social division. The difference is much smaller in access to political participation, although it follows the same pattern. It may be that exclusive political norms and structures are the hardest to change. The most striking difference emerges in whether villagers can access important social networks. Almost 70 percent of the communities with no initial social division have higher access today to social networks, but this falls by half among the communities with great social division. Our data, however, do not show a strong relationship between social divisions and mobility, and this may be because the influence of social structures operates indirectly through the functioning of local institutions and norms.

When reviewing the qualitative data about social divisions, we found widespread mentions in high- and low-MOP communities alike about the practices and norms associated with caste and other social differences. We also observed, however, more mentions of these social differences flaring up into acts of violence, petty theft, or sabotage in the high-MOP contexts. In high-MOP Hogalduri in West Bengal, for instance, there is mention of thefts harming area businesses and of poisonings of fish and poultry on area farms. Corruption is extensive there, and people say bribes may or may not get the police to take action. Such acts of clandestine sabotage, argues James Scott (1985), are common "weapons of the weak," the desperate gestures of poor people who are loosely organized but who nevertheless strike out to resist disadvantage, injustice, and powerlessness.

In other cases, however, incidents of violence and property destruction are clearly perpetrated by rich people seeking to maintain their privileged access to the community's rising wealth. In high-MOP Ibrahimpur in Uttar Pradesh, there are reports of upper-caste Thakurs sending their animals to destroy the fields of lower-caste farmers who try to grow more than a single crop. Should the farmers oppose the Thakurs, villagers say, they face beatings. In high-MOP Dostpur, Uttar Pradesh, a government initiative to reclassify land values and ownership sidestepped the local panchayat. Instead, decisions were made and bribes exchanged solely among the Thakurs and the land registration officials. Lower-caste farmers were left scrambling to sell jewelry, find loans, and start litigation in order to reclaim their land at a reasonable value.

The quantitative data portray a similar picture of higher tensions in high-MOP contexts. Twenty percent of the high-MOP communities rated the presence of social divisions as great or very great in 1995 compared to 11 percent of the low-MOP villages. By 2005, however, the share of communities with large social divisions had fallen to just 6 percent in the high-MOP villages, although substantial numbers of communities continue to report some divisions (figure 3.18).

One explanation for the higher prevalence of social tensions in communities with more mobility could be that as economic opportunities and government programs become available, this creates expectations among rich and poor alike that cannot be completely met. Frustrations, jealousies, and resentments build as people see some (but not others) getting further and further ahead. Moreover, the high-MOP communities are characterized by more effective but also more excluding political structures, and the increased prevalence of social strife in these contexts may be one face of their weak mechanisms for addressing the grievances that so often accompany development gains.

In addition to growth and government poverty programs, education is frequently held out as a panacea for easing inequalities. Yet, according to Azmat of Alampur in Uttar Pradesh, educational differences divide rather than unite the community: only "educated people have government jobs,

FIGURE 3.18
More high-MOP than low-MOP villages reported great social divisions 10 years ago

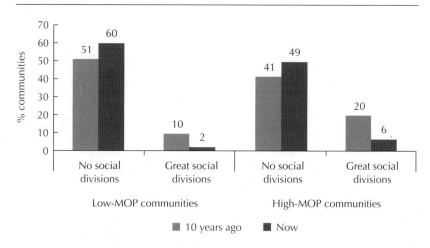

Note: The *t*-statistics for the difference in mean trends in "no social divisions" between now and 10 years ago are 2.81 for low-MOP communities and 2.39 for high-MOP communities (both significant at 5%). The corresponding statistics for the difference in mean trends in "great social divisions" are –1.00 (insignificant) and –2.73 (significant at 5%) for low- and high-MOP communities, respectively.

whereas the illiterate man keeps doing labor work in his fields and in the fields of others." In similar fashion, in high-MOP Baral in West Bengal, a village woman proclaimed that "there is inequality with education. Rich people are giving their children higher education. We are not getting that—maximum Madhyamik [middle level]."

But unequal and excluding power structures are not static, as this study attests. In high-MOP Gorithopu, Andhra Pradesh, villagers say their local leaders are extremely corrupt and capture all the benefits from local welfare schemes. Instead of the government, they credit their educated youth with bringing changes. The young people are living in towns to continue their education, where they are more exposed to modern ways through the media. As a consequence, a local man argued, attitudes are changing: "Young people do not bother about the caste and inequalities, but older people strictly follow the ways of discrimination according to the caste. They look down upon the lower-caste people."

The Correlates of More and Less Successful Communities

Whatever decisions governments make, they directly influence the lives of people living in that society. Whether construction of roads or water tanks, it is for the people.
> —Men's discussion group, Rassimata, Andhra Pradesh

There are no factories, and there is no possibility of getting work regularly, so we have to go outside the village in search of work.
> —Men's discussion group, Khalsi, West Bengal

Now that the government has made available good techniques for farming, farming has improved.
> —Women's discussion group, Lakhan Gaon, Uttar Pradesh

To consider several factors simultaneously that are important in villages with high poverty escapes, we ran a multivariate linear regression model using the ordinary least squares (OLS) methodology. We also examined whether community-level mobility factors differ among the poor and the rich—both for their movement up and for their falling down. The model consists of community-level economic, political, and social variables, including unequal access. The technical details of the model are presented in annex 3.1.

The leading mobility factors

The first column in table 3.7 presents the base model and significance levels for factors that are correlated with MOP. The final model builds in interaction terms, and the extended final model includes four additional variables—distance, irrigation, propensity for collective action, and share of initially poor. The extended final model has an explanatory power that is close to 43 per-

TABLE 3.7
Determinants of moving out of poverty index (MOP): OLS outcomes

Variable	Base model	Final model	Extended final model
Private employers in the community	−.0015	−.0318***	−.031***
Private employers x economic access		.0109***	.0101***
Improvement of market outlets in the community	.0465***	.0487***	.0445***
Government attention	−.0042	.0793***	.0694***
Government attention x political participation		−.0306***	−.028***
Women's membership in community council	.0013	.0016	.0015
Presence of private health center	.0031	−.0526	−.0691
Private health center x access to social network		.0137	.0181
Educational opportunities	.0076	.0023	.0033
Distance from the nearest city			−.0009**
Irrigation facility			.00011
Collective action to solve water problem			−.0227**
Share of initially poor population			−.3426***
Andhra Pradesh dummy	−.0551*	−.0307	−.0259
Assam dummy	−.1714***	−.1472***	−.1113***
Uttar Pradesh dummy	−.1065***	−.1075***	−.0847***
Constant	.1205***	.0901*	.4223***
Observations	291	288	288
R^2	0.19	0.28	0.43

*p < .10   **p < .05   ***p < .01 (white heteroscedasticity-consistent standard errors).

cent. We first present findings from the extended final model on the direct effects and then discuss interactions.

Both rising local government attention or responsiveness and improvements in market outlets are statistically significant at 1 percent. Responsiveness was measured by asking the respondent whether the local government pays less/same/more attention to what "people like you" think compared to 10 years ago. A 1-unit improvement in responsiveness is associated with an increase of 7 percentage points in a community's MOP. The gains are also very significant for villages reporting better market outlets: these are associated with an increase of 4 percentage points in MOP. In addition, the extended final model finds four factors to be negatively associated with MOP: greater distance from a city, the presence of private employers, collective action, and a large share of poor population.

We present three interaction effects that indicate that issues of access do matter, over and above the mere presence of a facility or village organization. Again, by themselves, private employers are negatively associated with MOP in all three models. But when present in communities with rising access to economic opportunities, private employers then contribute significantly to MOP. In similar fashion, the extended final model finds that the presence of private health care is no longer negatively associated with MOP when villages feature more open access to important social networks, although this outcome is not statistically significant. Access to social networks—and the information and (emergency) loans this can provide—may contribute indirectly to MOP by helping poor people access important services such as health care.

A more attentive local government independently contributes to MOP. Do communities with rising political participation further strengthen the contribution of government responsiveness to MOP? Unexpectedly, the model finds a negative relationship. There seems to be some substitutability between political participation and a responsive local government. It could also be that this outcome reflects problems of factionalism.

Other factors that have a positive but not significant association with MOP include women's membership on village councils, education, and irrigation.

Poor versus rich people's mobility factors

Table 3.8 compares the regression results for additional indexes related to movements up and down the ladder of life for the poor and nonpoor (rich) across the study villages.

TABLE 3.8
OLS outcomes across the key mobility indexes

Variable	MOP	MPI	MRI	FPI	FRI	FRIP	NPR
Private employers in the community	-.031***	-.0266**	-.0208*	-.0013	.0047	.0132	-.0167***
Private employers x economic access	.0101***	.0102**	.0078**	-.0023	-.0062	-.0072**	.0047*
Improvement of market outlets in the community	.0445***	.0469***	.0241***	-.012**	.0012	-.0157	.0047
Government attention	.0694***	.0527**	.0081	-.0043	-.0012	-.0084	.0276*
Government attention x political participation	-.028***	-.0259***	-.0099**	.005	-.0098	-.0071	-.0085*
Women's membership in community council	.0015	.0025**	.0008	-.0007	-.0015*	-.002***	-.0002
Presence of private health center	-.0691	-.1382**	-.0267	.067*	.0664	.0841	-.0244
Private health center x access to social network	.0181	.0418***	.0099	-.0165	-.0123	-.0207	.0078
Educational opportunities	.0033	.008	.0032	.0058	-.0022	.0008	-.0012
Distance from the nearest city	-.0009**	-.0014***	-.0002	.0006**	.0001	.0004	-.0009
Irrigation facility	.0001	.018*	-.0057	.0027	.0222*	.0318***	.0043
Collective action to solve water problem	-.0227**	-.0364***	-.0019	-.0032	-.0143	-.0074	-.0008
Share of initially poor population	-.3426***	-.1578**	-.252***	.0976***	.1426**	.219***	.0425
Andhra Pradesh dummy	-.0259	.0022	-.0294	-.0274*	-.0215	-.0394	-.0424**
Assam dummy	-.1113***	-.1759***	-.135***	-.033*	-.0538	-.051	-.078***
Uttar Pradesh dummy	-.0847***	-.1412***	-.171***	-.0236*	-.0369	-.005	-.0478**
Constant	.4223***	.4366***	.3873***	.0595*	.2287***	.0944	.0566
Observations	288	288	288	288	288	288	288
R^2	.43	.32	.35	.12	.14	.21	.12

Note: A positive coefficient with MOP, MPI, and MRI means that the corresponding explanatory variable helps upward movement; a negative coefficient with FPI, FRI, and FRIP means it prevents downward movement.

*p < .10   **p < .05   ***p < .01 (White heteroscedasticity-consistent standard errors)

Several of the findings presented above for correlates of MOP also hold for the other upward mobility statistics. For example, market outlets contribute to mobility of the poor (MPI) and nonpoor (MRI) alike. Also, both the rich and the poor benefit from communities that are closer to a city and that feature a combination of private employers and rising access to economic opportunities. And both face reduced prospects for upward mobility in communities with private employers, a large share of poor population, and a more responsive government when combined with rising access to political participation.

For other results, the significance of the factor or interaction of factors holds for mobility of the poor but disappears for the rich. A more responsive government is associated with increases in MOP and MPI by 7 and 5 percentage points respectively; for the rich, however, this factor has a positive but statistically insignificant association. This same pattern of significance emerges for women's membership on councils and for communities that combine private health centers and rising access to important social networks. As with the MOP results, collective action and presence of private health centers remain negatively associated with mobility of the poor (MPI); again this negative relationship holds for the rich but loses its significance.

Irrigation improvements help poor people move up (MPI), but not across the community poverty line. This same factor has a negative relationship with mobility of the rich, but the finding is not statistically significant. However, if we move across to the columns in table 3.8 that display findings for downward mobility, irrigation emerges as very important for small slides as well as for large ones that plunge the rich all the way into poverty. Many study communities report problems with the functioning of irrigation systems, and this may disproportionately affect the better-off landowners in the villages.

If several factors aid the upward fortunes of the rich and poor alike, this is not the case for factors associated with their downward movement. The sole statistically significant factor for pushing both the poor (FPI) and rich (FRI and FRIP) down the ladder is that of residing in a community with a large share of poor people in the population. Private health centers and greater distance from cities are significantly associated with falling of the poor, but they are not statistically significant for falling among the rich.

The statistics with a negative sign in the three falling columns indicate factors that help prevent downward mobility. Two such factors are women's membership on councils and the presence of private employers combined with rising economic access; however, these are only statistically significant for helping the rich. The poor alone seem to be protected from falling in communities where market outlets are improving.

In the last column are outcomes for net poverty reduction (NPR) as the dependent variable. These results especially signal the benefits of living in communities with a more responsive local government or that combine presence of private employers and rising access to economic opportunities.

Policy Reflections: Understanding Village Differences that Affect Poverty Outcomes

If there is rule of the public, then community prosperity will increase because only a poor and sad person can understand the problems of another poor and sad person. Those who are busy ruling don't understand the problems of others. They usurp the share of the people. If there is rule of the public, then all the people will meet and solve the problems of the village.
— Bhujdevi, a female villager, Lakhan Gaon, Uttar Pradesh

Despite rampant corruption, government schemes have brought important benefits to both Matka and Ashikabad, the villages that opened the chapter. In Matka, an inclusive irrigation program, a good road, and access to credit have combined to enable broad-based poverty reduction and the beginnings of a less unequal society. Ashikabad's infrastructure and services have also improved, but transport hardships, broken irrigation, and scarce credit have interacted in ways that ensure low returns for crops and labor and leave the village vulnerable to weather disasters and other shocks. Although they are only a short distance apart, the two villages offer starkly contrasting opportunities for poor families—a pattern repeated in the villages across the sample.

The Moving Out of Poverty study sought to explore whether there was significant variation in mobility across communities and the community-level factors associated with these variations. This section highlights four key findings and draws out some of their policy implications.

One: Community prosperity clearly varies and local economic opportunities matter

Community-level prosperity varies tremendously across communities. Our findings confirm the utility of community-targeted approaches for state, civil society, and private sector actors. The reasons for this variation have to do with a combination of economic, political, and social factors that determine whether economic opportunities exist at the local level and whether access is open to all or limited to a few.

Certain communities where a high proportion of people moved out of poverty had weak or average local economies in 1995 but managed to turn this around over the decade. In many cases, this improvement was due to the workings of entrepreneurial local governments that purposively persuaded a variety of actors to establish markets, transport networks, and financing systems—all of which the poor residents of these villages managed to take advantage of.

Half the villages reported the presence of private employers in 2005. But even where they are present, private employers don't contribute to poverty escapes unless poor people can access new economic opportunities. The key is measures that can expand both the presence of the private sector in the villages and, even more importantly, poor people's access to private employment. Equally important are measures to ease the flow of goods and people in and out of the village through improved roads and transportation. In addition, poor people's access to credit seems to contribute strongly to poverty escapes, particularly when combined with road access. The institutional mechanisms for increasing credit access require further innovation and partnerships between the private sector and civil society, including poor people's organizations.

Two: A responsive local government is strongly associated with higher MOP

In villages where local democracy functions well, communities and individuals benefit as community leaders manage to attract more programs and resources to the community. Where local democracy is not healthy, development funds get diverted to the more powerful and better-off sections of the community.

These findings suggest that geographic targeting to poor communities must take into account the responsiveness and functioning of local government. Local political leaders must be encouraged to see their role as creating local-level economic opportunities for their constituents while remaining accountable. Maintaining a flow of information about local government performance on key indicators is critical. And this information needs to be in the public domain. There should be more bottom-up citizen monitoring and top-down governmental monitoring of panchayats to ensure their transparency and accountability, and civic groups also should be strengthened to serve as watchdogs.[9]

Three: Infrastructure and public services by themselves do not necessarily translate into poverty reduction, but in combination with credit they have a powerful effect

The study finds that unequal social structures exercise a powerful influence over whether poor people can access the opportunities associated with local services and infrastructure. Certain factors, however, seem to interact in ways that reduce entrenched inequalities. Where poor people can access active markets, basic services, and other infrastructure in combination with reasonable credit sources, they can then frequently take advantage of livelihood alternatives beyond poorly paid seasonal farm jobs. And nonfarm activities change the landscape for rural poor people's mobility by making them less vulnerable to powerful patrons, landlords, and moneylenders, to the vagaries of the weather, and to many other sources of vulnerability that deplete assets and sustain the trap of poverty, insecurity, powerlessness, and exclusion. Roads and transportation that open up choices play particularly important roles in breaking social barriers.

Four: In low-MOP contexts, the propensity for collective action and political participation has not yet translated into higher mobility

In communities where MOP is low, we encounter more groups and greater participation in community affairs, but there is little evidence so far that this is helping people move out of poverty. Poor people organize and turn to one another to cope with exclusion from the more formal structures of village governance. Poor rural villagers repeatedly emphasized the mutual bonds between the economic and political elites in their villages and offered examples of how these elites collude to siphon off public and private goods. Given such excluding opportunity structures, merely pushing more "poverty money" down through the system will continue to have uneven results unless there is more effective and sustained demand from below for better performance. Over the long haul, there are few substitutes for building capacity for poor people's collective agency for civic engagement and entrepreneurship, particularly in an environment of decentralized governance.

However, in some low-MOP communities, particularly in Andhra Pradesh, poor people's organizations are helping them escape poverty (see chapter 5). But the study also reveals that much hard work remains to be done before this collective agency can function as more than a coping mechanism and really change poor people's lives. On the ground, grassroots groups of poor men and women need help with building their organizational capacities as well as with connecting to one another and to influential partners beyond their villages. By federating, poor people's autonomous groups can gain the clout they need to spread awareness of and effectively claim their rights and entitlements. Such networks have also been at the heart of several successful movements that are creating important new economic opportunities for poor people.[10]

Poverty reduction polices should be informed by community realities

These four findings point to the strong benefits of poverty policies that are sensitive to community-level characteristics and processes. To strengthen geographic targeting to communities and eventually improve the functioning of programs, we suggest some additional limited data collection at the community level on six topics: (a) mobility of the poor, (b) presence and strength of local and nearby markets, (c) responsiveness of local democratic bodies, (d) presence of infrastructure and services, (e) presence and role of social and economic inequalities and practices of dominant groups,[11] and (f) types and functioning of poor people's groups and organizations.

Statistics alone on these themes will take the analysis only so far, however. Again and again, we found ourselves turning to the qualitative accounts in order to accurately interpret the quantitative findings and to understand the processes driving them. This was certainly the case, for instance, with respect to the question of why the number of groups and political participation should be higher in low-MOP villages.

In contexts with good local governance and a growing local economy, the mobility outcomes indicate that existing policies are working well to move large groups of poor families out of poverty. In less favorable contexts, the information above would help policy makers design and monitor over time new approaches that could more effectively address the key local barriers to poverty escapes.

Annex 3.1 Background on Regression Model

To understand the associates of community-level variations in movement out of poverty in the four states, we ran a multivariate linear regression model at the community level using the MOP index as the dependent variable. We specify the following linear relationship for a representative community:

$$y_i = \alpha + Economic_i\,\beta + Political_i\,\delta + Social_i\,\theta + Interactive_i\,\gamma + \eta State + \varepsilon_i$$

y_i indicates the community-level MOP index, that is, the share of population in the mobility matrix of the ith community that has moved out of poverty in the last 10 years, based on the respective community poverty line.

$Economic_i$ is a vector of economic factors that influences the MOP index. Based on the MOP conceptual framework, we include factors associated with economic prosperity such as ease of getting a job with a private employer in the community, access of poor people to new economic opportunities, and improvement of market outlets in the community.

$Political_i$ is a vector of political factors entering in the MOP framework as local democracy. The variables in the category related mainly to attention paid by government in the community, participation of poor people in community-related political decision making, and women's membership in the community council.

$Social_i$ includes proxies for social factors related to social stratification and collective action in the MOP framework. It also includes variables that measure the extent to which people are involved in the community decision-making process as a proxy for people's agency. The variables we included in this category are the presence of a private health center in the community and access of poor people to social networks and opportunities. We also control for the level of educational opportunities in a community.

$Interactive_i$ is a vector of interactive terms that explores the effect of interaction between various inequality measures and economic, political, and social performances. This econometric design (Østby 2007; Keefer 2007) is intended to control for the possible impacts of horizontal inequality (Stewart 2000; Stewart, Brown, and Mancini 2005) and other socially divisive factors in moving out of poverty.

Finally, $State$ represents state dummies to control for state-specific effects, and ε_i represents the error term in the linear regression model.

Table 3.7 showed our base and final model outcomes based on the linear specification discussed above. The base model outcome finds positive correlations between MOP and the presence of private employers in the community, improvement of market outlets, women's participation in community council meetings, and the presence of educational facilities. The presence of private health centers and higher government responsiveness is found to be negatively associated with MOP.

As is evident from the table, the explanatory power of the model increases as we move from the base model ($R^2 = .19$) to the final model (.28) and the extended final model (.43). The outcome is robust and statistically significant for market outlets in the community and government attention. For women's membership in the village council and educational facilities, the coefficient holds the same sign across the models.

Access as a route out of poverty

Access is crucial. The development of services and infrastructure alone cannot help poor people move out of poverty unless they have access to these new opportunities. We examine this proposition empirically. For the regression, we use three variables measuring increases in social, political, and economic access: (a) whether more people have access to social networks and organizations, compared to 10 years ago; (b) whether more people participate in political decision making compared to 10 years ago; and (c) whether more people have access to new economic opportunities, compared to 10 years ago.

Annex table 3.A shows the correlations between these three variables measuring access. The correlation between economic and political access is .24, closely followed by correlation between economic and social access at .23. Both are statistically significant at 5 percent. Access to new economic opportunities therefore is almost equally correlated with access to political participation and access to social networks. The correlation between access to social networks and to political participation is somewhat lower at .13.

As shown in the OLS methodology, we introduce these access variables as an interactive term with some of the key facility and opportunity variables in the base model shown in table 3.7. In the final model, we interact access to new economic opportunities with presence of private employers in the

ANNEX TABLE 3.A
Correlations between social, political, and economic access

	Social access	Political access	Economic access
Social access	1		
Political access	0.13	1	
Economic access	0.23	0.24	1

Note: All correlations are significant at 5%.

community, government attention with higher political participation, and private health centers with access to social networks and opportunities for the poor.

Access to new economic opportunities in the presence of private employers. One can expect more jobs to become available with private employers when new economic opportunities open up in the community. In the base model, the impact of private employers without access to economic opportunities is positive, but the coefficient is negligible and statistically insignificant. In the final model, the relationship looks like the following equation:

$$\frac{\Delta \text{MOPIndex}}{\Delta \text{Private employer}} = -0.03^{**} + 0.01^{***} \times \begin{pmatrix} \text{Access to economic} \\ \text{opportunities} \end{pmatrix}$$

This can be interpreted as suggesting that if there is less access to new economic opportunities, the presence of private employers in the community does not help poor people move out of poverty. But if there is greater access to these emerging opportunities, the net impact of private employers becomes positive and statistically significant. Thus, private employers together with greater access to new economic opportunities helps poor people move out of poverty.

Government attention and political participation. Does it help if local government pays more attention to what poor community members think when it decides what to do? In the final model, higher government responsiveness is found to increase the likelihood of more people moving out of poverty. The interactive outcome of government attention and political participation is negative with the MOP index (as shown in annex table 3.A). If more people in the community have access to political decision making, then it lowers the influence of government attention on MOP and requires less governmental responsiveness to attain higher MOP.

Social networks and access to private health centers. Availability of health facilities is a crucial factor for the poor. Health facilities work as a safety net along with other primary institutional facilities. But what happens if access to social networks and opportunities does not improve over time? We find evidence that the presence of health facilities helps poor people move out of poverty only if more people in a community have access to social networks and associations. But the presence of health centers alone does not help in moving out of poverty.

Overall, we find that agricultural market outlets are an important factor for moving out of poverty. Increasing government attention and more participation by women in village councils also helps the poor. Educational facilities are important, but health facilities help only if more people have access to social networks and associations. The same is true for getting a job with private employers. Poor people benefit from getting a job with private employers and can use it as a mechanism to move out of poverty if more people in the community have access to new economic opportunities.

References

Bardhan P., S. Mitra, D. Mookherjee, and A. Sarkar. 2007. "Local Democracy in Rural West Bengal: Political Participation and Targeting of Public Services." Working paper, Boston University.

Bardhan, P., and D. Mookherjee. 2004. "Poverty Alleviation Efforts in Panchayats in West Bengal." *Economic and Political Weekly*, February 28, 965–74.

———. 2005. "Decentralization, Corruption and Government Accountability." In *International Handbook on the Economics of Corruption*, ed. S. Rose-Ackerman, 161–88. Northampton, MA: Edward Elgar.

———. 2006. "Pro-Poor Targeting and Accountability of Local Governments in West Bengal." *Journal of Development Economics* 79 (2): 303–27.

Barron, P., R. Diprose, and M. Woolcock. 2007. "Local Conflict and Development Projects in Indonesia: Part of the Problem or Part of a Solution?" Policy Research Working Paper 4212, World Bank, Washington, DC.

Bates, R. 2000. *Violence and Prosperity: The Political Economy of Development*. New York: Norton.

Chaudhuri, S., and M. Ravallion. 2006. "Partially Awakened Giants: Uneven Growth in China and India." Policy Research Working Paper 4069, World Bank, Washington, DC.

Coady, D., M. Grosh, and J. Hoddinott. 2002. "Targeting Outcomes Redux." FCND Discussion Paper 144, International Food Policy Research Institute, Washington, DC. http://www.ifpri.org/divs/fcnd/dp/papers/fcndp144.pdf.

Drèze, J., P. Lanjouw, and N. Sharma. 1998. "Economic Development in Palanpur, 1957–93." In *Economic Development in Palanpur over Five Decades*, ed. P. Lanjouw and N. Stern, 114–239. New York: Clarendon Press.

Elbers, C., T. Fujii, P. Lanjouw, B. Özler, and W. Yin. 2004. "Poverty Alleviation through Geographic Targeting: How Much Does Disaggregation Help?" Policy Research Working Paper 3419, World Bank, Washington, DC.

Epstein, T. S., A. P. Suryanarayana, and T. Thimmegowda. 1998. *Village Voices: Forty Years of Rural Transformation in South India*. New Delhi: Sage.

Foster, A., and M. Rosenzweig. 2004. "Agricultural Development, Industrialization and Rural Inequality." Paper presented at the World Bank, Washington, DC.

Galasso, E., and M. Ravallion. 2000. "Distributional Outcomes of a Decentralized Welfare Program." Policy Research Working Paper 2316, World Bank, Washington, DC.

Keefer, P. 2007. "Insurgency and Credible Commitment in Autocracies and Democracies." Policy Research Working Paper 4185, World Bank, Washington, DC.

Narayan, D. 2002. "Bonds and Bridges: Social Capital and Poverty." In *Social Capital and Economic Development: Well-being in Developing Countries*, ed. J. Isham, T. Kelly, and S. Ramaswamy, 58–81. Northampton, MA: Edward Elgar.

Narayan, D., and M. Cassidy. 2001. "A Dimensional Approach to Measuring Social Capital: Development and Validation of a Social Capital Inventory." *Current Sociology* 49 (2): 59–102.

Narayan, D., and S. Kapoor. 2008. "Beyond Sectoral Traps: Creating Wealth for the Poor." In *Assets, Livelihoods and Social Policy*, ed. A. Dani and C. Moser, 299–321. Washington, DC: World Bank.

Narayan, D., and P. Petesch. 2007. "Agency, Opportunity Structure and Poverty Escapes." In *Moving Out of Poverty: Cross-Disciplinary Perspectives on Mobility*, ed. D. Narayan and P. Petesch, 1–44. New York: Palgrave Macmillan; Washington, DC: World Bank.

Østby, G. 2007. "Horizontal Inequalities, Political Environment, and Civil Conflict: Evidence from 55 Developing Countries, 1986–2003." Policy Research Working Paper 4193, World Bank, Washington, DC.

Rao, V. 2005. "Symbolic Public Goods and the Coordination of Collective Action: A Comparison of Local Development in India and Indonesia." Policy Research Working Paper 3685, World Bank, Washington, DC.

Ravallion, M. 1993. "Poverty Alleviation through Regional Targeting: A Case Study for Indonesia." In *The Economics of Rural Organization: Theory, Practice, and Policy*, ed. K. Hoff, A. Braverman, and J. Stiglitz. New York: Oxford University Press for the World Bank.

———. 2007. "How Relevant Is Targeting to the Success of an Antipoverty Program?" Policy Research Working Paper 4385, World Bank, Washington, DC.

Roy, I. 2008. "Civil Society and Good Governance: (Re-) Conceptualizing the Interface." *World Development* 36 (4): 677–705.

Scott, J. C. 1985. *Weapons of the Weak: Everyday Forms of Peasant Resistance.* New Haven, CT: Yale University Press.

Srivastava, P. 2004. "Poverty Targeting in Asia: Country Experience of India." Discussion Paper 5, Asian Development Bank Institute, Tokyo.

———. 2006. "The Role of Community Preferences in Targeting the Rural Poor: Evidence from Uttar Pradesh." In *Poverty Strategies in Asia: A Growth Plus Approach*, ed. J. Weiss and H. A. Khan, 245–65. Northampton, MA: Edward Elgar; Tokyo: Asian Development Bank Institute.

Stewart, F. 2000. "Crisis Prevention: Tackling Horizontal Inequalities." *Oxford Development Studies* 28 (3): 245–62.

Stewart, F., G. Brown, and L. Mancini. 2005. "Why Horizontal Inequalities Matter: Some Implications for Measurement." CRISE Working Paper 19, Centre for Research on Inequality, Human Security and Ethnicity, University of Oxford, UK.

Tilly, C. 1999. *Durable Inequality.* Berkeley: University of California Press.

Woolcock, M. 1998. "Social Capital and Economic Development: Toward a Theoretical Synthesis and Policy Framework." *Theory and Society* 27 (2): 151–208.

Notes

1. Numerous governmental poverty programs are designed to transfer resources—cash, food, land, education, loans, housing, health care, jobs, and so forth—directly to the poor. A growing literature indicates, however, that such schemes are often more effective in reaching their intended beneficiaries when they target communities rather than higher levels of government such as states and districts. Galasso and Ravallion (2000), for example, analyze a food-for-education program in Bangladesh and find that the poor are reached more effectively when the resources are transferred directly to villages for local leaders to allocate rather than to higher levels of government, where political pressures to spread the resources seem to make targeting more difficult. In addition, Elbers et al. (2004) show that the use of disaggregated poverty data and detailed poverty maps constructed by sophisticated statistical techniques would also reduce the cost of government programs. In particular, their study of 1,594 communities in Cambodia finds that the same level of poverty reduction could be achieved with 31 percent of the budget that would be needed to make uniform payments to the country's entire population, if detailed poverty maps were used to select beneficiary communities for poverty programs.

   There is also some evidence that conditions within communities affect the distribution of resources where poverty programs and government resources are decentralized. Bardhan and Mookherjee's (2004) assessment of poverty-targeted programs in West Bengal suggests that high-level governmental poverty reduction and transfer programs fail due to elite capture and partisan practices. In particular, they find that communities that feature more land inequality, more illiteracy among the poor, more lower-caste households, and less contested elections (whether dominated by the incumbent or opposition parties) were the ones that received *smaller* grants from the government. Similarly, Bardhan et al. (2007) acknowledge the tendency of West Bengal villages with greater land inequality to allocate fewer poverty-targeted benefits to their lower-caste groups, while Galasso and Ravallion (2000) find in Bangladesh that communities that are less poor and unequal are likely to better target their food-for-education programs. Furthermore, even the decentralized programs with minimal benefits—designed precisely to discourage nonpoor participation—face important targeting problems. An assessment by Srivastava (2006) of a food-for-work scheme in Uttar Pradesh indicates, for example, that only 26 and 37 percent of the program beneficiaries were poor according to quintile and official poverty line measures, respectively. Because of diverse problems with targeting and its measurement, Ravallion (2007) urges policy makers to focus on evaluating programs based on poverty outcomes rather than on how well they target the poor or how cost-effective they are. Also see Srivastava (2004) and Coady, Grosh, and Hoddinott (2002) for a more general discussion of targeting gaps.

2. The sample is exceptionally diverse in terms of caste, ethnic, and other social groups. Scheduled castes (SC), scheduled tribes (ST), and other backward classes (OBC) are groups recognized by the government based on positive discrimination and are found across the four states. In Uttar Pradesh, caste groups include traditional Hindu (e.g., Brahmin priests and Vaishya traders); religious (e.g. Muslim

Pathans, Ansari, and Syed, and Hindu Brahmin, Avasthi, and Gupta); occupational (e.g., blacksmith Lohar, barber Nai); and socially inferior (e.g., Chamar, Harijan, and Valmiki untouchables). In Assam, we find people from the Hindu, Christian, and Buddhist faiths. Hindu subcastes include the Kalita, Nath, Vaishya, and Rajbanshi, while tribes such as the Tea Tribals and Bodos also exist. West Bengal has a mix of Hindus and Muslims. The SC here comprise castes such as Mondal, Pal, Ghosh, Hazra, and Tarafdar, and the ST include the Hembrem, Mani, Tudu, and Kisku. The unreserved "general" castes in West Bengal include the Mukherjee, Chatterjee, Das, and Palit. In addition to the SC, ST, and Harijans (formerly known as untouchables), Andhra Pradesh has high castes such as the Reddy and low castes such as the Kapu. Other castes include the Gondi, Savara, Kamma, Mangali, Sali, Chakali, and Kalinga.

3. In Uttar Pradesh, a northern state, the primary language is Hindi, but in a few communities people speak Bhojpuri, a dialect of Hindi, and less often, Braj Bhasha, a Hindu medieval language. In other states in the sample, Hindi is rarely spoken. In West Bengal, an eastern state, the principal language is Bengali. In Assam, in the northeast, people communicate mostly in Assamese and sometimes in Bengali and Nepali (Nepal being the bordering country). In Andhra Pradesh, a southern state, people usually speak Telegu.

4. In every study, community field teams interviewed key informants to complete a community profile of the village's demographic, economic, social, and political characteristics and trends. In addition, focus groups in each village were surveyed on a small but similar set of closed-ended questions and their responses were added to the community profile dataset.

5. These initial conditions in private employment opportunities inform the regression findings presented later in the chapter on the negative association between private employment and MOP.

6. Growth in India's agricultural sector lags far behind growth in the manufacturing and commercial sectors, and the disparity can even be seen in the countryside. Foster and Rosenzweig (2004) carried out longitudinal work between 1982 and 1999 with a National Council of Applied Economic Research panel of 242 villages in the 17 major states of India. They found that nonfarm employee income accounted for 40 percent of total rural income. In particular, the study found that rural factory employment in the tradable goods sector grew tenfold and accounted for twice as much rural wage growth as did improvements in agricultural productivity.

7. It is also surprising that market outlets, like the other facilities, are present in both high and low-MOP communities in roughly equal measure over the duration of the study. For the regression results presented later in the paper, a variable was used that captures not only whether markets were present but whether they were improving or deteriorating on a 5-point scale.

8. Tilly further specifies that the mechanisms operate very frequently on the basis of "bounded pairs," such as black/white, male/female, Jew/Christian.

9. See Bardhan and Mookherjee (2005) for recommendations for top-down watchdogging of panchayats. Rao (2005) makes a case for using gram sabhas as monitoring bodies.

10. See Narayan and Kapoor (2008).
11. The theme of inequalities was explored through questions that examined differences; the changes in the gap between rich and poor; and the extent of poor people's access to the major arenas of local economic, political, and social life.

Caste Dynamics and Mobility in Uttar Pradesh

Soumya Kapoor, Deepa Narayan, Saumik Paul, and Nina Badgaiyan

> *There is no freedom, sir. Only the Thakurs [upper caste] are free. Neither can we do any work, drink water, nor can we do anything else.*
>
> —A POOR 45-YEAR-OLD SCHEDULED CASTE MAN,
> Khiria Khurd, Jhansi district, Uttar Pradesh

> *Inequality on the basis of caste has decreased. People live in peace, with love and affection. They eat and live together without any difference.*
>
> —YOUTH DISCUSSION GROUP,
> Silori, Jhansi district, Uttar Pradesh

CHAPTER 4

I n no state or region of India does the word *caste* elicit such vivid descriptions of economic, social, and political inequalities as it does in the state of Uttar Pradesh. Caste divisions dominate community life in most villages in this state. Scheduled castes have historically represented the most backward and economically deprived segments of the state's population, along with scheduled tribes. Caste and class are inextricably intertwined, as the scheduled castes and tribes occupy the lowest status in terms of assets, income, employment, poverty, health, and education (Srivastava 2007; Lieten and Srivastava 1999). However, the past few years have witnessed a shift in the political fortunes of these lower social groups. The rise of the Bahujan Samaj Party, a party of the scheduled castes and tribes in the state, has given them a platform for economic, social, and political empowerment.

Caste Dynamics in Two Villages

Consider two villages, Khiria Khurd and Silori, both in the district of Jhansi. On the surface, Khiria Khurd and Silori are very similar. With nearly one-third of their populations belonging to scheduled caste groups, the two villages have an almost identical social distribution. Both are isolated farming communities located about 100 kilometers from the district center. A majority of households in both either engage in farming, cultivating wheat and other grains, or work as agricultural labor on farms. Yet only 8 percent of the initial poor in Khiria Khurd have moved out of poverty over a period of 10 years, from 1995 to 2005. In Silori nearly 25 percent have.

For all their surface similarity, the two villages differ greatly in their social relations and local governance. In Khiria Khurd, caste relations are deeply conflictual and are considered *the* main hindrance to improving one's prosperity, while in Silori, caste relations are not divisive and do not emerge as

167

an obstacle. In Khiria Khurd, there is a stark economic and political divide between the higher and lower castes. The higher-caste Thakurs do not allow the scheduled caste Chamars or Harijans to touch them or drink water from their wells. Thakurs maintain a strong hold on all economic opportunities available in the village, making the lower-caste laborers work on their farms for a pittance and blocking their attempts to start small businesses. Lower-caste men and women in Khiria Khurd spoke openly about the suppression by the Thakurs: "They do not let others move up and do not let [us] be equal to them. If someone wants to do anything, then they interrupt. They fight. When there was wiring of electricity, then these Thakurs broke the poles and threw them on the ground. They are free to interrupt others' work. They have the power to beat anyone."

Silori, by contrast, thrives on peace across all castes: people "eat and live together without any difference." Members of different castes in the village play seemingly unobtrusive roles in the lives of others outside their group. Although inequality exists, it has decreased. "People of high castes don't pressure the low-caste people as they did earlier," said the women. They attribute the difference to rising education levels within the village. Unlike Khiria Khurd, which has only a primary school, Silori also has secondary school facilities that are easily accessible to all.

In Khiria Khurd, exclusion and suppression along caste lines is reflected in local governance and in low levels of community prosperity. The Thakur-dominated panchayat, the local democratic institution, ensures that all development work that comes to the village, be it laying roads or setting up an *anganwadi* (childcare) center, is located in and around hamlets with Thakur families. In Silori, on the other hand, the local government seems to work for the well-being of all. Between 1997 and 2004, Silori witnessed many development activities including a link road connecting the village to the main road, access to Kisan (farmer) credit cards, and construction of a check dam and 40 or 50 wells for irrigation. The benefits of these works seem to have reached all caste groups including the scheduled castes.

A powerful and helpful village head is seen as the primary driver of prosperity in Silori. Villagers say he is proactive and responds to their concerns. "He gives more attention to the people because he believes that their opinion matters for taking decisions. He believes that if a decision is taken after listening to the opinion of the villagers, it will bring happiness to them," the women reported. In part, the village head is responsive because villagers themselves are now more aware of the government's responsibilities toward its people. The men in Silori attributed this to their better education, saying, "The villagers are more aware nowadays so the government does pay more attention to the people. It has to consider the likes and dislikes of the villagers."

In this chapter, we examine whether caste still casts a long shadow on prospects for moving out of poverty in Uttar Pradesh. We explore the role of local-level political, social, and economic institutions in mobility of poor people, with a special focus on the scheduled caste group. After setting the context, we first examine whether there is community-level variation in poverty outcomes. We then examine the role of caste in community-level variation based on the share of population that belongs to the lowest castes while considering many other factors. We then turn to the role of caste in household mobility while controlling for a host of other household and community characteristics. We end with a discussion of policy implications.

The Context: Uttar Pradesh in the 1990s

Rural poverty in Uttar Pradesh (UP) declined in the 1990s, but the state is still home to nearly one-fifth of India's rural poor. Recognized once as the "pacesetter for the country's economic and social development," UP is now one of the poorest states in the country (World Bank 2002). Estimates from the 61st round of the National Sample Survey (NSS) conducted in 2004/5 indicate that while the poverty headcount ratio in rural areas of the state declined from 43 percent to 34 percent over the previous 10 years, it remained higher than the all-India rural average of 29 percent (Himanshu 2007).[1]

With respect to growth, too, the 1990s on the whole was a lost decade for UP. While total income in India increased at a compounded annual growth rate of 6.8 percent per year in the early 1990s, the corresponding income growth in UP was considerably lower at 3.2 percent (annex table 4.A). This marked a complete reversal of fortunes from the days of the green revolution in the 1970s, when growth rates in UP were higher than the national average (Singh 2007). The deceleration in growth affected all sectors of the state economy, with agriculture showing near stagnation and even negative performance at the turn of the century (annex table 4.B).

Over the past few years, Uttar Pradesh has seen some acceleration in terms of both sectoral growth and poverty reduction. Growth rates in agriculture and industry suggest a turnaround after 2002/3 (annex table 4.B). According to the recent NSS data, the pace of poverty decline in UP between

1993 and 2005 was higher than the all-India average (0.84 percent annually compared to 0.77 percent for India).[2] Moreover, the state performed better on poverty reduction between 2000 and 2005 than between 1993 and 2000, mainly because it has been able to control the increase in prices of both food and nonfood items, keeping them lower than the national average since 2000 (Himanshu 2007).

Starting in the late 1980s and continuing into the 1990s, the economic and human development indicators, including literacy and school enrollment, of the scheduled castes and tribes in UP improved. They increased their ownership of land, a critical asset in rural economies (Srivastava 2007). They also found a new political voice. But the gap between these groups and people higher on the caste ladder persists.

The caste system is a core feature of Hindu society (Muslims, Christians, and followers of other religions are by definition not members of this social order). In the Hindu social hierarchy, different social blocs are divided according to their caste or *varna* (traditional occupation). In order of dominance, they are Brahmins, traditionally engaged in professions such as teaching and the priesthood; Kshatriyas, traditionally warriors; Vaishyas, traditionally engaged in agriculture, trade, and commerce; and Shudras, traditionally manual laborers and servants. At the bottom of the ladder are the groups traditionally considered outcastes; since independence, they have been known as scheduled castes or Dalits. The scheduled tribes, living in geographically isolated tracts, fall outside the caste hierarchy. While the tribes do not have a history of ritualistic discrimination like the scheduled castes, they are segregated and excluded by virtue of their physical isolation (Béteille 1991).

After India gained independence, the newly drafted national constitution provided for a separate category of "backward classes" who were distinguished as those socially and educationally backward. Due to their historical deprivation, all scheduled castes (SCs) and scheduled tribes (STs) were included in this category. However, the constitution also recognized that there were other castes that were not necessarily SC or ST but were nonetheless backward in most respects. They were called "other backward classes" (OBCs). Thus, the category of backward classes embraced all three groups—SCs, STs, and OBCs. While the SC and ST lists were drawn at the time of India's independence, the lines around the OBC category remain murky. Usually, the OBC category consists of peasant cultivators like the Jats and the Yadavs, who occupy low positions in the varna order. In the past they received little formal education and were poorly represented in government and white-collar jobs.[3] Over time, OBCs have emerged as an important force, both socially and politically.

Brahmins have traditionally ruled Indian society because of their position in the caste hierarchy. However, following independence, a series of actions by the state attempted to change this order. In UP, land reforms as early as the 1950s transferred lands from the upper castes (including Brahmins) to peasant cultivators, most of whom belonged to the upper strata of the OBCs. Under the leadership of the Lok Dal, a political party representing upper-strata OBCs in the 1960s, and later the Samajwadi Party, representing such groups in the 1990s, peasant cultivators such as the Jats and Yadavs gained political power. They tried in turn to protect the interests of middle-rung farmers like themselves, often at the expense of marginal farmers and the landless, who usually belonged to the SC/ST category or were lower down the OBC order. The Lok Dal, for instance, specifically targeted upper OBC farmers with landholdings of 2 hectares and above, trying to increase their economic clout and meeting their demands for remunerative prices and low input costs. The Lok Dal also blocked all subsequent efforts toward land reforms designed to benefit the marginal farmers and the landless, arguing that such measures would lower efficiency in agricultural production.

The 1980s witnessed the emergence of the Bahujan Samaj Party (BSP), initially a militant outfit representing the Dalits and strongly opposed to all upper castes. The BSP became a vehicle of identity consciousness for Dalits, who until then had neither political voice nor representation (Pai 2007a). The general Hindu, non-OBC category veered toward the Bharatiya Janta Party (BJP), which was initially successful in mobilizing mostly upper-caste Hindus along religious lines. But the BJP soon lost its mandate when it failed to bring Hindu upper-caste development issues to the policy table and failed to win the support of OBCs, who were emerging as a powerful "vote bank" in the state (Tiwari 2007; Dubey 2007). The Muslims, who make up 18 percent of the population, were left divided between the Congress Party and the Samajwadi Party, putting UP on a nearly 15-year path of political instability and hung state assemblies that were fractionalized along caste lines (annex table 4.C). The BSP's electoral sweep in the 2007 state assembly polls, with its new mantra of "Dalits together with *savarna* [upper castes]," suggests that a new social and political coalition may be in the offing.

Against this political backdrop, key economic and human development indicators for the OBCs improved between 1983 and 1999/2000.[4] The OBC category made gains as landowners: they constituted nearly 41 percent of the top quintile of landowning households in 1999/2000, even higher than the share of their general category counterparts (annex table 4.D). This could be a reflection in part of the agricultural policies favoring OBC farmers under the Jat and Yadav leadership of the state government since the 1960s. OBCs also seemed to be better educated than SC/ST Hindus.

The SC/ST Hindus improved their position, but they continued to fare worse than all other groups except Muslims. With redistribution of state land to SC/ST households from the mid-1970s to mid-1980s, the SC/ST Hindus increased their share of land ownership in the state. Together, they constituted 11.5 percent of the top quintile of landowning households in UP in 2000 compared to 9.3 percent in 1983. Literacy levels and school enrollments for SC/ST Hindus also improved during this period (annex table 4.E). But despite these positive developments, literacy rates of this category remained lower than those of other groups. This suggests a narrowing but not an elimination of the socioeconomic gap (annex table 4.F).

Sampling Methodology

In Uttar Pradesh, a multistage purposive sampling was undertaken to select rural villages in different contexts. It included villages in both low- and high-growth areas, as well as in areas with low and high concentrations of SCs and STs. Variations in growth rates were built in at the first stage of sampling when 11 districts in UP were chosen based on their relative ranking along two proxies for growth. The first proxy was the condition of infrastructure in the district as indicated by the infrastructure development index of the Centre for Monitoring Indian Economy (CMIE 2000). The second was growth in real wages between 1987/88 and 1999/2000. In addition, some consideration was given to geographic spread.[5]

While not strictly representative of rural realities in UP, the sample districts varied significantly in the proportion of people below the official poverty line so that the study results would broadly reflect the state's entire population (figure 4.1). The sample districts are among the richest and poorest in the state, ranging from Pilibhit in western UP, which has relatively few poor people, to Raebareli in central UP, where more than half the population is poor.

At the second stage of the sampling design, blocks within the chosen districts were divided into quartiles based on the proportion of irrigated area

FIGURE 4.1
Poverty distribution of all districts in Uttar Pradesh, with sample districts identified

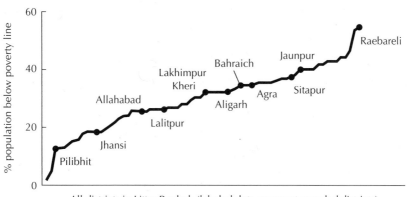

All districts in Uttar Pradesh (labeled dots represent sampled districts)

Source: Based on 2000 data from Indicus Analytics, http://www.indicus.net.

to total reported area (as a proxy for growth) and the proportion of SC/ST population in the block to total population. Three blocks that were among the highest and three that were among the lowest along both these dimensions were selected randomly from each district. Finally, three to four villages within each block were chosen randomly, representing 11 districts, 33 blocks, and 110 rural communities across UP (see annex 4.2 for details on the study blocks and districts).

Data were gathered through community visits using the mix of qualitative and quantitative methods described in chapter 1 and listed in appendix 2. At the start of fieldwork in each village, "ladder of life" discussions were held with focus groups of men and women, who ranked a random sample of about 150 households in their community according to their well-being status at the time of the study and 10 years earlier. They also set a community poverty line (CPL) between two steps of the ladder; households below the line were considered poor by local standards. Using the focus groups' placement of households on the ladder, the researchers constructed community mobility matrixes showing each household's mobility (or lack of mobility) over the 10 years. The matrixes then formed the basis for sampling households for detailed questionnaires and life stories. For details on the ladder of life exercise, see appendix 1 in this volume.

Summary Trends on Poverty and Mobility

Table 4.1 gives averages of some selected indexes for the entire UP sample. Most notably, it suggests that there has been a reduction of about 7.3 percentage points in poverty rates in our sample over the 10-year study period. While 66.7 percent of the sample population began in poverty in 1995, the percentage in poverty had declined to 59.4 percent by 2005. Our data, therefore, confirm the story of poverty decline in UP between 1993/94 and 2004/05. The numbers in table 4.1 also show that poverty reduction could have been even higher had the numbers of those falling into poverty been contained. Overall, 12.8 percent of all households moved out of poverty. But the impact of such movement is negated by those joining the poverty ranks: nearly 5.5 percent of all households had fallen into poverty, leading to net poverty reduction of only 7.3 percentage points for the sample.[6] Despite some movement up and down, 54 percent of the total sample population remained stuck in chronic poverty between 1995 and 2005.

Our results demonstrate that the standard practice in household surveys, which produces average poverty declines, hides two very different phenomena—moving out of poverty and falling into poverty. Their causes are different, pointing to a need for different policy actions.

It is important to note that our proxy poverty headcount figures—the percentage starting poor and percentage ending poor—are much higher than the official estimates. The official poverty headcount for rural areas in the state was 43 percent in 1993/94 and 34 percent in 2004/05, compared to our findings of 66.7 and 59.4 percent respectively. This is not surprising given that a large majority of both men's and women's discussion groups—almost 80 percent—placed the community poverty line on a higher step than the official poverty line, thus setting a higher benchmark of poverty (figure 4.2).

TABLE 4.1
Transitions in the sample population, 1995–2005, Uttar Pradesh

Mobility group	% of sample population
Movers	12.8
Chronic poor	54.0
Fallers	5.5
Never poor	27.7
Percentage starting poor (1995)	66.7
Percentage ending poor (2005)	59.4

FIGURE 4.2
Percentage of ladder of life focus groups in Uttar Pradesh that placed the community poverty line above, equal to, or below the official poverty line

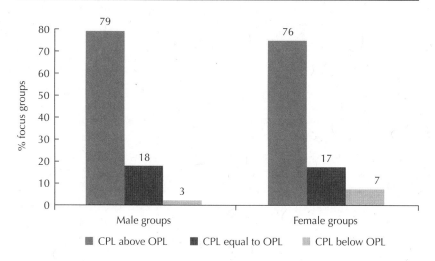

In other words, they considered the income at the official poverty line to be insufficient.

Community-Level Analysis

The community mobility matrixes provide a rich source of data for analyzing aggregate movement out of poverty or falling into poverty within each community, as well as variation across districts and communities. In this section, we first report variation between districts and communities within districts and then examine the factors associated with community-level variability.

Five summary indicators or indexes are used in this chapter to describe different types of transitions experienced by the communities during the study period. The statistics are derived from the household sorting exercise based on the communities' individual ladders of life. They relate to the community poverty line (see chapter 1, table 1.2):

- *MOP:* Moving out of poverty index. Measures extent of upward mobility by the poor across the CPL in a community.
- *MPI:* Mobility of the poor index. Measures extent of upward mobility by those who were initially poor, irrespective of whether or not they crossed the CPL.

- *MRI:* Mobility of the rich index. Measures extent of upward mobility by those who were initially above the CPL (nonpoor or "rich" by the study's definition).
- *FRIP:* Falling of the rich into poverty index. Measures extent of downward mobility of the rich across the CPL.
- *PI:* Prosperity index. Measures extent of all upward mobility in a community by both poor and nonpoor households.

Poverty and mobility trends by district

There is considerable diversity in economic and social development across the different regions of Uttar Pradesh, with the western region outperforming other regions. To confirm whether such variations are reflected in the communities in our sample, we calculated averages by district for MOP (percentage of initially poor households that moved out of poverty) and MPI (percentage of initially poor households that moved up to any extent). These figures use the community poverty line defined by the focus groups rather than official definitions of poverty. Table 4.2 summarizes these average scores.

Communities visited in Agra, Aligarh, Raebareli, and Jaunpur outperformed those in other districts in indicators of upward movement of the poor (MOP and MPI). In contrast, upward mobility of the poor was low in Allahabad and Lalitpur. The table also shows the distinctiveness of villages in Agra, Raebareli, Sitapur, Lakhimpur Kheri, and Jaunpur in the extent to which other people—particularly the nonpoor—experienced downward movement (reflected by FRIP, falling of the rich into poverty). In the sample communities of Agra, for instance, an average 20 percent of the population that began nonpoor fell into poverty. The numbers were higher in Sitapur and Lakhimpur Kheri, where roughly 30 percent and 25 percent of the nonpoor on average joined the poverty ranks. This explains in part the lower poverty reduction rates for Sitapur (8 percentage points) compared to, for example, Pilibhit (10 percentage points). While more poor people were successful in climbing out of poverty (MOP) in Sitapur than in Pilibhit, more people also fell into poverty (FRIP) in Sitapur. Finally, the numbers also suggest that poor people in our sample on average moved up more than rich people did. The MPI figures tracking all upward mobility of the poor are consistently above the MRI statistics for each district and for the sample as a whole. This conforms to the general pattern of pro-poor growth in rural UP over this period, as documented in other studies (World Bank 2007).

TABLE 4.2
Variations in poverty and mobility trends across sample districts, Uttar Pradesh

District	PI	MOP	MPI	MRI	FRIP	Movers	Fallers	PSP	PEP	Change in poverty
Aligarh	0.26	0.24	0.31	0.17	0.12	0.12	0.04	0.62	0.54	0.08
Allahabad	0.17	0.14	0.22	0.03	0.12	0.09	0.04	0.72	0.67	0.05
Agra	0.20	0.24	0.29	0.09	0.20	0.13	0.09	0.59	0.55	0.04
Bahraich	0.25	0.23	0.31	0.16	0.16	0.12	0.06	0.58	0.52	0.06
Lakhimpur Kheri	0.26	0.21	0.32	0.12	0.25	0.14	0.07	0.71	0.64	0.07
Lalitpur	0.19	0.16	0.23	0.12	0.17	0.09	0.05	0.64	0.60	0.04
Jaunpur	0.32	0.24	0.38	0.10	0.23	0.17	0.04	0.72	0.59	0.13
Jhansi	0.20	0.19	0.25	0.10	0.16	0.12	0.04	0.68	0.60	0.08
Pilibhit	0.23	0.20	0.29	0.09	0.14	0.14	0.04	0.69	0.59	0.10
Raebareli	0.39	0.29	0.51	0.22	0.22	0.11	0.04	0.64	0.57	0.07
Sitapur	0.32	0.22	0.39	0.12	0.31	0.16	0.08	0.73	0.65	0.08
UP sample	0.25	0.21	0.32	0.12	0.19	0.13	0.06	0.66	0.59	0.07

Note: PSP = percentage starting poor; PEP = percentage ending poor.

Average indexes, however, hide within-district variations, and they also get skewed by outlier villages. Figure 4.3 uses a box-and-whisker plot to illustrate the central tendency and dispersion of the MOP index across communities within each district. For each district, the line in the middle of the box is the median or 50th percentile of the data, the left edge of the rectangular box is the 25th percentile, and the right edge is the 75th percentile.[7] The lines extending from the box (the "whiskers") illustrate the more extreme values. Dots represent outlier villages. Districts are listed from top to bottom by the median value of MOP, so districts higher in the order had greater movement out of poverty. At the same time, one can see the variation across communities within the districts by the length of the boxes and whiskers. The median village in the Agra sample clearly does better on MOP than the median village in Raebareli, even though Raebareli has a higher average or mean MOP of 0.29 compared to Agra's 0.24 (table 4.2). The statistics for Raebareli reveal the wide variation among villages: one outlier village in the district has an MOP index of 0.06 and another has 1.00, the latter implying that everyone in that village who began poor climbed out of poverty. Similarly, of the 10 villages selected for Jaunpur, the MOP index ranged from a low of 0.09 to a high of 0.52.

FIGURE 4.3
Variations in MOP across sample districts and across communities within districts, Uttar Pradesh

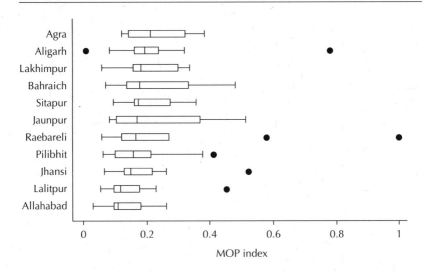

The box plot suggests that there are important village-level impacts on poverty. If poverty rates differed only by districts, then across-village differences would have been small. The wide variation shown in figure 4.3 implies that there are important village-specific features that lead to differential poverty rates. It also underscores the need for poverty mapping at a level lower than the district.

Correlates of community mobility

To understand why some communities are more conducive to the movement of poor people out of poverty, we explore the associates of community-level variations in MOP. For this, we turn to a series of multivariate linear regressions at the community level, using the ordinary least squares (OLS) method and using the MOP index derived from the mobility matrix as the dependent variable. We use initial conditions to avoid problems of endogeneity. The usual caution on regressions applies: that is, they are only a data summary device and indicate at best some associations between the dependent variable and a host of independent variables, without implying causation.

Our basic econometric model follows and builds on the main blocks defined in the conceptual framework outlined in chapter 1. Explanatory variables are constructed from the community-level data (a list of the explanatory variables used to measure each of the concepts is included in annex table 4.G).[8] These variables include proxies for our main building blocks in the conceptual framework: the economic prosperity in an area; the responsiveness of local democracy and cooperation of local leaders in community activities; collective action and the extent to which people are involved in community decision making; and the extent of social divisiveness and inequalities between children in schools based on caste or gender. We also control for educational facilities, share of initially poor people in the community, share of SCs in the village population, whether the community had a land reform program during the study period, and so on. In addition, we add a dummy variable for distance that takes the value 1 if there is a market within 12 kilometers of the community, 0 otherwise.

The results are reported in table 4.3. Our models explain on average around 44 percent of the variation observed in community-level MOP.[9] The main findings are as follows:

Local economic prosperity. Not surprisingly, changes in economic prosperity have a significant, positive association with mobility, as does the presence of educational facilities. A unit change in our economic prosperity measure is associated with a 1.4 percent increase in community-level MOP. When our sample of 110 communities is ranked based on their MOP index, we find that focus groups in the top third of the distribution had more positive perceptions of economic prosperity in their village than those in the bottom third. For instance, while 90 percent of male focus groups in the high-MOP villages thought it had become easier to make a living in the past 10 years, only 70 percent of those in low-MOP villages thought so. Similarly, 97 percent of focus groups in the high-MOP villages said that their community had become more prosperous over the study period; only 81 percent of those in the low-MOP villages spoke of an increase in prosperity. This suggests that expansion of economic opportunities in a community favors its population's chances of escaping poverty. Proximity to markets (within 12 kilometers) is associated with a 2 percent increase in MOP; this finding is robust but not statistically significant.

The initial share of poor people in a community is negatively associated with an increase in the MOP index and is significant at 1 percent. This suggests

TABLE 4.3
Factors behind community-level mobility in Uttar Pradesh: OLS outcomes for MOP index

Variable	Base model (1)	SC share (census) (2)	SC female/ male (3)	Total female/ male (4)
Changes in economic prosperity	0.0143**	0.0151***	0.014**	0.0122**
Market less than 12 kilometers	0.0207	0.0214	0.0188	0.0198
Initial educational facilities	0.0226*	0.0213*	0.0231*	0.0212*
Responsiveness of local democracy	0.0453***	0.0432***	0.0484***	0.0456***
Cooperation of local leaders	0.0575*	0.0554*	0.0609**	0.0542*
Participation in community affairs	−0.0595***	−0.0574***	−0.061***	−0.0616***
Index of collective action	−0.0199*	−0.0195	−0.0172	−0.0165
Social divisions	0.0095	0.0083	0.0119	0.0061
School inequality	0.0078	0.0067	0.0069	0.0035
Land reform	0.0278	0.0259	0.0233	0.031
Initial share of poor	−0.333***	−0.349***	−0.338***	−0.359***
SC share from census data		0.0945		
SC female-male ratio			0.0593	
Total female-male ratio				0.2475
Constant	0.419***	0.409***	0.362***	0.229
N	108	108	107	108
R^2	0.44	0.45	0.45	0.46

Note: Only OLS coefficients are reported in the table. Column 1 is the base model; different specifications are shown in columns 2 through 4.

*p < .10   **p < .05   ***p < .01 (White heteroscedasticity-consistent standard errors)

considerable divergence: people who live in poorer villages suffer an initial handicap in moving out of poverty. Intuitively, this makes sense. In villages with large concentrations of poor people, more workers are competing for a few jobs, depressing the price of labor and reducing opportunities for employment. Furthermore, when a poor person's friends, neighbors, and acquaintances are all poor themselves, they will be mostly unable to offer the valuable contacts and resources that can help in the climb up.

Local democracy. The two governance variables, responsiveness of local democracy and cooperation of local leaders, emerge as the two strongest correlates of community-level mobility. A more responsive local government and active cooperation of local leaders seem to help poor people move out of poverty by bringing more resources into the community that are available to all. A unit change in the responsiveness measure is associated with a nearly 4.5 percent increase in community MOP (the association is significant at 1 percent), and cooperation of local leaders is associated with a 5.7 percent increase. The importance of good local governance and leaders in mobility is also reaffirmed by our findings on land reform. Implementation of land reform has a positive association with community-level MOP, although the finding is not statistically significant.[10]

Our qualitative data, however, suggests that the caste of the local leader, or pradhan, is often an important factor in determining who benefits and who doesn't from actions taken by the local democratic structure and/or local leaders in a community. Governance improves in communities with free and fair elections and better access to information about local government programs, in part because people in such communities are more able to hold their leaders accountable. The stories from Dostpur and Shekhapur villages in Sitapur district are illustrative (box 4.1).

Collective action and empowerment. The two agency variables, participation in community affairs and propensity for collective action, have significant negative associations with community mobility. A unit increase in collective action and a unit increase in participatory decision making are each associated with a *decrease* in the chances of a community's people moving out of poverty, by nearly 2 and 6 percentage points respectively. This is surprising at first glance, but it suggests that poor people come together more in communities where moving out of poverty is more difficult. In other words, collective action may serve as poor people's only recourse for solving problems when all else fails. In a sense these findings reflect reverse causation.[11]

In a significant finding, women's share in the population of the community—a proxy measure of women's empowerment or agency—seems to make a big positive difference. A unit increase in the female-male ratio within the SC population is associated with an almost 6 percent increase in the MOP index. The coefficient is much higher for the total female-male ratio.[12] In fact,

BOX 4.1
How village leadership affects MOP

Dostpur village in Hargaon block, Sitapur district, is largely dominated by the scheduled castes. In the last census, the SC share of the village population was approximately 64 percent. The village has therefore been declared a "reserved constituency" for a Harijan (SC) candidate to the local leadership position. Chander Kanti, a 55-year-old Harijan woman, has been the pradhan of Dostpur since 1995 and is credited with most of the positive developments that have taken place in the village since then. These improvements include the opening of a junior high school, repair of a link road connecting the village to nearby sugar mills, construction of inner roads and drainages, installation of hand pumps, and initiation of self-help saving groups for men and women. The community mobility matrix of the village shows that an impressive 31 percent of households classified as poor in 1995 had moved out of poverty 10 years later.

A men's discussion group identified the pradhan as the main reason for this upward movement. According to Chhote, the "greatest strength of our village is our pradhan." While most of the infrastructure construction has been under the aegis of the Jawahar Rozgar Yojna employment program, Chander Kanti has played an influential role in getting the schemes to the village. She is said to have a "dominating personality," so that everyone is afraid of her. There are whispers that the pradhan favors Harijans; an example cited was a preferential reallocation of land to Harijan laborers in the village. Yet the move has lifted such families out of destitution and has presumably contributed to the high MOP figures of the village. And there is no denying the pradhan's positive role in infrastructure development in Dostpur. For young boys in the village, the pradhan "conveys problems that the community is facing to the government. The local government then solves them. The *khadanjas* [inner roads] and availability of drinking water are in that sense gifts of democracy."

Shekhapur, a village in the same block and district, has had lower movement out of poverty. Only 10 percent of households that were poor in 1995 had escaped poverty by 2005. As in Dostpur, scheduled castes are a large part of the population in Shekhapur, nearly 41 percent at the time of the last census. In this village, however, Thakurs and Brahmins dominate both economically and politically. The present pradhan, a Thakur, is said to consult only his kith and kin. "Whenever the village pradhan does any work, he just talks to the people close to him," complained a women's discussion group. The men lamented their inability to get useful information: "Only a few people have all the information regarding the decisions, and the rest are ignorant." The pradhan is also reportedly weak when it comes to decision making. The women continued: "We have to go to the police station to solve our disputes. No one goes to the pradhan because no one listens to him." Shekhapur has seen a string of negative events in the recent past, including floods in 2003 and a drought in 2004. The weakness of local leadership combined with the effects of these misfortunes seem to have restricted movement out of poverty in the village.

an increase in the share of women in a community has a significant association with the likelihood of people moving up from poverty (MPI). Overall, if we think of the female–male ratio as a proxy for women's participation and empowerment, then such empowerment and participation on average helps communities do better in moving up and out of poverty.

Belonging to scheduled caste. Finally, conventional wisdom and our own data on scheduled castes in UP would lead one to believe that villages dominated by SCs fare poorly on MOP. However, we find that the proportion of SCs in a village is *not* significantly associated with community mobility. On the other hand, most of the remaining variables in our conceptual framework, including proxies for economic prosperity, responsiveness of local democracy, and so on, retain the same level of significance as in the base model (see column 2 in table 4.3). In other words, we find no significant association between SC share and MOP index *after* controlling for other factors. We find similar evidence from the bivariate regression considering only SC share as an explanatory variable.

Any index constructed for movement out of poverty is subject to the placement of a threshold; in this study, it is the community poverty line (CPL). Placement of such relative thresholds can seriously affect reporting of changes in income or overall well-being. Given the problems that relative lines such as the CPL pose, we also used a broader index of all upward movement of the poor (MPI) in the community as the dependent variable and ran the same regression. The results are reported in annex table 4.H. Interestingly, while the signs on almost all associations remain the same as those observed for MOP, only changes in prosperity remain significant for community-level MPI. This suggests that provision of economic opportunities within a community could be one of the preconditions for upward mobility among the poor. But upward mobility does not guarantee movement out of poverty. As we find in our multivariate regressions for the MOP index (table 4.3), other factors such as responsiveness of democracy along with changes in economic prosperity are significant only for those who could move out of poverty.

Triggers for community prosperity

Given the importance of prosperity for community-level MOP and MPI, in this section we explore the major triggers or channels that have led to improvements in prosperity in the communities over the past 10 years. In each village, both key informants and focus groups of men and women were asked to rate the top two events that had affected the prosperity of their village positively during the study period.

In almost all districts, nearly one-third of key informant and ladder of life discussions rated improvements in connectivity through the building of roads and bridges as the most important factor explaining greater prosperity (annex table 4.1). The qualitative data also confirm the importance of roads, which connect people to markets, schools, and health clinics. This connectivity helps poor people take initiatives. A women's group in Dostpur, Sitapur, explained how roads within the village and connecting the village to markets have assisted farmers. "With the construction of *khadanjas* [brick roads] in the village, the people have benefited greatly. Commuting has become much easier. Earlier, it was very difficult for the farmers to transport their sugarcane to the sugar mills. Now it has become much easier, as they do not have to make many rounds up to the mills." Improved connectivity through roads also helps break the hold of the social elite. With an expansion of economic opportunities at the bottom, patron–client relations become less important for poor people's survival.[13]

Conversely, the bad condition of roads was reported as a major hurdle for individual agency. Respondents in Chhapra, Lalitpur, compared themselves to "a frog in the well," who jumps up only to slip back down. Reported the key informants: "The road is completely damaged. The villagers have become separated from all services. They cannot take a patient to the hospital. If someone has to go and sell his goods at the market, then he has to carry the bicycle and walk on foot on the road."

There are, however, variations on the trigger events that enhance community prosperity. While quite a few communities in Lakhimpur Kheri district singled out roads or improvement in connectivity as one of the top factors increasing their community's prosperity, sample villages in Sitapur seem to have benefited from commercial farming, particularly of sugarcane and peppermint. Use of hybrid seeds, chemical fertilizer, and other such agricultural inputs has also helped some villages in Sitapur and Jhansi prosper. Villages in Bahraich, on the other hand, reported high benefits from irrigation schemes, including construction of the Kheri dam. Across districts, communities assigned some weight to education, awareness, and literacy in improving their community's overall prosperity. Major events cited in this regard were the opening of primary and secondary schools. This was particularly noted in Lalitpur.

Strikingly, benefits from government poverty reduction schemes, including Indira Awas Yojna, the Ambedkar village scheme, and Sampoorna Grameen Yojna, seem to have had only a limited effect across districts and were seldom mentioned as the main trigger for improved community prosperity. There are three possible explanations: one, that these schemes were not active in these particular communities; two, that they were active but available to only a few people; and three, that the schemes benefit individuals rather than communities and hence did not receive mention at the community level.

Household-Level Analysis

Living in communities in which many people escape poverty, or living in communities with high levels of economic prosperity, responsive government, and a large share of women in the population may increase the likelihood of escaping poverty—but not necessarily for everyone. Even in the well-functioning village of Silori, reported in our opening village comparisons, not *all* or even *most* poor men and women managed to climb out of poverty. Consider the difference in outcomes between two households in Silori.

Arvinda is a 43-year-old man who has successfully moved out of poverty. Born in 1964 to a poor farmer in Silori and educated only through tenth grade, Arvinda recounts with much sorrow how he had to drop out of school due to poverty. He married at the age of 15 and started doing odd jobs in the village to support his family, trying different things to make ends meet. A grocery store venture failed when he could not repay the debt taken to finance it. He also tried farming after investing his savings in buying land. The turning point in his life came in 2001, when an irrigation canal opened in the village. The canal increased the yield from Arvinda's farms. Arvinda is now the proud owner of an insurance policy and has a flourishing business as a grain contractor in the grain market close to the village. He has two sons, one of them well educated, who he thinks will support him in his old age. He even provides financial help to his relatives.

The life story of 50-year-old Hari begins much like that of Arvinda, but it diverges sharply soon thereafter. The son of a poor laborer, Hari had to drop out of school after eighth grade. Like Arvinda, Hari tried different livelihoods and worked hard to improve his life and that of his family. He migrated to Delhi at the age of 20 to work as a security guard, then returned to Silori 15 years later to work as a laborer in other people's fields. Yet unlike Arvinda, Hari remains mired in chronic poverty. His land was claimed by the government for construction of the same irrigation canal that has brought wealth and prosperity to Arvinda, and Hari has no money to buy more land. He works as a security guard in the village and finds it difficult to support his large family that includes two daughters. His parents' death and division among the surviving brothers has left him with no support. He says there has never been a day in his life when he has felt secure.

These two narratives suggest the contrasting outcomes that can result when poor men and women take initiative to move out of poverty. They work hard, trying different occupations and ventures to improve their status. Some are successful; many are not. Why?

We begin this section with the reasons that people themselves cite as having facilitated their climb out of poverty or as having precipitated their fall into poverty. We then present results from the multivariate regression analysis, supported by a few descriptive statistics.

People's perspectives on reasons for upward movement

All households were asked to respond to the following questions: "On a 10-step ladder of well-being, where do you place yourself now and 10 years ago? What are the three most important factors that helped you move up/led to your fall on the ladder?"[14]

Among movers, the three reasons mentioned most frequently related to livelihoods. The most common was initiative to improve farming (28 percent). Jobs, including better wages, followed as the second most important trigger for upward mobility.[15] Establishing a new business or improving a business came third (figure 4.4).

We undertook in-depth analyses of the life stories of movers from a set of communities where commercial crops were grown and a set of communities where commercial agriculture had not developed. These provided two important insights. First, in all the communities, strategic life choices are most often made early, before the age of 25 years. Second, strategies for moving up differ depending on whether commercial agriculture is or is not viable in an area. In areas where commercial agriculture is well developed, people move up through gradual investment in cultivation of commercial crops. In areas with limited commercial cultivation, on the other hand, those who manage to move out of poverty generally use one of three strategies: they can migrate, pursue higher education, or get a government job, primarily through family connections. Even so, those households that are forced to look for livelihoods outside of agriculture often try to remain somewhat invested in farming by investing their savings in buying more land and assets to improve yields from agriculture (box 4.2).

FIGURE 4.4
Self-reported reasons for upward movement by movers in Uttar Pradesh

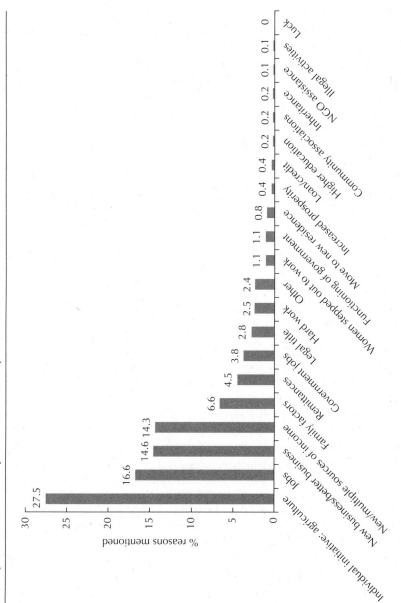

Note: Figures are percentages of reasons cited by movers when asked to name the top three reasons for their upward movement. For categories of responses, see annex 4.5.

BOX 4.2
Early choices and life trajectories

Poor people make strategic, calculated choices based on the opportunities available in their village. However, many of the most important decisions are made early in life, by the age of 25; this then sets up life trajectories. Sharp distinctions emerge between the life choices of people who live in areas where commercial agriculture is viable and those who live in areas where agriculture is not profitable. These findings are based on the coding of 61 life stories of movers across four districts in Uttar Pradesh.

In the districts where commercial crops are grown, Sitapur and Lakhimpur Kheri, moving out of poverty is attributed to gradual investment in cultivation of commercial crops like sugarcane. This includes purchases of agricultural equipment such as threshers, tractors, and sugarcane crushers, as well as high-yielding varieties of seeds. Thirty-five-year-old Rajesh, born to a poor family, said, "I thought of growing sugarcane when I was 25. I introduced new techniques, manure, and seeds, and in the next five years the yield and my income both increased. From my savings in the last three to four years, I have managed to buy an engine for irrigation and even an insurance policy. I am planning to buy a tractor now."

In contrast, in the districts where agricultural opportunities are limited, Raebareli and Jaunpur, young people make strategic decisions either to migrate, to invest in higher education, or to get government jobs. Forty-two-year-old Shivnath was born in a village with not much scope for commercial cultivation. He said, "Most people in my village are laborers, with little land for farming. But work as agricultural labor is not enough. I left my village when I was 25 years old. I had just had a son and my family responsibility and expenses had increased. I went to the state of Gujarat, where I knew a few people from our village. They helped me establish myself. With their help, I was able to open a small vegetable shop, and our income increased slightly."

As it did for Shivnath, early migration to a big city led to upward mobility for an astounding 48 percent of movers from villages with limited commercial cultivation. Many of those who migrated found low-level jobs in cities—pulling rickshaws or working in cloth mills, shops, or offices. Some started small businesses like vegetable vending with the help of their friends and relations already established in the city. They saved bit by bit and later returned to their villages to invest their savings in agriculture. "Every drop counted," said Shivnath. Even those forced to look for work outside agriculture, as Shivnath did, often try to remain somewhat invested in farming by investing their savings in buying more land and assets to improve their yields.

Other pathways to mobility for those in villages without commercial agriculture included getting more education—at a minimum, completing secondary school (52 percent)—and securing appointment to a government job, usually through family connections (44 percent). Most of these decisions that facilitated later upward movement were made by young adults before the age of 25.

Strategic decisions are made by movers before age 25

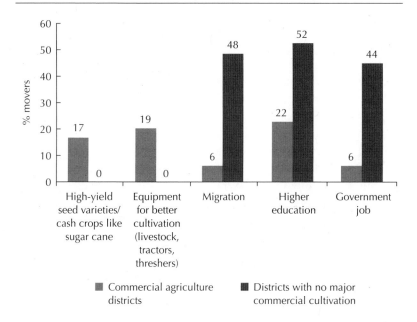

None of these strategies guarantees an escape from poverty. A majority of the chronic poor interviewed in both commercial crop-growing and other areas spoke of using the same strategies as those adopted by movers. However, their stories also featured shocks such as illness and death of the main earning member, leading in several cases to a burden of debt from which families found it difficult to escape.

People's perspectives on reasons for downward movement

There is no a priori reason to assume that there will be symmetry between the reasons for moving up and falling down—to assume, that is, that moving up results from absence of the factors that lead to falling down. Anirudh Krishna's work in India and in other part of the world establishes that reasons for movement up and out of poverty are not mirror images of the reasons for falling into poverty. The reasons for escaping poverty include diversification of livelihood activities, migration to cities for work, and improvement in irrigation facilities for farming; but ill health, high-interest private debt, and social expenses (such as for weddings) are the most common reasons for falling (Krishna 2004, 2006; Krishna et al. 2005). Our findings in Uttar Pradesh confirm the asymmetry of the reasons for mobility found in Krishna's studies.

Respondents in Uttar Pradesh cited two factors most frequently to explain their fall into poverty: decreasing community prosperity and health/ death shocks. About 18 percent of faller households believed that the worsening of their local market economy, including inconsistent availability of work opportunities, inflation in prices of basic necessities, and fluctuation in output prices, was a factor in their descent. Confirming Krishna's work, another 18 percent cited some combination of illness, injury, or death— especially devastating when the main income earner was affected—along with health- and death-related expenses. Excessive debt and inability to procure credit constituted the third most frequently cited reason for falling (figure 4.5). Against a difficult economic backdrop, an episode of illness in the family often pushed households into taking debt, mostly from private sources at high rates. Debt could also be taken to finance major household events like marriages. Ram's life story illustrates the multiple shocks that can propel households into poverty (box 4.3)

Caste Patterns in Mobility and Aspirations

Given our focus on understanding the influence of caste, we examined the distribution of movers, chronic poor, fallers, and never poor by caste group. We find that mobility rates for the scheduled castes seem similar to the rates for other groups, but proportionately more SCs are chronic poor and fewer are well-off compared to other caste groups. Despite these differences, we also find that there are no differences in aspirations along caste lines.

FIGURE 4.5

Self-reported reasons for downward movement by fallers in Uttar Pradesh

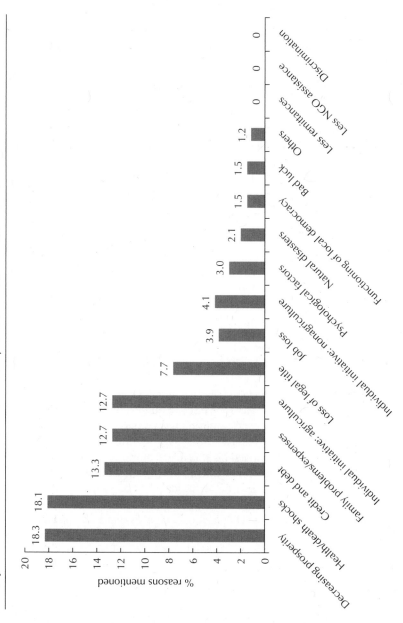

Note: Figures are percentages of reasons cited by fallers when asked to name the top three reasons for their downward movement. For categories of responses, see annex 4.5.

BOX 4.3
Falling into poverty: Hit by multiple shocks

When he was young, 55-year-old Ram never dreamed of the hardship that future years would bring. Born to a wealthy landed farmer in the village of Jigna in Lakhimpur Kheri district, Ram had an easy life as a child. Educated through the eighth grade, he left his studies at age 15 to help his father in farming. He regrets and at the same time is proud of the decision, which he says relieved his father, ailing with sciatica, of some of the burden of work in the fields.

A series of unfortunate events, beginning from the time of his marriage at age 16, pushed Ram into abject poverty. He spoke with much sorrow of how he lost his first four children, all daughters, to illness when they were infants. "I started believing that there was no child in my destiny." Soon, however, he was blessed with two sons.

As his family started to grow, Ram began to rear buffaloes in 1993 so he could sell their milk as a side business to farming. But the venture failed to take off, and the buffaloes soon died in an epidemic. "I felt sad that I could not treat them and further that my source of income had come to an end. I was quite worried. But in the year 1995, by the grace of God, I got a job as a watchman in the forest department. I worked there for a year."

A year later, illness struck. "One day, I had a very bad stomachache, and the doctor said that my intestines were bad and that I needed an operation as soon as possible, else anything could happen. At that time, I did not have sufficient money for the operation. I tried to arrange for funds but was unsuccessful. So at the end, I had to sell my share of land. That is how I got saved," he recounted.

Out of work and with no land to his name, Ram could not give his family anything to eat for days. Their troubles compounded with the death of Ram's parents in 2000, after which Ram and his brothers decided to separate. "I was drowned in sorrows," he said.

Not giving up hope, Ram and his wife began afresh. They performed labor for others in the village. In 2003, Ram married his elder son with much difficulty. The funds taken to arrange the wedding and buy jewelry for his future daughter-in-law left him buried in debt. "Our family was growing, and there was no source of income to come out of debt. Even after doing labor work, there were days when there was nothing to eat. Such was our condition that we worked the whole day and only ate once in the evenings. The days we did not work, we went to sleep with an empty stomach."

Weak from his illness and from harsh labor, Ram sees his two sons as his only remaining hope. "My future is in their hands," he said with resignation. "When they go out and find work for themselves, only then can I come out of this poverty and debt."

Scheduled castes still poor

Table 4.4 shows the distribution of the four mobility groups across caste categories. We combined SCs and STs, since there are 373 SC households but only six ST households in our sample, and we refer to this combined group as SCs. We do not discuss our findings on Muslims, as the total number of Muslims in our sample turned out to be too small to permit robust conclusions (128 households in a total sample of 1,635).[16]

There are striking differences between castes in the proportions of those stuck in chronic poverty. The SC group has by far the highest percentage of people in chronic poverty, 38 percent compared to 16–22 percent in other caste categories. There are also large differences in the proportions of the caste groups that were never poor (that is, who were well-off at the beginning of the study period and remain so now). The general caste category has the highest proportion of never poor, 37 percent, followed by the OBCs with 30 percent and the SCs with 16 percent.

At the same time, the distribution of movers across caste groups does not show a wide spread. Among OBCs, movers make up the largest mobility group at 37 percent, reflecting the progress that OBCs have enjoyed over the past few decades. But SCs, with 33 percent movers, have also made gains, although they lag behind a little. The general category, with 35 percent, is in the middle. A central conclusion is that although the SCs are the most represented among the chronic poor and the least represented among the permanently well-off,

TABLE 4.4

Distribution of mobility groups across caste categories, Uttar Pradesh

Mobility group		General	SC	OBC	Muslim
Movers	No. of households	206	124	204	58
	Percentage	35	33	37	45
Chronic poor	No. of households	92	145	118	26
	Percentage	16	38	22	20
Fallers	No. of households	69	49	60	15
	Percentage	12	13	11	12
Never poor	No. of households	215	61	163	29
	Percentage	37	16	30	23
Total	No. of households	583	379	545	128
	Percentage	100	100	100	100

Note: Percentages are within each caste group.

their mobility rates in the last decade are very similar to those of other caste groups.[17]

Aspirations for children are not related to caste

Does low mobility reflect low aspirations? Table 4.5 compares movers and chronic poor across different caste groups in terms of their aspirations for their children. The numbers point to three interesting conclusions. First, there are *no* major differences in aspirations for children between caste groups, either among the movers or among the chronic poor. SC movers have the same level of aspirations as OBC movers, 93 percent, which in turn is only 1 percent higher than the general category. Clearly, aspirations have little to do with caste.

Second, there is a clear distinction between the aspiration levels of the movers and of the chronic poor. More than 90 percent of the movers across caste categories expect that their children will be better off 10 years from now, compared to only 64 percent of the chronic poor. This implies that success reinforces higher aspirations and expectations for the next generation to do even better.

Finally, even though aspiration levels of the chronic poor and the SCs among them are lower than those of the movers, they are, nonetheless, high in absolute terms. This clearly establishes that poor people, in particular the SCs, are not poor because they lack aspirations to do well. Lack of motivation is not the problem; they face other obstacles.[18] While a poor person belonging to a scheduled caste may have the same desire for his children's future as one belonging to a general caste (table 4.5), it does not necessarily result in the same outcome (table 4.4).

The next obvious question is why some households, especially SC households, remain stuck in chronic poverty even though they aspire to a better future for their children. Our hypothesis is that poor people across caste cat-

TABLE 4.5
Aspirations for children's future, by mobility group and caste group, Uttar Pradesh

Mobility group	% that expect their children to be better off 10 years from now				
	General	SC	OBC	Muslim	Total
Movers	92	93	93	95	93
Chronic poor	67	62	65	62	64

egories have aspirations to do well and adopt similar strategies to move out of poverty, like increasing crop productivity or opening a small shop. But discriminatory local-level structures or the poor jobs and assets available to them hinder their ability to use these paths to escape poverty.

We, therefore, turn to multivariate regression analysis to examine the role of caste together with a range of individual and community characteristics, including social, political, and psychological variables, in upward mobility out of poverty. We use the regressions as a summarizing device to understand the associations between mobility and these individual and community characteristics. We also draw on our massive qualitative dataset to explain the findings and underlying mechanisms.

Why Do Some Households Escape Poverty and Others Do Not?

The regressions were run on a subsample of the data corresponding to the initial poor set, those who were classified as poor in 1995. Some moved up and some did not over the study decade; hence, the comparison is between movers and chronic poor.[19] The explanatory variables follow the conceptual blocks and the list of variables used to measure each concept, as described in appendix 3 of this volume. These include measures for economic opportunity, local democracy, social stratification, and individual and collective agency. For some of these measures, we differentiate between private benefits and social benefits. To ascertain associations between caste membership and movement out of poverty, we enter separate caste dummies as explanatory variables in the model. We also control for a range of household characteristics including assets, livestock, house ownership, education of the household head, and health shocks. The results do not imply causality.

A few methodological issues are worth highlighting. First, as far as possible, only initial conditions are used to measure each explanatory variable. This is to avoid halo effects or endogeneity biases that may emerge while regressing a change variable (movement out of poverty) against changes. Second, using community perceptions to identify the dependent variable, that is, the mobility status, helps ameliorate endogeneity biases or halo effects of regressing households' own perception of movement against their own perception of variables such as their assets. Third, people who answered the household survey were not representative of the village. Annex 4.6 reports the results of a weighted regression where we take into account the fact that households were stratified based on their mobility category and selected in a ratio favoring movers.[20] There are no significant differences in results. The subsequent discussion, therefore, is based mainly on the results for the unweighted regression. Finally, the regressions were subjected to tests for robustness, in addition to cluster correction. The averages for movers and chronic poor for all the variables used in the household regression are found in annex table 4.J.

Distinguishing private, community, and net impact

In the above framework, variables like responsiveness of local democracy, individual agency, and fairness can work as both a public good and a private good. For example, it could well be that some households said that their local democracy is responsive because they have had an opportunity to participate in it or derive benefits from it. However, one household's participation can have a strong "chilling" or "crowding out" effect on other households in the same community (Narayan and Pritchett 1999; Alatas, Pritchett, and Wetterberg 2007).

To disentangle private from public or social effects, we used the technique called leave-out mean (LOM). This method averages the responses of all households in the village excluding one household—say, "household A." For example, if we are considering the responsiveness of local government, the leave-out mean for household A is the average of all responses on this topic less A's own response. If household A's perceptions on responsiveness are influenced by participation in a local public works program, but A's participation served to exclude others, the private impact of the program may be positive, but its social impact could be negative.

The leave-out mean variable is therefore a good proxy of the extent to which local democracy or government can be captured by a few. If the net impact of local government responsiveness is negative, it suggests that the local government mainly redistributes zero-sum goods among the village population, benefiting some households at the cost of others. Similarly, one can calculate leave-out means for other individual variables like personal agency, aspirations, fairness, and so on, to distinguish between their private and public impact.

Based on the conceptual framework, we explore the relations between individual-level MOP and local-level economic, political, and social institutions as well as between mobility and a range of individual characteristics (ownership of assets, education, health shocks, sense of power and rights, control over everyday decisions, and aspirations, among others). The results

TABLE 4.6
Factors behind household-level mobility in Uttar Pradesh:
OLS outcomes for MOP index

Explanatory variable	Model (OLS)
Initial strength of economy	−0.020
Change in economic prosperity	−0.004
Responsiveness of local democracy	0.0447***
LOM of responsiveness of local democracy	−0.028
Corruption	−0.0254*
Fairness index	0.0264**
LOM of fairness index	0.015
Initial position on 10-step ladder of power and rights	0.0466***
LOM of initial position on 10-step ladder of power and rights	−0.0789***
Control over everyday decisions	−0.003
LOM of control over everyday decisions	−0.031
Household aspirations	0.1405***
LOM of household aspirations	−0.1767***
Index of collective action	−0.0287**
Access to networks and associations	−0.008
Social divisions	−0.010
School inequality	0.004
Violence against women	0.032
LOM of violence against women	−0.054
Present education status of household head	0.0313***
Health shocks	−0.015
Initial landholding	0.0109**
Ownership of house	0.169
Assets index	0.015
Livestock index	−0.012
Change in access to irrigation	0.003
SC dummy	−0.1001***
OBC dummy	−0.047
Constant	0.6662**
Observations	968
R^2	0.33

*p < .10   **p < .05   ***p < .01 (White heteroscedasticity-consistent standard errors)

are reported in table 4.6. We start with the most obvious variable, economic opportunities available at the local level, which we do not find to be significant. We then turn to our central variable, membership in the scheduled caste group, which turns out to have a significant, negative association with household mobility. Next, we examine the role of local-level political and social institutions before turning to individual characteristics. With respect to the latter, we focus particularly on the psychological dimensions, since these have been ignored in previous research and hence less is known about their influence.

Economic prosperity

Let us start with the most obvious variable: local economic prosperity. Neither the initial strength of the local economy nor change in economic prosperity emerges as having a positive association with moving out of poverty; in fact, the signs are negative, indicating some degree of convergence. In general, it makes sense that there would be some positive association between local economic prosperity and ability to move out of poverty. We can think of a few possible explanations for our counterintuitive finding. The most likely one is that living in a community with greater economic possibilities does not mean that every individual will have access to these opportunities. Differences in individual characteristics, as well as institutional norms of fairness, equality, and trust, may influence who has access and who does not. It is possible that in deeply divided societies, opportunities are distributed along social divides, which in UP follow caste lines.

We also found little difference between movers and the chronic poor in their assessment of change in the ease of finding jobs over the past 10 years (table 4.7). Overall, most households found it difficult to find jobs during the study period, with not much difference between movers and chronic

TABLE 4.7

Perceptions about economic opportunities, by mobility group and caste group, Uttar Pradesh

	% saying it has become easier to find a job in past 10 years				
Mobility group	General	SC	OBC	Muslim	Total
Movers	7.7	7.3	8.3	12.1	8.2
Chronic poor	8.7	6.9	3.3	7.6	6.3

poor. Only 27 of the 110 sample communities reported the presence of any formal private sector employment in their village.

However, if we consider the results of the weighted regression (correcting for the oversampling of movers) in annex 4.6, we find that prosperity in a community has a positive and significant influence on household mobility.

Scheduled caste status is a significant disadvantage

To test whether caste membership in any way influenced individual mobility out of poverty, the model includes dummies for SCs and OBCs (relative to the general category). Being an SC significantly lowers the probability of movement out of poverty even after we control for the effects of many other factors. An average SC household has a 10 percent lower likelihood of moving out of poverty than households in the general category. On the other hand, being an OBC does not significantly influence one's chances of an escape from poverty.

This finding implies that even after controlling for the independent effects of education and assets, belonging to a scheduled caste household, despite the gains in the past decade, is likely to dampen the probability of escaping poverty. This is likely linked to discriminatory institutions at the local level. So we explore in some depth the relationships between escaping poverty and other local-level economic, political, and social institutions, particularly local democracy and collective action. We also examine the role of individual psychological factors, including individual agency and aspirations. We end this section by briefly discussing the role of education and household assets.

Responsive local democracy helps household mobility

A more responsive local democracy favors movement out of poverty. We find significant evidence that in a more responsive democratic environment, a poor person is more likely to move out of poverty.

Responsiveness of local democracy was measured by four questions: households' trust in local government officials, their ability to influence their local government's actions, local government responsiveness to citizens' concerns, and overall satisfaction with local democracy.

Overall, almost 46 percent of the movers believed that their ability to contact their local government and influence its actions had increased in the past 10 years. In contrast, only 31 percent of those who remained in poverty over

TABLE 4.8
Rating on influence over local government, by mobility group and caste group, Uttar Pradesh

Mobility group	% saying their ability to contact and influence local government has increased in last 10 years				
	General	SC	OBC	Muslim	Total
Movers	42.2	40.3	47.5	65.5	45.9
Chronic poor	33.7	29.7	28.8	34.6	30.7

the study period believed this (table 4.8). Furthermore, among the households classified as movers, a lower proportion of SCs believed that they could contact and influence the actions of their local government, although the numbers were not dramatically different from those of the general category. Among the three categories considered (not including Muslims), the OBCs were most likely to report that they had influence over their local government.

Responsiveness helps some but excludes others

While a responsive local government seems to have a significant positive influence on individual mobility, a negative (though insignificant) coefficient on the leave-out mean for responsiveness suggests that local governments in UP could be reallocating or redistributing zero-sum goods, favoring some individuals over others. Although the net impact of local democracy—adding the coefficient on the responsiveness variable and the coefficient on its LOM—remains positive, our qualitative data show that there is some discriminatory exclusion in practice.[21]

Where it exists, unfair distribution observes deeply embedded social boundaries, with the ruling castes favoring those belonging to their own category. In the village of Nagara in Lalitpur district, for example, only households belonging to the Yadav and Lodhi (OBC) community have access to Kisan credit cards for buying agricultural equipment. The Lodhi pradhan is reported to favor those from his own caste group. In Dostpur, Sitapur, the Harijan pradhan works for the benefit of Harijans. According to a group of women in the village: "Our village head is a Harijan. She works only for the benefit of Harijans and consults them only before taking any decision."

In Sheopura, in eastern UP, the construction of a road linking the village to the main road and the opening of a sugar mill in a nearby town have changed the community's economic path from stagnation to dynamic growth. But a highly corrupt local government is fueling dissension and disunity by playing the caste affiliation card in the distribution of government schemes. "The upper caste have the most power here as the leader is from their community," said Kusum. "Whenever any scheme comes to the village, only they get its benefit. It doesn't reach the other people." The acting village head aids his cronies and lines his own pocket, while the titular village head—his wife—is unapproachable. Vimlesh, a woman in the village, said, "Only those people can reach them who are of the same caste or flatter them a lot." The fallout from such divisive politics is that the lower-caste Hindus get the shortest straw. Rani remarked, "The lower castes have the least power as they aren't able to get the benefits of any scheme. They just fight among themselves, and meanwhile someone else gets the benefit."

Some local panchayats and governments do bring benefits to their entire community. Where they do, our qualitative data confirm the presence of three factors: (a) active voting in elections that provides a check on the power of the local village head or pradhan; (b) information about the local government's programs in the village that promotes accountability; and (c) provision of quasi-public infrastructure such as roads that bring prosperity to the community irrespective of caste divides.[22] The example of Surjana in Bahraich district is a case in point (box 4.4).

Corruption hinders mobility

Corruption, both within the local government and at the national level, also seems to significantly reduce the chances for poor people in UP to escape poverty. Respondents across communities described in detail how corruption hinders their day-to-day lives. In a village in Raebareli, a youth said, "If there is a dead body in the hospital, then one has to give 20 or 30 rupees to the ward boy and tell him to get a stretcher and put the body in the car." Youths in a village in Jaunpur agreed: "Government employees right from the top to the bottom do not do any work without bribes. They speak of it as if we were giving offerings to a deity. They openly say: do something for us, and your work will be done. Policemen let goods worth lakhs [hundreds of thousands] go for a two-rupee bribe."

Bribe taking by officials also influences people's ability to start new livelihoods. Government schemes designed to help poor people make a living may fail to reach the intended beneficiaries as "all palms need to be greased." Respondents in a village in Bahraich lamented that credit cards from banks intended to benefit sugarcane farmers in the village have turned out to be

BOX 4.4
The case of Surjana: Local democracy as a positive-sum game

The village of Surjana in Tajwapur block, Bahraich district, has seen a considerable increase in its prosperity over the past 10 years (1995–2005). This is mainly attributed to a state government scheme called Daaks, implemented in 2000. The crop diversification and land preservation scheme provided (a) training and subsidies of key inputs even to small farmers; (b) land to poor farmers and SCs, allowing them to pursue farming and daily wage labor, thus boosting their income; (c) free well-drilling facilities to poor farmers and SCs, encouraging them to hire irrigation machines and grow crops not dependent on rain; and (d) easy provision of loans from government cooperative banks and through the Kisan credit card scheme.

Overall, the local government is reported to be active in implementing Daaks for village development, and this is reflected in high scores on local government responsiveness for this village. The villagers believe that in their community, at least, it is mainly the fear of not being reelected that keeps local leaders attentive. A men's focus group in the village reported, "In case the pradhan does not listen to the concerns of the people, then in the forthcoming elections, the people will not vote him to power." The women concurred, "When compared to the past 10 years, the pradhan has started paying more attention to the people of this village. Now whatever schemes come, they reach the people of the village. All the houses in the colony have been allotted to the deserving people. He [the pradhan] is afraid of any checking by the authorities."

What makes Surjana's story interesting is that it is a community divided along caste and economic lines, with higher castes dominant on the economic ladder. The pradhan himself was reported to be a landlord from a high caste. Yet the fear of not winning reelection has helped motivate him to share the economic pie widely. With the provision of land and housing through Daaks, the lower castes, who had historically been exploited by powerful patrons in the village, have now started pursuing multiple occupations. According to the villagers, the importance of social identity has weakened: "During the past 10 years, the gap [between the rich and the poor] has decreased. Earlier the lower-caste laborers worked in bondage with the big farmers who gave them a pittance for their hard work. They could not stand before the big farmers. Now this discrimination has decreased. The government has provided them with land and houses in the colonies. With this their living standards have improved."

more expensive than borrowing from landlords by mortgaging land. They said, "The peons to the manager of the bank harass the illiterate farmers, and they have to go to the bank again and again. Then they ask for a 10 percent commission, and only after paying that does one get a loan." In a village in Pilibhit, a photocopy of a land record that costs Rs 2 a page is usually done at government offices for Rs 100 a page. Access to a government housing scheme for the poor in a village in Allahabad is restricted to those who can pay Rs 1,000 at a minimum to the local government official.

Fairness facilitates MOP, while social divisiveness hinders it

Fair prices for agricultural produce and fairness in treatment by the law within the community have a significant association with an individual's chances of climbing out of poverty (table 4.9). Even where opportunities are readily available, fairness in accessing them can play a big role in how opportunity translates to actual movement out of poverty. The construction of a road or market can make it possible for poor people to sell their products, but if the pricing system is unfair, the potential benefits from the road or market may come to naught. A lower percentage of those classified by their communities as being stuck in chronic poverty thought that farmers received fair prices in their dealings, compared to those who were considered to have escaped poverty. However, there are no strong caste differences on this question.

Strong caste differences emerge in relation to treatment by local law enforcement agencies. When asked whether there was fair treatment under law in the community 10 years ago, half of the movers and 44 percent of the

TABLE 4.9
Perceptions about fairness by mobility group and caste group, Uttar Pradesh

Mobility group	% saying farmers' ability to receive fair prices has improved in last 10 years				
	General	SC	OBC	Muslim	Total
Movers	65	67	68	67	67
Chronic poor	53	55	55	50	54
	% saying law in their community was fair to all 10 years ago				
	General	SC	OBC	Muslim	Total
Movers	51	47	52	53	51
Chronic poor	51	36	53	31	44

chronic poor on average responded in the affirmative. However, these numbers dropped sharply for the SC group. Only 36 percent of the SC chronic poor thought that law enforcement in their community was fair to all. The perceptions of the OBCs matched those of their general counterparts. Further, no group reported improvement with respect to fair treatment under law over the study period.

In addition to fairness, divisions within the village along the lines of ethnicity, caste, and religion have a negative association with individual movement out of poverty. But the results are not significant, given the small difference in perceptions of movers and chronic poor on the extent of these divisions (53 percent compared to 60 percent).[23] However, our data suggest differences in such perceptions between castes, an interesting finding. Twelve percent of the SC movers said that their community was divided to a great or very great extent, but only 4 percent of OBC movers felt this degree of division.

Collective action does not yet help mobility

It is increasingly recognized that poor people's groups offer them an important channel to gain voice, representation, and identity and facilitate their overall well-being. Aggregating in groups, such as the women's self-help groups in Andhra Pradesh, can also help poor people increase their economic assets and protect them from shocks. Our data suggest, however, that in Uttar Pradesh, groups of and for the poor are limited in scope. Only 13 of the 110 communities visited in the state reported a presence of economic groups, and only 6 percent of all households surveyed for the questionnaire reported being members of any group.[24]

The regression results show a negative coefficient for both our measures of collective action (significantly so for community cohesiveness), indicating an inverse association with individual mobility. This implies that poor people participate in groups precisely because they are poor and have no other options. Collective action thus serves only as a coping mechanism among poor people.

The finding, though counterintuitive at first glance, can be explained by probing more deeply the forms of collective action that operate in UP. Our data reveal that most collective action undertaken is of the bonding type, where poor people came together in their own social groups to take action.[25] In fact, support from the family was the most common form of collective agency seen across communities, underscoring the importance of bonding social capital. Across communities, the family stood out as a source of power, either in terms of large family size, which leads to many earning members, or in terms of family unity, which may be tied in with the common ownership of property. Mechanisms of family collective action included informal partnerships between family members who work together, as well as migration of one family member who then sends home remittances to the rest. Often such strategies seem to have led to upward mobility and movement out of poverty. On the other hand, disunity within the family and/or division of property was seen as decreasing the collective strength of the family, leading to falls across communities.

But bonding by social groups over and above the family is mostly a coping strategy, not resulting in mobility, as poor people remain cut off from more prosperous members of their communities. Deep social divisions dampen the collective spirit needed for building bridges across social groups. In addition, the study revealed very few instances in which poor people were able to link with government or outside agencies for support, new ideas, capital, or access to markets. Availability of networks and associations improved on the whole over 10 years, but access to them remained limited to only a few.

Caste divisions in the village of Suchi, Raebareli, are quite common even though people speak of living together in unity. Below the surface, deep social divisions ensure that people only bond within their own castes. "Every caste has its own organization," noted the youths. A farmer in the village concurred: "There are differences by caste. The upper castes follow this inequality rule consciously. They don't think it is right to sit with the lower-caste people. The assistance of the lower castes is not considered in any governmental work in the village." Poor people's groups are not linked to any external government or nongovernment sources.

The MOP index for Suchi, which is only 0.16, suggests that social stratification and bonding along caste lines play a role in restricting mobility out of poverty. It is probably also true that a low MOP index reinforces stratification and caste bonding in Suchi since the poor are, on average, less able to assert their rights.

Individual agency plays a big role in climbing out of poverty

In addition to the usual set of human development and economic indicators, which we report later, we focused our lens on psychological factors. These are tied to motivation to work and to overcome obstacles.

Perhaps the biggest surprise is the strong independent association of psychological factors with mobility, even after we control for a large range of other independent variables. We used three proxies for individual agency: sense of power/rights and self-confidence, control over everyday decisions, and aspirations for oneself and one's children. For illustrative purposes, a unit increase on the ladder of power and rights is associated with 4.7 percent increase in the rate of moving out of poverty. The results are even more dramatic for aspirations. A unit increase in aspirations increases the rate of moving out of poverty by 14 percent.

Given that mobility status is not self-reported but assigned by the community, the findings on individual agency are clearly not attributable to the same subject bias. In addition, the agency measures such as position on a ladder of power and rights are based on initial conditions, that is, on the position 10 years ago, again minimizing bias. The pattern of results is confirmed by the descriptive statistics as well as the qualitative data across communities and life stories.

Respondents were asked, "On a 10-step ladder of power and rights, where are you today?" The movers on average placed themselves at 4.4, compared to an average of 2.2 for the chronic poor.[26] They also reported having greater control over everyday decisions than those in poverty (table 4.10). Again, OBC and general category movers did better than SCs. But it seems that organizational activity and the politics of dignity favoring the Dalits in the 1990s had some impact on their empowerment, as the chronic poor among the SCs report levels of improvement in sense of control over decisions close to that of the general category. But the biggest gainers were the OBC: in this category there was no difference between the chronic poor and the movers in scores on control over daily decision making.

The qualitative data also confirm the importance of individual agency. Across communities in UP, people speak poetically and passionately about the importance of self-confidence. A girls' group in Fateh Garh village in

TABLE 4.10

Perceptions about control in daily decision making, by mobility group and caste group, Uttar Pradesh

| Mobility group | % saying control over their everyday decisions has improved in the last 10 years | | | | |
	General	SC	OBC	Muslim	Total
Movers	47.5	41.7	46.1	48.3	46.1
Chronic poor	26.1	24.6	46.1	38.5	32.4

Jaunpur said, "If a poor person wants to be equal to the people above him, then he will have to have the courage and will to work very hard. Only then he can come out of poverty and can acquire his power." Men in the village of Dostpur, Sitapur, stressed the importance of applying oneself and believing in oneself: "If somebody works with full devotion and hard work, he can extract oil even out of stones."

Individual agency can have significant negative spillover effects. As with responsiveness of local democracy, we find a negative coefficient on the leave-out mean for aspirations, power and rights, and control over everyday decisions, suggesting that one person's agency or sense of power limits the opportunities for others. This negative impact is probably stronger in environments of limited economic opportunity. The net impact of agency (adding the coefficient of, say, the aspirations indicator with the coefficient of its LOM) is also negative. Metaphorically, one can compare it to a community-wide race where there is only one prize: if one wins, the other loses. In the villages, these races are being run between caste groups.

In the village of Teriya in Sitapur, for instance, the opening of a sugar mill has disproportionately benefited the landed households at the top of the ladder, leading to a rise in economic inequality. Groups of both men and women speak of a persistent social jealousy. "The inequality of self-interest still persists substantially. Destroying others' work makes one's own work easy," said a participant in the men's group. The women agreed, "The state of discrimination has reached to an extent that if their neighbor is eating bread and salt, then people are happy. But if he cooks pulses and bread, then they are jealous and will do everything to harm him."

The presence of such jealousy is further confirmed by quantitative findings on trust. When asked whether one has to be alert to someone taking advantage of them in their village, nearly 72 percent of all respondents interviewed for the questionnaire agreed strongly. Our qualitative data also revealed that affirmative action policies like reservations—reserving certain jobs for persons of specific social categories—are deepening social cleavages and increasing jealousy between groups in some areas. In a village in Bahraich, women said, "The government is increasing these [social] gaps. When there is an opportunity for employment, then we are told that this is a reserved vacancy. If there is a vacancy in the school, the post will remain vacant till the person of the reserved category comes to fill in the post. Those posts are not filled by capable people of the unreserved category, even though the person of the unreserved category is more competent."

Importance of assets, health, education, and livelihoods

The importance of education for higher returns to labor and of owning assets to get through hard times is widely understood. Our regression results also suggest direct and significant associations between mobility and higher education and between mobility and ownership of assets, especially homes and land. Health shocks, on the other hand, have a significant negative association with individual mobility, signaling once again the importance of affordable health care in supporting poverty escapes. In addition to directly influencing mobility, both asset ownership and a lower incidence of health shocks also work through individual agency to facilitate a move out of poverty by increasing the ability of individuals to take actions on their own behalf.[27]

The descriptive findings demonstrate the differences across mobility and caste groups. On average, the movers in our sample had completed their primary education, while those stuck in chronic poverty were either unschooled or had to drop out of school. Almost 50 percent of the general category movers had secondary education, followed closely by OBC movers at 40 percent, compared to only 25 percent for SC movers. In contrast, more than 40 percent of the SC movers are illiterate (annex figure 4.A). On average, the general and OBC category households are better educated than the SCs.[28]

The mobility groups also differ in land ownership, with nearly 87 percent of mover households holding legal title to land, compared to 70 percent of the chronic poor. The OBCs outscore all other categories in land ownership, even the general category. This confirms the gains made by OBCs as a landowning class in UP over the past few decades.

More movers are involved in high-return agriculture, while the chronic poor are predominantly involved in daily wage labor and casual work. But among both movers and the chronic poor, there are strong caste differences in sources of income. Among movers, the general category (48 percent) and OBCs (44 percent) rely primarily on agriculture; the SC group relies primarily on day labor. Among the chronic poor, day labor rises to 89 percent for the SCs, while for the general and OBC groups, it goes up to 55 percent and 66 percent respectively.

Our analysis thus confirms that the movers and chronic poor in our sample differ in terms of assets such as land and education level and that the SCs remain disadvantaged, despite gains reported in the broader literature. This could be another reason why temporary work is an important source of livelihood among the chronic poor, particularly the SCs. For people with no land and no education, daily wage labor is often the only way to meet their basic needs—and it is rarely sufficient to move out of poverty (box 4.5).

BOX 4.5
Caste and class

Bhadrasi village in Bahraich district illustrates how caste distinctions in Uttar Pradesh spill over into class differences. According to the key informants interviewed in this village, the SCs or Harijans "are the poorest ones." Those belonging to the general and OBC categories—Vermas, Yadavs, Thakurs, and Pandits—"enjoy good social status." While there is social harmony among all caste groups, there are clear differences in livelihoods practiced and lifestyles followed. The Harijans, both men and women, are laborers working in the fields, while the farmland belongs to those from the general and OBC categories. The informants added, "Most of the general and OBC group families have an electricity connection. Only five or six families of the Harijan caste have such a connection. They do not feel the need for electricity. They think that for them, the fan is sufficient. Moreover, even if they do get a connection, they cannot afford to pay the electricity bill."

In the village of Jigna in Lakhimpur Kheri district, Harijans and Muslims together occupy the lowest step on the ladder of life. A men's discussion group in the village described this population: "They do not have any land and do labor work on the farms or in other people's houses. Their wages range from 30 to 40 rupees. The women of these families also work on the farms. They are not educated people, and their children too do not obtain any education. There are many people in our village, especially the Harijans and the Muslims, who are in this condition and have remained so because they do not have any land. Hence today they are doing labor work. Some of these people have ancestral loans that they have to repay, and their entire life goes to pay these loans. They are unable to save as they earn daily and eat daily." Economic and social inequalities further spill into political inequalities. The Brahmins are "respected a lot and the Kurmis [OBCs] are economically prosperous. The Brahmins are also politically strong in the village because the local leader is also a Brahmin. These people are educated, and they have contacts with the politicians, whereas the Muslims and the Harijans have very little political power."

Factors influencing upward movement of poor households

Some poor women and men work hard and manage to move up, but not far enough to cross the poverty line. Are the factors influencing movement upward and out of poverty any different from the factors influencing movement upward that does not take one out of poverty? To test this, we ran the same set of regressions, but this time instead of focusing on movers who were initially poor and crossed the community poverty line, we included all initially poor people who showed any upward movement, irrespective of whether or not they crossed the CPL. The results are reported in annex table 4.K.

The factors associated with all upward movement of the poor (MPI) were mostly the same as those associated with movement out of poverty (MOP). Membership in an SC category had a significant negative association with any upward movement. Changes in access to irrigation inputs had a positive *and* significant association with upward mobility of poor households, indicating the crucial role that expansion of irrigation structures could play. Once again, local-level democracy played a significant positive role, but the leave-out mean for democracy was negative and significant, indicating a zero-sum game in the distribution of benefits among the poor.[29]

Conclusions and Policy Implications

The Moving Out of Poverty research in Uttar Pradesh establishes several important empirical findings that have policy implications.

First, the study confirms the lower mobility of scheduled castes in Uttar Pradesh, despite some progress. Individual caste membership does appear to act as a constraint on households' movement out of poverty. Interestingly, social divisions do not seem to affect mobility rates at the community level: these are not sensitive to the share of SC population in a community. This implies that social divisions act as a contextual variable—as a given in community life in rural UP. What matters for overall community mobility are factors normally associated with development, namely, a higher level of prosperity and a responsive local democracy. However, both economic institutions and local democratic institutions may act differently in relation to different social groups within communities; in particular, they may impose barriers to the mobility of SC households within a village.

Our findings suggest that SCs do not lack aspirations to do well, but they are more likely to suffer from unfair pricing in markets, and they have more limited ability to contact their local government. This group's chances of moving out of poverty could be improved by making the local leadership and democratic structure more responsive to their needs through mechanisms such as free and fair elections and better access to information on local government programs. The SC groups need assets like education, houses, and land. It is striking to note that reservation policies for OBCs in previous decades seem to have had a dramatic impact on the status of OBCs, who now either keep pace with or outperform even the general caste group on most development indicators.

Second, the study holds striking implications for the importance of individual agency in poverty reduction. Even after we control for a wide range of factors, the individual's own self-confidence, sense of power, and aspirations for the future emerge as a significant factor influencing mobility. People who manage to move up the ladder typically cite their own initiative to improve either their farming or their business ventures as the most important reason for their success. Their agency, however, occurs in a context of larger structural factors over which poor people have little control. Experience elsewhere suggests that belonging to self-help and civic action groups may enhance a sense of self-belief and empowerment among poor people, including women. The virtual absence of such groups in the sample communities of UP points to possible policy interventions to create them, based on borrowing and learning from experiences in other states, including Andhra Pradesh. Such policies would be critical in nurturing perhaps the only start-up asset that poor people have: confidence in their own abilities to improve their fate.

Third, the findings confirm that falling into poverty is primarily a story of shocks, particularly health-related shocks. Families facing serious illness or injury are forced to either sell their assets or go into debt. Such an event can launch an entire household into a downward spiral of poverty. Safety nets like health insurance coupled with improvements to public health infrastructure and access to credit could go a long way toward reducing poor people's vulnerability to falling further. Health shocks also contribute to keeping poor people poor, despite their hard work.

Fourth, the research finds that local panchayats, village-level democratic structures, can play a significant role in poor people's mobility. But corruption and clientelism within these structures means that their impact on mobility is often negative. The data suggest that these bodies typically benefit some at the cost of others, redistributing zero-sum goods to a chosen few. Social connections, caste, and contacts decide who gets a share of the pie and who doesn't. However, our data also show that local democracies can have positive spillover effects for all, provided that accountability mechanisms like better access to information and free and fair voting are in place.

Finally, the study confirms tremendous variation in mobility across communities and the importance of community prosperity for overall poverty reduction. Infrastructure, particularly roads that link communities to new economic opportunities, can be a strong trigger for improved prosperity, as can educational facilities. But increased opportunities are not necessarily equal opportunities. In the socially divided context of UP, what matters is who is able to take advantage of available opportunities; they and not others will have the chance to escape and stay out of poverty. For policy makers and practitioners, therefore, it is not enough to build a road to a market; one also needs to worry about how local processes of inclusion and exclusion will affect who gains access to and can sustain participation in the market, and whether the market gives poor farmers fair prices for their crops. Policies that ensure fair dealing in prices can be one mechanism to generate more pro-poor growth.

In the 60 years since independence, Uttar Pradesh has achieved a remarkable level of sustainable democracy at the local level. It has done so despite a socially heterogeneous population reflected in decades of coalition politics. Our study findings suggest that democracy and local leaders, when they are responsive to all citizens, can help poor men and women move out of poverty. The return to power of the Bahujan Samaj Party—originally a Dalit party, now a Dalit-Brahmin combination—means a return to one-party rule in the state and the end of the unstable politics that has hampered UP's development over the past few years. It also gives the poor in Uttar Pradesh, particularly the Dalits, a new chance to use local-level democratic structures as a means of improving their fate and catching up with other social groups.

The challenge will be to support economic, social, and political opportunities for Dalits while expanding opportunities for all, so that social cleavages do not grow wider. Increasing the size of the economic pie will be critical, and investment in roads and agriculture can play a crucial role here. While roads can lead to benefits for all, policies for agricultural improvement will need to be implemented with careful attention to fairness in access and distribution. Otherwise, the caste dynamics in places like Khiria Khurd, the village described at the start of this chapter, will defeat all efforts made by poor caste groups to access economic opportunities and move out of poverty.

Annex 4.1 Economic, Social, and Political Indicators, Uttar Pradesh

ANNEX TABLE 4.A

Compound annual growth rate (CAGR) of total and per capita income in Uttar Pradesh and India since 1951

Period	CAGR of total income (%)		CAGR of per capita income (%)	
	UP	India	UP	India
1951–56	2.0	3.6	0.5	1.7
1956–61	1.9	4.0	0.3	1.9
1961–66	1.6	2.2	−0.2	0.0
1966–69	0.3	4.0	−1.5	1.8
1969–74	2.3	3.3	0.4	1.1
1974–79	5.7	5.3	3.3	2.9
1981–85	3.9	4.9	1.5	2.7
1985–90	5.7	5.8	3.3	3.6
1990–92	3.1	2.5	1.1	0.4
1992–97	3.2	6.8	1.4	4.9
1997–2002	3.1	5.3	1.0	3.3
2002–05	3.7	6.7	1.6	4.9

Source: Singh 2007, using data from the UP government's Five Year Plan documents.

ANNEX TABLE 4.B

Annual percentage change in gross state domestic product in constant prices, Uttar Pradesh, 1994–2003

Period	Primary sector	Secondary sector	Tertiary sector	All sectors
1994–95	3.07	14.20	3.91	5.79
1995–96	1.94	5.68	4.25	3.69
1996–97	9.40	14.74	9.60	10.74
1997–98	−4.82	0.28	4.38	−0.09
1998–99	3.33	2.01	2.68	2.75
1999–2000	8.90	0.11	5.71	5.49
2000–01	−0.67	1.15	2.84	1.14
2001–02	2.34	6.83	4.70	4.33
2002–03	−4.90	5.00	2.50	0.14
2003–04[a]	4.90	7.20	6.20	5.90
2004–05[b]	4.10	4.80	6.20	5.20
CAGR	2.60	4.30	5.30	4.00

Source: Singh 2007.

a. Provisional estimates.

b. Quick estimates.

ANNEX TABLE 4.C
Assembly results, Uttar Pradesh, 1989–2007

Party	1989		1991		1993		1996		2002		2007	
	Seats	%	Seats	%	Seats	%	Seats	%	Seats	%	Seats	%
Congress	94	27.9	46	17.3	28	15.0	33	8.4	25	9.0	22	5.5
BJP	57	11.6	221	31.5	178	33.0	174	32.5	88	20.1	51	12.7
Janata Dal	208	29.7	92	18.8	27	12.4	7	2.6	0	0.0	0	0.0
SP	0	0.0	34	12.5	109	17.9	109	19.7	143	25.2	97	24.1
BSP	13	9.4	12	9.4	69	11.3	67	11.2	98	23.2	206	51.2
CPI	6	1.6	4	1.0	3	0.7	1	0.6	0	0.0	0	0.0
CPM	2	0.4	1	0.3	1	0.5	1	0.5	2	0.3	0	0.0
Others	5	3.9	2	1.8	2	2.3	3	0.6	31	17.4	10	2.5
Independent	40	15.5	7	7.4	8	6.9	9	6.1	15	4.8	16	4.0

Source: CSDS Data Unit, Centre for the Study of Developing Societies, Delhi.

Note: Percentages represent percentages of votes polled. BJP = Bharatiya Janta Party; SP = Samajwadi Party; BSP = Bahujan Samaj Party; CPI = Communist Party of India; CPM = Communist Party of India (Marxist).

ANNEX TABLE 4.D
Composition of landholding categories by social group, Uttar Pradesh, 1983 and 1999/2000

percent

Landholding category, 1983	SC/ST Hindu	Non-SC/ST Hindu	Muslim	Other non- Hindu	Total
Top 1 percent	3.1	82.4	10.5	4.1	100
Top 10 percent	5.8	85.2	7.7	1.3	100
Top 25 percent	9.3	81.1	9.0	0.6	100
Bottom 30 percent	33.2	47.0	19.3	0.6	100

Landholding category, 1999/2000	SC/ST Hindu	OBC Hindu	Upper- caste Hindu	Muslim	Other non- Hindu	Total
Top 1 percent	4.01	30.33	55.96	6.36	3.34	100
Top 10 percent	7.54	37.22	46.03	7.42	1.79	100
Top 25 percent	11.52	41.39	38.01	8.15	0.93	100
Bottom 30 percent	34.35	29.82	16.98	17.71	1.15	100

Source: Srivastava 2007.

Note: The 1983 survey did not give results for OBC Hindu and upper-caste Hindu households separately.

ANNEX TABLE 4.E
Distribution of adult males within social groups by education status, Uttar Pradesh, 1983 and 1999/2000

percent

Social group, 1983	Not literate	Literate through other means	Below primary	Primary	Middle	Secondary	Higher than secondary
SC/ST Hindu	27.2	22.0	18.4	16.1	14.5	9.5	5.1
Non-SC/ST Hindu	53.8	52.6	67.2	72.1	75.7	79.9	84.3
Muslim	18.7	24.3	13.7	10.9	8.5	9.0	8.4
Other non-Hindu	0.3	1.1	0.6	0.9	1.3	1.6	2.2
Total	100	100	99.9	100	100	100	100

Social group, 1999/2000	Not literate	Literate through other means	Below primary	Primary	Middle	Secondary	Higher than secondary
SC/ST Hindu	32.5	15.3	22.5	22.5	20.4	14.8	12.1
OBC Hindu	36.3	24.2	35.2	38.7	36.7	32.4	30.5
Upper-caste Hindu	9.9	16.9	22.5	22.6	31.8	42.2	50.0
Muslim	20.9	41.1	19.0	15.0	10.0	9.3	6.2
Other non-Hindu	0.5	2.5	0.9	1.2	1.0	1.3	1.2
Total	100	100	100	100	100	100	100

Source: Srivastava 2007.

Note: The 1983 survey did not give results for OBC Hindu and upper-caste Hindu households separately.

ANNEX TABLE 4.F

Disparities in socioeconomic status of social groups, Uttar Pradesh, 1999/2000

	SC/ST Hindu	OBC Hindu	Upper-caste Hindu	Muslim	Other non-Hindu	Total
Average landholding (ha)	0.30	0.65	0.88	0.33	1.20	0.58
Regular workers (%)	7.01	7.00	19.76	9.79	13.34	10.37
Literate (%)	49.26	61.52	86.55	48.67	81.58	63.63
Graduates (%)	3.34	3.65	16.92	2.36	12.29	7.01

Source: Srivastava 2007.

Note: Regular workers are those who have a job and earn a regular wage or salary. Graduates are those who have been enrolled in and/or completed college (a bachelor's degree or above).

Annex 4.2 Sample Blocks and Districts in Uttar Pradesh

Sample no.	Block	District	Region	Wage growth	Infra-structure	Irrigation	SC/ST concentration
1	Bijauli	Aligarh	Western	Low	High	Low	Low
2	Lodha	Aligarh	Western	Low	High	Low	High
3	Iglas	Aligarh	Western	Low	High	High	High
4	Etmadpur	Agra	Western	Low	High	High	High
5	Fatehbad	Agra	Western	Low	High	Low	Low
6	Achhnera	Agra	Western	Low	High	High	Low
7	Puranpur	Pilibhit	Western	Low	High	Low	High
8	Amariya	Pilibhit	Western	Low	High	High	Low
9	Bisalpur	Pilibhit	Western	Low	High	Low	Low
10	Talbehat	Lalitpur	Southern	Low	Low	High	Low
11	Bar	Lalitpur	Southern	Low	Low	Low	Low
12	Mandawara	Lalitpur	Southern	Low	Low	High	High
13	Bachawan	Raebareli	Central	High	High	High	High
14	Sareni	Raebareli	Central	High	High	Low	Low
15	Salon	Raebareli	Central	High	High	High	Low
16	Gondlamau	Sitapur	Central	High	Low	Low	High
17	Reusa	Sitapur	Central	High	Low	Low	Low
18	Hargaon	Sitapur	Central	High	Low	High	High
19	Isanagar	Lakhimpur Kheri	Central	High	Low	Low	Low
20	Mitauli	Lakhimpur Kheri	Central	High	Low	High	High
21	Phoolbehar	Lakhimpur Kheri	Central	High	Low	High	Low
22	Machhlishahr	Jaunpur	Eastern	High	High	High	High
23	Khutan	Jaunpur	Eastern	High	High	High	Low
24	Muftiganj	Jaunpur	Eastern	High	High	Low	High
25	Nawabganj	Bahraich	Eastern	High	Low	High	High
26	Jarwal	Bahraich	Eastern	High	Low	Low	Low
27	Tajwapur	Bahraich	Eastern	High	Low	High	Low
28	Soraon	Allahabad	Eastern	High	Low	High	High
29	Karchhana	Allahabad	Eastern	High	Low	Low	Low
30	Dhanupur	Allahabad	Eastern	High	Low	High	Low
31	Babina	Jhansi	Southern	Low	Low	Low	Low
32	Bamaur	Jhansi	Southern	Low	Low	Low	High
33	Bangra	Jhansi	Southern	Low	Low	High	High

Annex 4.3 Community-Level Analysis, Uttar Pradesh

ANNEX TABLE 4.G
Conceptual framework: Community level

Explanatory variable	Source	Coding/directionality
Changes in economic prosperity (PCA index)		
Whether easier or harder to make a living (rc904)	FGD	harder = 1, easier = 2
Trend in community prosperity (rc903)	FGD	less prosperous = 1, more prosperous = 3
Trend in available economic opportunities (rc912)	FGD	fewer = 1, more = 3
Trend in access to economic opportunities (rc917)	FGD	fewer have access = 1, more have access = 3
Local democracy		
Trend in responsiveness of local democracy (rc504b)	KI	less = 1, more = 3
Cooperation of local leaders 10 years ago (rc411)	KI	yes = 1, no = 0
Collective agency		
Trend in participation in community affairs (rc916)	FGD	fewer people participate = 1, more participate = 3
Index of collective action (PCA index[a])		
Coming together to solve water problems 10 years ago (rc412b)	KI	very unlikely = 1, very likely = 4
Coming together to assist each other 10 years ago (rc413b)	KI	very unlikely = 1, very likely = 4
Social stratification		
Extent of social divisions in the village (initial)		
Differences between people based on ethnicity, caste, etc., 10 years ago (c414b)	KI	no division = 1, to a very great extent = 5
Changes in school inequality (PCA index)		
Ethnic/religious discrimination in schools (c305b)	KI	improved = 1, deteriorated = 3
Gender discrimination in schools (c304b)	KI	improved = 1, deteriorated = 3

continued

Explanatory variable	Source	Coding/directionality
Control variables		
Initial share of poor	FGD	percentage of people below community poverty line in male ladder of life discussion
SC share	Census[c]	percentage of SCs in total village population
SC female-male ratio	Census	ratio of female SCs to male SCs in village
Total female-male ratio	Census	ratio of female to male population in village
Land reform program in last 10 years (rc216a)	KI	yes = 1, no = 0
Distance from market (c202bi)	KI	dummy: less than/equal to 12 kilometers = 1, more than 12 kilometers = 0
Initial education facilities rsum(c301i to c301vi)b[b]	KI	yes = 1, no = 0

Note: KI = key informant; FGD = focus group discussion.

a. A PCA was first done on current conditions, and weights were applied to initial conditions 10 years ago. A weighted average of initial conditions (with current weights) was then used as the independent variable on the right-hand side.

b. rsum(c301i to c301vi)b is the weighted sum of educational facilities in the village 10 years ago including primary, lower secondary, upper secondary, technical school, university, and other centers of learning.

c. Census 2001.

ANNEX TABLE 4.H
Factors behind community-level mobility in Uttar Pradesh: OLS outcomes for MPI index

Variable	Base model (1)	SC share (census) (2)	SC female/ male (3)	Total female/ male (4)
Changes in economic prosperity	0.0178**	0.0189**	0.0174**	0.0151**
Market less than 12 kilometers	0.0283	0.0291	0.0275	0.0271
Initial educational facilities	0.0277	0.0262	0.0272	0.0260
Responsiveness of local democracy	0.0049	0.0023	0.0060	0.0053
Cooperation of local leaders	0.0607	0.0581	0.0609	0.0564
Participation in community affairs	−0.0219	−0.0193	−0.0226	−0.0248
Index of collective action	−0.0232	−0.0227	−0.0214	−0.0188
Social divisions	0.0074	0.0059	0.0081	0.0030
School inequality	0.0193	0.0179	0.0186	0.0135
Land reform	0.0132	0.0108	0.0120	0.0174
Initial share of poor	−0.1340	−0.1544	−0.1351	−0.1690
SC share from census data		0.1190		
SC female-male ratio			0.0606	
Total female-male ratio				0.3256*
Constant	0.3974***	0.385***	0.3415**	0.148
N	108	108	107	108
R^2	0.16	0.17	0.16	0.19

Note: Column 1 is the base model; different specifications are shown in columns 2 through 4.

*p < .10   **p < .05   ***p < .01 (White heteroscedasticity-consistent standard errors)

ANNEX TABLE 4.I

Triggers for community prosperity, Uttar Pradesh

Trigger	% of times factor was cited as one of two top positive events in the community over 10 years
Roads/bridges/connectivity	32.3
Education	21.2
Other	14.7
Agricultural improvement	11.8
Irrigation	7.6
Government scheme	7.1
Commercial farming	5.3

Source: Key informants and ladder of life discussion groups (men and women); *N* = 660 positive events listed in 330 discussions in 110 sample communities.

Note: "Other" includes events not covered by the other categories (e.g., provision of electricity, improvements in provision or quality of drinking water, opening of health center, etc.)

Annex 4.4 Household-Level Analysis, Uttar Pradesh

ANNEX FIGURE 4.A

Education levels of movers, by caste group, Uttar Pradesh

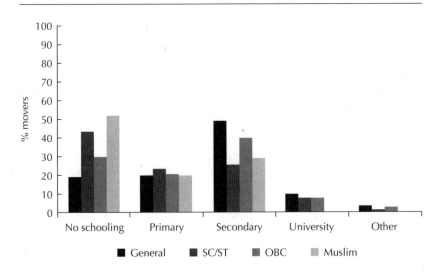

ANNEX TABLE 4.J
Average figures for movers and chronic poor on some key variables from household data, Uttar Pradesh

Variable	Movers	Chronic poor
Initial strength of economy	−0.047	0.077
Change in economic prosperity	−0.050	0.051
Responsiveness of local democracy	0.179	−0.438
LOM of responsiveness of local democracy	−0.013	0.035
Corruption	−0.014	0.028
Fairness index	0.135	0.228
LOM of fairness index	−0.011	0.026
Initial position on 10-step ladder of power and rights	2.878	2.123
LOM of initial position on 10-step ladder of power and rights	3.354	3.444
Control over everyday decisions	2.382	2.318
LOM of control over everyday decisions	2.341	2.348
Household aspirations	0.400	−0.655
LOM of household aspirations	−0.053	0.064
Index of collective action	−0.008	0.029
Access to networks and associations	3.203	3.286
Social divisions	2.275	2.252
School inequality	−0.030	0.025
Violence against women	1.495	1.507
LOM of violence against women	1.483	1.516
Present education status of household head	3.949	2.694
Health shock	0.285	0.391
Initial landholding	2.850	1.409
Ownership of house	0.980	0.969
Assets index	−0.191	−0.419
Livestock index	−0.013	0.020
Change in access to irrigation	3.833	3.856

ANNEX TABLE 4.K
Factors behind household-level mobility in Uttar Pradesh: OLS outcomes for MPI

Variable	Base model
Initial strength of economy	–0.006
Change in economic prosperity	0.002
Responsiveness of local democracy	0.043***
LOM of responsiveness of local democracy	–0.036**
Corruption	–0.011
Fairness index	0.014
LOM of fairness index	–0.019
Initial position on 10-step ladder of power and rights	0.035**
LOM of initial position on 10-step ladder of power and rights	–0.0836***
Control over everyday decisions	0.001
LOM of control over everyday decisions	–0.029
Household aspirations	0.1281***
LOM of household aspirations	–0.1767***
Index of collective action	–0.013
Access to networks and associations	0.013
Social divisions	–0.005
School inequality measure	0.012
Violence against women	0.030
LOM of violence against women	–0.024
Present education status	0.0317***
Health shocks	–0.039
Initial landholding	0.0085**
Ownership of house	0.103
Assets index	0.016
Livestock index	–0.012
Change in access to irrigation	0.0399***
SC dummy	–0.0842**
OBC dummy	–0.047
Constant	0.5735***
Observations	968
R^2	0.30

*p < .10   **p < .05   ***p < .01 (White heteroscedasticity-consistent standard errors)

Annex 4.5 Self-Reported Reasons for Upward/Downward Movement, Uttar Pradesh

Reasons for upward movement

1. Individual initiative: agricultural
   Crop diversification
   Increased crop production because of improved agricultural
      technology, irrigation, or high-yielding variety of seeds
2. Individual initiative: nonagricultural
   New business/better business
3. Job
   Steady job/increase in wages
   Got a job/got a better job
4. Got a government job
5. Higher education/received degree
6. Migration
   Remittances
7. Moved to new residence/made housing improvements
8. New sources/multiple sources of income
9. Hard work
10. Women stepped out to work
11. Increased prosperity
    Increase in community prosperity
    Improved national economy
    More work opportunities
12. Legal title
13. Loan/credit
14. Functioning of government
    Better national government
    Better local government
    Less corruption
    Government contacts
    Improved access to markets (roads, rails, etc.)
    Improved access to government services (water, power, etc.)
    More government assistance
    Improved security (less crime)
15. NGO assistance
16. Community associations/joined a group

17. Family factors
    Marriage
    Divorce/separation
    Fewer children
    Children got married/left home
    Children completed school/got jobs
18. Inheritance
19. Lottery/luck
20. Illegal activities (theft, selling drugs, etc.)
21. Other
    Family and community support
    Health

Reasons for downward movement

1. Health/death shocks
   Health problems/accident/high health expenses
   Death of earning member
   Aging
2. Individual initiative: agricultural
   Low agricultural yield/bad harvest
   Death of animal (cow, goat, etc.)
3. Individual initiative: nonagricultural
   Failure to achieve goal (educational/entrepreneurial)
   Lost a business
   Rise in housing costs/had to move
4. Job loss/unemployment
5. Received less remittances
6. Psychological factors
   Gambling/alcohol/drug addiction
7. Decreasing national/local prosperity
   Vulnerability to market price fluctuations (low output prices/high input
       prices)
   Economy got worse
   High inflation/increase in price of basic necessities
   Inconsistent work opportunities
   Increased restrictions on business/increased taxes
8. Loss of legal title/eviction
   Lost legal title to property
   Evicted from land

9. Credit and debt
   Failure to obtain credit
   Too much debt
10. Functioning of local democracy
    Worse local government
    Worse national government
    More corruption
    Less government assistance
    Rising crime
11. Less NGO assistance
12. Discrimination
    Communal/caste/racial discrimination
13. Family problems/expenses
    Marriage
    Divorce/separation
    Dowry/expenses on death feasts and weddings
    Family size (more children/dependents)
    Problems with children
14. Bad luck
15. Natural disaster (drought, flood, cyclone, river erosion)
16. Other

Annex 4.6 Factors Explaining Movement Out of Poverty in Uttar Pradesh: Outcome of Weighted Household-Level Regressions for Movers

Variable	Movement	Variable	Movement
Initial strength of economy	0.006 [0.40]	Social divisions	0.001 [0.10]
Change in economic prosperity	0.018 [2.97]**	School inequality measure	0.009 [0.82]
Responsiveness of local democracy	0.028 [3.22]**	Violence against women	0.033 [1.56]
LOM of responsiveness of local democracy	0 [0.42]	LOM of violence against women	0 [0.82]
Corruption	−0.011 [1.02]	Present education status of household head	0.027 [4.09]**
Fairness index	0.019 [3.10]**	Health shocks	−0.017 [0.65]
LOM of fairness index	−0.002 [0.63]	Initial landholding	0.015 [2.28]*
Initial position on 10-step ladder of power and rights	0.045 [3.05]**	Ownership of house	0.144 [2.15]*
LOM of initial position on 10-step ladder of power and rights	−0.097 [3.37]**	Assets index	−0.015 [0.38]
Control over everyday decisions	−0.003 [0.17]	Livestock index	0.009 [1.01]
LOM of control over everyday decisions	−0.112 [2.20]*	Change in access to irrigation	−0.007 [0.51]
Household aspirations	0.065 [7.59]**	SC dummy	−0.051 [1.84]
LOM of household aspirations	−0.001 [0.83]	OBC dummy	−0.021 [0.69]
Index of collective action	−0.023 [1.51]	Constant	0.583 [2.92]**
Access to networks and associations	−0.024 [2.00]*	Observations	966
		R^2	0.23

Note: All variables are weighted. Robust *t*-statistics in brackets.

*p < .05   **p < .01

References

Alatas, V., L. Pritchett, and A. Wetterberg. 2007. "Voice Lessons: Evidence on Social Organizations, Government Mandated Organizations, and Governance from Indonesia's Local Level Institutions Study." In *Membership Based Organizations of the Poor*, ed. M. Chen, R. Jhabvala, R. Kanbur, and C. Richards, 313–51. New York: Routledge.

Béteille, A. 1991. *Society and Politics in India: Essays in a Comparative Perspective*. LSE Monographs in Social Anthropology, no. 63. London: Athlone Press.

CMIE (Centre for Monitoring Indian Economy). 2000. *Profiles of Districts*. Mumbai: CMIE.

Dev, S. M., and C. Ravi. 2007. "Poverty and Inequality: All-India and States, 1983–2005." *Economic and Political Weekly*, February 10–26, 509–22.

Dubey, A. K. 2007. "A Case of Majoritarianism Unpacked: The Trials and Tribulations of the Bharatiya Janata Party in Uttar Pradesh." In Pai 2007b, 83–109.

Gupta, S. 2007. "The Rise and Fall of Hindutva in Uttar Pradesh: 1989–2004." In Pai 2007b, 110–35.

Himanshu. 2007. "Recent Trends in Poverty and Inequality: Some Preliminary Results." *Economic and Political Weekly*, February 10–26, 497–508.

Keefer, P., and S. Khemani. 2003. "Democracy, Public Expenditures, and the Poor." Policy Research Working Paper 3164, World Bank, Washington, DC.

Khemani, S. 2008. "The Political Economy of Equalization Transfers." In *Fiscal Equalization: Challenges in the Design of Intergovernmental Transfers*, ed. J. Martinez-Vazquez and B. Searle, 463–84. New York: Springer-Verlag.

Krishna, A. 2004. "Escaping Poverty and Becoming Poor: Who Gains, Who Loses, and Why?" *World Development* 32 (1): 121–36.

———. 2006. "Pathways Out of and Into Poverty in 36 Villages of Andhra Pradesh, India." *World Development* 34 (2): 271–88.

Krishna, A., M. Kapila, M. Porwal, and V. Singh. 2005. "Why Growth Is Not Enough: Household Poverty Dynamics in Northeast Gujarat, India." *Journal of Development Studies* 41 (7): 1163–92.

Lieten, G. K., and R. Srivastava. 1999. *Unequal Partners: Power Relations, Devolution and Development in Uttar Pradesh*. New Delhi: Sage.

Narayan, D., and L. Pritchett. 1999. "Cents and Sociability: Household Income and Social Capital in Rural Tanzania." *Economic Development and Cultural Change* 47 (4): 871–97.

Ojha, R. K. 2007. "Poverty Dynamics in Rural Uttar Pradesh." *Economic and Political Weekly*, April 21–27, 1453–58.

Pai, S. 2007a. "From Dalit to *Savarna*: The Search for a New Social Constituency by the Bahujan Samaj Party in Uttar Pradesh." In Pai 2007b, 221–40.

———, ed. 2007b. *Political Process in Uttar Pradesh: Identity, Economic Reform and Governance*. Delhi: Pearson Education.

Singh, A. K. 2007. "The Economy of Uttar Pradesh since the Nineties: Economic Stagnation and Fiscal Crisis." In Pai 2007b, 273–94.

Srivastava, R. 2007. "Economic Change among Social Groups in Uttar Pradesh: 1983–2000." In Pai 2007b, 345–66.

Tiwari, B. N. 2007. "BJP's Political Strategies: Development, Caste and Electoral Discourse." In Pai 2007b, 136–56.

World Bank. 2002. *Poverty in India: The Challenge of Uttar Pradesh.* New Delhi: World Bank.

———. Forthcoming. *Uttar Pradesh: Changes in Economic Conditions and Indicators of Service Delivery.* New Delhi: World Bank.

Notes

1. Nearly 61 percent of all rural poor in India in 2004–05 were concentrated in seven states: Bihar, Chhattisgarh, Jharkhand, Madhya Pradesh, Orissa, Uttarakhand, and Uttar Pradesh (Dev and Ravi 2007). The only states faring worse than UP on the rural poverty headcount ratio were Bihar, Chhattisgarh, Jharkhand, Madhya Pradesh, and Orissa.

2. UP's performance on poverty reduction was worse than the all-India average in earlier decades. In the 1980s, for instance, rural poverty in UP declined at a rate of 0.47 percent per year compared to a 0.93 percent annual decline for India as a whole.

3. No caste-based census has been undertaken in India since 1931. The first Backward Classes Commission used caste as an explicit criterion to judge backwardness. The government, however, rejected its recommendations because an explicit recognition of caste went against the spirit of the Indian Constitution. Furthermore, while SCs were clearly outcastes, the OBCs faced no such ritual discrimination (Gupta 2007). Later, the Mandal Commission recognized backward classes based on their educational and economic deprivation, but it ended up conflating those who suffered such deprivation with those also backward in the caste hierarchy.

4. These two endpoints were chosen because of the rare availability of caste data for both periods from the NSS. The years in question were covered by an NSS survey on employment and unemployment that distinguished between OBC, SC/ST, and other caste groups.

5. Uttar Pradesh had 71 districts at the time of the 2001 census. However, the number of districts has increased over time, especially in the last decade, and some recently created districts were not reflected in the databases available at the time of the study. Furthermore, in UP a new district may contain areas from several "original" districts. Therefore, it was not possible to extrapolate any indicator value of an original district to a newly created district. This limitation constrained selection, as the CMIE data were available for only 54 undivided districts of UP. Selection was therefore undertaken based on data for only 54 districts and not all 71 districts of the state.

6. In his recent study of the poorest districts in Uttar Pradesh, Ojha (2007) underlines the importance of safety net programs to reduce falling and make poverty reduction policies more effective. He finds that while 13.6 percent of the households in his sample districts moved out of poverty between 1998/99 and 2004/5, nearly 7 percent fell into poverty over the same period, leading to only a 6.6 percent decline in the poverty ratio.

7. Not all data are symmetric, so there is nothing to dictate that the 25th and 75th percentiles would be equidistant (though many people assume this because they are used to having mean plus/minus a standard deviation, which assumes symmetry).

8. We did not use any household-level variables because of the disproportionate household sampling in favor of movers.

9. An R^2 of 0.44 indicates reasonable goodness of fit. However, there is a drawback to overinterpreting this statistic, namely that one might try to include more variables in the model until there is no more room for improvement or until the R^2 becomes 1, indicating that the fitted model explains all the variability in the dependent variable (in this case MOP). In other words, one can try to reduce the omitted variable bias (what the model doesn't explain) by including other relevant control variables. But there is no certainty that the inclusion of additional control variables will reduce the bias or increase the R^2. The addition may increase or decrease the bias, and we cannot know for sure which is the case in any particular situation.

10. Land is an important asset in rural UP and was mentioned frequently in our study as a criterion for ranking households on the ladder of life. Communities that had experienced some kind of land reform spoke of it as a positive event. This was particularly true in villages where SC households had been given land under the state government policy. However, sustained benefits from the reform depended on a host of factors, including the amount of land granted, its quality (whether irrigated or nonirrigated), and whether households could use it for cultivating more remunerative commercial crops and/or combine it with non-farm activities. Access to support facilities like credit and agricultural inputs such as fertilizer also mattered. Thus land reform, while positively associated with mobility, was not sufficient to guarantee it.

11. Some other counterintuitive findings are that school inequality and social divisiveness tend to facilitate rather than hinder MOP. The association, however, is insignificant and nominal in absolute value.

12. This gap may be a reflection of the kind of activities that SC women engage in. Usually poor, scheduled caste women in our sample were found to be working as agricultural wage laborers or in low-return tasks like basket weaving. These activities helped them cope and move up from their initially poor state, but perhaps not to the extent that work helped women belonging to other social groups.

13. By their very nature, roads are nonexcludable, and anyone can use them. But although they undoubtedly helped improve prosperity levels in our sample villages, roads did not necessarily lead to community-wide mobility. Their impact on mobility was more likely to be cited if they were built recently. In communities that had had pucca roads for a few years, the old elites apparently had found new ways of dominating economic life and restricting the opportunities for poor people to prosper.

14. All three factors reported for upward/downward movement were aggregated, and the highest-scoring response was rated as the most important reason for upward or downward movement.

15. The frequencies with which jobs were mentioned by the four mobility categories also confirm the importance of jobs as a trigger for escape. Seventy-six percent of

those identified as chronic poor by their communities were found to be engaged in casual labor; by contrast, only 30 percent of the movers worked as casual labor. Nearly 25 percent of the movers had regular jobs, compared to only 5 percent of the chronic poor.

16. The lower proportion of Muslim households in our sample reflects their lower share in the state's total population. According to the Indian census of 2001, Muslims made up about 18 percent of UP's population. Moreover, Muslim households in UP tend to live in clusters, concentrated in districts such as Ghazipur and Faizabad in the eastern part of the state. Because our research did not cover these districts and because we sampled by mobility, not religious or caste affiliation, the sample includes relatively few Muslim households. Most Muslim households classified as movers in the study, unlike the Hindu caste groups, had a member of the family who had migrated abroad, often to the Middle East.

17. Analysis of data from the National Sample Survey indicates that the rate of poverty decline for SCs between 1994 and 2005 was actually higher than the average for other groups in Uttar Pradesh in rural and especially in urban areas (World Bank, forthcoming). However, despite the progress made, headcount poverty remained higher for SCs than for other groups: that is, SCs narrowed the gap but not enough to eradicate the distance between them and others. Also, while poverty declined among SCs, the pace of decline was faster in urban areas—a trend that is not captured in the study data as the research covered only rural villages in the state. In rural areas, the distribution of the poor actually shifted marginally against the SCs: more SCs in absolute numbers were counted in the ranks of the poor in 2005 than in 1994. This is consistent with their lower probability of moving out of poverty during this period.

18. The numbers in table 4.5 do, however, show that more than one-third of the chronic poor have low aspirations for their children and expect their children to be in a similar position or worse. Thus, a substantial proportion of the poor in the sample apparently believe that they are stuck in intergenerational poverty—a worrying indicator for policy purposes.

19. The dependent variable is a dummy that takes the value 1 if the household was classified by the community as having moved out of poverty from among the set of initially poor, 0 otherwise.

20. The weights are constructed using the actual weights of the movers, the chronic poor, the fallers, and the never poor in each community mobility matrix.

21. Earlier literature also uncovered this process in UP. Keefer and Khemani (2003) and Khemani (2008) show that political incentives can shape decisions made by local government for service delivery. In a socially divided state like UP, where the voter has poor access to information, such incentives lead to the channeling of benefits to those belonging to the leadership's own caste or religion.

22. The association between a responsive local democracy and these factors was confirmed when we ran a linear regression with responsiveness of local democracy as the dependent variable and a variety of independent variables that could potentially influence it (access to information about local government programs, people's voting patterns, whether there had been free and fair elections in the village in the past 10 years, etc.).

23. The positive (though insignificant) association between school inequality and household MOP is troubling. We find it hard to square this piece of evidence with our general storyline.
24. Households in UP recorded the lowest membership in groups compared to households surveyed for the study in other states. In Andhra Pradesh, 42 percent of households surveyed belonged to at least one group, in Assam 53 percent, and in West Bengal 22 percent.
25. The three types of social capital discussed in this section—bonding, bridging, and linking—can be summarized as follows. Bonding social capital includes formal and informal ties among people of similar backgrounds such as relatives, friends, and neighbors, as well as more established local groups like burial societies and dairy cooperatives. Bridging social capital refers to ties among people who are unlike each other. For purposes of this study, we use the term to mean horizontal ties between people who are different in some ways but who are basically of the same status or level of socioeconomic well-being. For instance, the term might describe contacts between different livelihood groups, such as a farmer's group and a watershed management group, or between people of different religious or ethnic backgrounds who have similar levels of well-being. Linking social capital refers to vertical ties between people of different status, such as between a patron and client, a doctor and patient, or a teacher and student.
26. When asked to place themselves on a similar 10-step ladder 10 years ago, the movers placed themselves at 2.9, compared to an average step of 2.1 chosen by the chronic poor.
27. The association between agency and these factors was confirmed when we ran a linear regression with an individual's current position on a ladder of rights as the dependent variable and independent variables that could potentially influence it (asset ownership 10 years ago, incidence of health shocks over 10 years, etc.).
28. In the survey, the education level of the household head is measured in 2005, but it is unlikely to have changed significantly over the previous 10 years for an adult head of household.
29. The association between the leave-out mean variable for responsiveness and individual movement out of poverty was negative but not significant.

People's Organizations and Poverty Escapes in Rural Andhra Pradesh

Deepa Narayan, Giovanna Prennushi, and Soumya Kapoor

Our hands used to shake earlier, now we can even talk to the chief minister!

> —MEMBERS OF A SELF-HELP GROUP,
> Pulagampalle, Anantapur district,
> Andhra Pradesh

Before we joined the group, we were limited only to the kitchen, without freedom. Now we have reached a stage where we can take independent decisions.

> —MEMBERS OF A SELF-HELP GROUP,
> Vellamaddi, Anantapur district,
> Andhra Pradesh

India
018   017
015
I32

Govindapalle village in Anantapur district, Andhra Pradesh, saw remarkable changes in the decade between 1995 and 2005. A water tank was constructed and clean water supplied to houses through the Satya Sai scheme run by a charitable faith organization. A cement and concrete road and a bus stand were built. The school was expanded to include grades 8 to 10. Employment opportunities improved after the central government opened a seed and dairy farm close to the village. A group of men in Govindapalle described these developments as "giving life to our villagers." They added, "We are living happily like *moodu puvvulu aaru kaayalu*," meaning "a tree with three flowers and six fruits."

Located in one of the mandals, or blocks, where self-help groups were launched earliest, Govindapalle also witnessed a remarkable expansion of these groups, from two in 1995 to 26 a decade later. The groups were reported to have helped reduce entrenched social divisions, including gender inequality and caste distinctions. They provided villagers a platform to demand greater accountability from local government, obliging local leaders to become more responsive to their constituents' concerns. The groups were also credited with empowering poor women through greater self-reliance, financial independence, and access to opportunities.

Still, all was not well in Govindapalle. During the same decade, the village experienced a prolonged drought that severely reduced people's chances of moving out of poverty. A group of men in the village talked about the farmers' plight: "All the crops here in our village are rain-dependent. Due to lack of rain, our wells and bore wells have dried up. There have been no crops in our village for many years. God has no mercy on us even if we worship."

The story of Govindapalle is emblematic of the situation in poor, rural Andhra Pradesh in the decade that began in the mid-1990s. With 76 million people, Andhra Pradesh (AP) is the fifth-largest Indian state. After trailing

235

during the first half of the 1990s, the state's growth rate, at almost 6 percent, exceeded the national average of 5.4 percent in the second half of the 1990s. Monetary poverty declined and social indicators improved. But the main driver of growth over this period was the services sector; agriculture experienced slow growth and households dependent on rainfed agriculture had a hard time coping. A rash of farmer suicides shook the state.

Poor people in Govindapalle credit the self-help groups (SHG) with bringing about notable collective and individual benefits. The groups are a key component of AP's poverty reduction strategy and received substantial public support under the state's Velugu program (later renamed Indira Kranti Patham) and other schemes.[1] Other public programs complemented support to SHGs, notably permanent housing and schools built under the Rural Development Trust, credit to farmers extended through cooperatives and government banks, and programs targeting scheduled tribes.

The data collected in Andhra Pradesh as part of the Moving Out of Poverty study provide some insights into poverty trends over time and into the role of these programs in helping households move out of poverty. This chapter examines the extent and dynamics of poverty in the study villages in AP and the influence of people's own organizations. While it does not evaluate the impact of self-help groups, the study looks at their contribution to helping poor people escape poverty over the long term. It finds that poverty is perceived to have declined and that self-help groups brought considerable benefits to the communities in which they operated and to their members, helping some of them move out of poverty.

Study Features and the State Context

In Andhra Pradesh, the study was conducted in 56 villages in three districts. The three districts visited—Adilabad, Anantapur, and Srikakulam—were among the poorest six in the state in 2000 and were therefore selected for the Velugu program when it was launched. Within each district, the study revisited the villages that had been surveyed in 2004 for the midterm appraisal of the first District Poverty Initiative Project, or DPIP I (CESS 2005). These villages, known as DPIP Phase I villages, were all in poor mandals (in Andhra Pradesh, a mandal is the administrative unit below district, equivalent to a block).[2] While the sample was not randomly selected and thus is not representative of rural AP or even of the three districts, it nonetheless provides a rich picture of the lives of poor people in 56 rural villages in relatively remote and less prosperous parts of the state.

Data collection tools

In each sample village in Andhra Pradesh, the study teams conducted interviews with three or four key informants; held focus groups with men and women to discuss factors that help or hinder movement out of poverty, as well as ideas about freedom and democracy; asked youth groups about their aspirations for the future; and conducted in-depth interviews, including both surveys and life stories, with 15 households (most often with a female respondent). The information gathered reflects the sometimes contrasting views of different segments of society.

As in the three other Indian states where the study was conducted, an exercise called ladder of life provided key input (see appendix 1 in this volume). Participants in a focus group, usually five or six men or women, defined steps on a "ladder" corresponding to levels of well-being in their village and then placed each household in the village on a step. The group was next asked to identify the step at which households were no longer considered poor. The imaginary line between this step and the ones below was designated the community poverty line (CPL), thus providing a context-specific definition of poverty. Finally, they were asked to identify households that had moved up or down the ladder over the 10 years prior to the survey (1995–2005). This exercise generated a community mobility matrix with four categories:

- *Movers:* households that were poor in 1995 but moved out of poverty by 2005
- *Chronic poor:* households that were poor in 1995 and remained poor in 2005
- *Fallers:* households that were not poor in 1995 but fell into poverty by 2005
- *Never poor:* households that were not poor in 1995 and remained not poor in 2005 (also called the "chronic rich")

Figure 5.1 reproduces the mobility matrix of one of the AP sample communities, Seedhi village in Srikakulam district. In this community, focus group participants identified five steps on the ladder of life and placed the poverty line between steps 3 and 4. One hundred twenty households were considered to be in poverty in 1995; in the ensuing decade, 105 of them remained poor while 15 moved above the poverty line. Six households fell into poverty in the same period.

FIGURE 5.1
Community mobility matrix for Seedhi village, Andhra Pradesh

Steps		Now					
		1	2	3	4	5	Total
10 years ago	1	6, 11, 19, 37, 38, 39, 41, 47, 48, 51, 53, 54, 55, 58, 62, 63, 69, 76, 77, 79, 81, 83, 87, 95, 97, 104, 107, 108, 120, 143, 144, 145, 146	2, 4, 9, 10, 13, 21, 22, 25, 32, 36, 40, 42, 45, 46, 49, 52, 65, 74, 78, 85, 86, 105, 127, 142, 147	50			59
	2	14, 59, 123	43, 67, 72, 89, 92, 122, 132	1, 8, 24, 28, 29, 60, 84, 94, 106, 109, 118, 130, 148, 149	121	5	26
	3		124	7, 20, 26, 27, 35, 71, 75, 90, 96, 102, 103, 110, 112, 113, 115, 117, 119, 128, 131, 134, 137	64, 70, 80, 125, 141	18, 31, 68, 88, 93, 99, 100, 150	35
	4			101, 129, 133, 136, 139	116, 126, 138	30, 135	10
	5			16		3, 12, 15, 17, 23, 33, 34, 56, 66, 73, 82, 111	13
	Total	36	33	42	9	23	143

Note: Bold lines indicate the community poverty line. A total of 150 households were sorted; participants could not give the status for seven households.

The ladder of life exercise makes it possible to look at poverty dynamics both at the community level, by using the whole matrix, and at the household level, by looking at a particular household's movement up or down. While the problems common to recall data are relevant here, the exercise is a good way to get information on changes over time in the absence of panel data.[3]

Historical and socioeconomic context of the study villages

The three districts visited in Andhra Pradesh share a common story of under-development and isolation. The Centre for Monitoring Indian Economy (CMIE) index ranks individual districts on availability of infrastructure in relation to an all-India average. It confirms that the six DPIP I districts, including the three covered by the Moving Out of Poverty study, fell well below the AP average in 2000 (table 5.1).

The economy of rural Andhra Pradesh has been centered on agriculture for centuries. Nearly 70 percent of the state's rural population depends on rainfed agriculture for their livelihood. The state has a tradition of barrage and canal water irrigation dating to the time of the British, but most such assured sources of irrigation remain concentrated in South Coastal Andhra, which has the highest agricultural output per hectare in the state (Dev 2007). The other parts of AP, including all three districts in our sample, depend primarily on tank or well irrigation. In the regions of Telangana (where Adilabad is located) and Rayalseema (where Anantapur lies), well irrigation has become the dominant irrigation mode, replacing tanks, because of improper maintenance of tanks or encroachment on tank beds by farmers. This has brought about a gradual depletion of groundwater tables, leading to acute water scarcity in times of persistent drought.

TABLE 5.1
Infrastructure rankings of Andhra Pradesh districts, 2000

District	Average CMIE index
Hyderabad district	153.7
Non-DPIP I districts (without Hyderabad) (16)	102.3
DPIP I districts (6)	88.8
All AP districts (23)	102.1

Source: CMIE 2000.

Note: The infrastructure indicators used for computing the CMIE index include access to transport, energy, irrigation, banking, communication, education, and health.

Figure 5.2 shows the three study districts in Andhra Pradesh. While similar to each other in some respects, they differ in others. Anantapur has been most severely affected by drought. This district, now recognized as one of the poorest and most backward in all of South India, received in recent years an average rainfall of 521 millimeters per year, compared to a state average of 925 millimeters (Ghosh 2004). In contrast, Srikakulam, which is on the coast and has some dense forest cover, received only slightly less than adequate rainfall over the last decade. Adilabad fell in between the other two. Lack of water proved to be disastrous for cultivation of rainfed crops like maize, which is grown in large quantities in Anantapur (World Bank 2006). The high level of risk faced by households in Anantapur is illustrated by the fact that

FIGURE 5.2
Sample districts in Andhra Pradesh

75 percent of all households surveyed there for the DPIP midterm appraisal in 2004 had faced at least one incident of drought, compared with 50 percent in Srikakulam and 12 percent in Adilabad. The population of Srikakulam is also relatively protected from the impact of drought because fewer people are engaged in farming than in Adilabad or Anantapur. Erratic rainfall coupled with dependence on groundwater irrigation contributed to slow growth in Anantapur in the study period. Between 1993 and 2004, the district's gross domestic product grew on average 3.8 percent per year, compared to 5.3 percent in Adilabad and 6 percent in Srikakulam (Dev 2007).

Beyond such economic disparities, the three districts in our sample also followed very different historical trajectories of social and political development (Srinivasulu 2002). The state of Andhra Pradesh was formed in 1956 by bringing together three regions—Telangana in the northwest, Coastal Andhra along the coast, and Rayalseema in the southwest—that shared the Telugu language but had separate governance systems. Until 1956, the Telangana region (where Adilabad lies) was a separate state under the rule of a Muslim ruler called the Nizam, while Coastal Andhra (where Srikakulam lies) and Rayalseema (where Anantapur lies) were part of the British Madras Presidency. Villages in the Telangana region were primarily feudal and remained outside the reach of most development activities that were taking place in the provinces of the British Madras Presidency, such as construction of canals. A dominant landowning class included Muslim and Hindu upper-caste landlords called *doras*. They imposed a system of forced labor, called *vetti*, in which peasants worked for free on their farms in exchange for the patronage they received from their "benefactors."

Anti-feudal agitation under the Nizam's rule and tenancy reforms after India's independence led to migration of the doras from this region. In most cases, the absentee landlords sold their land to their former tenants. But the groups that benefited from these reforms were those, like the Kapus and the Reddys, who were already dominant in the village society, occupied the middle rung in the caste hierarchy between the Brahmins and the Dalits, and constituted the vast majority of the tenants. These erstwhile peasant cultivator tenants made the most of the reforms, while the lower-caste Dalits mostly remained landless and confined to the ranks of the vetti laborers. In other words, the reforms merely replaced one landlord class with another, perhaps an even more aggressive one (Srinivasulu 1999), and the practice of vetti continued in districts such as Adilabad. Later, the antifeudal agitation broadened into a wider movement, with Dalit and youth activists demanding better labor practices and separate statehood for Telangana. In all its stages and forms, however, the movement remained primarily a struggle of low-class people against their high-class oppressors rather than a conflict between castes per se.

In contrast to the class politics of Telangana, districts in Coastal Andhra (including Srikakulam) witnessed mobilization along caste lines. Such mobilization coincided with four broad events in the history of the state. First, while districts like Srikakulam along the northern coastline were part of the British residency, they were amalgamated in the residency at a later stage. In these districts, the British continued with a form of permanent revenue settlement, appointing the village landlords as collectors of tax on their behalf. Thus, in northern districts like Srikakulam, as opposed to other districts like Anantapur in Rayalseema, a tradition of landlord-tenant relations dominated all forms of economic life. Divisions between landlords and lower-caste laborers were therefore more evident historically in Srikakulam than in, say, Anantapur.

Second, the arrival of the Green Revolution and more capital-intensive techniques in agriculture strengthened the hold of landowners in North Coastal Andhra. Better farming techniques ended up disproportionately benefiting the landowning class, which used them to increase their stranglehold on local village economies. Third, the emergence of the Telugu Desam Party in the early 1980s gave peasant cultivator groups like Kamma and Kapu landowners from North Coastal Andhra a political vehicle and a base in state politics, which until then had been dominated by the Reddys. Fourth, better education among the Dalits in this region, along with the formation of a Dalit political body (the Dalit Maha Sabha) in 1985, deepened social fissures between them and their upper-caste patrons. The latter slowly started using political power to suppress the Dalits even further. As a result of all these factors, the 1980s witnessed a string of upper-caste atrocities including mass killings of Dalits in the region (APCLC 1991). The Kammas and Kapus tried to exploit their newfound political voice to gain further dominance, while the Dalits tried to find a voice for the first time.

In sum, it is clear that Andhra Pradesh has had a checkered history of widespread caste- and class-based antagonism. These inequalities are deeply rooted in the social structure of the state and have played out in their worst forms in districts like Adilabad and Srikakulam. It is in this milieu that self-help groups began to operate. Supported on a small scale in the 1980s and 1990s by nongovernmental organizations and development agencies like the United Nations Development Programme, UNICEF, and the World Bank, they have emerged over the past decade as a serious policy tool for reducing poverty. Recognizing both the potential of the groups and the possibility of tapping into a constituency of poor women voters, successive state governments launched a series of initiatives to scale up SHGs (Suri 2002). Any assessment of these groups' contribution to increased mobility out of poverty and improved well-being has to take into account the difficult and varied circumstances in which they operated.

Poverty Dynamics in the Study Areas

In this complex context, what does it mean to be poor? The ladder of life exercises provide part of the answer. Table 5.2 presents ladders constructed by focus groups in two communities in different districts. The bottom step of each ladder is occupied by those who are the poorest and worst off in the community, while the top step is reserved for the richest and best off. The bold lines indicate the position of the community poverty line as defined by the focus groups.

These examples illustrate several characteristics of poverty and mobility in all the sampled communities. First, land is key to socioeconomic stratification in these agricultural villages. Second, the bottom and top steps are remarkably similar across communities. Landless laborers almost always occupy the bottom step and big farmers and landlords occupy the top step. Third, government employees are consistently placed near the top of the ladder (see step 4 in Koncha). Fourth, there is virtually no mention of formal private sector jobs; the only nonagricultural jobs mentioned are low-paying occupations (e.g., washermen and barbers) as well as forms of self-employment such as engaging in trade. Fifth, the position of the community poverty line and the amount of land a household needs in order to be above the CPL vary across communities. While this may seem odd at first, it actually reflects variations between communities in the productivity of land. As one would expect, a household needs more land in drought-stricken Anantapur to rise above the poverty threshold than in Srikakulam. In Srikakulam, where collection and marketing of forest products is an essential component of livelihoods, possessing even 1 acre of land is enough for a household to be considered above the CPL. So the position of the line captures the reality of different needs in different agro-climatic areas.

More importantly, however, the descriptions of well-being categories provided by focus group participants are multidimensional and go well beyond the basic land and occupational criteria. These include housing characteristics and children's education. The very poor are described as living in huts, not sending their children to school, and going hungry if they get no daily work. They are usually unable to save and have little hope of bettering their

TABLE 5.2
Ladder of life steps in two Andhra Pradesh communities showing caste, political connections, and irrigation inputs

Step	Kamthanahalli, Anantapur	Koncha, Srikakulam
6	Landlords and politicians: They own 50–60 acres of land. Only seven families in the village are at this step and they all belong to the Reddy caste. They have wells and bores for irrigation and nearly half the people in the village work for them. They also engage in politics.	Landlords and politicians: They own 50 acres of land, enjoy respect in the community, and earn income from farming and politics. They have good irrigation facilities, live in well-furnished houses, and educate their children through university. Only the local assemblyman's family is at this step.
5	Traders: Shettys form this class and their main occupation is the groundnut business. Apart from this, they also do agriculture, as they possess nearly 10 acres of land. They live in big newly constructed houses and send their children to towns for higher education.	Big farmers: They own 8 acres of land and belong to the Kapu caste group. Some are government employees like teachers. They mainly grow paddy and sugarcane and their main source of irrigation is either the canals or rainfall. They have their own bores and pump sets. They live in proper houses and educate their children in towns.
4	Big farmers: They have 20–30 acres of land and are purely dependent on agriculture. Their lands are moderately irrigated, but they work hard to get high yields. Everyone in the village respects these people. Families at this step send their children to towns for education.	Medium farmers: People at this step belong to the Kapu caste (a backward class group). They mostly grow vegetables and paddy but are dependent on rains. They don't have wells and bores. They live in proper houses and educate their children.
3	Farmers and private jobholders: They have 5 acres of land and private jobs. Some have irrigation facilities for their land. They live in pucca houses and send their children to school.	Small farmers: They own 1 acre of land. They lease land for cultivation. They have all agricultural tools, houses provided by government, and sufficient food and clothing. People in caste-based occupations like barbers and washermen and people belonging to Mala, Kapu, and other backward classes are at this step.
2	Small farmers: They have 1–5 acres of land. Their cultivation is dependent on rainfall and they work as labor during the off-season. Some are in caste-based occupations. They live in houses provided by the government and don't have any other assets.	Poor landless laborers: They are totally dependent on wage labor. As there is no work in the village, they migrate to towns for 4–5 months a year or even the whole year. They have no houses and cannot educate their children. They mostly belong to the Mala, Chakali, and Kapu caste groups.
1	Agricultural laborers: They have no land or other assets. They live in permanent houses provided by the government and get their children educated in nearby government schools.	

Note: The Koncha, Srikakulam focus group did not identify a sixth step. Bold lines indicate the community poverty line defined by each group. 1 acre = 100 decimals or 0.4 hectare or 3 bighas (approximately).

condition. A woman on the first step in Chennampalle, Anantapur, described her condition: "We have nothing in our house. I get up early in the morning, go for labor work and bring my daily wage to have food at least once in a day. Usually we starve as we cannot have food for the second time in the day." Those who are a step above the very poor live slightly better. They sometimes have pucca houses—built of permanent materials rather than mud, straw, or thatch—and generally send their children to school.

The ladders also reiterate social identities in village hierarchies. Those from the lower castes are placed at the bottom rung of the ladder and generally work as agricultural laborers. The higher-caste Reddys and Shettys usually operate at the top of the ladder as landlords, traders, or politicians; in Kamthanahalli, Anantapur, "nearly half the people in the village work for them," according to focus groups. This is in consonance with historical evidence presented in the preceding section.

Finally, the ladders emphasize the importance people give to ownership of irrigation assets. Those at the higher steps are generally described as possessing their own borehole pumps and irrigation sets, crucial for survival in a drought-affected context. For example, the landlords and politicians "have good irrigation facilities," as noted by participants in Koncha, Srikakulam.

Trends in the incidence of poverty: Progress over 1995–2005

The ladder of life exercises showed that many people lived below the community-defined poverty lines in the sample communities—on average, 56 percent of households in 2005. Not surprisingly, the incidence of poverty was higher in the Anantapur communities than in the other two districts (table 5.3).

However, even these poor, rural communities have seen improvements over 1995–2005. Across the sample villages, the incidence of poverty declined

TABLE 5.3

Percentage of households below the community poverty line in the Andhra Pradesh sample communities, 1995 and 2005

District	% of households below CPL, 1995	% of households below CPL, 2005	Change in incidence of poverty (percentage points)
Adilabad	53.4	46.9	−6.5
Anantapur	80.0	75.6	−4.4
Srikakulam	49.9	36.6	−13.3
Average	63.8	56.3	−7.5

7.5 percentage points. The largest drop took place in the Srikakulam villages and the smallest in the Anantapur villages.[4] Since the villages in Srikakulam had fewer poor households to begin with, based on villagers' perceptions, the disparities across the villages in the three districts grew.

Two other indicators of mobility confirm the picture of diversified improvements across districts: the percentage of initially poor households that moved above the community poverty line (MOP), and the percentage of initially poor who moved up, irrespective of whether they crossed the community poverty line or not (MPI). Across the study villages, 36.8 percent of initially poor households moved up and 21.5 percent managed to cross the poverty line (table 5.4).[5] Significantly more poor households moved up in the Srikakulam villages than elsewhere, and fewer rich households fell down.

These findings, based on communities' definition of what it means to be poor, mirror those derived from quantitative studies using a basic-needs poverty line. Table 5.5, based on the Indian government's National Sample Sur-

TABLE 5.4

Percentage of initially poor households that moved up or out of poverty in the Andhra Pradesh sample communities, 1995–2005

District	% of initially poor households that moved up (MPI)	% of initially poor households that moved out of poverty (MOP)
Adilabad	34.6	21.2
Anantapur	27.1	10.1
Srikakulam	53.4	38.9
Average	36.8	21.5

TABLE 5.5

Adjusted poverty headcount estimates for four southern Indian states, 1993/94 and 1999/2000

percent

State	1993/94 (NSS 50th Round)			1999/2000 (NSS 55th Round)		
	Urban	Rural	Overall	Urban	Rural	Overall
Andhra Pradesh	17.8	29.2	26.2	10.8	26.2	21.6
Tamil Nadu	20.8	38.5	30.3	11.3	24.3	20.0
Karnataka	21.4	37.9	33.2	10.8	30.7	24.1
Kerala	13.9	19.5	17.8	9.6	10.0	9.9
All India	17.8	33.0	29.1	12.0	26.3	22.2

Source: Deaton and Drèze 2002, based on data from the National Sample Survey.

TABLE 5.6
Adjusted poverty headcounts in Andhra Pradesh and India, 1993/94, 1999/2000, and 2004/05

percent

| | Andhra Pradesh | | All India | |
Period	Urban	Rural	Urban	Rural
1993/94	17.8	29.2	17.8	33.0
1999/2000	10.8	26.2	12.0	26.3
2004/5	8.4	20.9	10.2	23.1

Source: Dev 2007.

vey (NSS), indicates that monetary poverty declined in rural AP in the second half of the 1990s, albeit less rapidly than in other southern Indian states.

Analysis of data from the 2004/05 NSS round by Dev (2007) confirms a further dip in rural poverty levels in the state, from about 26 percent in 1999/2000 to 21 percent in 2004/05 (table 5.6). Dev notes that the rate of poverty reduction in rural AP was in fact faster between 1999/2000 and 2004/05 than over the earlier period, primarily because of low inflation and low relative food prices.

Poverty dynamics: Reasons for moving up or down

Poverty incidence figures at any point in time are influenced by two contrasting flows: people who successfully move up and out of poverty, and those who fall down and join the poverty ranks. Decomposing the change in the incidence of poverty can thus be very informative. Table 5.7 decomposes the *net* change in poverty incidence in our sample into the percentage moving

TABLE 5.7
Change in poverty incidence in the Andhra Pradesh sample communities: Moving up and moving down

District	Change in incidence of poverty (percentage points)	% moving up	% moving down
Adilabad	6.5	11.1	4.6
Anantapur	4.4	7.0	2.6
Srikakulam	12.7	15.8	3.1
Average	7.4	10.6	3.2

out of poverty and the percentage falling into poverty. While more than 10 percent of the sample population moved up and out of poverty over the study period, nearly 3 percent fell into poverty, reducing the net percentage change.

Looking separately at movers and fallers is useful also because the reasons given for falling were not mirror images of those given for escaping poverty. About one-fifth of the faller households cited a decrease in available opportunities in their local economy due to drought as the primary trigger of their descent (table 5.8). Negative shocks including ill health, death of a breadwinner, and aging were identified together as the second most important reason leading to a fall. Lack of work and failure of crops, coupled with health problems, forced some households to borrow money at high interest rates, and inability to service this debt was an additional reason for declines in well-being.

In contrast, the reasons given for moving out of poverty reflected the households' own ability to get jobs or to improve their income, primarily in agriculture, through crop diversification or better farming techniques (table 5.9).

Overall, therefore, our data suggest a decline in poverty as defined by the communities themselves. The decline was fastest in Srikakulam and slowest in Anantapur. The data also show that the factors associated with upward and downward mobility are not necessarily the same. Policies aimed at reducing poverty in rural Andhra Pradesh must therefore be designed with attention both to poverty avoidance mechanisms and to strategies that can help people move out of poverty.

TABLE 5.8

Self-reported reasons for downward movement by faller households, Andhra Pradesh

Reason	% of faller households
Decreasing national/local prosperity	21
Health/death shocks	14
Credit and debt	10

Note: Decreasing national/local prosperity combines (a) vulnerability to market price fluctuations, (b) worsening economy, (c) high inflation/increase in price of basic necessities, (d) inconsistent work opportunities, and (e) increased restrictions on business/increased taxes. Health/death shocks combines (a) health problems, accidents, and high health expenses, (b) death of a breadwinner, and (c) aging. Credit and debt combines (a) failure to obtain credit and (b) too much debt.

TABLE 5.9

Self-reported reasons for upward movement by mover households, Andhra Pradesh

Reason	% of mover households
Individual initiative (agricultural)	26
Jobs	20
Family support	9

Note: Individual initiative (agricultural) combines (a) crop diversification and (b) increased crop production because of improved agricultural technology, irrigation, and/ or high-yielding varieties of seeds. Jobs combines (a) steady job/increase in wages, (b) got a job/better job, and (c) increase in work opportunities. Family support includes (a) children completing school/getting jobs, (b) inheritance, and (c) marriage.

Impact of People's Organizations and Other Factors on Poverty

What lies behind these changes in the incidence of poverty? In looking at the impact of various factors, we rely on information from two main sources: qualitative evidence from focus group discussions and women's life histories and quantitative data collected with the household and community questionnaires.

Our main hypothesis is that people's organizations, and self-help groups in particular, had a positive impact, but dependence on rainwater remained a crucial source of vulnerability. Women, but also men, attributed an important role to the SHGs. In 19 of the 56 communities sampled (34 percent), female focus group participants listed self-help groups as the key factor responsible for greater prosperity. Men cited them too, albeit less frequently (tables 5.10 and 5.11). Water is the other key variable; it was cited as the most important factor by women in 25 percent of the villages and by men in 41 percent. Coastal AP communities like those in Srikakulam experience cyclones and floods that destroy property and fields, and inland communities deal constantly with water scarcity. The last decade in particular has been marked by a persistent drought in large parts of the state. Despite numerous water management interventions cited in focus group discussions, these poor, largely agricultural communities remain very vulnerable to the vagaries of the weather.

Education, cited by both men and women in 10 percent of the villages, comes next for women, with men also citing housing improvements. Housing is one example of public investments that reduce vulnerability and provide at least some elements of a safety net. Other examples cited by focus

TABLE 5.10
Positive factors responsible for community prosperity, according to female focus groups, Andhra Pradesh

Factor	Frequency	% of villages
Self-help groups	19	33.9
Water	14	25.0
Education	6	10.7
Economic opportunity	5	8.9
Roads	4	7.1
Housing	3	5.4
Social	2	3.6
Agriculture	2	3.6
Sanitation	1	1.8
Total	56	100

TABLE 5.11
Positive factors responsible for community prosperity, according to male focus groups, Andhra Pradesh

Factor	Frequency	% of villages
Water	23	41.1
Housing	8	14.3
Roads	7	12.5
Education	6	10.7
Economic opportunity	4	7.1
Agriculture	3	5.4
Self-help groups	3	5.4
Social	2	3.6
Total	56	100

group participants are distribution of land to the landless and provision of compensation for disasters (fires, pests).

Collective benefits derived from people's organizations

Why do self-help groups matter? Our qualitative data suggest two sets of impacts: collective benefits accruing to a community as a whole as a result of the presence and activities of groups, and individual benefits accruing to group members. Among collective benefits, people cited reduced social divisions, greater empowerment of women, greater accountability of local government, and last but not least, economic benefits.

Groups helped reduce social divisions. Perhaps the most remarkable collective impact of SHGs, considering the historical background of these villages, is that they have contributed to an easing of social cleavages and inequalities along both caste and gender lines.[6] In 13 of the 19 villages where women rated SHGs as the most positive factor, respondents also mentioned a considerable decline in social divisions. By comparison, in only 18 of the remaining 37 villages was a decrease in inequality mentioned. In regressions with a 0–1 dummy for "SHGs cited as the most important positive event" as the dependent variable, the coefficient for social divisions in the community 10 years ago is significant and negatively correlated. Trends over time reflect the different histories of the three districts studied. In 1995, caste-based inequalities were the highest in villages in Adilabad, part of the Telangana region where social cleavages along lines of caste, class, and land ownership were historically deeper; they were lowest in Anantapur. Fortunately, the reduction in such inequalities was also sharpest in Adilabad (table 5.12).

Some examples illustrate how groups helped reduce social divisions. In villages

TABLE 5.12

Percentage of Andhra Pradesh sample communities with high social divisions, 1995 and 2005

percent

District	1995	2005
Anantapur	12.5	0
Adilabad	37.5	0
Srikakulam	18.8	6.2
Total	21.2	1.8

Note: Based on perceptions of key informants in the 56 sampled villages.

of Anantapur, SHGs that were formed across castes helped women from lower castes break old cultural barriers and claim equal status with those of higher castes. An upper-caste SHG member in Atmakur village described the effect of the groups: "We used to keep the Mala and Madiga [scheduled caste] people away from us and never used to allow them to enter our houses. After the formation of the groups, we came to know that not the caste or religion, but living together is more important for life. Now all of us are living together and visiting one another's houses. This is a good change in us." Pedakka, a member of a self-help group in the same village, said, "The SHGs help you realize that the blood in you and me is the same. In the meetings [now] everyone sits together. There is no discrimination. This is one major change that has taken place after the establishment of SHGs in the village."

Groups helped empower women. Empowering women is one of the first objectives of SHGs. The campaign against liquor is a striking example of women's empowerment. In Dhampur, Adilabad, a focus group of young women explained, "If any injustice is done to our women, we do not keep quiet. Recently one husband thrashed his wife in a drunken state. Our group came to know about this and we all went to him and abused him and threatened him, saying that if it happens again, we will take serious action against him. The power of women's groups is up to that extent." In the same village, SHG members started their own movement to curb consumption of the potent spirits called *arrack*. A woman in a focus group said, "One year back we initiated a movement to eradicate the consumption of arrack. We went to the liquor shops and threw away all the liquor." Possibly related to these strides by women, most chronic poor and mover households interviewed reported a dip in violence against girls and women in their villages.

Groups fostered greater local accountability. Where groups function well, they are credited with increasing the collective ability of people to approach local government and demand better services. Nearly 40 percent of the households interviewed said that the local government now acts more in the interest of the people than it did 10 years ago, while only 24 percent said that it acts more in its own self-interest. Households' trust in local government officials also registered an improvement. People provided examples of how groups began to hold gram panchayats and service providers accountable (box 5.1).[7]

Thus there is strong evidence in the community reports that groups have fostered local accountability, demanded and monitored the provision of infrastructure and services, and conveyed the needs of poor people to local authorities. But there are also examples of how nonfunctioning local institutions have hampered the working of groups. Corruption in particular has derailed efforts in some locations (box 5.2).

Groups brought about economic benefits. Markets set up by Velugu in Anantapur reportedly changed local market dynamics by lowering the prices of essential commodities. Elsewhere, SHG members opened up shops and expanded services available in the community. In Kotham, Srikakulam, women opened a shop selling cashew seeds, pineapple, and turmeric; they purchased the produce directly from local people and cut out the middlemen and agents. The women made a profit, which they invested in a second shop. The groups received training from government officials and nongovernmental organizations on new livelihood opportunities and served as agents of the government for procuring crops like maize and distributing agricultural inputs like fertilizers.[8]

Individual benefits to group members

In addition to benefits accruing to the whole community, self-help groups brought benefits to their members. Group members learned to save and gained greater access to credit, which was used for both consumption and productive activities. They also received information that otherwise would not have reached them, including information about government programs and education on various topics from AIDS awareness to better farming practices to business skills. Underlying these changes, a fundamental shift in women's role in the family and in the community helped increase incomes and improve expenditures.

BOX 5.1
Groups enhance accountability of local institutions

Chedulla, Anantapur
Women in Chedulla recounted an incident where a schoolteacher had demanded an extra Rs 200 from each student, which had caused an SHG member to stop sending her child to school. The other women went to the school to make enquiries. This turned into a confrontation, at which point the SHG set a date for a formal meeting and informed the teacher that she would be required to submit details of her expenditures to the village organization (VO), a village-level federation of SHGs. VO representatives listened to the opinions of teachers from neighboring villages before facing the accused teacher in the formal meeting. The women recalled, "She then got nervous and returned all the money, and soon after that had herself transferred to another district." The VO gained a new social standing in the community. The members said, "Now we're being called to attend functions even by officials. We realized that the school was short one teacher; we discussed this matter in the meeting of the VO and appointed one member's daughter as teacher for Rs 300."

Korrapadu, Anantapur
Before self-help groups were formed in Korrapadu, women left the panchayat to the village elders. After the groups were formed, the head of the panchayat, known as the *sarpanch*, began to attend SHG meetings at least once every couple of months. VO leaders also attended gram panchayat meetings. The gram panchayat and the VO began to work together: they invited revenue officers to discuss land issues, and whenever there were problems with the water and hand pumps the VO approached the panchayat to have them repaired. In the words of a men's focus group: "The representatives are [now] working in fear of the people. They realized that the people respond to their mistakes. Earlier, work took people to the offices; now the government goes to people for work. Thus people have become the government."

Groups helped members save, and pooled savings were available to help with unforeseen expenditures. Many women cited higher savings and greater access to credit as an important factor in improving their families' well-being. Self-help groups usually began by inculcating a habit of thrift and collective saving. Savings by group members were pooled and loaned to members who needed funds. In addition to supporting immediate daily consumption, these loans

BOX 5.2
Poorly functioning local institutions hamper SHGs

Bestharapalle, Anantapur
The Baba group is a self-help group of poor women in the village of Bestharapalle, Anantapur. The group had recently faced a scarcity of funds, and a
member attributed the group's financial problems to corruption among government officials. *"Devudu varamichchina poojari varamiyyaledu annatlu,"*
she said, meaning even if the God gives a boon, the priest stands in the way
of receiving the benefits of it. Corruption apparently took two forms. First, the
women were sold equipment like tools needed for weaving at double their
actual price. "The cost of the equipment provided would be Rs 2,000 to Rs
2,500. But they charged Rs 5,000," complained Rajni, a member. "It is like
spending 50 paise on spices for a curry worth only 25 paise." Second, loans
were apparently given only to those women who abided by the officials' dic-
tates and to those belonging to one particular caste. The others were largely
ignored. Losses on account of higher input prices meant inability to repay
the amount borrowed and subsequent disqualification from borrowing in the
future. "Even though many kinds of assistance are provided to us from the
top, we are not able to reap the benefits at the local level," concluded one
member.

Chintada, Srikakulam
Members of the Santoshi Mata Group in Chintada, Srikakulam, purchased
cattle with a loan of Rs 16,000 from Velugu. The initial years saw their
business booming as the group received a contract to supply milk to a
hostel attached to a school for tribal children located in the village and
constructed by the Integrated Tribal Development Agency. The hostel residents, all students, guaranteed a regular demand for milk from the SHG
members. "Apart from the milk supply, we were also handed the responsibility of cleaning the hostel and taking care of the sanitation. In a very short
span of time, our entire group prospered and earned money. We cleared
all our dues. But things changed when a new warden took over the hostel.
The warden was not giving proper food to the children. One day we had
an argument with him regarding this and subsequently all our orders were
cancelled, both for milk supply and for the hostel sanitation works. The
local officials do not listen to our complaints. We now find it difficult to
even feed our cattle."

---

were used to cope with sudden shocks such as illness and to finance social expenses such as weddings.[9] A women's focus group in Malkapur, Adilabad, explained, "We save Rs 30 every month [one rupee a day] and whenever we are in need of the money, we borrow from the groups. The rate of interest is very low. By the end of the year we are able to save Rs 300–400 that is useful for sending our children to school by getting them the required clothes and books. At the time of our daughters' marriage, many of us borrow amounts as high as Rs 15,000."

Such collective savings provided an important fallback mechanism or a safety net. The pool of savings was particularly helpful for survival in times of drought and helped members reduce their borrowing for consumption purposes. While on average 41 percent of our sample households reported borrowing from any source for consumption purposes in the year before our survey, only 33 percent of the sample households who reported joining a group had done so. Among those who borrowed, the amounts still owed were smaller.

After gaining some experience with collective savings, groups were linked to government banks that provided credit at low rates of interest. SHG members across our sampled villages mentioned the ease with which they could secure government loans. Those in Lingatla village, Adilabad, said they opened their personal saving accounts and that of the SHG "simply on the pledge of the pass book." Expansion of government bank branches in Andhra Pradesh over the study period significantly improved accessibility. Nearly one-third of the 19 villages where women cited SHGs as the most positive event also reported SHG-bank linkages, with government banks serving as a primary source of credit in the community. In comparison, government banks were a primary source of credit in only one-fifth of the other villages.[10]

Credit facilitated by SHGs provided an alternative to moneylenders and the ever-increasing burden of debt. In Korrapadu, Anantapur, members of a self-help group recounted the difficulties they used to have in paying moneylenders: "The wages were not enough for our daily bread. If there were any problems, we took loans from the landlord and paid interest at a rate of Rs 41–51 [on Rs 100] compounded on the original amount. The landlords took advantage of our situation and us. It was as if we were already in a well, and yet they were stoning us."

Group savings and bank credit were also used for productive activities. These included activities like rearing cattle, dairying, weaving thread and baskets, growing flowers and vegetables for sale in nearby markets, and opening petty shops and businesses. In Ratti, Srikakulam, self-help groups of women united under a *mahila samakhya* (a women's federation). The federation purchased cashew nuts from households in the village and sold them directly to the government or in the weekly market. The financial benefits derived from the business reportedly helped member families move up the ladder in the village.

Groups also helped households build assets. A higher proportion of those who joined groups during the study period reported an increase in their assets, particularly land (22 percent of members compared to 16 percent of nonmembers). Improvements in access to land titles were also more common in the 19 villages where SHGs were rated as the top positive event in the community than in the villages where they were not. In several communities, group members received gas connections from the government after they joined the group.

Starting new activities or acquiring land, however, did not always guarantee an escape from poverty. Often many members of a group started the same activities, like livestock rearing or vegetable farming, and demand did not always grow to absorb the increased supply, especially where drought was most severe. So prices plunged and households who had borrowed to buy buffaloes or grow vegetables were not able to repay the loans. This happened, for instance, in Govindapalle and Appilepalle in Anantapur. The villagers did not complain; the money they made was sufficient to maintain their families, but the investment did not help them move out of poverty. Owning land without an assured source of irrigation did not help in a context of prolonged drought.

Self-help groups facilitated access to information. Groups in Vellamaddi, Anantapur, were able to participate in food-for-work programs and AIDS awareness programs initiated by the local government. Women in Govindapalle received training on new inputs for their crops. "We also find out about prices by talking with others and through discussions among ourselves," they said. "Our meetings are held on the 16th of every month and through these we become aware of many things."

Self-help groups supported a fundamental shift in women's roles in the family and outside. The improvements in the economic well-being of households whose women belonged to groups were mirrored by a fundamental change in women's roles in the family and community, which helped increase incomes and shift expenditures. Women spoke proudly of being able to stand up to their husbands because of the confidence they had gained in their groups. A woman in Govindapalle said, "People now think that both men and women are equal. Previously in a family the husband used to take decisions on his own. But now things are different. For example, when my husband purchases land I ask him to include my name also in the document. Earlier he used to take decisions on his own before taking loans. But now he discusses all the issues with me before taking the decisions, like the matters of buying houses, business loans, and marriages of sons and daughters." Members of a self-help group in Vellamaddi recounted, "Before we joined the group, we were limited only to the kitchen without freedom. We used to be like prisoners to our husbands, working like machines. We had no independent views. Even the kind of food to be cooked in the house was decided by elders. Now we have reached a stage where we can take independent decisions."

In Govindapalle, women were "very confident that we are no longer inferior to men in earning money for livelihoods. We are taking some livelihood, small or big, to earn money and we are not sitting idle at home. Money thus earned is being saved and we can use that money when needed. Now we can take decisions on our own. We need not depend on our husbands for money and we have the capacity to live independently." In Ratti, Srikakulam, women said, "We now earn our own livelihoods without depending on our husbands or other male members. Often we have a big share in running the family— not just as homemakers but also as breadwinners."

Men recognized the subtle changes occurring. In Kurumala, Anantapur, men said, "Both men and women have equal freedom. The women are now aware of everything. Earlier they used to depend on us to solve problems. But now they are taking responsibilities. They now participate in decisions about marriages, land and loans." Basic literacy played a role. Many women across groups spoke with pride of how they had learned to read and write thanks to their membership in groups. "We are [now] educating our children," said a group of women in Lingatla, Adilabad. "Hopefully all our children will get good jobs. They need not face problems like we do."

Greater empowerment of women within the home was mirrored by a greater role in the public sphere. Women in Shivanoor, Adilabad, said, "Earlier we couldn't speak outside like men. Our men scolded us if we went outside. Ten years ago we didn't know anything about banks. But now we know the bank manager and the cashier and we know how to tackle them. We know how to deposit and withdraw money and we have learned how to sign. Ration cards are now being issued in our names." The proportion of those who contacted their local politicians or sent them letters was higher among those who reported being members of groups (15 percent) than among those who did not (7 percent). In Chedulla, Anantapur, a woman recounting her life story said, "Before, I was just one person; now I am 10, and so I feel I would dare to go up to any government official." Women in a focus group in Chintada, Srikakulam, felt they have achieved something that had been unthinkable: "Talking to officials and bankers is like a dream for us. We never thought that some day we would handle them."

Women who belonged to groups were now seen across communities as the ones who wielded power because they had valuable access to credit, livelihood opportunities, and government programs. A male respondent in the village of Powerguda, Adilabad, summed up, "Those who are not a part of any group lack power. They don't know anything. They have much less influence. So they are powerless."

Groups may affect youth aspirations. Nearly 24 percent of all youths interviewed for the study wanted to own a business by the age of 30. Such entrepreneurial aspirations were second only to hopes of engaging in agriculture or horticulture, which 32 percent of youths said they wanted to do. Interestingly, aspirations for starting a business were higher among youths whose parents were members of two or more groups: 35 percent of youths from families with membership in two or more groups hoped to set up a business, compared to 21 percent whose parents were members of one group or none.

In sum, the qualitative evidence collected through focus group discussions, life histories, and case studies of self-help groups documented the role these groups played in improving the lives of their members. As we will now see, our quantitative evidence supports these findings.

Quantitative analysis of the role of people's organizations

Quantitative analysis of data from household and community interviews confirms the qualitative findings that SHGs help their members improve their lot. Using data from household interviews, we ran regressions with a dummy capturing movement out of poverty as our dependent variable and a set of explanatory variables including the number of groups household members belonged to at the time of the study (*totgroups05*) and change in their membership over 10 years (*groupch*).

A caveat is in order. We dealt with nonrandomness in the selection of households within villages by using information from the cluster-level ladder of life exercise to construct approximate weights (annex 5.4 describes how the approximate weights were constructed). We then ran weighted regressions. While this is a reasonably satisfactory way to address nonrandomness at the household level, having randomly selected observations would have been better and might have yielded somewhat different results.

Our dependent variable was a 0–1 dummy (*moverm*) indicating whether a household that started off poor at the beginning of the recall period (1995) stayed poor (0) or moved out of poverty (1) by the end of the period (2005). The dummy was based on the classification of households into movers and chronic poor provided by male focus group participants. The sample included 531 households that started poor.[11] For simplicity, we used an ordinary least squares (OLS) specification, but results for a logit specification, as well as two other alternative specifications, are similar and are reported in annex 5.2.[12] Table 5.13 shows that the change in the number of groups that household members belonged to (*groupch*) was positively correlated with moving out of poverty and strongly significant. The more groups household members belonged to, the more likely they were to have moved out of poverty.[13] This result supports the earlier findings and points to the importance of active membership, as captured by belonging to several groups rather than just one.

There are two reasons why our regression is likely to underestimate the impact of groups. First, the regression captures individual benefits only. Because groups were active in all our villages, we did not have a "control" group of households living in villages where there were no groups and so we could not assess collective benefits. Overall benefits—collective and individual—may well be larger than the regression indicates. Second, the quantitative survey did not distinguish between different types of groups, or between groups that functioned well and groups that did not, and it did not provide information on the number of years a group had been active. Thus we were not able to make these distinctions in the regression analysis. Treating all groups as the same, regardless of their age and other characteristics, is clearly not satisfactory, especially considering the rich debate about the impact and efficacy of groups in AP (for example, see Jones, Mukherjee, and Galab 2007). But the data did not allow us to do otherwise. Our estimates therefore are likely to understate the impact of well-functioning groups.

Other factors affecting movement out of poverty

Our explanatory variables included a number of other variables in addition to the number of groups a household belonged to in 1995 or 2005 and the change over the decade. In line with the analysis done in other Moving Out of

Poverty study sites (Narayan, Pritchett, and Kapoor 2009), we grouped these variables in six main conceptual blocks, outlined below. Annex 5.3 provides details on how the variables were constructed.

Household-level factors. We took into account the education level of the respondent, usually a woman (the name of the variable used in the regressions and in the results tables is *educ*); whether the household had suffered a health shock during the study period (*healthshock*); and ownership of land, assets, and livestock (*land, assets*, and *livestock*). Interestingly, the education level was not significant, although it had the expected positive sign (respondents with higher levels of education were more likely to move out of poverty, but not significantly so).[14] Health shocks, on the other hand, were very significant. Households that had suffered a health shock were much more likely to have remained poor, in line with what households report when asked about reasons for downward movement. Assets and livestock were also significant in explaining upward mobility of the poor, while land was not. Education and assets to some degree controlled for unobserved household characteristics that may have affected membership in groups and mobility, such as greater activism and ability to lead.

Economic opportunities. We hypothesized that more households would move out of poverty in communities where the local economy was stronger, based on the perception of key informants (*econstrength-KI*) or focus group participants (*econstrength-FGD*). However, neither variable was significant, possibly because both are imperfect measures of opportunities.

Local democracy. We expected that better-functioning local institutions and lower corruption would help households move out of poverty (*locdemocracy, corruption*). Local democracy and corruption indicators were positively correlated with moving out of poverty but were not significant.

Fairness. Greater fairness in treatment of people under the law (*fairlaw*) was, as expected, positively correlated with moving out of poverty, but it was not significant. Fairer treatment of women, measured by lower perceived violence against women in households in the village (*violencewomen*), was positively and significantly correlated with moving out of poverty.

Individual and collective agency. Control over everyday decisions (*control*) and aspirations (*aspirations*), both considered indicators of individual agency, were not significant. The only individual agency variable that showed some significance was the leave-out mean of control over everyday decisions, with lower control associated with more movement out of poverty. (The leave-out mean is the mean of the variable for all households in the cluster except the one in question; see chapter 1 and appendix 1 of this volume.)[15] This result is hard to explain and disappears when initial conditions are considered, as shown in column 3 of annex table 5.E.

Indicators of collective agency are negatively correlated: greater collective action (*collectiveaction*) and greater cohesiveness in 1995 (*cohesiveness*) are correlated with less movement out of poverty—significantly so for collective action. At first glance this seems counterintuitive, especially given the significance of group membership for moving out of poverty. But this is probably explained by the fact that groups were started first in the poorest communities in AP, where people's ability to come together and solve common problems and social cohesiveness are likely to have been low. Another possible reason why collective action may have a negative sign is that the type of collective action present in 1995 might have been of the bonding type, given deep social divisions. If so, stratification along caste and class lines would have dampened social capital of the bridging or linking type that is helpful for movement out of poverty.

Social stratification. Indicators of discrimination by gender or ethnic/caste background in schools (*inequality*) and in village society at large were not significant. Caste dummies, while having the expected signs, were not significant and are not included in table 5.13.[16] These results do not suggest a strong pattern of exclusion along ethnic/religious/caste lines, which is remarkable given the history of these regions and the experience elsewhere in India.

Conclusions

Qualitative and quantitative data collected by the Moving Out of Poverty study shed light on movement in and out of poverty in drought-prone rural communities in Andhra Pradesh and the role of people's self-help organizations in this process. The study's main findings are that poverty declined between 1995 and 2005, albeit at different rates in different districts, and that people's organizations improved their members' chances of escaping poverty.

While people in the sample villages continued to perceive a high level of poverty, living conditions generally improved during the study period. Improvements varied across districts and localities, partly on account of

TABLE 5.13
Correlates of moving out of poverty in Andhra Pradesh

Variable	OLS weighted (MOP)	Variable	OLS weighted (MOP)
econstrength95-KI	−0.012	cohesiveness95	−0.037
	[0.35]		[1.38]
econstrength-FGD	−0.007	inequality	−0.032
	[0.18]		[1.11]
locdemocracy	0.021	educ	0.024
	[1.28]		[0.86]
locdemocracy-LOM	0.031	healthshock	−0.088
	[0.89]		[2.97]***
corruption95-KI	0.022	land95	−0.001
	[0.86]		[0.16]
fairlaw95	0.037	assets95	0.061
	[0.84]		[1.98]**
violencewomen95	0.046	livestock95	0.026
	[1.89]*		[1.71]*
control	−0.037	totgroups05	−0.024
	[1.60]		[0.93]
control-LOM	−0.12	groupch	0.068
	[1.78]*		[2.02]**
aspirations	0.013	Constant	0.777
	[1.11]		[2.28]**
aspirations-LOM	−0.03	Observations	531
	[0.93]	R^2	0.14
collectiveaction95	−0.079		
	[1.98]**		

Note: KI denotes information from key informants and FGD stands for focus group discussions; variables without suffix are from household interviews. LOM indicates leave-out mean (weighted). 95 and 05 denote variables referring to 1995 and 2005; where no date is indicated, the variable combines information for the two periods and/or changes.

*p < .10   **p < .05   ***p < .01

historical legacies and partly because of differences in the extent to which areas were struck by drought during the decade. Water, especially for irrigation, was a key concern in these poor agricultural communities, which remained largely vulnerable to the vagaries of the weather and suffered when droughts (and other natural calamities such as pests or cyclones) struck.

People's organizations played an important role in these changes, as reflected in the testimonies of women and men alike. Self-help groups helped women gain greater dignity and become more empowered in both the household and the community. They also reduced social divisions and fostered greater accountability of local institutions. The SHGs expanded economic opportunities in the communities in which they operated. They also benefited their members directly by expanding savings and access to credit for both consumption and productive activities and by providing a means for poor women to receive information on topics such as better farming techniques and business skills. Quantitative evidence confirms that group membership has a significant positive impact on household mobility.

The changes captured by these results are truly epochal. Centuries-old social cleavages are diminishing in importance. Public policy has helped spur this transformation by supporting self-help groups through Velugu and its successor program. Through their group membership, poor scheduled caste women have gained a political voice; as a result, they are wooed by politicians and are increasingly integrated into the panchayats. These developments are significant for creating local governments that are more responsive to local people.

The findings of the AP study have several policy implications. First, vulnerability to drought needs to be reduced through more and better water management investments and possibly through introduction of crops that are less water-intensive (World Bank 2006). Second, given the negative impact of health shocks, safety nets such as insurance schemes, food security, and further expansion of bank credit at reasonable rates of interest can be steps toward protecting the most vulnerable households from falling further and could complement improvements in health systems. Finally, the study confirms the multidimensional impacts that people's own organizations—particularly self-help groups—have had in poor, rural Andhra Pradesh. The AP experience establishes that, when properly financed and supported over a decade, SHGs can be used as a policy tool for helping poor people move out of poverty and for breaking down persistent caste barriers. The challenge is to strengthen the local institutions on which these groups depend for funds and other services and to support sustainable income-generating actions undertaken by the groups.

Annex 5.1 Sample Selection for the Study in Andhra Pradesh

The AP sample for the Moving Out of Poverty study was not selected randomly. The community data were collected in 56 villages distributed over 19 mandals (blocks) in three districts (annex table 5.A). The household data come from 839 households, roughly 15 per village.

District and mandal selection. The selection of districts and mandals was done as part of the DPIP midterm appraisal (CESS 2005). The three districts selected were among the state's six poorest in 2000,[17] and the mandals selected within each district were among those where DPIP activities started earliest (that is, during DPIP Phase I). These mandals satisfied certain criteria including high poverty, illiteracy, rainfed agriculture, and in some cases, the presence of self-help groups.

Village selection. All villages surveyed in the DPIP midterm appraisal (MTA) were selected for the Moving Out of Poverty study. Of the 16 villages in each district, 12 were DPIP Phase I villages and four were control villages where DPIP activities started later. While the distinction between Phase I and control villages might have been meaningful in 2000, it was definitely no longer so by the time of the study in 2005, as DPIP activities had spread. In addition to the 16 DPIP MTA villages, the sample included eight villages in Anantapur where the United Nations Development Programme (UNDP) had started self-help groups under the South Asia Poverty Reduction Program, before DPIP activities began. In sum, none of the villages sampled was a true "control" village in the sense of *not* having been covered by one or another of the SHG expansion programs.

Within each village, a random subsample of about 150 households was selected and listed, and these households were placed on the steps of the ladder of life by focus group participants. Effectively, these subsamples represent our clusters. (In the text, we use "village" and "cluster" interchangeably. In reality, however, a cluster is a hamlet of households. A village may have many such hamlets or clusters, which are grouped together within the definite surveyed boundaries of a "revenue village," whose boundaries were traditionally determined by the state for purposes of collecting revenue.)

ANNEX TABLE 5.A
Andhra Pradesh study sample

District	Villages visited	Households interviewed
Adilabad	16	239
Anantapur	24	360
Srikakulam	16	240
Total	56	839

Household selection. The selection of households was also not entirely random. Of the 15 households surveyed by the study in each village, 10 were to be DPIP MTA households (with female respondents), to construct a panel. The DPIP households were selected randomly after stratification based on the Participatory Identification of the Poor (PIP) lists prepared by the Society for the Elimination of Rural Poverty to assess entitlement to ration cards. The global Moving Out of Poverty study guidelines indicated that households were to be selected randomly after stratification into mover, faller, chronic poor, and never poor categories based on the ladder of life mobility matrix (figure 5.1), in proportions equal to 40, 10, 20, and 30 percent respectively. Movers, at 40 percent, were to be oversampled since the purpose of the study was to examine factors leading to movement out of poverty. Apparently, the five non–DPIP MTA households were selected to approximate these percentages. As it turns out, of the 839 households for which we have data, only 114 are movers—13.6 percent instead of 40 percent that the study guidelines call for. The proportions for the other categories are also off the targets, with 50 percent of all interviewed households being chronic poor.

Since all 150-odd households in a cluster were classified into the mover, faller, chronic poor, and never poor categories during focus group discussions, we know the proportion of each category in the population. The overall proportions in the population and in the sample are not too dissimilar (annex table 5.B), but the differences at the village and mandal levels are significant and warrant the use of weights (annex 5.4).

The nonrandom nature of the sample has three main consequences. First, the results are (at most) representative of poor parts of three poor districts—not of AP as a whole, not of all poor parts of AP, not even of the three districts as a whole. While village-level census data can be used to compare

ANNEX TABLE 5.B
Distribution of households by mobility group in household sample and villages, Andhra Pradesh

Mobility group	Frequency in household sample	% of household sample	Frequency in villages	% of villages
Mover	114	13.6	889	10.7
Chronic poor	417	49.7	4,442	53.2
Faller	27	3.2	278	3.3
Never poor	281	33.5	2,739	32.8
Total	839	100	8,348	100

ANNEX TABLE 5.C
Sample villages as a share of total villages in three districts, Andhra Pradesh

District	Villages in study data	Villages in census data	Study/total villages (%)
Adilabad	16	1,729	0.9
Anantapur	24	952	2.5
Srikakulam	16	1,814	0.9
Three districts	56	4,495	1.2

the sampled villages to other villages in the three districts, the study sample is too small to yield very meaningful comparisons (annex table 5.C).

Second, we do not have a true control group in terms of the policy intervention. All the households and all the villages in our sample have seen an expansion of self-help groups. While households in control villages did indeed report belonging to fewer groups in 1995, the change in the number of groups and the average number of groups in 2005 were higher in control than in UNDP villages. Moreover, community data provide a different picture (more groups in control villages). So, in sum, we do not have proper control groups.

Third, because households were selected on the basis of stratification of what is effectively the main dependent variable—moving out of poverty—this is not neutral to the results and household-level regression results should be weighted (annex 5.4).

Annex 5.2 Results of Alternative Specifications, Andhra Pradesh

We report the results of three alternative specifications: (a) a logit regression instead of an OLS regression; (b) regressions (OLS and logit) capturing initial conditions only; and (c) regressions using a different dependent variable, namely whether an initially poor household moved up or not, regardless of whether it crossed the community poverty line.

Logit specification

Since the dependent variables are 0–1 dummies, we checked whether results are sensitive to using a logit specification instead of OLS. Annex table 5.D compares OLS and logit specifications with basic regressors; column 1 is reported from table 5.13. Apart from some minor differences in the significance level of a couple of variables, the results are unchanged.

Regressions (OLS and logit) capturing initial conditions

Columns 3 and 4 in annex table 5.E report results obtained with regressors capturing initial conditions only, rather than also including variables that measure changes over the decade (annex table 5.G describes the initial-condition indicators used in this table). The findings do not change substantially compared with column 1 in annex table 5.D: belonging to groups is positively correlated with moving out of poverty and significant at the 5 percent level even after controlling for the number of groups household members belonged to in 1995.

Among other variables, the only differences are that now initial conditions on fairness under the law are significant and positively correlated with moving out of poverty, and the leave-out mean of control over everyday decisions is no longer significant. The fact that initial conditions on local democracy are not significant is interesting, as it suggests that households in communities with initially poor local institutions were not destined to suffer from this. Local democracy improved markedly over time and our local democracy indicator for 2005 is only weakly correlated with local democracy in 1995, and negatively so: at the margin, communities where local institutions were less trusted and less responsive saw larger gains in local democracy over time.

ANNEX TABLE 5.D
Correlates of moving out of poverty in Andhra Pradesh, OLS and logit specifications

Variable	OLS weighted (MOP) Model 1	Logit weighted (MOP) Model 2	Variable	OLS weighted (MOP) Model 1	Logit weighted (MOP) Model 2
econstrength95-KI	−0.012	−0.196	cohesiveness95	−0.037	−0.257
	[0.35]	[0.67]		[1.38]	[1.25]
econstrength-FGD	−0.007	−0.002	inequality	−0.032	−0.2
	[0.18]	[0.01]		[1.11]	[1.24]
locdemocracy	0.021	0.207	educ	0.024	0.207
	[1.28]	[1.37]		[0.86]	[1.01]
locdemocracy-LOM	0.031	0.436	healthshock	−0.088	−0.787
	[0.89]	[1.25]		[2.97]***	[2.54]**
corruption95-KI	0.022	0.125	land95	−0.001	−0.008
	[0.86]	[0.54]		[0.16]	[0.21]
fairlaw95	0.037	0.416	assets95	0.061	0.438
	[0.84]	[1.07]		[1.98]*	[2.32]**
violencewomen95	0.046	0.511	livestock95	0.026	0.17
	[1.89]*	[1.82]*		[1.71]*	[1.90]*
control	−0.037	−0.356	totgroups05	−0.024	−0.255
	[1.60]	[1.68]*		[0.93]	[1.31]
control-LOM	−0.12	−1.259	groupch	0.068	0.533
	[1.78]*	[1.88]*		[2.02]**	[2.13]**
aspirations	0.013	0.149	Constant	0.777	3.625
	[1.11]	[1.06]		[2.28]**	[1.15]
aspirations-LOM	−0.03	−0.367	Observations	531	531
	[0.93]	[1.30]	R^2	0.14	
collectiveaction95	−0.079	−0.568			
	[1.98]**	[1.96]*			

Note: KI denotes information from key informants, and FGD stands for focus group discussions; variables without suffix are from household interviews. LOM indicates leave-out mean (weighted). 95 and 05 denote variables referring to 1995 and 2005; where no date is indicated, the variable combines information for the two periods and/or changes.

*p < .10 **p < .05 ***p < .01

Regressions using upward movement as the dependent variable

Columns 5 and 6 in annex table 5.E report OLS and logit results using a different dependent variable, namely whether an initially poor household moved up (dummy = 1) or not (dummy = 0), regardless of whether it crossed or did not cross the community poverty line (MPI, for mobility of the poor index).

The results are similar: changes in group membership are significantly correlated with upward movement. Interestingly, health shocks are not significant when the dependent variable is upward movement, suggesting that households may move up a bit even in the event of a health shock but generally remain below the poverty line. Education and assets are strongly significant. Initial conditions on cluster households' views on local democracy are negative and significant: more movement up of poor households occurred where local democracy was rated lower in 1995. Households that felt they had little or no control over everyday life in 1995 also moved up more frequently (or, possibly, households that moved up felt they had more control in 2005 than 10 years earlier). Apart from these small variations, the results are substantially the same.

ANNEX TABLE 5.E
Correlates of moving out of poverty and moving up in Andhra Pradesh, initial conditions, OLS and logit specifications

Variable	OLS weighted (MOP) Model 3	Logit weighted (MOP) Model 4	OLS weighted (MPI) Model 5	Logit weighted (MPI) Model 6
econstrength95-KI	0.004	0.004	0.003	0.012
	[0.12]	[0.02]	[0.08]	[0.08]
locdemocracy95	–0.02	–0.155	–0.007	–0.033
	[1.11]	[1.01]	[0.32]	[0.29]
locdemocracy95-LOM	–0.016	–0.216	–0.122	–0.619
	[0.47]	[0.70]	[2.46]**	[2.44]**
fairlaw95	0.074	0.545	0.023	0.155
	[2.18]**	[1.68]*	[0.40]	[0.50]
violencewomen95	0.073	0.76	0.133	0.833
	[2.94]***	[2.56]**	[3.63]***	[3.55]***
control95	–0.021	–0.18	–0.066	–0.344
	[1.28]	[1.33]	[2.27]**	[2.32]**

continued

Variable	OLS weighted (MOP) Model 3	Logit weighted (MOP) Model 4	OLS weighted (MPI) Model 5	Logit weighted (MPI) Model 6
control95-LOM	−0.001	−0.019	0.055	0.256
	[0.02]	[0.06]	[0.82]	[0.79]
collectiveaction95	−0.061	−0.45	−0.074	−0.366
	[1.70]*	[1.79]*	[1.63]	[1.71]*
cohesiveness95	−0.033	−0.243	0.01	0.039
	[1.33]	[1.27]	[0.33]	[0.26]
educ	0.04	0.323	0.071	0.355
	[1.53]	[1.77]*	[2.39]**	[2.59]**
healthshock	−0.104	−0.903	−0.067	−0.338
	[3.21]**	[2.78]**	[1.49]	[1.48]
land95	−0.001	−0.002	−0.001	−0.002
	[0.14]	[0.05]	[0.09]	[0.07]
assets95	0.052	0.336	0.068	0.318
	[1.81]*	[2.01]**	[2.28]**	[2.32]**
livestock95	0.026	0.174	0.018	0.086
	[1.77]*	[1.90]*	[1.17]	[1.18]
totgroups95	−0.005	−0.074	−0.035	−0.165
	[0.17]	[0.38]	[0.97]	[0.94]
groupch	0.041	0.241	0.042	0.192
	[2.33]**	[2.58]**	[2.36]**	[2.37]**
Constant	0.009	−3.664	−0.236	−4.142
	[0.03]	[1.65]	[0.64]	[2.25]*
Observations	531	531	531	531
R^2	0.12		0.13	

Note: KI denotes information from key informants and FGD stands for focus group discussions; variables without suffix are from household interviews. LOM indicates leave-out mean (weighted). 95 and 05 denote variables referring to 1995 and 2005; where no date is indicated, the variable combines information for the two periods and/or changes.

*p < .10   **p < .05   ***p < .01

Annex 5.3 Variables for Household Regressions, Andhra Pradesh

ANNEX TABLE 5.F

List of variables for household regressions in Andhra Pradesh: Basic conceptual framework

Explanatory variables	Source	Coding/directionality
Economic opportunity		
econstrength95-KI: Strength of local economy in 1995 (PCA index[a])		
Strength of local economy (rc205b)	KI	very weak = 1, very strong = 5
Presence of private employers (rc208b)	KI	yes = 1, no = 0
Difficulty in finding a job (rc209b)	KI	very difficult = 1, very easy = 6
Changes in economic prosperity		
econstrength-FGD: Trend in community prosperity (rc903m)	Male FGD	less prosperous = 1, more prosperous = 3
Local democracy		
locdemocracy: Responsiveness of local democracy (PCA index)		
Trust in local government officials (rh415bi)	HH	not at all = 1, to a very great extent = 5
Satisfaction with democracy in local government (rh511)	HH	very dissatisfied = 1, very satisfied = 4
Extent to which local government takes into account concerns (rh502b)	HH	less = 1, more = 3
Ability to influence actions of local government (rh504)	HH	decreased = 1, increased = 3
corruption95-KI: Corruption (PCA index)		
Corruption in government officials at the country level (rc505b)	KI	almost all = 1, almost none = 4
Corruption in government officials in village (rc506b)	KI	almost all = 1, almost none = 4
Fairness		
fairlaw95: Fairness in treatment under law within community in 1995 (rh606b)	HH	yes = 1, no = 0
Violence against women		
violencewomen95: Violence against women in 1995 (rh609b)	HH	very much = 1, none at all = 4
Individual agency		
control: Household's perception of control over everyday decisions (rh501b)	HH	less = 1, more = 3

continued

Explanatory variables	Source	Coding/directionality
Household aspirations		
aspirations: Individual aspirations (PCA index)		
Aspirations for self (rh716)	HH	worse off = 1, better off = 3
Aspirations for future generations (rh717)	HH	worse off = 1, better off = 3
Collective agency		
collectiveaction95: Extent of collective action in 1995 (PCA index[a])		
Coming together to solve water problems (rc412b)	KI	very unlikely = 1, very likely = 4
Coming together to assist each other (rc413b)	KI	very unlikely = 1, very likely = 4
Social stratification		
cohesivenesss95: Differences between people based on ethnicity, caste, etc., in 1995 (rc414b)	KI	to a very great extent = 1; no division = 5
inequality: Trend in ethnic/religious discrimination in schools (PCA index)		
Ethnic/religious discrimination in schools (c305b)	KI	improved = 1, deteriorated = 3
Gender discrimination in schools (c304b)	KI	improved = 1, deteriorated = 3
Control variables		
educ: Current education level of respondent (h106)	HH	(regrouped into fewer categories) illiterate = 1, at most primary = 2, some secondary and above = 3
healthshock: Health shocks over 1995-2005 (h305)	HH	yes = 1, no = 0
land95: Total farmland owned in 1995 (h204 i+ii+iii+iv)b	HH	number of hectares owned
assets95: Assets owned in 1995 (h201 i-xiii)b (PCA index[a])	HH	whether owned (yes = 1, no = 0)
livestock95: Livestock owned in 1995 (h203 i-x)b (PCA index[a])	HH	whether owned (yes = 1, no = 0)

Source: Adapted from Narayan, Pritchett, and Kapoor 2009.

Note: Reference questions in the community questionnaire are indicated by *c* and in the household questionnaire by *h*. Prefix *r* means variable was recoded. Suffix *a* means current (at time of study); *b* means initial (approximately 10 years ago). KI = key informant; FGD = focus group discussion; HH = household; PCA = principal component analysis. In the farmland variable, the symbols i, ii, iii, and iv signify irrigated land, unirrigated temporary crop land, unirrigated permanent crop land, and grazing land/wasteland respectively.

a. A PCA was first done on current conditions, and weights were applied to initial conditions 10 years ago. A weighted average of initial conditions (with current weights) was then used as an explanatory variable.

ANNEX TABLE 5.G
List of variables for household regressions in Andhra Pradesh: Conceptual framework with indicators of initial conditions

Explanatory variables	Source	Coding/directionality
Economic opportunity		
econstrength-KI: Strength of local economy (rc205b)	KI	very weak = 1, very strong = 5
Local democracy		
locdemocracy95: Responsiveness of local democracy in 1995 (PCA index)		
Trust in local government officials (rh415bi)	HH	not at all = 1, to a very great extent = 5
Extent to which local government takes into account concerns (rh502b, reconstructed)	HH	absolutely not = 0, very, very much = 4
Fairness		
fairlaw95: Fairness in treatment under law within community in 1995 (rh606b)	HH	yes = 1, no = 0
Violence against women		
violencewomen95: Violence against women in 1995 (rh609b)	HH	very much = 1, none at all = 4
Individual agency		
control95: Household's perception of control over everyday decisions in 1995 (rh501b, reconstructed)	HH	absolutely no control over decisions = 0, absolute control over all decisions = 6
Collective agency		
collectiveaction95: Extent of collective action in 1995 (PCA index[a])		
Coming together to solve water problems (rc412b)	KI	very unlikely = 1, very likely = 4
Coming together to assist each other (rc413b)	KI	very unlikely = 1, very likely = 4
Social stratification		
cohesivenesss95: Differences between people based on ethnicity, caste, etc., in 1995 (rc414b)	KI	(recoded so more is better) to a very great extent = 1; no division = 5

continued

Explanatory variables	Source	Coding/directionality
Control variables		
educ: Current education level of respondent (h106)	HH	(regrouped into fewer categories) illiterate = 1, at most primary = 2, some secondary and above = 3
healthshock: Health shocks over 1995-2005 (h305)	HH	yes = 1, no = 0
land95: Total farmland owned in 1995 (h204 i+ii+iii+iv)b	HH	number of hectares owned
assets95: Assets owned in 1995 (h201 i-xiii)b (PCA index[a])	HH	whether owned (yes = 1, no = 0)
livestock95: Livestock owned in 1995 (h203 i-x)b (PCA index[a])	HH	whether owned (yes = 1, no = 0)

Source: Adapted from Narayan, Pritchett, and Kapoor 2009.

Note: Reference questions in the community questionnaire are indicated by *c* and in the household questionnaire by *h*. Prefix *r* means variable was recoded. Suffix *a* means current (at time of study); *b* means initial (approximately 10 years ago). KI = key informant; FGD = focus group discussion; HH = household; PCA = principal component analysis. In the farmland variable, the symbols i, ii, iii, and iv signify irrigated land, unirrigated temporary crop land, unirrigated permanent crop land, and grazing land/wasteland respectively.

a. A PCA was first done on current conditions, and weights were applied to initial conditions 10 years ago. A weighted average of initial conditions (with current weights) was then used as an explanatory variable.

Annex 5.4 Weighting the Andhra Pradesh Sample

How to construct approximate weights?

While exact sampling weights cannot be reconstructed for Andhra Pradesh because the selection was not random (annex 5.1), it is possible to construct approximate weights by using the proportion of households in each mobility group in the village listing done by focus group participants and in the household sample. Let us consider the list of about 150 households classified by the (male) focus group participants in the ladder of life exercise as our population. If $N(i, j)$ is the number of households in category i in village j, with i ranging from 1 to 4 for the four categories, and $n(i, j)$ is the number of households in category i in the sample for village j, then the selection probability of a household belonging to category i in village j is simply $n(i, j)/N(i, j)$ and its weight is the inverse of this selection probability, $N(i, j)/n(i, j)$. Annex table 5.H provides an example.

Intuitively, we can assume that sampled households provide information on nonsampled households in the same category, and weights tell us how many households in the population a sampled household "represents." So, for instance, every chronic poor household in the sample for village 1 gives us information about, or represents, 12.25 households in the population for that village. On average, each sampled household in this village represents 10.53 households in the populations (158/15). Households from categories that are oversampled will have weights below this average (in village 1, the never poor) and households from categories that are undersampled will have weights above the average (in village 1, the chronic poor).

Note that the sum of weights over the 15 households is equal to the number of households in the population. In more formal terms, the sum of

ANNEX TABLE 5.H
Selection probabilities and weights for households in village 1

Mobility group	No. of households in community list	No. of households in sample	Selection probability	Weight
Movers	35	3	0.0857	11.6667
Chronic poor	49	4	0.0816	12.2500
Fallers	10	1	0.1000	10.0000
Never poor	64	7	0.1094	9.1429
Total	158	15	0.0949	10.5333

the 15 $N(i, j)/n(i, j)$'s, for i ranging from 1 to 4, is equal to $N(j)$, or the total number of households in the village.

In what sense are these weights approximate? They are approximate in the sense that, while we take into account one dimension in which the sample was not random, we cannot take into account others. Since households were not randomly selected, we cannot reconstruct true sampling weights. If, for instance, households were selected from among those closest to the main road, or among the friends of the village head, we should not assume that our approximate weights reasonably correct for that.

These weights take into account only selection of households, not of villages. In the Andhra Pradesh study, villages were purposively selected and we did not attempt to construct approximate village selection probabilities. So even after weighting, our sample only represents the population of the selected villages and not any larger population.[18]

How to deal with unrepresented categories?

The approach to obtaining approximate weights described above is appealing in its simplicity but unfortunately runs into problems wherever no household was selected from a given category. In some cases, no household was selected because there was none in that category, for example, no fallers in a community. This is fine. In other cases, there were such households but none was selected, as in village 2 (annex table 5.I).

In theory, this should not have happened. Even if the 10 households selected a priori from the DPIP MTA list had all been in one category, the interviewers still had five slots to fill, and they could have selected at least one household in each of the remaining three categories. In practice, however, they did not do so, perhaps because it was not possible to find households belonging to each category that were willing to be interviewed (maybe the seven movers in village 2 were all away at a wedding or busy all day in their fields). Whatever the reason, as in village 2, in several villages in the sample one or two categories are not represented. This happened most often with the least numerous category, the fallers.

ANNEX TABLE 5.I

Households in each category in the community and the sample, village 2

Mobility group	No. of households in community list	No. of households in sample
Movers	7	0
Chronic poor	15	0
Fallers	16	4
Never poor	112	11
Total	150	15

If we compute selection probabilities and weights for village 2 as we did for village 1, we will have zero selection probabilities for chronic poor and movers and consequently infinite weights (which is irrelevant, since there are zero observations to use these weights on). Note that this is not just a statistical artifact. What we face is a real problem: there is no one in the sample to represent those chronic poor and movers in village 2. They simply have no voice in our sample.

There are basically two ways to deal with this problem. The first is simply to ignore unrepresented households. The second is to assume that households that are close in some sense to those unrepresented can represent them. Each solution has its advantages and disadvantages, as we shall see.

Ignoring unrepresented households. This is not as absurd as it may seem at first. We do not have information on any of them and cannot invent it, so we simply conclude that our sample represents not all households in the communities but only those for whom we have "representatives" in the sample. We would then calculate selection probabilities and weights for those households that are represented; zero weights really are infinity (annex table 5.J).

It is important to note that if we sum these weights over the sampled households, we get 128, not the total number of households in the community (150) as we did earlier. Intuitively, this makes sense: our sample only represents fallers (16) and never poor (112), that is, 128 households in total. We have indeed ignored the others.

Weights constructed in this manner have a desirable property. Suppose we wanted to calculate a weighted mean at the community level. We simply sum the variable we want to average multiplied by each weight for each observation and divide by 128. In other words, these weights divided by the total number of households represented sum to 1. That this is a desirable property

ANNEX TABLE 5.J
Selection probabilities and weights for households in village 2

Mobility group	No. of households in community list	No. of households in sample	Selection probability	Weight
Movers	7	0	0	—
Chronic poor	15	0	0	—
Fallers	16	4	0.2500	4.0000
Never poor	112	11	0.0982	10.1818
Total	150	15	0.1000	10.0000

can easily be seen if we consider calculating the weighted mean of a variable that has the same value for all sample households in a community; in this case, we would want the weighted average to be exactly equal to that value, no more and no less. Weights summing up to 1 do the trick.

Naturally, there is also a downside: we ignore all those unrepresented observations. This means that in the end our sample represents fewer households in the population than we originally expected. Take the AP population and sample: the total population in the 56 communities surveyed is 8,348 households (a little less than 56 × 150, as on average there are just under 150 households per community). Now, take the population represented in our sample if we ignore all households in categories from which no one was selected; our population goes down to 7,889 households. We have "lost" 5.5 percent of the sample, which is not negligible. What is worse, we have lost proportionally more households in the less numerous categories, as annex table 5.K indicates.

Using "close" households to represent households not represented. Reducing the population represented by our sample, particularly if it penalizes small categories, is clearly not ideal. Can we not do better? One option is to assume that the households from the represented categories represent the others also. In other words, we can assume that households that are "close" in the sense of living in the same village can well represent our missing households.

In the case of village 2, this would mean assuming that the fallers and never poor in the sample also represent the chronic poor and movers. This is certainly possible, but unconvincing. We could compare the characteristics of households in the four categories in villages where we have them all and develop a metric to tell us to whom the chronic poor and movers are most

ANNEX TABLE 5.K
Total population by category and population represented by households in the same category and village

Mobility group	No. of households in population	No. of households represented in the sample	Difference (%)
Movers	889	729	18.0
Chronic poor	4,442	4,351	2.0
Fallers	278	142	48.9
Never poor	2,739	2,667	2.6
Total	8,348	7,889	5.5

similar. We could also assume that the unrepresented households are represented by a weighted average of the categories present. So, for example, each faller household sampled in village 2 would also represent $(4/15) \times (15+7)$ chronic poor plus mover households, and each never poor household would also represent $(11/15) \times (15+7)$ chronic poor plus mover households. In the latter case, the desirable property that weights sum to total population is respected. Whichever way we go, this is not an ideal solution.

There is another way in which we could interpret "close," namely by taking households in the same category but in nearby villages to represent our missing households. So, for example, we would consider the movers sampled in the four villages in the same mandal as village 2 to represent not just movers in their village but movers in the whole mandal. Annex table 5.L has information on category frequencies in the four communities in Gudihathnur mandal, which we call mandal 1.

If we were to follow this approach, the 7 + 11 + 5 never poor in villages 1, 2, and 3 would represent not only the 64 + 112 + 48 never poor in the same villages, but also the 19 never poor in village 4. Instead of the selection probabilities and weights calculated at the village level, we would assign mandal-level selection probabilities and weights. In this mandal, we have missing observations in at least one village for each category, so the mandal-level weights would substitute the village-level weights for each category and village. In some cases they are higher, in some cases lower, but on average they will be higher: more households are now represented by our sample.

In the AP sample, using households in the mandal to represent unrepresented households is not always enough; in some mandals, no household was interviewed in the faller category. In this case, the only option is to go up to the next level of aggregation, the district.[19] A final, simpler option would be to use weights by district and mobility group for all households, even those that are represented at lower levels of aggregation.

The beauty of weights constructed this way is that they sum up to the population: by going up to the lowest level of geographic aggregation for which we have some observations in our sample, we can represent all households in the population. As usual, though, there is a flip side: these weights do not sum to 1 at the community level.

Which weights to use for what?

Both solutions outlined here attempt to deal with the problem that there are no sampled households from some categories in some communities. Both have advantages and disadvantages, and they work well for different purposes.

ANNEX TABLE 5.L
Frequencies by category in four villages of mandal 1

Village no.	Village name	rhhclassm	rmovers	rfallers	rneverpoor	rchronicpoor	one	Movers	Chronic poor	Fallers	Never poor
1	Kamalapur	158	35	10	64	49	15	3	4	1	7
2	Guruj	150	7	16	112	15	15	0	0	4	11
3	Malkapur	150	30	1	48	71	14	4	5	0	5
4	Dhampur	150	23		19	108	15	4	11	0	0

Specifically, we need weights for two purposes: (a) to obtain cluster means that take into account nonrandom selection within clusters, and (b) to obtain weighted sample and subsample means, regression results, and so on. From the preceding discussion, it is clear that the first type of weights, those that ignore unrepresented households, are appropriate to calculate village means. Weights obtained in this way are used to calculate the weighted cluster means used in regressions. The second type of weights, which use geographically "close" households in the same category to represent those unrepresented, are appropriate to weigh observations for the sample as a whole and major subsamples (such as districts). In the end, the regressions reported in the text use weights by district and mobility group for all households, even where we could have calculated weights for smaller geographic units. This approach was done because selection probabilities and weights vary greatly across villages, ranging from 1 (when all households in a category were selected) to 77 (when very few households were selected from a numerous population), and very high weights increase the impact of outliers or near-outliers in regressions.

References

Aiyar, S., D. Narayan, and K. Raju. 2006. "Empowerment through Self-Help Groups: Andhra Pradesh Shows the Way in India." In *Ending Poverty in South Asia: Ideas that Work*, ed. D. Narayan and E. Glinskaya, 104–35. Washington, DC: World Bank.

APCLC (Andhra Pradesh Civil Liberties Committee). 1991. "The Chundur Carnage: August 6, 1991." Vijayawada, India: APCLC.

CESS (Center for Economic and Social Studies). 2005. "Mid-Term Appraisal of District Poverty Initiatives Project." Hyderabad, India: CESS.

CMIE (Centre for Monitoring Indian Economy). 2000. *Profiles of Districts*. Mumbai: CMIE.

Christen, R., and G. Ivatury. 2007. "Sustainability of Self-Help Groups in India: Two Analyses." Occasional Paper 12, Consultative Group to Assist the Poor, Washington, DC.

Deaton, A., and J. Drèze. 2002. "Poverty and Inequality in India: A Re-Examination." *Economic and Political Weekly*, September 7, 3729–48.

Dev, S. M. 2007. "Inclusive Growth in Andhra Pradesh: Challenges in Agriculture, Poverty, Social Sector and Regional Disparities." Working Paper 71, Centre for Economic and Social Studies, Hyderabad, India.

Dev, S. M., S. Galab, and C. Ravi. 2007. "Indira Kranthi Patham and Poverty Reduction in Andhra Pradesh." Paper presented at International Conference on Andhra Pradesh Experience with Membership-Based Organizations of the Poor, Hyderabad, India, June 5–6.

Ghosh, J. 2004. "Despair and Determination in Anantapur." *MacroScan*, October 15. http://www.macroscan.org/the/food/oct04/fod151004Anantapur.htm.

Jones, N., M. Mukherjee, and S. Galab. 2007. "Ripple Effects or Deliberate Intentions? Assessing Linkages between Women's Empowerment and Childhood Poverty." Paper presented at International Conference on Andhra Pradesh Experience with Membership-Based Organizations of the Poor, Hyderabad, India, June 5–6.

Narayan, D., L. Pritchett, and S. Kapoor. 2009. *Moving Out of Poverty: Success from the Bottom Up*. New York: Palgrave Macmillan; Washington, DC: World Bank.

Srinivasulu, K. 1999. "Regime Change and Shifting Social Bases: The Telugu Desam Party in the Twelfth General Elections." In *Indian Politics and the 1998 Elections: Regionalism, Hindutva and State Politics*, ed. R. Roy and P. Wallace, 210–34. Delhi: Sage.

———. 2002. "Caste, Class and Social Articulation in Andhra Pradesh: Mapping Differential Regional Trajectories." Working Paper 179, Overseas Development Institute, London.

Suri, K. C. 2002. "Democratic Process and Electoral Politics in Andhra Pradesh, India." Working Paper 180, Overseas Development Institute, London.

World Bank. 2006. *Overcoming Drought: Adaptation Strategies for Andhra Pradesh, India*. Directions in Development Series. Washington, DC: World Bank.

Notes

1. Velugu (meaning "eternal light") was launched by the Andhra Pradesh state government in 2000 with support from the World Bank under the first District Poverty Initiative Project (DPIP I). The program supported women's self-help groups as a way to trigger economic development and alleviate poverty at the community level. By the end of 2005, the program had organized 7.8 million poor women into 617,472 self-help groups. These groups mobilized up to $250 million in savings every year, obtained additional credit of up to $475 million from banks, and used the credit and government grants to improve livelihoods and community infrastructure. They also worked for the abolition of social evils like child labor and temple prostitution, created community-based health systems, and established residential schools to promote education of girls (Aiyar, Narayan, and Raju 2006). The program was extended in 2004 under a second DPIP.

2. For more information on the selection of the Andhra Pradesh study sample, see annex 5.1. Constructing a panel later turned out not to be feasible.

3. At the time the Moving Out of Poverty study was launched, no India-wide panel study existed. Panel data are not widely available in India. Existing panel studies include Palanpur in Uttar Pradesh, the ICRISAT (International Crops Research Institute for the Semi-Arid Tropics) villages, the National Council of Applied Economic Research panel surveys, and the Human Development Survey conducted in 2004/05 by the National Council of Applied Economic Research and the University of Maryland.

4. These findings differ from those of Dev, Galab, and Ravi (2007), who found greater declines in Anantapur than in the other two districts. But their data refer to the period 2003–06, while the data used here cover 1995–2005.
5. Obviously, MPI is higher than MOP because MOP is a subset of MPI (only those poor who, in rising, cross the community poverty line are counted in the MOP index).
6. Studies including the DPIP midterm appraisal (CESS 2005) and more recent work by Dev, Galab, and Ravi (2007) have found the program to be efficient in targeting the very poor and the socially marginalized. Both studies suggest a faster decline in poverty levels among the very poor, particularly those belonging to scheduled and backward castes, after they join SHGs.
7. Other studies on SHGs in Andhra Pradesh have also reported the positive externalities that such groups have had on local government functioning. The DPIP midterm appraisal, for instance, notes that awareness of and participation in local government bodies was higher in DPIP districts, that is, in those where the Velugu program had been implemented, than elsewhere (CESS 2005). It is possible that some groups may have been more successful than others in holding service providers to account or encouraging collective action. However, our data did not allow us to differentiate between groups to see if that indeed was the case.
8. The state government, for example, now deals directly with self-help groups and village organizations that act as procurement agents for maize. In 2005 the maize procured from SHGs was estimated to be worth $26 million. Non–group members benefited from the increase in farmgate maize prices that resulted from cutting out the shares of middlemen. It should be noted that groups generally need support in livelihoods and actual day-to-day operations to be able to perform some of these more complex roles. In a recent study evaluating the operational structure and performance of four leading SHG programs in other Indian states, Christen and Ivatury (2007) conclude that unless external support is provided to SHGs in a sustainable way and paid for by revenue that the programs themselves generate, groups will degrade over time and eventually collapse.
9. In the midterm appraisal of the DPIP project in AP, it was estimated that the proportion of households in the intervention area able to withstand drought increased from 4 to 11 percent, while households able to withstand health shocks increased from 5 to 13 percent. The percentage of households selling assets in distress was estimated to have declined from 14 to 3.5 percent over the project years, and that of households with members seeking work as bonded/ attached labor from 2 to 0.7 percent (CESS 2005).
10. Loans to SHGs have now been mandated as priority sector lending in India, with the National Bank for Agricultural and Rural Development (NABARD) refinancing all loans to SHGs. Through the end of 2005, SHGs in Andhra Pradesh had received nearly $475 million from commercial, government, and cooperative banks (Aiyar, Narayan, and Raju 2006). Being one of the first states to experiment with SHGs, AP accounted for nearly two-fifths of the total finance disbursed by banks to all SHGs in India, according to the state government's Department of Rural Development (http://www.rd.ap.gov.in/).

11. Household interviews were conducted with 839 households, but 308 of them were not poor in 1995, so we do not consider them when studying movement out of poverty.

12. We also took into account the fact that households are clustered and corrected standard errors.

13. We also looked at the number of groups present in the village and its change (as opposed to the number of groups a household belonged to and its change), but the former variable is noisily measured so we do not believe it is reliable.

14. In the survey, the education level of the respondent was measured in 2005, but it is unlikely to have changed significantly over the previous 10 years for adults in the household.

15. To control for halo effects, that is, the fact that a person's view on different subjects may be colored by a generally positive (or negative) outlook on life, we have in some cases included in the regression the value of a variable as well as its leave-out mean.

16. Caste dummies were used for general category, other backward classes (OBC), scheduled castes (SC), and scheduled tribes (ST). Caste composition was also not a significant predictor of changes in poverty at the village level. Villages that experienced high percentages of households moving out of poverty did not have fewer ST or SC than villages with less positive performance. Conversely, predominantly ST villages did not appear to have experienced lower declines in poverty than other villages. Villages with a high percentage of SC households fared slightly worse than the average, but the difference was not significant. The presence of a religious minority (Christian, Muslim) was also not a good predictor of the percentage of households that moved out of poverty.

17. In addition to Adilabad, Anantapur, and Srikakulam, the list included Mahabubnagar, Chittoor, and Vizianagaram.

18. This last paragraph oversimplifies matters a bit. To be more precise, first, villages in the AP sample had apparently been randomly selected for the original DPIP study (either the baseline or the midterm assessment) among villages in districts and mandals selected for the first phase of DPIP. Second, in many cases, the approximately 150 households that represent our population were selected from the larger population of a revenue village.

19. If mandals were contiguous, we could aggregate them more finely than by district, but generally they were not.

Politics of the Middle Path: Agrarian Reform and Poverty Dynamics in West Bengal

Klaus Deininger, Deepa Narayan, and Binayak Sen

I got 2 kathas of patta land from the Government in the year 1978. Though this property had not helped me too much in the angle of economy, it gave me mental satisfaction. Since I have some land, I can now claim to be a permanent resident of this village.

—MITHUN, A CHRONIC POOR MAN,
Kuchut, West Bengal

To live in this society, one has to link himself with politics, otherwise living and doing business will be impossible. If any danger comes, I go to the party leaders for help. I never go to government employees for any help.

—SUKAHN, A MALE MOVER,
Biruha, West Bengal

Liton lives in Halapara village in South 24 Parganas district in West Bengal. In 1980, at the age of 35, he was a petty trader selling vegetables. What he describes as a turning point in his life came when he received a single bigha of land from the state government—through the local panchayat—as part of the agrarian reform drive. "Although the land was little, this was the first time I owned any property," he said. "I then started cultivation besides doing vegetable selling. After that I never looked back." After 12 years he bought another 4 bighas of land, and in 1994 he opened an LIC (life insurance) account and started depositing quarterly. When asked about his other involvements, he said, "My wife is my best friend. I do not belong to any particular community. I do politics, I am doing politics since 1960. I make regular visit to the party office, but I never took any political advantage." Liton is seen is his community as a mover, as someone who has crossed the poverty line.

Amzad, another mover in the same village, narrated a similar climb out of poverty. After the land reform, his break came through a combination of cultivation on the land he received and agribusiness. Of his other involvements, Amzad said, "I am not attached with a club or financial organization. Also, I am not aware of such organization. I am doing politics since 1990 as majority of the population here is attached with politics. I make regular visit to the party office."

In Mayahauri, a nearby village in the same district, Mohiuddin, also classified as a mover, recounted a typical upward trajectory. "I started work as day laborer with my father in 1968. After that I got land from the panchayat pradhan in 1980. This is the first big thing in my life. I started cultivation alongside with day labor. In 2000 with the help of my sons I bought another 4 bighas. Now we have adequate food." Mohiuddin, however, ended his story with a twist. Of his other involvements, he said: "I am not related with politics in such way. Though the circumstances around me force me to mingle with them and take part in their party affairs. If I do not do so, I will never be able to stay here and earn my livelihood here. So I am taking part in party's affairs and have relation with them. I cannot say anything more and depict more vividly about it though they never tried to harm me."

Another resident of Halapara, Prokash, is classified as chronic poor. He received 4 kathas of land from the government in 1984 (about one-fifth of a bigha). But he did not have enough money to cultivate the land, so he sold it. He did not get much from the sale. Last year, he came down with malaria and had to borrow from informal sources of credit for subsistence. When asked about other involvements, he said, "I am not involved in politics. Also, I have no interest in this."

Which of these accounts of the political process reflects the reality in rural West Bengal? All four life histories feature access to land reform, and two of them explicitly refer to the panchayat. But they give different accounts of involvement in the political process, suggesting the varying roles that politics can play in a person's ascent from poverty.

Liton is a party activist and at least indirectly a beneficiary of the prestige and power that the party commands, even though he denies getting any privilege. The denial actually confirms his activist position: he represents the view of the ideological enthusiast. Amzad, though a loyalist like Liton, feels almost obligated to support the ruling party ever since he got access to redistributed land. Recognizing the widespread politicization at the village level, he made a pragmatic decision to be part of it: he represents the view of the pragmatic supporter. In contrast, Mohiuddin symbolizes the silent opposition. For him, ordinary people and party activists are in an us-them binary relationship of mutual opposition. Although he too benefited from the agrarian reform during its initial phase, he did not like the subsequent politicization. He managed to put up with his erstwhile benefactors and continued to take part in party activities, keeping his opposing views to himself.

Prokash's position is that of the indifferent spectator. Though he too received land and had a chance for a breakthrough, he could not reap the benefits of agrarian reform. Strikingly, the amount of land he got is much smaller than what the movers received—a pattern consistently borne out by the life stories data.[1] He lacked capital to invest in the land and he needed to meet immediate consumption needs, so he quickly sold the meager plot. He also suffered health shocks that resulted in debt. Once he returned to agricultural wage labor, his interest in politics quickly disappeared; in fact, he sounded quite passive and indifferent. He is a nonmover, stuck in chronic poverty.

All four life stories show that the agrarian reform initiated in West Bengal in 1978 was a pivotal life event for the beneficiaries. Land was targeted to the land-poor, not just to marginal and small farmers, but also to those who were virtually landless and working as agricultural laborers. The average amount of land received by each beneficiary under the reform was modest. Nevertheless, as seen in the life stories of the three movers, it represented a significant point of departure, a break with the past on at least two counts. First, it provided a durable foundation on which poor households could plan for the future. For food-poor households, having even an extra bigha of land was important in addressing the problem of food insecurity. Households with more favorable initial conditions—higher aspirations, a well-functioning family network, and better skills—could use the land as a base for developing diversified strategies for moving ahead. Second, access to land reform provided scope for remaining connected with politically influential forces at the local level. Such a connection meant the possibility of gaining access to nonland opportunities, including access to antipoverty programs, recommendations for placement in educational institutions or salaried jobs for sons or daughters, rights to a trading space in the marketplace, and access to farm or nonfarm loans.

However, the life stories also imply that the land distribution was implemented through an initial screening by the panchayat and mediated through grassroots politics, with prospective beneficiaries required to maintain a certain level of political allegiance if not activism in support of the ruling party. In other words, political clientelism benefits the politically connected households—the movers in the above cases—but not others. Those who did not benefit may have been excluded from the process by choice or because their personal characteristics and circumstances relegated them to the sidelines.

Competing Narratives on Rural Institutional Reforms

The package of rural institutional reforms initiated in 1978 comprised two main parts. The first was decentralization through three-tier panchayats at the district, block (subdistrict), and village levels. This structure was introduced in West Bengal more than a decade before the 73rd amendment to the Indian constitution mandated it countrywide in 1992.[2]

The second part of the package was land reform.[3] This was carried out through two routes:

- Through tenurial security. This scheme, known as Operation Barga, resulted in access to "barga land." The program involves registration of sharecroppers, providing them permanent and hereditary rights. This reduces tenants' probability of being evicted and often also increases their share of the crop. Given the security of tenure for registered sharecroppers (*bargadars*), such tenancy reforms are expected to have significant productivity effects compared to tenancy lands cultivated by unregistered sharecroppers during the pre-reform period.[4]
- Through land distribution under the ceiling legislation, resulting in access to "patta land." Ceiling laws provide the basis for expropriating land held by any given owner in excess of a state-specific ceiling and subsequently transferring it to poor farmers or landless agricultural workers (*pattadars*). In most states of India, even where the government has been able to acquire above-ceiling land, overcoming political pressures in the distribution of such land has been very difficult. In West Bengal, by contrast, lands acquired under ceiling legislation have been transferred in a relatively pro-poor fashion (World Bank 2007).[5]

As a result of significant efforts in the area of decentralization and land reform, West Bengal was top or close to top among Indian states in terms of both the share of land area transferred and the share of population that benefited from it (World Bank 2007; see also annex table 6.B). There is wide consensus in the literature that these institutional reforms initially had beneficial effects on the poor, especially in the context of decentralized governance in West Bengal.[6] The present study, using both qualitative and quantitative methods also found support for such a positive appraisal of the impact of land access for the rural poor during the initial phase of agrarian reform, 1978–90. Opinions, however, diverged on the assessment of what happened in the later phase, as detailed below.

The early optimistic view

According to the most optimistic interpretation, decentralization and land reform implemented by local government strengthen local democracy by leading to better-functioning local government, improved reach and targeting of service delivery, maintenance of social peace, and greater social inclusion. All these positive developments tend to favor the initiatives, aspirations, and empowerment of local residents, especially poor people. Community-wide, they should stimulate faster local growth and poverty reduction. Indeed, some initial results of the reforms in West Bengal, mainly in the 1980s, supported this optimistic view. The sharp drop in rural poverty in West Bengal between 1977 and 1993 was one of the fastest among all Indian states (Datt 1998).

A remarkable feature of this development was the decline in rural inequality, often attributed to the egalitarian influence of agrarian reform.[7] There is some debate as to whether the poorest rural households shared in the dividends of the agrarian reform package: there were very few share-croppers among the poorest to begin with, so barga reform would not have touched most of them, and patta reform was probably too modest in scale to have much tangible effect. But the laboring class in rural West Bengal benefited through another route. As elsewhere in eastern India, the rural poorest, whose main occupation is agricultural wage labor, gained indirectly from the labor-intensive growth in the agricultural sector spurred by the green revolution (Hossain et al. 2002).

The dissenting view

Dissenters contend that the early optimistic view, based on evidence from the 1980s, largely ignores the contrasting dynamics of development in the 1990s and the changing nature of the state's political economy. There are two reasons why the initial decentralization and land reform may not have led to sustained rural revitalization and upward mobility of the poor. The first relates to a gradual slowdown of rural reform under the rule of the Left Front (LF), an alliance of leftist parties that came to power in 1977 in West Bengal. The LF administration was shaped by competition to secure often narrow electoral victories in a large number of marginal constituencies, resulting in inevitable class compromises among different landowning groups (Williams 1999).

The second reason has to do with persistent shortcomings in macroeconomic management and policy indecisiveness that undermined the effort to bring about deep structural reforms and modernization, making it more difficult to tap rural development potential (Banerjee et al. 2002). The process of land reform, which focused on sharecroppers from the beginning, slowed considerably in the 1990s with respect to both barga and patta reforms. Some observers attributed this to the Left Front's conscious decision to appease and consolidate the power of the middle peasantry (Bhattacharya 1999). Others cited the declining activism of the gram panchayats as reflected in the dramatic drop in attendance at gram sabhas (local assemblies). Still others pointed to the corrupting and exclusionary influence of political clientelism encouraged by party middlemen (Maharatna 2007).

The 1990s also witnessed considerable difficulties in macro-managing the economic affairs of the state in terms of exercising prudent fiscal oversight, creating an enabling business climate, and encouraging growth of the modern sector. While West Bengal continued to do well with respect to agricultural growth, there was faltering performance in the formal manufacturing sector (dominated by state-owned enterprises and older industries in the jute and cotton textile belts), so that West Bengal lagged behind other advanced states of South India in manufacturing. This was seen as part of a long-term urban/industrial decline that started in the mid-1950s.[8] For many, this was surprising, given the state's early industrialization experience and its relatively ample supply of skilled workers (Banerjee et al. 2002; Lahiri and Yi 2008).

One consequence of the slow development of the modern sector, with a virtual absence of small and medium entrepreneurs in the 1980s and 1990s, was a persistence of dualism between traditional and modern sector activities. This in turn slowed the absorption of rural surplus labor. State finances were also weak (the fiscal deficit at one point reached 9 percent of state's gross domestic product). This made it difficult to support any sustainable expansion of modern infrastructure to promote growth of the nonfarm sector in rural and periurban areas, further undermining the scope for absorption of agricultural surplus labor (Maharatna 2007). The fiscal deficit also led to lackluster performance in providing rural access to basic education and health. In this regard West Bengal stood in sharp contrast to Kerala, a state that experienced a similar fiscal crisis during the same period.

All these factors—the slowing of land reform, the decline in popular involvement in local government activities, the crisis in state finances, the long-term urban/manufacturing decline, and the limited absorption of rural surplus labor—suggest a political economy dominated by an "intermediate regime," a social block consisting of middle-class urbanites and rural sharecroppers, small farmers, and middle peasants.[9] Adopting a so-called middle path, the Left Front sided with these sectors, including white-collar state employees and trade union lobbies, at least until 2001. This kept the regime from undertaking deep institutional reforms to stimulate growth in the manufacturing and service sectors and led to incomplete reforms in the rural areas. In short, the dissenting view sees the regime's "middling" strategy as responsible for the limited nature of the gains reaped from decentralization and land reform.

In this chapter, we recognize the potential of both arguments and empirically explore the factors that contributed to moving out of poverty in West Bengal, focusing mainly on the changing institutional and economic dynamics during 1995–2005. Using life histories, community time lines, and community focus group discussions, we also attempt to shed light on the importance of institutional factors such as local democracy, land reform, nonfarm sector development, political clientelism, and agency of poor people that figured in both the optimistic and dissenting views. We blend this discussion with the evidence collected from a structured qualitative and quantitative survey to subject the data to econometric investigations.

The Macro Context: Contrasting Decadal Dynamics

Given its significant agrarian reforms and decentralization efforts in the early 1980s, why did not West Bengal take off and join the league of top performers among Indian states in the subsequent period? Why, for that matter, could it not emulate the progressive experiences of China and Vietnam in the 1980s and 1990s? In the literature and the public policy debate, this problem has sometimes been termed the "West Bengal paradox." The explanation appears to lie, at least in part, in the faltering implementation of land reform in the 1990s, a decade in which rural growth slowed and inequality rose.

Initial growth followed by slowdown

Implementation of agrarian reforms did contribute to several positive changes in the first 15 years of Left Front rule (1978–93). These included higher agricultural growth, favorable redistributive outcomes, faster poverty reduction, and greater social inclusion across gender, caste/tribal, and religious lines. Growth in food grain production accelerated after 1980 and averaged 2.4 percent between 1981 and 1999, one of the highest among Indian states during that period. The annual rural poverty reduction rate, as recorded by the 38th and 50th rounds of the National Sample Survey (NSS), was remarkable in the 1980s. Rural consumption inequality remained virtually unchanged during this period (for details on poverty trends, see Chatterjee 1998).

Though the precise contributions of land reform, decentralization, and expansion of groundwater irrigation are yet to be determined (Chatterjee 1998), the importance of the first two factors in driving these changes is now generally accepted. The agricultural growth effects are attributable to producer incentives from secure land tenure and greater output share, resulting in higher land productivity.[10] Decentralization also led to better delivery of agricultural inputs and sustained the implementation of agrarian reform itself, at least in the initial phase.

By the early 1990s, however, there were signs of slippage. The pace of agrarian reform, in terms of further registration of bargadars and distribution of patta lands acquired under the ceiling legislation, slowed after 1990. Studies show that the development performance of gram panchayats, measured in terms of implementation of land reform efforts, was better in settings where local elections were more contested and worse in areas with higher illiteracy, higher asset inequality, and a greater concentration of scheduled castes and scheduled tribes (Bardhan and Mookherjee 2006). The performance of gram panchayats varied depending on these factors. Furthermore, the ruling LF regime was also increasingly concerned about its own political survival. As a result, over the years, the agrarian reform efforts in West Bengal became increasingly susceptible to local electoral dynamics. This often led to electoral class compromises and to an apparently weaker commitment to the declared objectives of broad-based popular participation in the reform.

At the same time, a large part of West Bengal agriculture remained locked in low-value-added cultivation of high-yielding varieties (HYV) of rice. By the mid-1990s, 60–70 percent of acreage was brought under cultivation of HYV *boro* paddy (dry-season rice). Moreover, the scope for further expansion of diesel tube wells and canal irrigation, a process driven by the private sector, was relatively limited. Our study also found a very high proportion of irrigation users in the sample, with little variation across dynamic poverty categories. As a result, cereal production started slowing down: after rising 28 percent between 1985/86 and 1990/91, it rose by only 15 percent and 11 percent in the subsequent five-year periods. The overall growth rate of agricultural output fell from a high of 15–16 percent during 1985–95 to 9 percent over the period 1995/96 to 2000/01.[11]

New data suggest a slower pace of rural poverty reduction in the post-1990 period compared to the preceding decade.[12] The growth in per capita consumption expenditure in rural areas declined from 2.7 percent in 1983–94 to just 1.1 percent in 1993–2005 (Dev and Ravi 2007). As a result, the rate of rural poverty reduction slowed considerably in the latter period as well. According to one recent estimate based on grouped distribution data, the rural poverty headcount in West Bengal dropped from 64 percent to 41 percent during the decade between 1983 and 1994—a decline of about 2.1 percent per year, compared to the all-India average of

0.9 percent. Over the next decade, however, the poverty headcount declined only to 29 percent, implying a much slower pace of poverty reduction of 1.2 percent annually, compared to the all-India average of 0.8 percent (Himanshu 2007).

The slowdown in rural growth and poverty reduction performance was accompanied by rising inequality. The Gini index of consumption inequality increased from 25 to 27 percent during 1993–2004, which was a *reversal* of the trend of declining inequality in the previous decade (from 30 percent to 25 percent between 1983 and 1993).[13]

Faltering implementation of land reform

As mentioned earlier, the movement out of poverty in West Bengal took place against a backdrop of agrarian reform. When we compare the share of households that benefited from tenancy legislation to the share of total land area transferred, we see a large variation across states (annex table 6.B; see also World Bank 2007). In West Bengal, under barga reform, 11 percent of the population benefited from a transfer of only 6 percent of the land area, and plot sizes remained considerably below the average for the 15 major states. This suggests that the goal was to maximize the number of beneficiaries (the same pattern is noticeable in Kerala). In most other states, by contrast, the share of population is significantly below the area share, indicating transfers of above-average-size plots. In Maharashtra, 27 percent of the land area was distributed to 11 percent of the population; corresponding figures in Karnataka were 15 percent and 5 percent, in Andhra Pradesh 4 percent and 0.8 percent, and in Madhya Pradesh 2 percent and 0.6 percent.

As for ceiling legislation, which requires greater government effort to appropriate land and redistribute it, the shares of both area and population are much lower in most states than under tenancy reform. Although some states such as Rajasthan, Uttar Pradesh, Bihar, and Andhra Pradesh transferred more land under ceiling than under tenancy legislation, the evidence indicates transfer of above-average-size plots of patta land. This suggests that even where the state was able to acquire above-ceiling land, it was difficult to overcome political pressures affecting its distribution. The exception here is West Bengal. Not only did the state record higher figures under patta than under barga reform, but the share of population that benefited under ceiling legislation was significantly above the share of land transferred. West Bengal appears to have been able to avoid pressures to transfer above-ceiling lands in large chunks, which in turn suggests a formidable—in the Indian context—level of grassroots organization.

Both types of reform increased access to land for poor sharecroppers and marginal/small farmers in West Bengal. This is likely to have had a positive poverty reduction effect, at least initially. The problem is that there has been a considerable slowdown in land reform efforts since the early 1990s. The number of registered bargadars rose rapidly between 1978 and 1981, showed slower but respectable growth in the 1980s, and dropped sharply in the first half of the 1990s. The same goes for patta land distribution. The Moving Out of Poverty life history data show that more than 80 percent of the plots obtained through land reform, under both the patta and barga schemes, were distributed between 1978 and 1990.

The question of why the process of land reform stumbled goes beyond the scope of this analysis, but it has important implications for poverty reduction. Those who gained access to land in the 1980s stood apart from the rest of the poor community, creating a schism within the rural poor and almost predetermining who would move out of poverty in the subsequent decades.[14]

Understanding Community Prosperity: The Changing Face of Villages, 1995–2005

Macro data cannot provide information about local growth and local inequality. Villages differ considerably across districts and even within a given district. Our study used key informant interviews and community focus group discussions to shed light on how ground-level realities changed in the villages between 1995 and 2005. This provides essential local context for understanding poverty dynamics and serves as an indirect cross-check on macro state-level trends.

Sample selection

In West Bengal, the sample selection was done in two stages. In the first stage, districts were categorized as high-growth or low-growth in terms of wage rates and levels of infrastructure development, based on their relative positions above or below the median value. The selection was done on a pro-rata basis from each cell, but with some element of geographic spread as a consideration. This yielded five districts from four regions (eastern plains, western plains, central plains, and Himalayan).

The second stage was the identification of communities within these districts. Because of the availability of panel data from a state government survey conducted in the late 1990s, the identification of communities was done directly based on the level of implementation of land reforms at the grassroots level. The indicator used for selection related to the proportion of households within a community who were *pattadars* or *bargadars*. It was assumed that the higher the proportion of pattadars or bargadars, the higher the level of implementation of land reforms. For West Bengal, it was decided to cover five districts and a total of 40 gram panchayats. Two villages were randomly selected from each sample gram panchayat, making a total of 80 communities.[15]

Identification of mobility groups

In each sample village, focus groups of residents created a "ladder of life" for their community, showing local levels of household well-being on a figurative ladder. The groups also defined a community poverty line, indicating the ladder step at which households were considered no longer poor by local standards. Finally, they ranked about 150 households in their community according to their well-being status at the time of the study (2005) and approximately 10 years earlier (1995). For details on the ladder of life exercise, see appendix 1 in this volume. In West Bengal, the size of a household's landholding and its main occupation are among the factors that determine which step of the ladder an individual household is on.

Based on the ladder of life exercise, each sample household was classified into one of four mobility groups: movers (poor in 1995 but moved out of poverty by 2005); chronic poor (poor in 1995 and remained poor in 2005); fallers (not poor in 1995 but fell into poverty by 2005); and never poor (not poor in 1995 and remained not poor in 2005).

We use two sets of data: (a) information generated from the key informants and community focus groups, and (b) information generated from the perspectives of the poor. The poor, in this context, refers to the initial poor set, those households that were poor in 1995 irrespective of their later movement—that is, the movers plus the chronic poor. Since opinions can diverge for a host of political and economic reasons, we discuss here only those indicators with the least divergence between these two groups. The idea is that the convergence indicators can provide a more objective assessment of local growth and inequality trends.

Trends in community prosperity

Community discussions point to overall positive trends in West Bengal villages during the study period (annex tables 6.C and 6.D). We use data from key informants and households. The most notable improvements concern key issues of infrastructure especially rural-urban link roads that increase the connectivity of villages. Currently 96 percent of the villages are reached by an all-weather road. Village-level electricity coverage has increased from 51 percent to 83 percent. With respect to market access, 61 percent of the communities reported improvements over the past decade, compared to only 3 percent that reported deterioration. Similarly, 43 percent of communities reported improved supplies of agricultural inputs as against 5 percent giving a negative rating.

Other aspects of infrastructure, however, did not show the same level of across-the-board improvement. A large differentiation across surveyed communities is noted with respect to credit access: 30 percent reported improvement while 12 percent reported deterioration. Surprisingly, the state that earlier recorded one of the highest expansions in irrigation coverage now faces problems in this regard: 17 percent of communities reported deterioration in irrigation access compared to 37 percent that reported improvements. The new problem areas include the expansion of canal irrigation, flood control and drainage, and arsenic contamination of water due to excessive groundwater irrigation. But the most important area of recent neglect seems to be agricultural extension: only 28 percent of communities reported improvement in extension services, while 22 percent gave a negative assessment. Naturally, these trends have had a negative impact on productivity, a sign noted earlier by others (Banerjee et al. 2002).

While these infrastructural developments present a mixed picture, the local growth assessments from community focus groups give a rather upbeat signal. Seventy-six percent of the groups reported that communities have become more prosperous, and 63 percent thought that economic opportunities now are greater than 10 years ago. At first glance, this view from the community level does not readily square with the rather modest growth assessment derived from the NSS rounds between 1993/94 and 2005/06 discussed earlier. However, qualitative reporting by the community only gives a picture of the directionality of change; it does not estimate the growth rate. Even though statewide growth was modest, a majority of communities say that they have become more prosperous. There need not be any contradiction between the two claims.

The picture on the employment front is more disconcerting, with opinions almost equally divided as to whether it has become easier or harder to make a living and get ahead. This suggests that even if there are more economic opportunities than before, people also need to work even harder than before (perhaps combining more than one job and working longer hours) to become more prosperous.[16]

Trends in inequality are also uneven across the communities. First, on economic inequality, 48 percent of communities reported increased polarization between the top 10 percent and the bottom 10 percent, while 33 percent thought the gap has decreased. On balance, the picture appears to be of modestly rising inequality, consistent with data from the NSS rounds. Second, as regards social inequality, communities report greater social inclusion through networks and associations. Other evidence, notably a narrowing of the social gaps in fertility and human development indicators, also suggests that the social/caste divide has diminished in West Bengal over the past two decades.[17] The term "social inequality" implies not only social categories such as caste, ethnicity, and religion but also agrarian classes based on landholding size. And it appears that the land-based class structure has become less skewed over time. The proportion of communities in which more than 50 percent of households are landless has declined in the past 10 years (annex table 6.C). This was expected, given the background of land reform, but the fact that it actually happened indicates increasing social mobility and a decline in the semi-feudalism that characterized Bengal villages until the mid-1970s (Boyce 1987). Third, the level of corruption, a proxy indicator of current political inequality, is very high: 66 percent of communities have "high corruption," according to the community focus groups. This appears to be cause for concern, not so much for the impact on local growth as for the impact on the distribution of growth dividends.

Do these perspectives expressed in community focus group discussions vary from the judgments of the initial poor, those who were below the community poverty line 10 years ago? In the main, the results show similar trends (annex table 6.E). The only noticeable difference is that poor people seem to give a bleaker picture regarding local democracy. While the information about local government has increased in 32 percent of communities and ability to contact local government has increased in 63 percent, in only 12 percent of communities do poor respondents say the local government is paying greater attention to people's needs. Even where majority opinion favors local democracy, there are signs of slippage: in 43 percent of cases the impact of local democracy was rated as either negligible or negative. In only 17 percent of cases did poor people think that the local government is now run more in the public interest (as opposed to self-interest) compared to 10 years ago.

The declining enthusiasm for local democracy is also reflected in the dwindling attendance at village assembly meetings (known locally as both gram sangsads and gram sabhas). These are mandated, institutionalized but informal forums where all villagers can come together with local government functionaries to discuss local problems and priorities. The assemblies provide people an opportunity to air their grievances collectively, and they were initially seen as a tool for empowering the masses. Data available from the state's Panchayats and Rural Development Department for 2000 show that there were more than 3,000 gram sangsads in West Bengal and that almost 90 percent held their meetings. The worrying point was the rapidly decreasing attendance at these meetings, which declined from 30 percent of all villagers in 1996 to only 5 percent in 2000 (Raychaudhuri 2004). The data from our study also confirm this negligible attendance. This raises the question: Does a well-functioning local democracy matter for moving out of poverty?

The Impact of Local Democracy

One indicator used in the Moving Out of Poverty study was whether households' ability to influence local government has increased over the past 10 years. On the basis of this indicator, we classified West Bengal communities into those where local democracy has improved, deteriorated, or stayed the same. We then compared the two polar categories—communities where local democracy has improved or deteriorated—on an array of governance outcomes. We used responses from the initial poor set, that is, those households that were poor in 1995, as we give more weight to the opinions of poor people in judging governance and social outcomes.

Our basic finding is that responsive government leads to improved governance and greater well-being of households. Noticeable differences in governance outcomes at the community level were found between communities that scored high or low on responsiveness of local government (annex table 6.F). In a more responsive local democracy, the level of corruption goes down perceptibly: in communities where local democracy has improved, only 10 percent of the initial poor reported a high level of corruption, compared to 40 percent in the communities where local democracy has deteriorated. Similarly, access to information on the part of poor people goes up sharply in the improved-democracy communities (83 percent vs. 7 percent), and the ability to express religious belief freely is also better (97 percent vs. 73 percent). There are also signs of improved law and order (peace recorded in 82 percent vs. 71 percent of communities), and less violence against women (no violence recorded in 96 percent vs. 88 percent of communities).

Responsive local democracy is also associated with less discrimination in schools based on gender and with improved health and schooling services. Note that with respect to freedom of religion, law and order, violence against women, and schooling services, both sets of communities rank very high, implying that social preconditions for well-functioning democracy are well established in rural West Bengal in contrast to the lagging states of India.[18]

The general easing of social inequality in West Bengal is also reflected in panchayat elections, which seem to have produced some noticeable increases in political representation of the socially excluded groups in gram panchayats. The proportion of seats allocated to scheduled castes and scheduled tribes in different gram panchayat elections increased from 23 percent in 1978–83 to 33 percent in 1998–2003 (Bardhan and Mookherjee 2006). However, the combined share of landless, marginal (0–2.5 acres), and small (2.5–5 acres) farmers has increased only slightly, from 66 percent to 71 percent. This is because households owning more than 5 acres of land are still vastly overrepresented (compared to their demographic share) in gram panchayats. Medium and large farmers represented less than 4 percent of households in the village but held approximately one-third of seats throughout the period.

Improved governance may lead not just to good governance outcomes but to favorable economic outcomes as well. Communities with vibrant democracy also tend to have better employment prospects and a higher rate of movers than communities where democracy functions less well. Thus, in improved-democracy communities only 27 percent of the poor expressed difficulty in getting access to jobs, as opposed to 66 percent in declining-democracy communities. Similarly, 65 percent of the initial poor in improved-democracy communities said setting up a business has become less difficult, as opposed to only 26 percent in declining-democracy communities. One would have expected, then, the proportion of the movers to be higher in the first category than in the second category. This is borne out empirically: in improved-democracy villages, 68 percent of the initial poor were judged to be movers, compared to 46 percent in the declining-democracy communities.

Note that with or without local democracy, the proportion of movers is considerable in West Bengal compared to other state samples included in the study, suggesting that factors other than local democracy were also important in poverty escapes. These results, however, need to be confirmed through a regression framework where we control for initial local affluence and recent prosperity as well as district-level fixed effects to judge the independent impact of vibrant local democracy on governance and social outcomes.[19]

Factors Influencing Ascent

Differential access to economic assets is the most common narrative used to explain movement out of poverty. Movers—and upwardly mobile households, generally speaking—tend to have greater *initial* economic assets compared to households that do not move up. There are two caveats to this otherwise plausible explanation. First, usually formation of initial conditions as an outcome of historical processes involving interactions among economic, geographic, social, and political factors remains outside the purview of the analysis. As a result, what we get is a statistical snapshot at a given point in time of differences in initial asset conditions between movers and chronic poor; the reasons for the historical differences in asset conditions between the two groups remain a mystery. Hence, a study of poverty dynamics needs to explore the importance of institutional (political, social, and geographic) factors in creating more favorable initial conditions for take-off among the movers. In some contexts these factors may be tied up with social exclusions relating to caste, ethnicity, or religion; in other contexts they may be influenced by political mechanisms of inclusion and exclusion.

Second, while initial conditions matter, subsequent factors also matter. Two poor households with the same initial level of economic assets can have very different savings/accumulation rates if they take different initiatives based on differing aspirations. Hence, a poverty-dynamics analysis needs to take into account the independent importance of initiatives and aspirations.

Third, the political, social, and economic context in which people use their assets to take initiatives also makes a difference. Poverty dynamics analysis is often based on what individuals and households possess or do, when actually the community or neighborhood where the individual lives may be the crucial factor. On this dimension we also remain vulnerable, as information on households residing in adjacent villages and *paras* (neighboring areas within the same village) was not collected during the survey.

One key reason why these dimensions are not often integrated into analysis is that it is difficult to capture them through the conventional quantitative survey. In this study we try to partially compensate for this by using multimethod tools. Thus, we shed light on the formation of initial conditions through the use of community synthesis reports and life histories of movers and chronic poor. We probe the role of initiatives and aspirations by integrating quantitative data with qualitative information from life histories and discussions with youth groups.

Effect of initial conditions

Among households that were poor at the beginning of the study period, those that escaped poverty in the decade that followed—the movers—seem to have had higher initial education, more land and nonland assets, and greater organizational networking capacity than those that did not move out of poverty.[20] The average education score of household heads in the mover category is 36 percent higher than the average in the chronic poor category. A similar difference is noticeable when the education of all working members of the household is considered. The *current* land ownership of the movers is about 68 percent higher than that of the chronic poor. Given the thinness of the land market in the state, it is likely that current difference also reflects past difference. We suspect that the observed difference is partly due to differential access to land reform in the 1980s between the two groups of households. For initial nonland assets, similar differences are seen: the movers, for example, were twice as likely as chronic poor to own radios 10 years ago.

On the whole, however, the difference in other initial conditions does not appear to be particularly striking. For one thing, there is very little difference in the initial sources of income between mover and chronic poor households. Ten years ago, 57 percent of movers and 42 percent of chronic poor still derived income from casual daily labor. The two groups had similar involvement in the crop sector (39 percent of movers vs. 41 percent of chronic poor), livestock sector (5 percent vs. 9 percent), and fishery (2 percent vs. 3 percent). In fact, movers had much lower initial involvement than chronic poor in the nonfarm sector (7 percent vs. 18 percent). A look at the initial income sources of households that were poor in 1995 would give no indication of who would successfully move out of poverty in the subsequent decade. Clues must be sought elsewhere, outside the realm of initial asset conditions.

An element that may help explain the different trajectories of the two groups is networking capacity. In the West Bengal context, this has less to do with membership in self-help, nongovernmental, or community-based groups than with the nature of political activism itself.[21] Movers and chronic poor differed in terms of the types of networking they engaged in. Movers displayed higher initial organizational membership, and they also preferred groups with more heterogeneous membership. Movers belonged to groups that were religiously homogeneous in only 6 percent of cases, while chronic poor preferred same-religion groups in 21 percent of cases. Corresponding figures for same-ethnicity groups are 3 percent for movers and 13 percent for chronic poor, and for same-caste groups, 3 percent and 8 percent. The pattern holds for gender: 11 percent of movers and 25 percent of chronic poor belonged to all-male or all-female groups. The preference for heterogeneity among movers suggests that they have a greater propensity to look beyond their narrow universe and forge links with a diverse set of players. However, the most important difference between the two groups lies in the higher political activism of the movers.

Hidden role of political activism

Information on current political activism shows that about 17 percent of movers reported membership in political groups or associations, compared to only 5 percent of the chronic poor (the corresponding figures for fallers are 2 percent and for the never poor, 25 percent). Were the movers more politically active than the chronic poor 10 years ago? There is some evidence that they were.

Political activism is not limited to organizational membership but also includes participation in political activities. About 16 percent of movers reported having signed petitions to make demands on local or national government; by comparison, only 3 percent of the chronic poor, 8 percent of the never poor, and 11 percent of the fallers had done so. The difference is equally striking for participation in a protest or demonstration: 10 percent of movers versus 5 percent of chronic poor and 4 percent of fallers did so. The same pattern appears with respect to participation in information and election campaigns.

Does greater political activism lead to better access to economic opportunities? Since there is no direct way to judge from the quantitative survey, we rely here mainly on the life history tool. For many movers, entry into the "political club" was a turning point in their lives. Political connections benefited the movers, besides providing land reform opportunities, by giving them access to salaried government service, housing loans, spaces for stalls in the marketplace, and access to antipoverty schemes (both centrally sponsored schemes and state-level programs).

However, political activism can only help people move out of poverty if there is a political demand for such activism on the part of the regime in power. For the ruling Left Front regime, this was a matter not just of ideological positioning but of political survival in a context of often acute electoral competition. While the LF was able to maintain a stable political regime at the state level, this did not come easily. First, the share of votes that went to the Communist Party of India (Marxist), the principal constituent of the Left Front, remained stable during the 1990s at around 37 percent in both assembly and parliamentary elections.[22] In contrast, the share of other major parties such as the Indian National Congress-I and the Bhartiya Janta Party (BJP) fluctuated considerably from one election to another. Thus, in parliamentary elections, the share of votes polled for the Congress Party increased from 36 percent in 1991 to 40 percent in 1996 but dropped to 15 percent in 1998. The BJP's share of votes initially dropped from 12 percent to 7 percent, then rose to 10 percent during these three elections. Active mobilization at the grassroots level clearly played a key role in ensuring voter loyalty, resulting in the remarkable stability of votes polled for the LF.

Second, in many constituencies the margin of victory secured by the LF was modest. Consider the 1996 parliamentary election results. In that year the Congress Party actually received a higher share of votes than the Communist Party of India (Marxist)—40.17 percent vs. 36.7 percent; however, the seat distribution (82 vs. 138 seats) was largely in favor of the latter. Of course, seat distribution was influenced by the supporters of other partners of the LF in a constituency and was not the main factor behind the victory. In most such additional seats the electoral edge of the LF was marginal and depended on careful block-by-block electoral planning, reflecting the embedded political tensions of the regime. Against a backdrop of such acute competition, the model of political clientelism becomes advantageous both for the regime and for poor people.

Electoral imperatives as a factor influencing policy actions

One big question is why the state regime did not use land reform to reach out to the chronic poor as well and thereby consolidate its electoral base. After all, the evidence suggests this would have been a win-win strategy for both the party and the poor. The proportion of movers in West Bengal in that scenario of development would have been much higher. The left-out poor, those who did not gain in the initial phase of land reform (1978–90), would have benefited from an expanded land reform and might have climbed out of poverty, following the example of the movers. For its part, the regime would have increased its political popularity. Why, then, did the agrarian reform stop halfway? Some of the contributors to the *Sonar Bangla* volume considered this question.[23] We add our own speculations.

First, while the regime used agrarian reform as a means of entry into the rural areas, it needed to gain the support of the middle peasantry in order to win the electoral battle. The initial land reform drive was popular among the marginal and small peasantry, but an expansion of this campaign—requiring more land acquisition under ceiling reform—would have alienated not only the rural rich but also the rural middle peasantry.[24] The regime did not want to risk this. In the first wave of the reform, the poorest of the poor—whose main occupation was agricultural labor rather than sharecropping—were largely left out. The regime intended to secure their support by expanding antipoverty programs and by creating greater wage employment opportunities through expansion of irrigation in the winter season. Some homestead land was provided for those without any shelter. But the option of giving landless laborers access to enough land to enable them to become small farmers had to be weighed against the political costs of bringing additional surplus land into the agrarian reform program.

Second, in West Bengal rural progress was initiated by a political movement of the left and not by a social movement rooted in the socially excluded classes, castes, and communities. In the case of the Dravidian social mobilization in Tamil Nadu, removing barriers to social inclusion set the conditions for rural progress and broad-based development. In contrast, West Bengal still suffered from the lack of an inclusive social movement, a point frequently stressed by critics on the extreme left. Many of the rural laborers, who did not benefit as much as the movers, belonged to the social groups of untouchables, tribals, and Muslims. The Left Front regime, while not encouraging social exclusion, did not actively seek to overcome it by expanding the reach of land reform. This may also partly explain the relatively slow progress in basic education during the reform decades of the 1980s and 1990s. This is not to suggest any ex ante complicity of the regime with the *bhadralok* (gentleman) culture, but only to point out its ex post limitations.

Three, by the early 1990s the regime had already started considering a development path beyond agrarian reform, namely, revitalization of the urban growth agenda and diversification in rural areas. The argument was that the agrarian reform of the 1980s had created the basis for home market development, providing space for subsequent development of nonfarm diversification (as in the case of Chinese township and village enterprises) and linkage industries and services. It was expected that the new growth agents of the 1990s would constitute the social basis of the party in the countryside as well as in the periurban areas. Although political indecisiveness and constrained fiscal space limited the actual progress on these fronts (Maharatna 2007), it is clear that agrarian reform was downplayed in favor of these new approaches.

These three circumstances—curtailment of land reform for fear of alienating the middle peasantry, inability to overcome social exclusion, and a shifting development agenda—in a sense constitute a "middle path" politics that sought to strike a balance between the interests of the rural/urban middle class and those of the rural poor. This also put a ceiling on the agrarian radicalism that informed the process of institutional reforms that took place during 1978–90.

Economic benefits of political connections

The life history tool is useful for capturing the diverse economic benefits that can be gained from political connections at the village level. Political contacts have long been an important factor of differentiation among poor people in many parts of South Asia. In many cases these contacts are mediated through caste-based politics, although in some cases they are based on ethnic allegiance. Traditional forms of clientelism also turn on inequalities in landholdings, with large landlords locked in semifeudal patron-client relationships with landless and marginal farmers. While such relationships persist in the Indian countryside, modern forms of political clientelism based on party connections have become important as well—especially in West Bengal.

Political connections in the state are used for a variety of purposes, but they are particularly helpful in enabling a person to diversify his or her livelihood away from farm sector work to include work in other sectors. They are nearly essential for anyone, whether poor or nonpoor, who wants to set up a business. Party contacts can help the aspiring entrepreneur obtain a business license, get a government loan, and gain access to business contracts. Intervention by the political party may be needed at various stages to ensure the survival and success of the business. One obvious area of patronage was providing access to land during the patta distribution phase of land reform and during Operation Barga.

The case of Ajit, a mover from Ballartop village in South 24 Parganas district, illustrates how moderately poor people can gain a leg up through political connections. Ajit already had some land in 1975, but he obtained more in 1978 through his connection with a local political leader, which put him firmly on the upward trail.

> The biggest thing in my life was when my father gave me 2.5 bigha land
> in 1975. By that land I was able to improve my family condition. I had
> good relations with all with whom I worked. They always helped me.
> When Pancha Singh came to my house, it was a significant event in my
> life. In 1978 he was the MLA [member of the legislative assembly] from
> our area. He came to our house and after seeing our poor financial condi-
> tion gave me 1.5 bigha of government land. I saw a ray of hope in my life.
> After getting that land I began to improve my condition more. Thereafter
> I acquired another 4 bigha lands. I began to cultivate *aman* [wet-season]
> paddy. In 1997 and 2000, I bought an additional amount of 3 bigha
> lands. I am now cultivating on my 7 bigha land. Due to that I have no
> poverty in my family now. In 1998 I got a house from government—now
> I am living in a well-built house. Now I do not have to work as laborer for
> others. I am living happily.

Some mover households got access to both patta and barga lands. In
fact, as the life story evidence suggests, without such a big push very few of
the poorest could aspire to escape poverty. Dharmadas, 42, a mover in Gar-
gara village in Birbhum district, narrated the confluence of fortunate circumstances. Before the land reform, he said,

> we were struggling for existence. Most of the times, we did not have any-
> thing to eat. At times we ate rice in the afternoon and did not eat anything
> at dinner, only drank water. My father died in 1984. As a result, I had to
> stop my studies. I could study only up to class five. All the household
> responsibilities fell on my shoulder. In 1983 I got 2.5 kathas of patta land
> from the government. But that was not enough to change the situation.
> I still used to work as day labor in our village as well as in our neighbor-
> ing villages. Mother did the work of preparing *muri* [puffed rice] at other
> people's houses. In 1989 I got another 2 acres barga land from the govern-
> ment. Since then I started farming while working as day laborer on the
> side. I got married in 1990 and my first child was born in 1994. I got one
> cycle and one watch at my wedding. I bought one pump set for irrigation
> in the year 2000. I was able to cultivate the same land two times in a year.
> From then onwards, I have been able to overcome my financial crisis. I
> have got one LIC [life insurance] policy done in 2004. The most significant
> thing is I have improved techniques of cultivation in 1996 and installation
> of the pump in 2000, through which I have been able to progress.

The political link is important even for the never poor—those who were
above the community poverty line in both 1995 and 2005. The case of Mukul
of Jamalhati village, South 24 Parganas, is illustrative. In 1978, when the land
reform program started, the family had 400 bighas, a large part of which

was taken by the government as vested property under ceiling legislation. However, the family had a husking mill and received access to other nonfarm businesses in compensation for the loss of land. One of the reasons for such compensation was the family's party connections: Mukul's father was a long-time member of the Communist Party of India (Marxist), and in 2000 Mukul himself became secretary of the village committee, which he considers as the high point in his life. Mukul explained the advantage:

> Our father and we were doing CPI(M) work, now also we are doing the same party work. So we have some influence in party. Now I am the secretary of Jamalhati village committee. My father was also a party member, so we did not face much difficulty at the time of land distribution. Though we felt some sorrows but there was some savings. By that savings I had started a business from that time. From the year 2000 I am the secretary of the village committee. For five years I am holding the same post. Due to that post I came closer to the villagers. I am trying to solve the problems of the village.

Some chronic poor got their houses repaired through the help of the panchayat. This was especially true of those who displayed some upward mobility but remained below the community poverty line. Pengu of Bana-gram village, Burdwan district, described the event:

> In 1983, when I was given a land by our government, I was 23 years old. I was very delighted then. After getting this land, I started cultivating paddy. After getting land from our government, a home was built up by our panchayat in 1991. As a result my standard of life became better.

A similar story is told by another chronic poor, a one-time land reform beneficiary in Randiha village:

> The first property I received was in the year 2004, which was a loan of Rs 10,000 from IAY [Indira Abashik Yojana, a centrally sponsored housing scheme]. With that amount it was possible for me to rebuild and decorate my house and make it a better place for our shelter. This is a matter of importance to poor people like me. Earlier, in the year 1978, my mother received 2 kathas of land from the government.

Local political connections also helped people get loans from institu-tional sources. Credit is especially important for poor people, who may lack even minimal savings to buy the agricultural inputs they need to start farming on land accessed through patta or barga reforms. There are many instances among the movers in which the party or local government functionaries mediated to help party cadres access loans from the Integrated Rural Development Programme, a government program that promotes self-employment of the rural poor.

Lack of political connections was a distinct disadvantage in accessing credit. A youth group in Dwarshini village reported that no matter what the aspiring entrepreneur does, "the BDO [block development officer, a government functionary] is unwilling to put his signature for a nonparty man." Government aid is allotted to the village, but it cannot be accessed by nonparty members. In Gutri, the focus group put it as follows: "The loans, government aid that comes for the village people never reach for the general public and when reaches them they don't have the right to say anything. So the business man finally doing progress and with the increase of their number of business, are becoming more rich."

Licensing was another area where political connections made a difference. It is not always mandatory to obtain a government license to do business, but it is required in some communities and for specific businesses. In such cases it is only "by help of party or after giving bribe they can get license," as a resident of Baintala village said. Party members may be exempt from giving bribes, but if one is not a party member, one must give a bribe. In Randiha, Kartik said, "In order to get some signature, there are such officials who say, either to bring party certificate or give bribe. Those who are in party, they do not have to bribe the officials." What is not paid as a bribe to government officials is often paid as a "donation" to the party fund. Nomita in Dulki village reported that only after paying a donation "they can start business." An even more acute comment was made by Sheikh Nurul in another village, giving a rather startling definition of "freedom" in a politically sensitive context: "Earning money, to be self-reliant is some kind of freedom. Besides this, doing party, working for the party, flattering the party leaders, to realize or gain certain facilities and opportunities for someone is also an instance of freedom."

While loans and licenses figure prominently in the life stories of movers, political connections are used to gain other economic benefits as well. In Nanagar village, Kanta expressed his gratitude to the party for helping him secure space for a market stall. "Since 1996 I am attached with the party and the involvement with the party brought me peace of mind. At the initiative or effort of the party I was allotted a space in the market for opening of my business. This beneficial or benevolent act of the party would be acknowledged with respect for all of my life. If I could have the opportunity to serve the party under any circumstance I would be glad to come forward." Another mover reported that his son got jobs in the rural works program because of a panchayat connection.

Political connections also mattered in gaining access to salaried employment, which usually ensures a higher and more regular flow of income. The position of teacher in a government school, in particular, was a highly popular aspiration among youths in focus groups. Teachers play a multidimensional role in village society: they enjoy social prestige as educators and are also widely seen as politically influential, being called frequently to participate as presiding officials in local or national elections. Getting access to a teaching job thus can be a trigger for moving out of poverty. Dinesh of Sunia village, Burdwan, reported that "1995 was a turning year in my life. That year I got the job of a primary school teacher in the village school. I got that job on my own merit though." The question is whether others can secure such coveted jobs without any political backing. For that we need to turn to the youth group discussions. Most of the youths agreed that "without connections, the prospect for getting even a fourth-class employee job is minimal." There is also direct evidence in some of the movers' life stories that political connections help in getting formal jobs. Dinabandhu, a 48-year-old mover in Tola village, said, "The best evidence of change in my life is when I got the government service with the party source. After receiving this job there is a change in my life. I now work for the progress of the society. I got the job, and behind this is my education, my party and my duty towards society. My life style has changed. Now I work in a responsible job of the society.

Political exclusion contributes to disenfranchising the most deprived segment of the rural poor. As Budhai in Kamalpur village put it, "All the facilities are enjoyed by the members of the party. The poor persons go outside the village in search of job." The sense of being excluded economically has made many poor people reluctant to participate in community decision making or even in voting. In Sipta village, a discussion group said that "participation in local government is not so much encouraging, because there have been many political clashes and today it has increased, which has discouraged people to take part in elections and participate in local administration."

This may be a perception of the most deprived segment of the rural poor, who are excluded in the competition for scarce resources. However, the qualitative case studies make clear that even if these voices are a minority, they are a significant minority. In short, the emerging picture of local democracy, as revealed from the perspectives of different groups of poor people, is a complex one of hope and disappointment, promise and frustration, that resists sweeping generalizations.

Differential rating of local democracy by movers and chronic poor

If our hypothesis regarding political clientelism is correct, one would expect movers to rate changes in local democracy more positively than the other mobility groups.[25] There is some evidence to support this hypothesis (annex table 6.H). All five indicators considered reflect on the performance of local government from different angles. Three aspects are noteworthy here.

First, one common thread is that movers give a consistently higher score to local government than chronic poor. Among poor households, 40 percent of movers but only 27 percent of chronic poor place high trust in local government functionaries. Only 17 percent of movers think local government functionaries are highly corrupt, compared to 29 percent of chronic poor. Satisfaction with local government is extremely high for the movers (85 percent). Movers are more positive about their ability to influence local government: 23 percent reported increased ability to influence, while 9 percent reported decreased ability. This is in contrast to the chronic poor, where increase and decrease are almost evenly balanced.

Second, although the movers' appraisal may be overoptimistic, certain progressive aspects of local democracy in West Bengal seem indisputable. On several indicators, even chronic poor households on balance rate local government in a positive light. For instance, more of the chronic poor households are satisfied (65 percent) than dissatisfied with local government. Both groups rate corruption relatively low compared to other states such as Uttar Pradesh.

Third, despite divergences in the opinions of movers and chronic poor, certain problem areas stand out. One such area is trust in local government, where even the movers seem equally divided, with 40 percent reporting high trust and 38 percent low trust. Responses to the query as to whether local government mainly serves the interest of the few (elite capture) are also equally revealing. A high proportion of both movers (52 percent) and chronic poor (65 percent) report persistence of elite influence.

Building on land reform: Occupational choice and the nonfarm sector

Although political contacts often helped movers get ahead economically, it would be a gross oversimplification to attribute the movers' success entirely to political connectedness. Rather, the life history data bring out the importance of occupational diversification and particularly of transition into the nonfarm sector as a means of moving up.

The most common trajectory from the qualitative evidence in life stories runs as follows. In the beginning, most of the movers (and chronic poor) belonged to the class of landless and marginal farmers, owning up to 150 decimals of land. Typically they worked either as agricultural laborers or as sharecroppers on the lands of others. Then came the first wave of land reform. Some of the land-poor got small plots through patta or secured tenurial rights on land through barga. According to the life stories, the amount of land allotted varied from a few kathas to at most 1–2 bighas.

Gaining access to land changed the occupational pattern for the recipients. Many of them started cultivating the small plot they had received, planting mainly rice during the rainy season and vegetables the rest of the year, and selling the produce in the market. Most, however, did not leave their previous occupation of day labor, at least not yet. With hard work and a strong family support network, including the active support of the spouse or spouse's family, a household head would be able to save money to buy or lease some additional land. A dose of good luck was also essential; notably, good health in the family during the first three or four years of land reform was sometimes critical to the capital accumulation process.

By the end of the 1980s most mover households had managed to purchase another 2–3 bighas of land, adding to the initial 1 or 2 bighas they received through the land reform. This was also the period in which irrigation coverage became widely available, allowing the movers to start agricultural diversification on a larger scale. By this time, too, many of the mover families had children who were adolescents or young adults and could help their parents with the household occupation.

The next step was to attempt the leap into the nonfarm sector. Households with at least one educated member were best positioned to do this. While some adult children had only a primary education or less, others had completed secondary school and in some cases had gone beyond. These educated children could help their families by getting salaried jobs or by applying their skills to starting a business. Mover households often used their savings from farm income or (in a few cases) secured institutional loans to start nonfarm small businesses that allowed for self-employment. For these households, upward mobility came through successive occupational transitions: from working mainly as agricultural labor prior to land reform, to doing both labor and farming in the second phase, to doing both farming and nonfarm jobs in the third phase. This trajectory highlights the importance of diversification in moving out of poverty, a hypothesis we tested further with quantitative data.

Life stories and community interviews indicate two main routes of transition from the farm to the nonfarm sector. If the initial landholding was very small or farming was not a viable activity for one reason or another, the household could sell some plots and invest the returns in a business such as pulling a rickshaw, driving a motorized van, opening a small shop, selling vegetables in the market, or doing fish-pond cultivation. The other route involved continuing with farming but diversifying crop production and buying more land to make farming more profitable.[26]

The first route was most profitable in cases where small farmers faced obstacles to continued farming. These obstacles often concerned water—either persistent irrigation problems due to lack of irrigation canals and the rising costs of hiring irrigation pumps, or problems of poor drainage and waterlogging. Sadhana, a member of a female focus group in Kantipur, pointed out, "Now nothing is to be gained from cultivation. In the boro season, one has to spend a lot to get irrigation water. Very often, the cost of cultivation cannot be raised from the selling price." According to a female focus group in Bhada, some land-poor households were "selling their land due to the poor condition of cultivation and started their business. Now they are earning more money from business than cultivation." The choice of farm or nonfarm activities in the initial stage of ascent was also influenced by local production and market conditions, including vulnerability of the land to flooding and erosion, irrigation access, proximity to urban markets, availability of family labor, and difficulties in accessing loans, where loans are granted based on the size of the land mortgaged as collateral.

Differential entry into the nonfarm sector by chronic poor and movers

If the movers could escape poverty through this farm-nonfarm transition, why could the chronic poor not do the same? It is instructive to compare the case studies of land reform beneficiaries who were all poor at the time of land reform. Our analysis is based on the accounts of approximately 40 individuals whose lives appear to have been differentially impacted by land redistribution, based on their different outcomes. The majority of them received either patta or barga land in the period between 1978 and 1985. Of the 40, more than half were able to move out of poverty, while the others remained stuck there.

Evidence points toward three proximate reasons for divergent outcomes. First, those who moved out of poverty generally received larger amounts of land under the land distribution program. Second, movers were able to convert the land they received through land reform into an income-generating asset. And third, movers displayed superior entrepreneurship.

Unequal amounts of land accessed through land reform. A review of land allotments to those who became movers and those who remained poor shows that the former received more land than the latter. Two examples from the same community, Tola, illustrate the different initial access to land. A chronic poor woman received just 2 kathas:

> In 1980 my father came to stay with my uncle's house. Uncle arranged for us to stay in a combined room. Father worked as field labor. In 1990 we got 2 kathas of land in patta in which we built up a hut and started living independently. After that my father died in 1998. After his death I took the responsibility of the family. I still run my family by working as a day laborer in a field.

A male mover in Tola received five times as much land:

> My life is changed in the year 1998 after getting 10 kathas of land from the government . . . My income increased and I started thinking of going far in my life. In 2001 I started business of growing and selling vegetables in our village market. I started first with Rs 500 as initial capital and slowly I got hold of the business. Now my monthly income from the business is Rs 2000. I can now run my family smoothly.

Most movers in Tola seem to have received at least 1 bigha of land, approximately twice as much as the 10 kathas received by the mover in the second account. In fact, across communities, most movers received patta land in bighas, while chronic poor received patta land in kathas. With respect to barga land, movers received as much as 3 acres. This was the case of Shakti, a 45-year-old mover in Ganeshpur village:

> I started cultivating 3 acres of barga land since 1980. I am using borrowed plough and cow; in return, I am giving him [landlord] half of the production. I have given my son education up to class nine by doing cultivation. Now both of us doing cultivation and earning our livelihood comfortably. I bought a cycle for my son in 2000 from my earning. Now I have opened a savings account in Mayurakshi Grameen Bank. I am much happier than before.

In contrast, most of the chronic poor respondents seem to have been given patta land in allotments of 1.5 kathas to 10 kathas. Even when such small amounts did not allow a move out of poverty, they apparently improved poor people's lives somewhat. Rakhal of Sunia village got 1.5 kathas of patta land in 1978 and used it to build a house: "That time I had a change in my life because before that I had no place for living. But now it is my property."

Land asset with and without income generation. Not only did chronic poor receive less land than movers, but the pattern of land use was different as well. In the example of Rakhal above, the tiny plot of land he received was just big enough to build a small house, which is exactly what this respondent and many other chronic poor did. Building huts or houses on the land allotted to them was an important first step, providing shelter for poor people who had lacked even homestead land, but it was clearly not enough to trigger income generation and a climb out of poverty.

What prevented the chronic poor from transforming their land allotment into income-generating assets? It seems that shocks played an important role. A sudden health shock or a social obligation (to finance the marriage of a daughter or sister, for example) can erode initial savings considerably and lead to indebtedness. Thus many of the respondents who remained in poverty found themselves compelled to sell their land to meet expenses or repay loans, either soon after receiving the land or many years later. Three examples from different villages show the debilitating impact of social obligations, health shocks, and covariate shocks (in this case related to the drying up of the village canal).

Kanchan, a 41-year-old chronic poor man in Gangua, Burdwan:

> In 1982 we got 5 kathas of land as a patta from the government. But we had to sell the land for Rs 10,000 for the marriage of my sister. If we had owned that land we could prosper in life by farming in that land. But after selling the land we have fallen down to our original level. I am still a day laborer as I was in the past.

Anjan, a 45-year-old chronic poor man in Halapara, South 24 Parganas:

> Got 8 kathas patta land in 1982. Due to ill health I had to sell off the land in 1983 for Rs 8,000. I repaid loans with that amount and also I did the repairing of my house.

Amulya, a 60-year-old chronic poor man in Gutri, South 24 Parganas:

> Year 1980: That was a good time in my life as that year I got 5 katha patta land from government. Before that I was a daily laborer. But after getting that land I became self-dependent. I cultivated in my land and got food twice a day. I was happy with that. Year 1998: That year I lost everything as I sold my land that year. For cultivation our main source of water was our water of canal. But in 1996 water of the canal dried up. So cultivators faced difficulty and their conditions became worse. They did not get money from their cultivation that year. So to return money which I borrowed earlier, I had to sell my land in 1998.

A second theme that emerges is the mediating role of credit access. Some chronic poor who received land were unable to turn it into an income-generating asset because they lacked initial capital. Niamat, a 28-year-old chronic poor man in Halapara, recalled:

> Got 4 kathas of patta land in 1984. Due to poverty I had no money to cultivate the land, so I sold off the land in 1984. Compared to the past my condition has remained the same. I still have no savings. Whatever I earn gets spent in running the household.

Niamat started working as an agricultural laborer in 1984, and he remains a laborer today. His life story contrasts to that of Kanta, a 44-year-old mover in Pardahana, who received land and also the initial capital needed to make the land profitable:

> In 1981, I got land from government and loan too. This was the turning point of my life. It helped me a lot. I could see a ray of hope in my life. With that loan I started farming and now I consider myself a successful farmer. Now I can afford my family well. I have bought TV and cycle for my household members. I have opened a bank account this year so I consider myself a lucky man. My main source of income at present is farming as it was 10 years ago.

Role of entrepreneurship and gainful diversification

The stories of movers who received land suggest that they often used the land as a platform to undertake a series of successful diversification attempts. After receiving the initial land allotment, they either focused purely on farming or cultivated the land given to them while also continuing the livelihood activities they had been doing before. Either way, they slowly accumulated savings, and in 15 or 20 years they had funds to invest. At that point, the movers either acquired more land (typically 2 to 7 bighas) and increased their profits by producing more crops, or they used their savings to diversify. This might involve diversification within agriculture, such as by going into pisciculture (fish-pond cultivation) or vegetable horticulture, or diversification into a nonfarm activity such as opening up a tea shop. Ayub, a 55-year-old mover in Mayahauri, illustrates the pattern:

> The most valuable thing in my life is the patta of 1 bigha land by the panchayat. After getting that land I started the work of cultivation while I was still engaged as a laborer. In the year 1990 I bought 2 bighas of land and in the year 1998 another 3 bighas of land. I also bought 2 bighas of land by the help of my sons. I have now become the owner of 8 bighas of land and I do not have to work as day laborer as my sons do the work of tilling and selling the crops. In the season of *aman* [rainy season] I also cultivate ladies-finger [okra], brinjal [eggplant], and bitter gourd, besides the aman rice. When I started this work I used to earn Rs 8,000 to 10,000 per season of paddy and from my vegetable garden I earn another Rs 8,000 to 10,000. At present I earn Rs 40,000 to 50,000 per year from my 8 bighas of land.

Others benefited in different ways. In the case of the mover Dinesh from Sunia, his father had received 1 bigha of land and used it to save money and educate his sons. Thanks to his education, Dinesh was able to secure a teacher's job when he grew up and elevate his household from step 3 on the ladder of life to step 7.

Concurrent involvement in a number of jobs had different meanings for different groups of households. For the chronic poor, multiple occupations meant "distress diversification," in which they tried to combine day labor with homestead gardening to earn a livelihood. For the movers, diversification meant concurrent involvement in several different types of gainful employment, to earn a daily living but also to generate savings for the future and eventually climb out of poverty. As for the land-rich, diversification opens up new routes for mutually supportive capital accumulation: profits earned from the nonland sector are plowed back into the land sector and vice versa.

Of course, this story of transition from agricultural to nonfarm jobs is familiar in many agrarian contexts. What stands out in the life stories of movers and chronic poor in West Bengal is the importance of political support and intermediation in the process of making this transition.

Political mediation in the transition to nonfarm activities

If moving from farm to nonfarm activities is a common route out of poverty, this raises the question of the impact of political clientelism on such ascents. A focus group in Gutri village stated outright that one can move out of poverty through party affiliation: "People can come out of poverty by becoming powerful. If someone supports the party they can take advantage of financial help and can come out of poverty." A youth group in Dwarshini village affirmed, "To carry on business taking financial help from the state, to gain land from the state, or to have a service with the help of the party is an important freedom in our village . . . So it is most urgent to work for the party for our quick prosperity." The importance of party-based connections in West Bengal villages would seem to put the nonparty poor at a disadvantage in setting up a business. Even those with a nominal party affiliation may receive help that is too limited.

Besides providing assistance in conducting a business, the party is also said to help people get government jobs, and this appears to be a very clear route out of poverty in the ladder of life discussions. The story of Shivakumar is revealing in this respect:

> I am doing politics from the year 1989. And this helped me a lot. I got the government job with the help of political party. It changed my life, I am happy with the party. I cannot repay the loan of this help to the party. In 1998 I got a service in the Block Agriculture Department as fourth-class staff. I got this service from the recommendation of the party leaders. I get Rs 6,000 per month as salary. From that peace came to my life and changes came into my life economically, socially, and mentally. . . . Today I am prospering. Previously I was running my family by doing the work of farm hands. But now I have got a permanent job. My income increased and income is secured. I can overcome any problem with my savings.

The central lesson from these case studies is not that diversification and transition to nonfarm sector matters for moving out of poverty; that narrative is well established in the literature. What is of note here is that the movement to diversification and to nonfarm sectors is not random. There is a selection bias in terms of who can gain access, and the process can be considerably mediated through politics, an aspect often neglected in the standard discourse on the farm-nonfarm transition.

The quantitative survey also supports this story (annex table 6.I). In terms of occupational mobility, more movers than chronic poor transitioned into nonfarm sectors. The comparison between 1995 and 2005 for movers shows the magnitude of increase in household participation in different non-farm activities: nonfarm business (27 percent), livestock/dairy (13 percent), crop and vegetable production (12 percent), and salaried jobs (4 percent). Chronic poor display much less mobility, increasing their involvement only in livestock (mainly goat and poultry rearing). In fact, over time they tend to withdraw from the crop sector, perhaps selling off whatever meager land they received through land reform.

Results of the Multivariate Analysis

To summarize the evidence and to look simultaneously at many factors, we used multivariate analysis to identify individual, household, group, and community-level factors that helped poor people move out of poverty. The qualitative and descriptive evidence led us to several expectations. First, we expected (initial) household assets in general to have a positive impact. Second, while we expected well-functioning local democracy to have a positive impact on movers, we also predicted some exclusion of chronic poor because of lack of political connections—a factor stressed in the previous section—with negative consequences for their mobility. Third, we expected diversification of income sources and occupational transitions from farm to nonfarm activities, triggered initially by land reform, to have a strong positive impact. Fourth, we foresaw a pronounced positive impact of personal characteristics—a positive mindset, commitment to hard work, and alertness to new economic opportunities—reflecting the psychological dimensions of empowerment and aspiration.

Our econometric analysis does not imply causality. We can only talk about the presence or absence of statistical association between the movement out of poverty and these factors. Although we have tried to include as much as possible the initial conditions and changes that can be considered exogenous to the prospects of escaping poverty, the problem of endogeneity cannot be satisfactorily overcome in this kind of econometric setup.[27] Hence this analysis should be considered supplemental to the results already presented.

The model

We consider a range of factors that may affect mobility in the agrarian context of West Bengal. The most important aspect of the model relates to testing for congruence or divergence of public and private interests, a factor likely to be particularly relevant in the context of political clientelism. To do this we use a statistical technique called leave-out mean (LOM). The leave-out mean was created for the following factors: strength of local democracy, unfairness in access, level of initial empowerment, personal aspiration, and violence against women. For each of these variables, both the household rating and the average rating for the rest of the community have been included at the same time. The idea is to statistically test whether some of these factors function as a public good, benefiting all residents of the community, or as a private good, benefiting the fortunate few (for discussion of the leave-out mean technique, see chapter 1 and appendix 1 of this volume).

The model considers a range of variables/factors that can be grouped as follows:

Economic vibrancy. The first group of variables relates to local economic vibrancy. Two indicators considered here are initial strength of the economy (a proxy for initial level of income) and change in economic prosperity (a proxy for growth).

Local democracy. The second group of variables captures various dimensions of the "local state." Here we consider two indicators: the level of corruption in the local government and the responsiveness of local democracy. Given the tendency toward political clientelism in West Bengal, we expect corruption to be positively related to mobility. Similarly, we expect local democracy to be positively related to movers, but insignificant or even negative for the rest of the community.[28]

Fairness. The third group of variables captures a broad measure of "fairness." The latter is empirically constructed based on three aspects of accessibility: ability of rural producers to get fair prices for their crops, the degree of fair treatment by law, and access to credit. The rapid expansion of the road network in recent years has increased the ability of farmers even in remote areas to get fair prices for their output. Moreover, agrarian reform has removed or at least diminished the power of middlemen. From this angle, one would expect a positive impact. However, credit access is unevenly distributed, which may cancel out the other effects. Hence we remain uncertain regarding the ultimate sign of this indicator.

Empowerment. The fourth group of variables pertains to three distinct dimensions of empowerment: rights, agency, and aspiration. Individuals or households that were located initially higher on the ladder of power and rights are expected to be better prepared to take advantage of opportunities to improve their life situation, livelihood, and future prospects for upward mobility. The precise channels through which personal empowerment can have an independent effect on income growth and mobility is still debated. Does it work through better connectivity with the existing power structure—in which case the empowerment route for movers may be the disempowerment route for the rest of the poor, as we have seen in earlier case studies of political connectivity? Does it imply better networking capacity or bargaining power in the marketplace? Perhaps an empowered individual is a person "with a plan" under even most adverse circumstances.

Being empowered can also mean freedom from *extra-economic* coercion (a much-discussed issue in West Bengal until the 1970s). According to this view, empowered individuals represent economic actors who do not depend on landlords or moneylenders for their livelihood. They may simply be working in occupations that are more formalized, perhaps in salaried jobs or in self-employed trading, or they may be involved in some self-help group activities that confer a measure of independence from the traditional rural middlemen/landlords.

The economic impact of positive aspiration is well known: it has an important bearing on savings and investment behavior. Does it also work through better personal initiatives on the work front? It is quite possible that the so-called culture of poverty has an important effect on mobility outcomes through the aspiration channel. While poverty of aspiration may be one of the crucial aspects of poverty in general, it is not altogether clear whether it is conditioned by more deep-seated class factors such as family and inheritance. The two aspiration indicators used in this study focus on individual (current generation) and family (future generation) mobility prospects. From this perspective, poverty of aspiration can be considered as sign of hopelessness about the future—an indirect indicator of intergenerationally transmitted chronic poverty. What we need to test is whether empowerment picks up some independent effects even when the aspiration factor is significant.

Social capital and social discrimination. Factors in the fifth group capture the presence of social capital, while those in the sixth group focus on the theme of discrimination based on ethnicity/caste, gender, or social class. Social capital is captured by indicators such as collective action (a statistical index was constructed based on the willingness to help others in times of crisis) as well as access to organizational networks and associations. An indicator of fair treatment of students belonging to different caste and religious groups as well as boys and girls has been considered as a key indicator of social discrimination. We also included the conventional social identity indicators such as statistical dummies for scheduled caste (SC) and scheduled tribe (ST). In addition, we also consider "violence against women" as the indicator of family dysfunctionality.

Conventional controls. The seventh and eighth groups of variables draw attention to the conventional factors of importance such as human capital (education levels specified as separate dummies) and health shocks. We also include assets and livestock assets, given the context of agrarian reform where possession of nonland assets is closely correlated with land assets. We expect these assets to be characterized by considerable return in the context of West Bengal, which has been experiencing relatively high income growth since the 1990s. The model also includes some conventional control variables such as household demography—the age and sex of household head and religion. We also include district-level fixed effects to control for the omitted variable biases.

Policy variable: Diversification of income sources. Finally, we have a variable of policy interest: whether the household is able to make the transition from single to multiple livelihood sources and diversify into nonrice, noncrop, and nonfarm sources of income. As discussed earlier, based on qualitative evidence, most movers achieved such diversification on the foundation laid down by initial access to land reform. This is not to say that nonland beneficiaries did not diversify, but as the life histories suggest, they were usually either chronic poor exhibiting distress diversification or never poor who were engaged in multiple sectors from the outset and did not depend on land reform. The purpose here is to test whether there is indeed a statistical association between income source diversification and the likelihood of moving out of poverty, controlling for other factors of interest including particularly whether respondents received land.

Nearly all the factors considered here are in the form of two types of indicators: (a) variables capturing initial conditions prevailing in the community (or household as applicable) 10 years ago, and (b) variables capturing changes in the community (or household as applicable) that can be considered as exogenous to the individual mobility process of the households. The first group of variables includes strength of economy, index of responsiveness of local democracy, initial location of the household on the ladder of power and rights, index of collective action, extent of social divisions, home ownership, index of household assets (consumer durables and amenities), index of household ownership of livestock, sources of income and extent of diversification, and membership in groups. Change variables that are considered exogenous here are generically formulated as questions regarding changes over the past 10 years ("better, worse, or stayed the same"). These relate to questions regarding change in personal control over everyday decisions that affect one's life, violence against women, access to networks and associations, inequality measures, health shocks, and fairness. Some variables are more susceptible to endogeneity than others; these include rating of the current level of corruption and rating of future aspiration.

A linear probability model is estimated to perform multivariate analysis of factors that may influence upward movement for the two groups: the initially poor who moved out of poverty, crossing the community poverty line (MOP), and the initially poor who moved up any amount, whether or not they crossed the poverty line (MPI).[29] (See table 1.2 in chapter 1 for an explanation of the summary indicators of mobility.) We mainly focus on the *results for those who escaped poverty* for the base OLS (ordinary least squares) model and compare them with the extended OLS model (table 6.1). In both cases our discussion in the next section follows the results of the unweighted regressions.[30]

Main results

Several findings are noteworthy. First, local democracy is positively associated with the probability of escape from poverty in the base model, the effect being stronger in the weighted regression. The positive poverty-reducing role of local democracy is a reassuring feature, especially for a state that embarked early on the path of devolution and decentralization. But the promise of local democracy is not without pitfalls, as the benefits may not be equally accessed by various poverty groups.

Second, local democracy benefits movers at the cost of others. In fact, the association is negative in both base and extended versions of the model. The emerging picture is one of relative *political advantage* on the part of the movers vis-à-vis the chronic poor when it comes to accessing the benefits of local democracy. This is also consistent with the picture of political patronage through local government generated through the qualitative evidence. Again, this should not depreciate the importance of local government in general. It only shows the need for further democratization of the local state as a public service agency.[31]

Third, both individual empowerment and aspirations emerge as statistically independent factors having positive influence on upward mobility.

Here both weighted and unweighted models show similar results, upholding the positive association of empowerment and aspiration with poverty escape for the movers while indicating the relative disadvantage for the chronic poor. Again, this is consistent with poor people's perceptions of being left out and excluded from the stream of developmental benefits that went into rural areas, which possibly resulted in lower expectations on the part of the chronic poor.

Personal empowerment is a significant predictor of mobility even when personal aspiration is separately accounted for. This means there is more to empowerment than the element of aspiration as such: each of these aspects of greater power and freedom should be accorded individual importance. Perhaps the movers are characterized by higher *internal* empowerment before *external* (such as economic and political) empowerment can take place; perhaps both take place simultaneously. Case studies of movers do show that they invariably have better family relationships, more positive attitudes toward educating their children even in the face of adverse circumstances, and a core will to succeed incrementally by saving, working hard, and grabbing whatever fleeting chances come their way.

Fourth, among the conventional considerations, accumulation of physical assets, including land, and accumulation of livestock assets continue to be significant explanatory factors underlying the movement out of poverty.

Fifth, turning to the policy variable of interest, we find that initial diversification of income sources has a strong positive impact on the prospect of upward mobility. This confirms the qualitative evidence that income/occupational diversification built on the platform of initial land reform is an important route for moving out of poverty in the agrarian context of West Bengal. We found that 62 percent of the initial poor had only a single source of income 10 years ago, but those who could switch over to managing multiple sources of income had a strong chance of escaping poverty during the subsequent period. Transitions into regular wage employment, vegetable horticulture, or fish-pond cultivation appeared to be the most profitable strategies.[32]

The study finds evidence of both distress-driven diversification and gainful diversification. The distinction is important. The chronic poor often cannot subsist on a single source of income alone. As the life stories show, some depend on agricultural wage labor with occasional vegetable selling on the side. This is a case of distress diversification. In contrast, movers tend to combine farming with more remunerative activities: fish-pond cultivation, trade, and transport business, for example. Access to capital, social links, and a will to seize market opportunity—all these factors stand out in the life stories

TABLE 6.1

Factors influencing poverty escapes in West Bengal: Results for those who crossed the poverty line (MOP) and those who moved up (MPI) among initial poor set

Variable	MOP (base model)	MOP (extended model)	MPI (base model)	MPI (extended model)
Initial strength of economy	0.001 [0.05]	−0.006 [0.47]	0.003 [0.28]	−0.001 [0.07]
Change in economic prosperity	−0.004 [0.53]	0.002 [0.16]	−0.012 [1.24]	−0.001 [0.06]
Responsiveness of local democracy	0.029 [2.18]**	0.023 [1.68]*	0.029 [2.26]**	0.026 [1.96]*
LOM of responsiveness of local democracy	−0.046 [2.03]**	−0.097 [2.68]***	−0.025 [1.14]	−0.085 [2.86]***
Corruption	0.023 [2.63]**	0.013 [1.77]*	0.02 [2.26]**	0.011 [1.28]
Fairness index	0.015 [0.82]	0.007 [0.39]	0.012 [0.70]	0.006 [0.37]
LOM of fairness index	0 [0.02]	0.009 [0.32]	0.008 [0.30]	0.021 [0.75]
Initial step on the ladder of power and rights	0.08 [5.34]***	0.074 [4.73]***	0.075 [4.41]***	0.07 [4.02]***
LOM of step on the ladder of power and rights	−0.073 [3.39]***	−0.081 [4.08]***	−0.075 [2.90]***	−0.08 [3.16]***
Control over everyday decisions	0.154 [5.00]***	0.171 [5.37]***	0.152 [4.81]***	0.172 [5.13]***
LOM of change in control over everyday decisions	−0.222 [3.60]***	−0.124 [1.88]*	−0.238 [3.42]***	−0.161 [2.21]**
Household aspirations	0.201 [9.82]***	0.202 [9.53]***	0.193 [9.53]***	0.191 [9.25]***
LOM of household aspirations	−0.141 [4.90]***	−0.175 [5.43]***	−0.121 [3.83]***	−0.154 [4.60]***
Index of collective action	−0.004 [0.20]	0.039 [1.35]	−0.018 [0.92]	0.016 [0.75]
Access to networks and associations	0.001 [0.04]	−0.009 [0.51]	0 [0.03]	−0.012 [0.80]
Social divisions	−0.007 [0.52]	0.005 [0.44]	0.012 [0.90]	0.027 [2.29]**
School inequality	−0.001 [0.11]	0.004 [0.45]	−0.005 [0.43]	−0.008 [0.88]
Violence against women	−0.035 [0.84]	−0.028 [0.67]	−0.026 [0.68]	−0.017 [0.47]
LOM of violence against women	0.035 [0.69]	0.074 [1.48]	−0.024 [0.43]	0.008 [0.17]

TABLE 6.1 *(continued)*

Variable	MOP (base model)	MOP (extended model)	MPI (base model)	MPI (extended model)
Health shocks	−0.029 [0.70]	−0.019 [0.45]	−0.009 [0.25]	−0.007 [0.18]
Ownership of house	0.04 [1.01]	0.033 [0.71]	0.011 [0.19]	−0.012 [0.21]
Assets index	0.041 [3.42]***	0.038 [2.76]***	0.028 [2.46]**	0.03 [2.26]**
Livestock index	0.012 [0.85]	0.012 [0.97]	0.022 [1.72]*	0.02 [1.66]
Religion		−0.03 [0.61]		0.035 [0.90]
Scheduled caste (SC dummy)		−0.027 [0.80]		0.002 [0.06]
Scheduled tribe (ST dummy)		−0.056 [1.33]		−0.019 [0.34]
Education of head of household		0.004 [0.58]		0.004 [0.60]
Income source diversification		0.146 [3.11]***		−0.126 [2.77]***
Age of head of household		0.004 [0.42]		−0.006 [0.63]
Age of head of household^2 (squared)		0 [0.41]		0 [0.47]
Sex of head of household		0.032 [0.54]		0.038 [0.63]
Membership in groups		0.033 [1.60]		0.022 [1.07]
Political activism		−0.014 [1.26]		−0.015 [1.40]
Constant	0.73 [4.54]***	0.385 [1.43]	0.884 [5.16]***	0.806 [3.04]***
Observations	655	648	655	648
R^2	0.44	0.47	0.42	0.44

Note: Robust *t*-statistics in brackets based on clustered standard errors; all regression models control for district fixed-effects. Some key institutional variables and their expected signs are as follows. Corruption: higher value indicates higher corruption; expected sign is negative. Fairness index: higher value indicates more fairness (it is a synthetic index of fair access to credit, fair access to remunerative prices, and fair treatment by law); the expected sign is positive. Violence against women: higher value indicates lower violence; the expected sign is positive. One of the empowerment indicators ("step on the ladder of power and rights") relates to the initial location of the household on the ladder of power and rights. All indexes are constructed through principal component analysis (PCA) on initial status (value) of the variables, but using the current weights. LOM stands for the community average for the variables concerned but is generated through the leave-out mean approach.

*p < .10   **p < .05   ***p < .01

of movers. This is what we call gainful diversification. We find in the movers' regression that people who have multiple sources of income have higher chances of moving out of poverty than people with single source of income. The chronic poor are not able to diversify into multiple sources of gainful employment and income.

Finally, we also find that using dummies for *current status* as land reform beneficiaries does not yield any statistically significant result on moving out of poverty.[33] The study speculates that this may be partly due to the fact that those who *currently* hold land reform plots are locked into the land sector because of legal restrictions on the sharecropper who becomes owner of the sharecropped land. Deininger et al. (2008) provide supportive evidence for this. Perhaps the statistical insignificance of the "current dummy for patta/barga beneficiary" shows that even with land reform, remaining locked into the crop sector does not offer an adequate path to long-term mobility. Only those who graduate into nonfarm activities after an initial period of climbing through land reform can escape the poverty trap. This is upheld by the statistically significant results for nonfarm occupations as factors of upward mobility compared to the reference category of agricultural labor. These are, however, current problems of agrarian transition, and they do not negate the historical importance of land access as an initial trigger of ascent for beneficiaries of the land reform that started more than two decades ago.

As mentioned earlier, qualitative studies on movers point to the importance of initial access to land as a vehicle of poverty reduction. The qualitative evidence also points to the dynamic effects: those who received land were more able to diversify their income, acquire more land, and move out of poverty in a virtuous cycle. We argue that this part of the dynamic story of land reform–induced upward mobility over time is better captured through the qualitative data.[34]

Conclusions

Several findings emerge from the preceding analysis. First, institutional reforms, specifically local government and agrarian reform, strengthened local democracy in West Bengal. Past studies have suggested that the profile of local actors in local democracy has undergone considerable changes in recent decades, with greater representation of socially backward groups than was the case before 1978. The Moving Out of Poverty study shows that the *functioning of local democracy along with increased (albeit partial) political representation of the poor has mattered for climbing out of poverty.* The impact of local democracy (as in the case of the base model) has been positive and significant.

Second, movers out of poverty seem to follow a much more organizationally connected trajectory than did the chronic poor. Movers were more likely to be members of organizations, both political and economic. Within the realm of economic organizations, movers preferred more socially heterogeneous settings. At the same time, movers were much more likely to be politically connected and to participate in political organizations and political activities. With respect to organizational involvement, *the key difference between movers and chronic poor in West Bengal seems to lie in the sphere of political participation.* The lesson here is that the exclusionary processes that come with the functioning of local democracy need to be changed so that the excluded poor too can join the movers' league. The need to strengthen local democracy, given the exclusionary tendencies so emphatically voiced by those left out, is consistent with the previous findings in the literature.[35]

Third, qualitative life history evidence for movers suggests that *initial access to land* gained during the period of land reform (1978–90) played an important role in shaping the escape route from poverty. Movers got access to more land than the chronic poor, they succeeded much more in transforming their land into viable income-generating assets, and they displayed greater entrepreneurship in terms of investing in new technology or new lines of business. Part of their success (compared to the chronic poor) can no doubt be attributed to their good luck in not being affected by disrupting shocks in the early phase of their ascent. If they did suffer shocks, they may have had greater capacity to cope with them by mobilizing family resources.

Fourth, and most important, movers were able to use the platform of land reform to *diversify their income sources.* They made the difficult transition from depending on a single source of income to managing multiple occupations, typically graduating from rice farming to various nonrice, noncrop forms of agriculture and from there to nonfarm self-employment businesses or in some cases to regular wage employment jobs. To accomplish this transition, they worked hard for at least a decade or two to generate savings and educate their children. They typically encouraged their spouses to participate in income-earning or cost-saving activities, they used their connections, they planned for the future, and they continued to seize opportunities as they came along.

Fifth, the process of diversification and transition to nonfarm activities at times can be considerably *mediated through politics,* an aspect often neglected in the standard discourse on farm-nonfarm movement. The movement to greater diversification and nonfarm sectors is not random: there is a selection bias in deciding who can make this transition. Political connections enabled individuals to gain access to timely loans, space in the local marketplace, business permits and information needed to start a business (such as commercial pisciculture or vegetable selling), and even salaried jobs.

Sixth, as expected, agency, rights, and aspirations—three dimensions of empowerment—had a strong positive effect on the chances of escape from poverty. But the results also showed that these should not be seen as psychological attributes alone. The leave-out mean results for all three dimensions showed that empowerment for the movers may often mean disempowerment for the chronic poor. This is consistent with the story of political connectedness favoring movers and disfavoring the chronic poor that runs throughout the West Bengal findings. However, this also means that policies to strengthen empowerment cannot be based on individual targeting. More effective, perhaps, would be separate class actions and organizations for the chronic poor and the ultrapoor to avoid the skewed distribution of empowerment that has contributed to greater social differentiation within the rural poor witnessed in the past two decades.

The seventh finding begins with a question: Why did the state regime not extend the land reform program to reach the chronic poor and reap electoral benefits? Perhaps it feared losing the support of the middle peasantry, an important constituency that would have been affected by land acquisition under ceiling legislation. Quite possibly, the rural poorest were never the main social base of the regime, and the regime expected to secure their support directly by expanding antipoverty programs and indirectly by creating greater wage employment opportunities—expanding irrigation during the winter season or encouraging migration to periurban areas. The option of converting them into small farmers by providing land beyond the amount needed for minimal homesteading would have required bringing additional land into the agrarian reform program and this, in turn, would have entailed political costs.

Annex 6.1 Supplementary Tables

ANNEX TABLE 6.A
Trends in poverty headcount, West Bengal, 1987/88–1999/2000

percent

Period	Official		Deaton and Drèze 2002		Kijima and Lanjouw 2003		Sen and Himanshu 2005	
	Rural	*Urban*	*Rural*	*Urban*	*Rural*	*Urban*	*Rural*	*Urban*
1987/88	48.8	33.7	36.3	22.3	36.0	. .	45.9	30.4
1993/94	41.2	22.9	25.1	15.5	25.1	15.5	35.5	18.2
1999/00	31.7	14.7	21.9	11.3	26.4	14.3	31.9	14.9
Change over 1987–93	–7.6	–10.8	–11.2	–6.8	–10.9	. .	–10.4	–12.2
Change over 1993–99	–9.5	–8.2	–3.2	–4.2	1.3	–1.2	–3.6	–3.3

Note: Deaton and Drèze (2002) and Kijima and Lanjouw (2003) use the same Deaton-Tarozzi poverty line, but they use different procedures for adjusting the consumption expenditure (the so-called single regressor "30-day intermediate goods expenditure" for Deaton and Drèze as opposed to the multivariate model that includes a set of household characteristics but excludes 30-day intermediate goods consumption for Kijima and Lanjouw). Results from Sen and Himanshu (2005) cited here refer to the so-called "mixed (30/365) days reference period" and are based on the official state-specific poverty line.

ANNEX TABLE 6.B
Land reform efforts in 15 states of India: Share of land area transferred compared with share of population that benefited
percent

State	Tenancy		Ceiling	
	Area	Population	Area	Population
Andhra Pradesh	3.5	0.8	8.3	3.8
Bihar	0	0	4.4	4.0
Gujarat	15.0	11.2	2.0	0.3
Haryana	0.5	0	1.3	0.3
Himachal Pradesh	0.2	3.2	0.1	0.1
Karnataka	15.4	5.3	1.7	0.3
Kerala	8.5	12.5	1.3	1.0
Madhya Pradesh	2.2	0.6	2.7	0.7
Maharashtra	27.0	10.7	7.7	1.1
Orissa	0.2	1.4	2.2	1.3
Punjab	1.9	0	1.5	0.3
Rajasthan	0	0.2	6.6	0.8
Tamil Nadu	3.7	3.2	2.5	1.2
Uttar Pradesh	0	0	5.8	3.7
West Bengal	6.4	10.8	14.9	19.7
Total	5.5	5.4	4.4	2.3

Source: World Bank 2007.

ANNEX TABLE 6.C
Village-level indicators from the perspective of community focus group discussions, 1995 and 2005, West Bengal

percent

Indicator	10 years ago (1995)	Now (2005)
Access to infrastructure		
Bus terminal in community	60	70
All-weather village-city connection	—	96
Daily bus service	—	89
Electricity access	51	83
Community market	76	86
Public library	15	24
Public place to phone	9	64
Post office	64	70
Access to clean water	55	79
Strength of local economy		
Strong	11	26
Weak	33	16
Landlessness		
<20%	7	5
20–30%	18	28
30–40%	25	26
40–50%	15	12
50%+	35	29

ANNEX TABLE 6.D
Change in village-level indicators from the perspective of community focus group discussions, 1995–2005, West Bengal
percent

Indicator	Change over 10 years	Indicator	Change over 10 years
Access to infrastructure		*Local growth* (cont.)	
Credit access		Economic opportunities (C912)	
Improved	30	Greater	63
Deteriorated	12	Fewer	9
Agricultural input access		*Corruption*	
Improved	43	Very high	6
Deteriorated	5	High	60
Irrigation access		Low	23
Improved	37	Very low	11
Deteriorated	17	*Local inequality*	
Agricultural extension		Economic (C910)	
Improved	28	Gap (top 10%–bottom 10%) increased	48
Deteriorated	22	Gap (top 10%–bottom 10%) decreased	33
Market conditions		Social (C918)	
Improved	61	Community networks/ associations open to	
Deteriorated	3	Many people	68
Local growth		Few people	32
Community (C903)		Compared to 10 years ago, these networks give (C919)	
More prosperous	76	More access	45
Less prosperous	5	Less access	16
To make living (C904)			
Easier	53		
Harder	46		

ANNEX TABLE 6.E
Change in village-level indicators from the perspective of the initial poor set, 1995–2005, West Bengal

percent

Indicator	Change over 10 years
Local prosperity (C903ml)	
More	77
Less	5
Expansion of economic opportunity (C912ml)	
Greater	64
Fewer	9
Economic inequality (C917ml)	
More people get opportunity	51
Fewer people get opportunity	22
Ability to contact local government (h504)	
Increased	63
Decreased	5
Local government pays attention (h502b)	
More	12
Less	8
Information about local government (h515b)	
Improved	32
Deteriorated	8
Impact of local democracy (C922)	
Positive	57
No impact	15
Access to organized network (C919ml)	
More	48
Less	11
Access to participation in community affairs (C916ml)	
More people	44
Less people	19
Access to networks	
Open to many	67
Local income inequality (C910ml)	
Increased	52
Decreased	31
Compared to 10 years ago local government run for (h507)	
Greater public interest	17
Own self-interest	10

Note: Household and community data combined. The initial poor are those households that were poor in 1995, regardless of whether or not they moved out of poverty in the subsequent decade.

ANNEX TABLE 6.F
Impact of improved local democracy on outcomes in West Bengal:
Views of initial poor set

percent

Indicator	Communities where local democracy improved	Communities where local democracy deteriorated
Local government pays attention		
Local government works for more people	49	0
Local government works for fewer people	3	56
Satisfaction with local government		
Very satisfied	30	0
Very dissatisfied	0	23
Corruption		
Very high	1	28
High	9	12
Low	46	55
Very low	44	5
Information about local government		
Improved	83	7
Deteriorated	1	45
Setting up a business		
Less difficult	65	26
More difficult	4	33
Religious expression		
Freely express religious belief	97	73
Crime and violence		
Very peaceful	82	71
Violence against women		
None	96	88
Employment opportunity		
Very difficult	27	66
Primary schooling		
Improved	83	71
Deteriorated	0	9
Secondary schooling		
Improved	81	68
Deteriorated	0	9

Fair treatment in schools		
Improved	89	1
Deteriorated	1	70
Health		
Improved	43	32
Deteriorated	16	30
% of movers	68	46
Average no. of organizations in village	0.36	0.05

Note: Communities were assigned to one of three categories, depending on whether the ability to influence local government was seen to have improved, stayed the same, or deteriorated. This table contrasts the results in the two polar categories. Figures represent percentages of initial poor reporting development outcomes. The initial poor are those households that were poor in 1995, irregardless of whether or not they moved out of poverty in the subsequent decade.

ANNEX TABLE 6.G
Differential rating of economic trends by movers and chronic poor, West Bengal

percent

Indicator	Mover	Chronic poor
Finding job		
Harder	39	60
Easier	24	6
Business environment		
More conducive	40	23
More difficult	7	20
Control over everyday decisions		
More	46	13
Less	4	9
Aspiration (current generation)		
Better self-prospect	75	17
Worse self-prospect	2	18
Aspiration (future generation)		
Better prospect	78	39
Worse prospect	4	11
Fair price in market		
Improved	24	18
Deteriorated	10	18
Credit access		
Expectation of denial	4	11

ANNEX TABLE 6.H
Differential rating of political trends by movers and chronic poor, West Bengal
percent

Indicator	Mover	Chronic poor
Trust in local government		
High trust	40	27
Low trust	38	47
Local government run		
In the interest of all people	48	35
In the interest of a few	52	65
Satisfaction with local government		
High	80	65
Very low	2	8
Ability to influence local government		
Increased	23	18
Decreased	9	17
Corruption in local government		
Negligible	27	16
High	17	29

ANNEX TABLE 6.1
Occupational mobility by movers and chronic poor, West Bengal

percent

Mobility group	Wage employment		Regular salaried job		Crop		Livestock		Fishery		Nonfarm business		Remittances	
	1995	2005	1995	2005	1995	2005	1995	2005	1995	2005	1995	2005	1995	2005
Movers	57.21	47.62	29.55	33.33	38.77	50.59	5.20	18.91	1.89	2.84	6.86	33.33	0.95	0.95
Chronic poor	41.83	32.62	32.18	32.43	41.06	36.94	8.49	12.87	3.09	2.57	17.50	16.86	0.26	1.03

ANNEX TABLE 6.J
Factors explaining movement out of poverty in West Bengal:
Outcome of household-level regressions under alternative methods
of estimation (movers vs. chronic poor within initial poor set)

Variable	OLS weighted	OLS unweighted	Probit weighted	Probit unweighted
Initial strength of economy	−0.022	−0.006	−0.333	−0.369
	[1.25]	[0.47]	[2.41]**	[2.95]***
Change in economic prosperity	0.018	0.002	0.236	0.086
	[1.14]	[0.16]	[2.04]**	[0.86]
Responsiveness of local democracy	0.049	0.023	0.359	0.235
	[4.44]***	[1.68]*	[3.85]***	[2.87]***
LOM of responsiveness of local democracy	0.002	−0.097	0.006	0.009
	[1.79]*	[2.68]***	[0.98]	[1.58]
Corruption	−0.01	0.013	−0.01	0.036
	[0.88]	[1.77]*	[0.14]	[0.52]
Fairness index	0.001	0.007	−0.014	0.04
	[0.06]	[0.39]	[0.14]	[0.53]
LOM of fairness index	0.000	0.009	0.007	0.01
	[0.32]	[0.32]	[1.04]	[1.67]*
Initial step on ladder of power and rights	0.062	0.074	0.427	0.422
	[5.99]***	[4.73]***	[5.97]***	[5.81]***
LOM of initial step on ladder of power and rights	0.000	−0.081	−0.005	−0.007
	[0.37]	[4.08]***	[0.82]	[1.26]
Change in control over everyday decisions	0.136	0.171	0.981	0.931
	[4.28]***	[5.37]***	[4.19]***	[4.41]***
LOM of change in control over everyday decisions	−0.002	−0.124	−0.017	−0.012
	[1.85]*	[1.88]*	[1.19]	[0.88]
Household aspirations	0.113	0.202	0.972	1.023
	[6.16]***	[9.53]***	[6.24]***	[6.31]***
LOM of household aspirations	−0.001	−0.175	−0.016	−0.021
	[1.38]	[5.43]***	[1.77]*	[2.60]***
Index of collective action, 10 years	−0.056	0.039	−0.418	−0.355
	[2.59]**	[1.35]	[2.57]**	[2.53]**
Trend in access to networks and associations	−0.005	−0.009	−0.207	−0.114
	[0.32]	[0.51]	[1.87]*	[1.23]
Social divisions	−0.025	0.005	−0.138	−0.202
	[1.61]	[0.44]	[1.36]	[2.14]**
Trend in school inequality	−0.018	0.004	0.017	0.02
	[1.65]	[0.45]	[0.24]	[0.35]
Initial violence against women in households	−0.037	−0.028	−0.58	−0.419
	[1.60]	[0.67]	[3.31]***	[2.47]**
LOM of violence against women in households	0.007	0.074	0.063	0.061
	[5.87]***	[1.48]	[4.61]***	[4.04]***

Variable	OLS weighted	OLS unweighted	Probit weighted	Probit unweighted
Health shocks, 10 years	−0.034	−0.019	−0.434	−0.366
	[1.07]	[0.45]	[2.21]**	[1.99]**
Initial ownership of house	0.101	0.033	0.578	0.356
	[2.24]**	[0.71]	[1.49]	[1.30]
Initial assets index	0.053	0.038	0.486	0.56
	[3.43]***	[2.76]***	[3.37]***	[2.90]***
Initial livestock index	0.02	0.012	0.22	0.169
	[1.84]*	[0.97]	[3.02]***	[2.34]**
Religion of household head	0.082	−0.03	0.433	0.541
	[1.93]*	[0.61]	[1.46]	[2.02]**
SC dummy	−0.004	−0.027	−0.073	−0.07
	[0.14]	[0.80]	[0.45]	[0.44]
ST dummy	0.036	−0.056	−0.236	−0.451
	[0.96]	[1.33]	[0.80]	[1.62]
Education of head of household	−0.002	0.004	0.029	0.037
	[0.21]	[0.58]	[0.54]	[0.84]
District dummy 2	−0.194	0.038	−1.374	−1.127
	[3.06]***	[0.61]	[3.06]***	[2.89]***
District dummy 3	−0.062	0.225	−0.334	−0.142
	[1.15]	[3.77]***	[0.88]	[0.41]
District dummy 4	−0.012	0.044	−0.165	−0.039
	[0.24]	[0.83]	[0.40]	[0.11]
District dummy 5	−0.029	0.098	−0.402	−0.612
	[0.53]	[1.77]*	[1.00]	[1.48]
Initial income source diversification	0.078	0.146	0.566	0.399
	[1.91]*	[3.11]***	[2.39]**	[1.89]*
Age of head of household	0.003	0.004	−0.015	0.007
	[0.42]	[0.42]	[0.36]	[0.16]
Age of head of household^2 (squared)	0.000	0.000	0.000	0.000
	[0.36]	[0.41]	[0.69]	[0.12]
Sex of head of household	0.028	0.032	0.139	0.237
	[0.66]	[0.54]	[0.46]	[0.81]
Initial membership in groups	0.033	0.033	0.18	0.178
	[2.51]**	[1.60]	[1.47]	[1.43]
Political activism, 10 years	−0.021	−0.014	−0.174	−0.124
	[2.38]**	[1.26]	[3.29]***	[2.17]**
Constant	−0.131	0.385	−2.746	−2.784
	[0.67]	[1.43]	[2.41]**	[2.11]**
Observations	648	648	648	648
R^2	0.61	0.47		

Note: t/z statistics in brackets.

*p < .10 **p < .05 ***p < .01

References

Banerjee, A., P. Bardhan, K. Basu, M. D. Chaudhuri, M. Ghatak, A. S. Guha, M. Majumdar, D. Mookherjee, and D. Ray. 2002. "Strategy for Economic Reform in West Bengal." *Economic and Political Weekly*, October 12, 4203–18.

Banerjee, A., P. Gertler, and M. Ghatak. 2002. "Empowerment and Efficiency: Tenancy Reform in West Bengal." *Journal of Political Economy* 110: 239–80.

Bardhan, P. 2002. "Decentralization of Governance and Development." *Journal of Economic Perspectives* 16 (4): 185–206.

Bardhan, P., and D. Mookherjee. 2005. "Political Economy of Land Reform in West Bengal 1978–98." Institute for Economic Development, Boston University.

———. 2006. "Pro-Poor Targeting and Accountability of Local Governments in West Bengal." *Journal of Development Economics* 79 (2): 303–27.

Besley, T., and R. Burgess. 2000. "Land Reform, Poverty Reduction, and Growth." *Quarterly Journal of Economics* 115 (2): 389–430.

Bhattacharyya, D. 1999. "Politics of Middleness: The Changing Character of the Communist Party of India (Marxist) in Rural West Bengal (1977–90)." In Rogaly, Harriss-White, and Bose 1999, chap. 10.

Boyce, J. 1987. *Agrarian Impasse in Bengal: Institutional Constraints to Technological Change.* New York: Oxford University Press.

Chatterjee, B. 1998. "Poverty in West Bengal: What Have We Learnt." *Economic and Political Weekly*, November 21, 3003–14.

Datt, G. 1998. "Poverty in India and Indian States: An Update." FCND Discussion Paper 47, Food Consumption and Nutrition Division, International Food Policy Research Institute, Washington, DC.

Deaton, A., and J. Drèze. 2002. "Poverty and Inequality in India: A Re-Examination." *Economic and Political Weekly*, September 7, 3729–48.

Deininger, K., S. Jin, and V. Yadav. 2008. "Impact of Land Reform on Productivity, Land Value and Human Capital Investment: Household Level Evidence from West Bengal." Paper presented at the annual meeting of the American Agricultural Economics Association, Orlando, FL, July 27–29.

Dev, S. M., K. S. James, and B. Sen. 2005. "Causes of Fertility Decline in India and Bangladesh." In *Economic Development in South Asia*, ed. M. S. Khan, 258–312. New Delhi: Tata McGraw-Hill.

Dev, S. M., and C. Ravi. 2007. "Poverty and Inequality: All India and States, 1983–2005." *Economic and Political Weekly*, February 10–26, 509–22.

Drèze, J., and A. Sen. 2002. *India: Development and Participation.* New York: Oxford University Press.

GoWB (Government of West Bengal). 1999. *1999 Statistical Abstract of West Bengal.* Kolkata: Department of Statistics, Government of West Bengal.

———. 2004. *West Bengal Human Development Report 2004.* Kolkata: Development and Planning Department, Government of West Bengal.

Himanshu. 2007. "Recent Trends in Poverty and Inequality: Some Preliminary Results." *Economic and Political Weekly*, February 10–26, 497–508.

Hossain, M., M. L. Bose, A. Chowdhury, and R. Meinzen-Dick. 2002. "Changes in Agrarian Relations and Livelihoods in Rural Bangladesh: Insights from Repeat Village Studies." In *Agrarian Studies: Essays on Agrarian Relations in Less-Developed*

Countries, ed. V. K. Ramachandran and M. Swaminathan. Kolkata: Tulika Print Communication.

Kijima, Y., and P. Lanjouw. 2003. "Poverty in India during the 1990s: A Regional Perspective." Policy Research Working Paper 3141, World Bank, Washington, DC.

Lahiri, A., and K. M. Yi. 2008. "A Tale of Two States: Maharashtra and West Bengal." Working Paper 06-16/R, Research Department, Federal Reserve Bank of Philadelphia.

Maharatna, A. 2007. "Population, Economy and Society in West Bengal since the 1970s." *Journal of Development Studies* 43 (8): 1381–1422.

Mehta, P. B. 2003. *The Burden of Democracy*. New Delhi: Penguin.

Rajan, S. I., and K. S. James, eds. 2004. *Demographic Change, Health Inequality and Human Development in India*. Hyderabad: Centre for Economic and Social Studies; New Delhi: Manohar.

Raychaudhuri, A. 2004. "Lessons from the Land Reform Movement in West Bengal, India." Paper presented at "Scaling Up Poverty Reduction: A Global Learning Process and Conference," Shanghai, May 25–27. www.eldis.org/static/DOC17932.htm.

Rogaly, B., B. Harriss-White, and S. Bose, eds. 1999. *Sonar Bangla? Agricultural Growth and Agrarian Change in West Bengal and Bangladesh*. New Delhi: Sage.

Ruud, A. E. 1999. "From Untouchable to Communist: Wealth, Power and Status among Supporters of the Communist Party (Marxist) in Rural West Bengal." In Rogaly, Harriss-White, and Bose 1999, chap. 9.

Sarkar, A. 2006. "Political Economy of West Bengal: A Puzzle and a Hypothesis." *Economic and Political Weekly*, January 28, 341–48.

Sen, A., and Himanshu. 2005. "Poverty and Inequality in India." In *The Great Indian Poverty Debate*, ed. A. Deaton and V. Kozel, 305–70. Delhi: Macmillan India.

Sen, B., M. Mujeri, and Q. Shahabuddin. 2007. "Explaining Pro-Poor Growth in Bangladesh: Puzzles, Evidence, and Implications." In *Delivering on the Promise of Pro-Poor Growth*, ed. T. Besley and L. J. Cord, 79–118. Washington, DC: World Bank; New York: Palgrave Macmillan.

Williams, G. 1999. "Panchayati Raj and the Changing Micro-Politics of West Bengal." In Rogaly, Harriss-White, and Bose 1999, chap. 8.

World Bank. 2004. "State Fiscal Reforms in India: Progress and Prospects." Report 28849-IN, Poverty Reduction and Economic Management Sector Unit, South Asia Region, World Bank, Washington, DC.

———. 2007. *India: Land Policies for Growth and Poverty Reduction*. New York: Oxford University Press.

Notes

1. Chronic poor received much smaller amounts of land than movers across the 240 life stories collected in West Bengal. Chronic poor generally received land in kathas, while movers received land in bighas. Units of land measurement in this chapter follow Bardhan and Mookherjee (2006): 1 acre is equivalent to 100 decimals of land, while 1 bigha equals 33 decimals—roughly one-third of an acre. The term *katha* has slightly different meanings in different areas, possibly

depending on local land productivity. In some places 20 kathas equal 1 bigha, while in others 16 kathas make a bigha.

2. The process of panchayat formation started around 1978 in West Bengal, but it was only in the early 1980s that these bodies started to function in a regular way. The West Bengal Panchayat Act of 1983 mandated elections to three-tier panchayats, and elections to each of these three tiers have been held regularly. The panchayats were given significant responsibility for implementing the land reforms in the state.

3. Land reform efforts in West Bengal date back to the 1950s; however, before the Left Front government came to power in 1977, very little was achieved in terms of land distribution. A survey of 88 villages found that 70–75 percent of all patta land recorded in 1998 had been distributed *after* 1978 (Bardhan and Mookherjee 2005).

4. Operation Barga has not been without pitfalls. "As tenants will still have to pay rent, their incentive to undertake (non-contractible) land investment and to exert effort in cultivating it will be reduced, compared to what would be the case under full ownership. . . . In West Bengal, purchase and sale of tenancy land is only allowed to occur between the landlord and the tenant. Tenancy land is also allowed to sublease to third party regardless whether the tenant household is still able to cultivate the land. This together with the relative lower productivity effect [compared to the case under full ownership] is expected to be associated with a lower purchase and [sale] price of tenancy land relative to the own land" (Deininger, Jin, and Yadav 2008, 13).

5. Apart from the political pressures that can slow the pace of land distribution to the poor under ceiling legislation, other factors can also reduce its impact. Deininger, Jin, and Yadav (2008), for instance, point out that patta reform lands are of lower quality than owned nonpatta lands. Failure to provide land recipients simultaneous access to credit and other inputs can also reduce the positive effects of patta land reform.

6. See Bardhan (2002) and Banerjee, Gertler, and Ghatak (2002).

7. See Chatterjee (1998), Besley and Burgess (2000), and GoWB (2004).

8. This was initially attributed to the adverse impact of the partition. West Bengal became virtually cut off from its hinterland in East Bengal, which had been a major source of raw materials.

9. This is a variation of the old Kaleckian argument, with the difference that he postulated a block consisting of the urban middle class and rural rich peasants. The "middling" position of West Bengal is a widely prevalent notion; see, for instance, Rogaly, Harriss-White, and Bose (1999).

10. See Banerjee, Gertler, and Ghatak (2002) and Besley and Burgess (2000).

11. Growth in the rice sector is likely to plateau at a level close to zero without further technological innovations and improvements in rice productivity. The state's yield per hectare is still considerably below that of other rice-producing states such as Andhra Pradesh and Tamil Nadu, and much below that of China, Vietnam, and Thailand.

12. A slowdown in consumption growth and poverty reduction was already evident in the analysis of trends between the 50th and 55th rounds as compared to the trends in the 1980s (annex table 6.A).

13. The state's performance on human development indicators is also largely disappointing, as evidenced by slow progress between the second and third rounds of National Family Health Survey (Maharatna 2007). What has caused the state's underperformance in this regard? The fiscal crisis of recent years provides one important clue. While there has been deceleration in the average growth of expenditure in social sectors for most of the 16 major states during the 1996–2002 period compared to the 1990–96 period, the drop was much more pronounced for the low-income states (World Bank 2004). For West Bengal this can be seen in the declining share of education, which fell from 16.6 percent of total public expenditure in 2000/1 to 11.7 percent in 2003/4. The corresponding share of health dropped from 5.6 to 3.9 percent during the same period. Clearly, the pressure of fiscal crisis has affected public investments in the social sectors. However, the low priority given to the education and health sectors was already visible at the beginning of the 1990s, well before the fiscal crisis entered its acute phase. The fiscal crisis of recent years has *aggravated* the adverse allocation pattern for these social sectors and cannot be taken as an explanation of underperformance during the 1980s and the first half of the 1990s. If anything, the quality of fiscal deficit was poor throughout the 1990s, when the fiscal deficit increased from just 3 percent to 9 percent of state domestic product. It should be noted that the state has historically given low priority to investing public resources in basic education and health, and the pattern did not change much in the 1980s and 1990s. In this respect, the state's experience stands in sharp contrast to the experiences of Sri Lanka and the Indian state of Kerala (Drèze and Sen 2002).

14. Having said that, we should hastily add that land reform was not the only variable influencing upward mobility. By the middle of the 1990s, the profitability of the land sector, which remained restricted to high-yield varieties of rice, had already started declining. A new set of nonfarm households that made their profits from diversified income/occupational sources started to emerge in rural West Bengal and aspired to buy new lands for commercial and contractual cultivation. The existing land laws were, however, not very conducive to the operation of this set of cultivators. The success of agrarian reforms also possibly meant that a large number of registered sharecroppers were almost locked in a situation of semi-permanent settlement, for it did not allow them to exit the land sector even if they wanted to. This undermined the efficiency of land market transactions (on this issue, see World Bank 2007).

15. Of course, 80 communities culled from only five districts cannot be considered as statistically representative of overall trends at the state level. Nevertheless, one would not expect sharply divergent trends if the development experience of the period between 1995 and 2005 were widely shared at the spatial level. Communities refer to villages (up to 200 households); for larger villages, it refers to the most representative part (neighborhood) of the villages.

16. That seems to be the trend in most growth-seeking communities in South Asia that are trying to move from low-income to middle-income status while maintaining a certain standard of rural consumption (which nowadays includes color TV, CD player, sewing machine, tube well, and bicycle).

17. See, for example, Dev, James, and Sen (2005) and Rajan and James (2004).

18. See Mehta (2003) for a discussion of social preconditions for a well-functioning democracy.

19. There is, of course, a question of causality here, but we shall probe this in a multivariate framework, purging the confounding influence of other mediating factors (table 6.1).

20. In this study, "initial" conditions are mainly those prevailing 10 years ago, at the beginning of the study period (1995). The life history tool traces dynamics over a longer period, often 30–35 years.

21. By contrast, the movers in Bangladesh seem to engage in a different kind of network building, with much less emphasis on political links and greater emphasis on making connections with nongovernmental organizations and their *samities*, or associations (Sen, Mujeri, and Shahabuddin 2007).

22. Figures are from the *Statistical Abstract of West Bengal* for 1999 (GoWB 1999). We cannot claim originality with regard to the last argument. It was made in several recent writings that discuss the stable vote share, victory in the marginal constituencies, and the poor's continued political allegiance. Sarkar (2006) contends that such political allegiance is more likely to happen in the context of rural and urban informal sectors where people have a much more acute need to access housing, loans, jobs, and government programs through party mediation and party arbitration.

23. See Rogaly, Harriss-White, and Bose (1999), Bhattacharyya (1999), Ruud (1999), and Williams (1999).

24. This is partly because of West Bengal's high population density—the highest among the Indian states—which potentially reduced the amount of surplus land available for redistribution under the existing land-ceiling laws.

25. The more positive (optimistic) rating by the movers as compared to chronic poor is also noticeable in case of perception-based economic indicators such as access to employment and a conducive business environment (annex table 6.G). Such differences are expected in case of economic outcomes among individuals with differing economic mobility. However, what interests us here is the considerable gap in the rating of political institutions by movers and chronic poor, which one would not have expected in a well-functioning democracy.

26. An ideal strategy is to combine both routes, and indeed the never poor often did so. Some movers also combined different activities in order to maximize their earnings, buying farmland to add to what they already had and at the same time opening a small business like a shop. These strategies were reported by female ladder of life groups in Biruha and Baral, among other communities.

27. It is possible that even the ratings of so-called initial conditions and of the seemingly exogenous changes that occurred in the past 10 years, obtained through individual recall, are also influenced by the current poverty status of the respondents. Such biases are may exist, although one cannot be too sure about their directionality. Should we expect that those who have achieved success (the movers) would overstate their past level of economic and social well-being and the level of their institutional access? The opposite is also possible. Clearly, more research is necessary to address such questions.

28. The strength of local democracy is a statistical index that takes into consideration several dimensions of the supply and demand sides of democracy such as community trust in local government officials, ability to contact local government and influence its actions, level of responsiveness of local government to local problems, and overall level of satisfaction with the way democracy works in the local government.

29. The dependent variable takes the value of 1 if the household is identified by the community as an escapee/mover, 0 otherwise. The model explaining escape from poverty or, broadly speaking, mobility within and above poverty, is estimated for the sample of the *initial poor* only. Although we present here the results of the linear probability model, we also checked the robustness with an alternative specification such as the probit model. We find our results relating to the positive impact of local democracy, personal empowerment, aspiration, initial asset index, and violence against women to be broadly upheld (table 6.1).

30. However, we have also checked the validity of our results with both unweighted and weighted regressions (annex table 6.J). Although the results are broadly similar across different variants, there are some differences across weighted and unweighted versions that we highlight only when they seem to be consequential.

31. In the weighted model, however, local democracy has a positive sign but statistically weak association with movement out of poverty.

32. Additional model results controlling for the same set of factors described above.

33. We implemented additional exercises (not shown in the table) to check the possible effects of past land reform on the current difference between movers and chronic poor by including a "land reform period" dummy—that is, whether those who got land during the initial phase of land reform (1978–85) were better off than those who got land in the subsequent periods. We found, rather surprisingly, a negative association, implying that the early beneficiaries did not perform well later. We also tried to include separate dummies for the patta and barga reform beneficiaries to see whether they currently explain any difference; the results suggest some positive effects only for the upwardly mobile households in general (MPI) but not for the movers (MOP)—and that only for the barga indicator. We also considered a third possibility to test whether a statistically significant household asset effect in the regression result is actually picking up some of the effects of land reform. We tried to test this proposition by interacting the household asset variable with the land reform (patta/barga) variables but could not confirm such effects.

34. The question may arise as to why the qualitative evidence is taken as the guide here. The present study found that the bulk of the land reform was carried out during 1978–90, and it documented the positive impact of that phase of land reform on the beneficiaries in terms of their higher chances of moving out. This documentation was done through (and could be done only through) life history interviews, since the time frame for the quantitative survey for the overall study was the last 10 years (1995–2005). That is the reason qualitative evidence is privileged over the quantitative evidence in judging the *initial* positive effects of land reform on moving out of poverty.

35. See, for instance, Bardhan and Mookherjee (2005, 2006).a

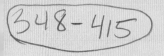

Who Benefits from Conflict? Some Evidence from Assam

Deepa Narayan, Binayak Sen, and Ashutosh Varshney

> *Being powerful and being poor are like two banks of a river. As the riverbanks never join, the poor also never become powerful. Poor can get power when they get rid of poverty.*
>
> —A CHRONIC POOR MAN, Assam

> *Extremists threatened the company, who gave them Rs 50,000 monthly, and then the government banned the permit to import wood from this area. In 2000 the company closed and that was the last of my service and employment.*
>
> —PANIKHAITI, A NEVER POOR MAN, Assam

CHAPTER 7

India

018 017

015 D74 R23

I32

E scapes from poverty in the state of Assam take place in a particularly difficult context. Since the late 1980s a separatist insurgency has challenged the central government's control, provoking counterinsurgency operations by the Indian army. Throughout the state, people struggle to earn livelihoods, and if they move out of poverty they do so against a backdrop of persistent low-intensity conflict. Simultaneously, the "normal" practices of democracy also play out. According to a close observer of political dynamics in Assam:

> Deaths, injuries and humiliations resulting from "insurgencies" and "counter-
> insurgency operations" as well as the hidden hurt that citizens quietly
> endure have become part of the texture of everyday life in the region. They
> coexist, somewhat awkwardly, with elections and elected governments,
> a free press, an independent judiciary and investments in the name of
> development—in sum, the institutions and practices of a normal democ-
> racy and a developmentalist state. (Baruah 2005, 4)

Two villages in the districts of Nalbari and Jorhat provide examples of the different ways in which poverty reduction can take place despite conflict. Kardohola village, in Nalbari, experienced intense conflict until 2003. The situation began to improve rapidly that year following a large counterinsurgency assault on the rebels. This ushered in a period of peace lasting at least two years (the survey was done in 2005). Kardohola now ranks very high in terms of its poverty reduction performance, with 39 percent of its residents having moved out of poverty; in fact the village displayed the second-highest incidence of escape from poverty over the past 10 years in Assam, based on the perceptions of its residents. In a sense, the rapid improvement following the transition from conflict to peace is not surprising. After all, that *is* the promise of peace: peace is supposed to enable communities to use their assets, capabilities, and talents to the fullest, and the Kardohola narrative can be read in that light.

However, there is also evidence that long-term development initiatives in the village were only minimally interrupted by the long-lasting conflict. When our teams visited in 2005, the village had a middle and a lower primary school and a youth arts group. People talked about changes in attitudes toward education, noting that higher education had enabled youth to take jobs in private firms or engage in self-employment activities. Women who were skilled in cottage industries had started weaving on a larger scale, and a local bazaar was set up to give better market access. Local self-help groups emerged even before the conflict, bearing names of hope—Nabadeep (new light), Pragoti (progress), and Nabamilan (new unity). Electricity came to the village. There were village panchayat members and a village headman, and a village development committee. Religious meetings and community discussions were held in the local *namghar* (prayer hall). Although there were vague complaints about the efficiency of local government, it seemed that the latter had functioned reasonably well in developing education, health, and transport facilities and providing homes to households below the poverty line.

The villagers expressed broad agreement that things had changed for the better in the decade between 1995 and 2005. The question is why. Did public policy at the central, state, and local levels play an important role—or any role at all—in facilitating the recovery? Or is it simply that the resilient Kardohola villagers came together in the midst of disaster, motivated by their faith in a better future?

Upper Deuri village, in Jorhat district, offers an interesting contrast. Here conflict remained high throughout the study period and was still going on in 2008. At the time of the study, in 2005, conflict in the village was increasing in intensity. The combined impact of insurgent operations and patrols by the security forces created anxiety and disrupted daily life. As one respondent put it, "There is a feeling of terror that has been created in the minds of the people." Unexpectedly, Upper Deuri also displays a high incidence of moving out of poverty, 28 percent, again according to the perception of local people themselves.

How should one explain this? Household interviews and community focus group discussions revealed some favorable initial conditions in the village, such as a very high level of literacy ("there are educated people in every household of the village") and a strong inclination among young people to pursue higher education. Beyond this, however, village youths took initiatives to adopt and spread new agricultural practices and technologies, resulting in a considerable increase in the production and marketing of foods. Proximity to the Jorhat market linked the village to the wider world and encouraged agricultural diversification. Electricity came to Upper Deuri in 1985, but coverage within the community expanded in recent years—a sign of rising economic prosperity. Most importantly, the people talked about the "high spirit of unity" and about the public works initiatives they had taken independent of government programs. A community focus group remarked,

> Our society has unity. There is a *gaon parichalana samity* [village management organization] in our village. In this organization all people get together to discuss about social development work. For instance, our people are trying to rebuild the *namghar* [prayer hall]. In the same way, there are some rules of the organization, like in the low-lying areas of our village, where cultivation prospect is not good, lands are given to the fishermen for fish farming. These lands are given to them on rent and they give a due share of profit to the organization. The *samity* then supports public works with that money.

Such expressions of cohesiveness are remarkable not just because of the conflict situation but also because the village experienced a very high rate of immigration. People from "outside places like Nagaon, Bihar, and Nalbari"—from outside the village as well as outside the state—moved to Upper Deuri and started small businesses such as jeweler shops, pharmacies, and barbershops.

The experience of Upper Deuri presents an often puzzling picture of economic vibrancy and social unity in the face of the fear and disruption resulting from the long-running insurgency and counterinsurgency operations. Taken together, both community narratives point to the possibility of resilience, recovery, and even mobility out of poverty in environments of recent and continuing conflict. Several preliminary observations stand out. First, it is clear that public policy had an important developmental role in both communities, providing proximity to markets, access to infrastructure (roads, electricity, schools, health centers, irrigation), support to self-help groups, access to antipoverty programs, and maintenance of local peace. Second, collective action by residents, independent of government action, seems to be important both in peacekeeping and in promoting local social development through public works. Third, the adoption of new farm practices and agricultural diversification, development of cottage industries, and drive for higher education are all encouraging signs of individual and entrepreneurial initiative that offers development potential for the future.

Reading these two community accounts as development narratives may suggest that conflict has no effect on economic well-being. This is, of course, not true: persistent conflict in a community discourages long-term investment, interferes with development, and lowers the quality of life. In Upper Deuri people are "afraid to move outside at night and often they have to guard their crops at night." In Kardohola, young people were often targeted by security forces when conflict was high. There is widespread relief that students don't have to "lose their study years" now that peace has returned to the community.

The central point, however, seems to be that some initiatives did take place at the village level, despite the conflict and perhaps even *because* of the conflict. In both communities, people's initiatives, development policy efforts, and market-driven changes showed significant structural continuities throughout the conflict years. This made possible a degree of economic healing and even, for some people, escape from poverty. Of course, these two villages may be atypical. But the example of Assam as a study of movement out of poverty amid long-term conflict contains many such unexpected scenarios, and hence the situation in the state demands fresh scrutiny.[1] Does democracy perhaps generate some processes, even during insurgencies, that systematically increase government's concern with citizen welfare in conflict-ridden parts of the country?

This chapter raises the question of effective policy responses to conflict in democracies that may not be possible in authoritarian regimes. It summarizes the conventional wisdom about the consequences of civil conflict and considers theoretically some possibilities about how poor people might escape poverty under such conditions. After an overview of India's policy responses to the conflict, we turn to the statistical results of the Moving Out of Poverty study in Assam and their explanation through qualitative narratives. Finally, we consider the question of local democracy in a conflict context, with a focus on the inclusiveness of the local state.

Differential Responses to Conflict: Does Democracy Make a Difference?

It is reasonable to suppose that democratic and authoritarian systems deal with conflicts and civil wars very differently. On the whole, dictatorships would be likely to rely primarily, or only, on military counterinsurgency operations to vanquish the insurgents. But democracies would offer a *political as well as a military* response. They would deploy the nation's military to crush the rebel militia, but they would also tend to allocate higher fiscal resources to conflict areas to wean the rebels' base of support away from them. This resource transfer can end up helping poor people in several ways. The theory that civil conflicts hurt the poor has not yet drawn a distinction between the ways that democratic and authoritarian polities respond to the same set of crisis circumstances.

Supportive evidence comes from India, the longest-lasting democracy in the developing world. Since independence in 1947, India has witnessed insurgencies in a few states, mainly in the northeastern and northern parts of the country. The states of Nagaland, Mizoram, and Assam in the northeast and Kashmir and Punjab in the north have been the sites of civil conflicts. In addition to waging counterinsurgency operations against rebel organizations, the central government has responded with a two-pronged political approach. It has sought to persuade the underground leaders of the rebellion to participate in elections and run governments, if they win power electorally. At the same time, it has allocated more fiscal resources for developmental purposes to the disaffected states as a way to deal with the discourse of grievance, undermine the mass base of the rebels (where it exists), and win over regional political elites.

The roots of conflict in Assam lie in part in decades of uncontrolled migration from East Pakistan and Bangladesh, which fueled Assamese resentment against the Indian central government.[2] The economic underdevelopment of Assam as a whole deepened the sense of exploitation. Assam saw violent conflict in the late 1970s and early 1980s, but in the beginning the rebels did not challenge the sovereignty of India. In the late 1980s a full-blown insurgency broke out, led by the United Liberation Front of Assam (ULFA). The ULFA attacked both governmental and civilian targets in its fight for a *swadhin* (independent and sovereign) Assam.

Not all Assamese organizations supported the ULFA's demands, but the rebels enjoyed enough support, both economic and political, to keep the insurgency alive. The government launched a counterinsurgency operation. At the same time, however, elections were held in Assam, political parties continued to participate in them, and elected governments continued to function. Central government fiscal transfers to the state increased over time, underwriting centrally sponsored development schemes.[3]

Of course, greater allocation of fiscal resources to a zone of insurgency does not mean that the resources will be used optimally. Democracy has three theaters of operation in India: at the center, in the state capitals, and in the local governments. The first two have been part of India's democratic experience since independence. Since 1992–93, a constitutional amendment has required communities to elect local governments every five years. The objective of the amendment was to improve governance at the local level on the assumption that the closer the government is to the people, the greater its concern for them will be. Many development projects, especially those involving education, health, sanitation, roads, and buildings, are routed through local governments, even if the resources come from the center. Our respondents report that they have greater voice in governance than before, but they also say that resources have been disproportionately captured by the local elite.

It is possible that this has something to do with the relative newness of India's elected local governments, for it can be argued that as local governments become more institutionalized, they respond better to local concerns. It is also possible that conflict intensifies elite capture, as normal political processes are not fully in operation when a civil conflict is under way. But we really cannot be sure. Only future evidence will settle the question of whether the longevity of local democracy, or the absence of acute conflict, makes local governments more responsive.

It is clear, however, that some of these resources, even if subject to elite capture, do help poor people. If a road or bridge is built, the military can more easily reach the insurgents, who often hide in the villages to avoid arrest. But once a road or bridge is built, poor producers can also take their wares to the nearby town market in the morning and come back home in the evening. Buses run faster on paved roads.

While we have not yet been able to investigate *empirically* whether other democracies in the developing world follow the logic we uncover in India, our sense is that our results are not India-specific. Rather, it is in the nature of democracies to deploy political as well as military approaches to insurgencies. This is not to deny that some authoritarian systems may also allocate greater public resources to an area of insurgency, but the tendency in democracies appears to be systematic, not dependent on the whim of authoritarian leaders.

Our claim, it should be stressed, is not that civil conflicts are good for the poor; that notion would be quite ridiculous. Civil conflicts destroy precious resources, and ending such conflicts remains the first-best option for development. But we cannot abandon poor people in a region affected by civil strife. We know from the comparative literature that civil conflicts tend to last a long time. As poor households, even in normal times, are especially vulnerable to losses of income and livelihoods, one can imagine how difficult the situation must be for them when they are engulfed by fighting.

India's experience may suggest some ways to ameliorate poverty in times of civil conflict. In any case, it presents empirical materials at odds with the conventional wisdom.

Economic Consequences of Civil Conflicts: Alternative Possibilities

In 1998 I got a house from the government. This made a change in my life, because the earlier house was in a broken condition and rainwater used to run through the hole in the roof.

—A chronic poor person,
Kardohola, Assam

The local government keeps busy, scheming how to rob the seeds and plunder the government grants. They gulp all facilities and grants like a crane.

—Men's discussion group,
Upper Deuri, Assam

Although others have written on the subject, arguments about the economic consequences of civil conflict have by now become a dialogue with Paul Collier and his colleagues.[4] They argue that civil conflict is a "conflict trap" for poor countries, a view now prevailing in policy circles. Conflict affects economic growth and the well-being of the general populace, and prolonged conflict, according to this view, leads to a slowing of growth and an increase in poverty. A vicious circle of conflict and decline sets in (Collier and Hoeffler 2004).

In a recent formulation, Collier (2007) takes this argument further. He has divided up the population of the so-called Third World into two blocs: "the bottom billion," 58 impoverished countries mostly in sub-Saharan Africa, and "the rest of the developing world," countries such as China, India, Thailand, Indonesia, and South Africa. The per capita income of the bottom billion grew by 0.5 percent per year in the 1970s, but it declined by 0.4 percent per year in the 1980s and by 0.5 percent per year in the 1990s. By the turn of the millennium, these countries were poorer than they had been in 1970. In contrast, the per capita income of the rest of the developing world grew by 2.5 percent per year in the 1970s and by 4.0 and 4.5 percent annually in the 1980s and 1990s. Civil war, argues Collier, is a conflict trap in general, but it is especially so for the very poorest: "The bulk of the countries that fall into civil war are from the bottom billion" (2007, 34–35). The lower the per capita income of a country, the longer the civil war typically continues.

But what are the mechanisms that produce the trap? In an earlier work, Collier identified five aspects of conflict that have devastating economic effects: destruction, disruption, diversion, dissaving, and portfolio substitution.

> The most obvious way in which civil war damages the economy is through the *destruction* of resources. For example, part of the labor force is killed or maimed and bridges are blown up . . . A second effect is the *disruption* caused by warfare and the often concomitant social disorder. For example, some roads become unsafe and so extra costs are incurred in achieving the same outcome. . . . A third effect is the *diversion* of public expenditures from output-enhancing activities. For example, as the army and its powers are expanded, the police force and the rule of law diminish. The enforcement costs of contracts consequently rise and the security of property rights is reduced . . . Fourthly, to the extent that these income losses are regarded as temporary, there will be *dissaving*, an effect analytically similar to the destruction of the capital stock. Finally, in response to the deterioration in the economic environment, private agents will engage in *portfolio substitution*, shifting their assets out of the country. Here, assets should be understood to include human as well as physical and financial capital. (Collier 1999b, 168–69, emphasis in original)

All of these mechanisms have an income-reducing effect, and lower incomes in turn make civil wars more likely. The implications for the poor should be obvious. The overall loss of economic dynamism means that they have fewer opportunities to step out of poverty. Elsewhere, Collier (1999a) argues that only four kinds of people "do well out of the war": opportunistic businessmen, criminals, traders, and the rebel organizations. A civil war hurts everybody else, especially poor people.

We argue that a variation on this theme is possible. While conflict affects the general well-being of poor people at first, most start adapting to the circumstances eventually and some even go on to become net gainers while the conflict continues. We particularly stress the importance of having a democracy as the overarching framework for such recovery.

But how can democracy have an economic healing effect? The key mechanism, at least in the medium term, is the execution of a public redistributive policy. Public policy can play an important role even in low-growth contexts by providing redistributive transfers from outside to the area affected by conflict.[5] The role of compensatory fiscal transfers is especially important. Democracies are likely to be sensitive to redistributive conflicts both within a region and across regions, and one typical response of the democratic political regime is to address regional grievances through fiscal measures and other economic incentives that encourage investment. This may be especially true of Indian democracy, given the growing importance of coalition politics and regional parties since the mid-1990s.

Available evidence for India, which we will examine later, does suggest that fiscal transfers from the center to the states have been redistributive in nature, with lagging states getting higher transfers per capita than richer states. For the lagging states the average annual fiscal transfer per capita has increased over time; sharp rises have been recorded since the mid-1990s, coinciding with the era of coalition politics. It is possible that with the onset and intensification of conflict in Assam, per capita transfer to that state has increased even faster than to the other lagging states. The terms of transfer are likely to be more beneficial as well. Ninety percent of the transfers to Assam from the center are in the form of grants; this is because Assam is a "special category state," that is, a low-income and conflict-prone state.[6]

Much depends, of course, on the conflict itself. The possibility of recovery is obviously much less in cases where high-intensity conflict threatens the very fabric of civil society and even leads to state insolvency. This is clearly not the case with Assam. Gleditsch et al. (2002) distinguish three levels of conflict: (a) minor conflicts producing more than 25 battle-related deaths per year, (b) intermediate conflicts producing more than 25 battle-related deaths per year and a total conflict history of more than 1,000 battle-related deaths, and (c) "wars" that result in more than 1,000 battle-related deaths per year. In none of the calendar years since 1979 did the death toll from conflict in Assam cross the benchmark of 1,000.[7] The annual number of conflict-related fatalities between 1992 and 2001 in Assam, though higher than elsewhere in the northeast, still places the state in the intermediate category according to the criteria set forth by Gleditsch. In statistical terms Assam's insurgency, underway since the 1970s, has been a low-intensity conflict, but it is civil conflict nonetheless.

For poor people, the impact of increased fiscal transfers from the center to the states differs depending on the reach of such transfers. Have the benefits typically been restricted to the rich and the powerful, or have they also percolated to the poor, including those who remain at or around the poverty line and those stuck far below the line? This remains a largely empirical question not explored in the literature; it is explored in the case of Assam with our Moving Out of Poverty data set.

Part of the reason why escape from poverty can occur during civil conflict is that people learn to adapt to difficult circumstances, just as they do in case of the recurrent floods that plague Assam. Conflict is disruptive, but as it continues, people's responses can become more orderly, creative, and sustainable. Innovative conflict-adaptive and conflict-mitigating institutions may emerge and assume mitigating or healing functions. Even if these institutions do not lift the poor out of poverty, they may well protect them from falling down further.[8] Again, this is largely an empirical and unexplored question that we address in this chapter.

Response to Conflict: Is There a Role for Economic Policy?

There is no problem in doing business. All can do it. But where there is no light, no bridge, and no roads, what business will you do?
—Women's discussion group,
Biralipara, Assam

Generally speaking, conflict destroys human lives and economic assets; it warps social interactions between communities and between people within a community. And conflict in a region inevitably slows its growth, constraining economic opportunities. Individual aspirations for upward mobility give way, all too often, to the struggle for survival.

As we have suggested, Assam presents a variation on this theme. We consider two possibilities. First, the conflict in Assam has been sporadic and generally of low intensity, although there have been high-intensity phases. At no time has conflict engulfed all parts of the state simultaneously: zones of peace have always coexisted with zones of conflict, even within high-conflict districts. As a result, the conflict has produced slow growth but not no growth. The general trend has been in line with the state's long-run growth since the early 1950s; in none of the conflict years since 1980 has per capita economic growth in the state been negative. Assam never fell to the level of the "bottom billion."

Second, the negative impact of slow growth may have been mitigated at least partially by the favorable policy response to conflict on the part of the Indian central government. Central transfers appear to have had a moderating influence on the adverse growth effects of the conflict, and they may have benefited some sections of the poor population even in the presence of slow growth.

Although policy attribution is difficult, it appears that not all was lost during the decades of conflict in Assam. In fact, modest gains were achieved in some key aspects of well-being at the aggregate level. The limited quantitative and qualitative evidence at our disposal relates to a few key dimensions of well-being, namely poverty, child malnutrition, human development, and employment. Changes in these broad indicators suggest a mixed picture: progress has been considerable in some areas (greater than the average for the low-income states or even than the all-India average), while in other areas the state lagged considerably. What is remarkable is that even modest positive trends could be sustained during a period of conflict and low economic growth.

The magnitude of central transfer

In the smaller states of India, especially those in the northeast, central transfers have customarily made up a much higher proportion of state budgets than in the bigger Indian states. The Institute for Social and Economic Change in Bangalore, which presents a comparative scenario for a typical year in the mid-1990s, points to two noteworthy patterns (Rao 2000). First, only 27 percent of the state revenue budget for the smaller states comes from their own revenue; the rest comes from central government sources. The corresponding figure is 49 percent for the larger low-income states and rises secularly for the middle-income (67 percent) and high-income states (84 percent). The figure for Assam is 29 percent, which is higher than the figures for the remaining states in the northeast. These patterns do not change if one considers the other indicator of interest, the ratio of states' own revenue to total expenditure.

Second, many of the smaller states are conflict-prone states. As the intensity of conflict rises, dependence on central government sources is also likely to increase. However, we do not have current data on conflict intensity across the Indian states that would show whether central government transfers respond to a higher intensity of conflict. Available evidence only suggests that in conflict-prone states of the northeast, in general, current spending accounts for a higher share of state domestic product (40 percent) than in the low-income (20 percent), middle-income (18 percent), and high-income (16 percent) states. This shows the importance of government spending, and particularly the role of central transfers, in the economy of the smaller conflict-prone states. Again, Assam seems to be on a stronger footing economically than the other northeastern states, the corresponding ratio being 21 percent, comparable to other low-income states in India.

The striking effect of central transfer is illustrated in annex table 7.A. Per capita central transfer is much higher in the "special category states" marked by ongoing conflict than in the general category states (Rs 2,896 as against Rs 660 in 2000/01). The figure for Assam (Rs 1,216) is roughly twice as high as the average for the general category states. The figures for other more conflict-prone states are much higher (for example, Rs 3,376 for Tripura, Rs 3,971 for Manipur, Rs 6,332 for Nagaland, and Rs 9,602 for Mizoram). The other noteworthy aspect is that per capita central transfer as a proportion of current state spending is also higher for the conflict-prone states than for the general category states. For Assam, this figure is 36.7 percent, compared to 30.0 percent for the low-income, 19.4 percent for the middle-income, and 11.4 percent for the high-income states.[9]

Poverty trends

According to official estimates, the poverty headcount dropped only marginally in Assam, from 41 percent to 36 percent, during the period between 1983 and 2000 (table 7.1).[10] The rate of reduction was much slower than the all-India average. This confirms the generally dampening effects of slow growth in Assam in relation to the rest of India. However, there are important variations by subperiod and by sector. In general, the overall poverty headcount in the state stayed unchanged between 1983 and 1993 and dropped modestly thereafter. The incidence of rural poverty increased slightly during 1983–93 and decreased slightly in the latter half of the 1990s. The main beneficiaries during the entire period between 1983 and 2000 appear to have been urban residents: the incidence of urban poverty decreased dramatically from 26 percent in 1983 to only 8 percent in 1993, where it remained in the subsequent period.

TABLE 7.1
Long-term poverty trends in Assam, 1973–2000

Period	Rural poverty headcount index (%)	Urban poverty headcount index (%)	Combined poverty headcount index (%)	Rural poor (millions)	Urban poor (millions)	Total poor (millions)
1973/74	52.7	37.2	51.2	7.6	0.6	8.2
1977/78	59.8	37.6	57.6	9.8	0.7	10.4
1983	42.6	26.4	40.9	8.1	0.6	8.7
1987/88	39.4	9.9	36.2	7.4	0.2	7.6
1993/94	45.0	7.7	41.0	9.4	0.2	9.6
1999/2000	40.0	7.5	36.1	9.2	0.2	9.5

Source: Planning Commission estimates based on expert group methodology (www.Indiastat.com), cited in GoI 2002, 65.

Note: There are well-known comparability problems between 1993/94 and 1999/2000, as discussed in the edited volume by Deaton and Kozel (2005). However, we restrict our discussion to the official poverty numbers because of our interest in studying long-term trends on a consistent computational basis.

The disaggregated regional data available for the 1990s based on the poverty numbers calculated by Deaton (2003) show additional aspects of regional variation. In areas with a high initial level of poverty, the pace of decline was faster. Thus, a drop in poverty was registered only in the western region of the state, while poverty worsened in the eastern and hill regions. In the western region poverty fell at a slightly higher pace in urban areas than in rural areas. The exacerbation of poverty was most striking in the hill region: the rural poverty headcount increased from 31 percent to 51 percent, while the urban headcount rose from 5 to 18 percent. This is consistent with the picture of intensified conflict, driven by deprivation, among the tribal population of the hills during this period.

There has been a dramatic change in recent years, as suggested by data from the 61st round of the National Sample Survey (NSS) for 2004/05. The rural poverty headcount, which remained stagnant at around 45 percent between 1983 and 1993/94, dropped to just 22 percent in 2004/05: in other words, the level of rural poverty was cut almost in half (Himanshu 2007). The urban poverty headcount dropped from 8 percent to 4 percent during the same period. Although the estimates for 2004/05 are based on published grouped distribution data while the previous rounds are based on the unit-record data, the encouraging trends in the post-1993 period appear indisputable; Dev and Ravi (2007) also suggest the same trends based on the "mixed reference" period. These results seem to be consistent with one of our central arguments regarding the response of democracies to conflict: that is, counterinsurgency operations create disincentives for insurgency while expanded development programs create incentives for peace.

Human development trends

Education and health are two areas where Assam did better than the low-income states despite the climate of conflict. This improvement is due to comparatively favorable initial conditions in terms of literacy, including female education. Female adult literacy in Assam in 1991 was 37 percent, which was higher than the all-India average and also much higher than the levels observed in low-income and some middle-income states such as Rajasthan (17 percent), Bihar (18 percent), Uttar Pradesh (20 percent), Madhya Pradesh (23 percent), Andhra Pradesh (26 percent), and Orissa (29 percent). The picture is the same for the male adult literacy rate. Assam's edge over other low-income and some middle-income states with respect to literacy was maintained during the conflict years of the 1990s. According to the population census of

2001, the overall literacy rate in the state stood at 64 percent (GoA 2004), which was higher than the rate in Bihar (48 percent), Uttar Pradesh (57 percent), Rajasthan (61 percent), and Andhra Pradesh (61 percent).

With respect to infant mortality, the estimates for Assam show marked improvements between 1992/93 and 1998/99, closing the gap with the all-India average. The National Family Health Survey (NFHS) round for 2005/06 shows further modest progress, as the infant mortality rate dropped from 70 deaths per 1,000 live births in 1998/99 to 66 in 2005/06. Assam also did better than the above-mentioned states, and it retained this advantage during the conflict decade of the 1990s.[11]

NFHS data for 1998/99 show that enrollment rates at both the primary and upper primary levels in Assam were higher than the all-India average (GoA 2002, table 10.7). There is also some evidence that access to basic education is more equitably distributed in Assam than in other low-income states. For instance, the enrollment rate at the primary and secondary levels for the bottom 30 percent of the population is higher in Assam than the all-India average and also higher than in the other low-income states. Progress in the educational dimension was broadly shared by all the districts in Assam; the coefficient of variation in the expansion of literacy actually dropped over 1991–2001.

One of the key factors underlying Assam's relatively strong performance in basic education and health indicators, compared to other low-income states of India, is the higher share of state domestic product spent on these sectors. In terms of public expenditure on primary education per child (ages 6–14) as well as per student enrolled in primary school, Assam spent more in 1998/99 than Bihar, Uttar Pradesh, Madhya Pradesh, Orissa, Rajasthan, Andhra Pradesh, and West Bengal (Deolalikar 2005). Even though the state was largely dependent on central government largesse, the ruling coalition has made an effort to prioritize human development expenditures. One study showed that in terms of the performance of government health services on a number of indicators such as access, usage, reliability, and user satisfaction, Assam ranks 12th out of 22 states in India and is actually superior to Bihar, Madhya Pradesh, Rajasthan, Orissa, Andhra Pradesh, and West Bengal (Public Affairs Centre 2002). This should not, however, distract attention from the issue of quality of services. Like other low-income states of India, Assam suffers from extremely inadequate physical infrastructure in areas such as road access, electricity, communication, and sanitation. Rough living conditions have made it difficult to retain service providers such as doctors and teachers in the villages.

Employment trends

Unemployment, especially among youth, shows disturbing trends in the 1990s, and this in turn has worrisome implications for the persistence of conflict. In 1983/84 the rate of joblessness among young people ages 15 to 29 in Assam was high, but not as high as in some other states such as Tamil Nadu, West Bengal, and Punjab.[12] In fact, it was slightly better than the all-India level (annex table 7.B). The situation changed dramatically during the course of the conflict. The rate of youth unemployment registered the sharpest increase in Assam among 15 major Indian states during the decade between 1983/84 and 1993/94. By the latter year, at around the time a large counterinsurgency operation called Operation Rhino was under way, youth unemployment in Assam was about three times higher than in the rest of India. These data indirectly support the argument, implied by the Collier model, that high unemployment during civil conflict makes it easier for the insurgents to recruit new cadres among disaffected youth.

We used NSS data from various rounds to determine the overall unemployment rate for the entire working-age population, rather than for youth only. Table 7.2 shows that the employment situation severely deteriorated during the course of the conflict in the 1980s and remained at a high level in the 1990s. The overall unemployment rate for the state increased from only 3.6 percent in 1983/84 to 10.3 percent in 1993/94, dropping slightly to 9.1 percent in 1999/2000. Since conflict was widespread in the rural areas of Assam, it is important also to track the unemployment trends separately for rural and urban areas. Additional data show that although rural unemployment has been lower than urban employment in all years, the sharpest increase in unemployment was recorded in the rural areas. In short, the rural population was more affected than the urban population during the intensified phase of conflict between 1983 and 1993. There are signs of improvement in the overall employment situation by 1999/2000, especially in the rural areas. Although Assam has not yet reached a turning point in its recovery, the modest progress achieved may signal that the redistributive transfer policy on the part of the central government in response to the conflict has played a compensatory role, encouraging some positive rural changes in recent years.

Who Moved Out of Poverty during Conflict?

We turn now to the question of who benefited from the government's developmental response to the conflict. Our focus is on those who, starting poor,

TABLE 7.2
Trends in the unemployment rate over NSS rounds in Assam and other Indian states, 1983–2000

State	1983/84 (NSS 38th round)	1987/88 (NSS 43rd round)	1993/94 (NSS 50th round)	1999/2000 (NSS 55th round)
Andaman and Nicobar Islands	6.6	4.5	8.2	7.0
Andhra Pradesh	3.6	4.8	2.7	2.9
Arunachal Pradesh	—	1.8	1.3	2.2
Assam	3.6	5.5	10.3	9.1
Bihar	3.6	4.5	4.7	5.3
Chandigarh	8.3	6.4	5.2	4.3
Dadra and Nagar Haveli	0.7	0.6	1.5	0.9
Daman and Diu	—	—	3.9	2.8
Delhi	3.6	5.4	0.8	3.8
Goa	6.5	9.4	11.9	13.2
Gujarat	2.8	3.0	2.2	1.3
Haryana	4.0	6.0	3.4	2.2
Himachal Pradesh	5.2	5.5	2.6	5.5
Jammu and Kashmir	2.8	4.2	7.0	5.0
Karnataka	3.3	3.9	3.1	2.4
Kerala	14.9	18.2	11.2	12.8
Lakshadweep	—	21.1	20.3	18.8
Madhya Pradesh	1.7	2.9	3.1	2.4
Maharashtra	2.7	3.7	3.1	3.8
Manipur	0.3	2.8	2.5	3.4
Meghalaya	4.9	1.2	1.1	2.4
Mizoram	0.7	0.2	1.0	2.7
Nagaland	0.4	4.4	4.5	6.7
Orissa	3.9	6.0	5.3	5.1
Pondicherry	6.7	7.2	5.2	5.1
Punjab	4.2	4.7	2.8	3.5
Rajasthan	1.6	3.2	1.4	1.8
Sikkim	5.6	4.1	2.0	5.7
Tamil Nadu	5.6	6.5	4.4	3.2
Tripura	7.8	8.7	6.3	3.5
Uttar Pradesh	3.0	3.3	2.5	3.2
West Bengal	7.1	7.2	6.5	6.9

Note: Unemployment rates are defined for usual principal status of male workers in the 15–59 age group and have been estimated by the authors based on data from the primary NSS rounds.

improved their situation or even managed to cross the poverty line despite the growth-depressing climate of conflict. In order to address this question, we make use of primary data revealing the profiles of those who moved out of poverty, those who remained stuck in poverty, and those who fell into poverty over the study period. Both quantitative and qualitative data are important. It is well known that reliance on any single instrument is not desirable for reasons of verification, supplementation, and integration of evidence. Quantitative data indicate broad patterns of empirical regularities, while qualitative data provide glimpses of key moments in the life experiences of individuals and households as they move into and out of poverty. For a description of the data collection tools see appendix 2 in this volume.

Sampling strategy

In 2005, a primary survey of a total of 746 households was carried out in 50 communities (villages) across five districts in Assam, using a multistage sampling technique. The districts chosen provide examples of both high and low infrastructural development. However, the sample does not include the areas of most intense conflict, where administration of the survey was not feasible. Also excluded were the extremely flood-prone parts of the state, which were virtually impossible to access during June–August 2005, when the survey was carried out.[13]

The list of the actual communities was drawn up through consultation with key informants including the block development officer, the in-charge of police station, and the panchayat samity chairman at the block level. They provided information that enabled us to identify villages according to gradations of conflict (high-medium-low) and conflict trajectory (villages of endemic conflict, villages that moved from peace to conflict, villages that moved from conflict to peace, and villages that have remained more or less outside the direct influence of conflict). The term "conflict" was understood to indicate any insurgency-driven activity that resulted in civilian casualties. Upon discussion with the key informants, eventually 50 communities were selected on a purposive basis from each of the identified blocks. The list of districts and blocks in the sample is shown in table 7.3.

Measuring poverty

At the start of fieldwork in each village, focus groups of men and women created a "ladder of life" for their community, showing local levels of household well-being on a figurative ladder. The groups also defined a community poverty line (CPL), indicating the ladder step at which households were

TABLE 7.3
Distribution of sample districts and blocks in Assam

District	NSS region	Block	Development profile
Nalbari	Eastern Plain	Paschim Nalbari Amguri	High wage growth + high infrastructure index
Sonitpur	Eastern Plain	Biswanath Dhekiajuli	High wage growth + low infrastructure index
Jorhat	Western Plain	Titaber Teak	High wage growth + high infrastructure index
Kamrup	Western Plain	Sualkuchi Bezera Kamalpur	High wage growth + high infrastructure index
Darrang	Western Plain	Sipajhar Pub-Mangaldoi	High wage growth + low infrastructure index

Note: Development profiles are based on information provided on wage growth at NSS-region level by Kijima and Lanjouw (2004) and on the Relative Infrastructure Development Index generated by the Centre for Monitoring Indian Economy (CMIE 2000).

considered no longer poor by local standards. Finally, they ranked about 150 households in their community according to their well-being status at the time of the study (2005) and approximately 10 years earlier (1995). For details on the ladder of life exercise, see appendix 1 in this volume.

In Assam, as in the other study states, this process defined four main groups of households in each community. The first group, and the most important from the perspective of the study, consists of *poor households that crossed the poverty line* over the 10-year period, according to the rating of the community where they live. These households are viewed as having moved out of poverty; for the sake of brevity, we call them movers. Two aspects of the definition are noteworthy. First, the focus is on long-term escape from poverty rather than on temporary movements around the poverty line that are characteristic of agrarian societies. Second, the rating is done by the community and not by individuals, thus avoiding the problem of subjectivism in self-rating. One could even say that the poverty rating is owned by the community: through collective consultation, debate, and clarification, the community reaches a sociological understanding about whether a particular household has moved up or down or stayed at the same level on the well-being ladder.[14]

The second group consists of people who remained stuck in poverty over the 10-year period; we call them the chronic poor. The third group consists of households that were not poor in 1995 but slipped into poverty by 2005; they are called fallers. The fourth group consists of those who started above the poverty line and remained there throughout the period; we call them the never poor.

In addition to these four mobility groups, the study also considers a broad group of initially poor households that experienced upward mobility of any kind, irrespective of whether or not they crossed the poverty line. This provides a broad-based measure of well-being improvement among the poor. This group includes the movers (those who did cross the community poverty line) as a subset.[15]

Of particular interest to the study is community-level mobility. The ladder of life exercise enabled the researchers to calculate the number and percentage of households in each village that moved up or down on the ladder during the study period. The moving out of poverty index (MOP) measures the extent of upward mobility by the poor across the CPL in a community. The mobility of the poor index (MPI) measures extent of upward mobility by those who were initially poor, irrespective of whether or not they crossed the CPL. For details on the calculation of these and other indexes used in the study, see chapter 1, table 1.2.

Summary numbers on poverty and mobility

Consistent with the overall growth performance of the state's economy, microsurvey data collected for the present study show that the rate of poverty reduction in Assam has been quite slow compared to other Indian states (table 7.4). Among the initially poor households, those that were poor in 1995, only about 10 percent escaped poverty over the next 10 years, a much lower rate than in Uttar Pradesh (21 percent), Andhra Pradesh (21.5 percent), and West Bengal (31 percent). In Assam, nearly 7 percent of *all* households sorted by the communities' subjective rankings escaped poverty over the study period. However, 5 percent of the households ranked also fell into poverty, leading to a net poverty reduction of less than 2 percent. More than 90 percent of the households that began in poverty in 1995 remained stuck there 10 years later.[16]

Most poor men and women in Assam who were successful in escaping poverty cited diversification of income

TABLE 7.4

Summary trends on poverty and mobility in Assam

Movers as % of initially poor	9.6
Movers as % of all households	6.9
Fallers as % of all households	5.4
Net poverty reduction (%)	1.5
Chronic poor as % of initially poor	90.4

sources as the most important trigger of their mobility. Nearly 26 percent of them mentioned opening a shop or a small side business or sending their children to work in cities as having helped them expand their income and move out of poverty. Another 16 percent cited jobs in government or the private sector as reasons for ascent, while 12 percent mentioned improvements in farming.[17] All of the strategies for upward movement mentioned in Assam echoed those cited by poor people in other states visited for the study.

Likewise, the stories we heard about falling mirrored the ones heard in the more peaceful states. People spoke of slipping into poverty due to poor economic conditions in their community, agricultural failures, or health shocks. One-third of the faller households in Assam singled out decreasing community prosperity as the reason for their downfall, while another 16 percent cited crop failure. Decreasing prosperity may indirectly reflect the effects of conflict, while agricultural failures may reflect the adverse impact of floods. Only 9 percent of fallers cited health shocks as the key trigger for their descent into poverty. This is a much lower proportion than in Uttar Pradesh, where roughly 18 percent of faller households cited health shocks as a key reason for their impoverishment.[18]

It is notable that relatively few people explicitly mentioned conflict as a reason for falling down. This supports our argument that the people of Assam seem to have largely adapted to the situation. Men and women living in conflict-affected sites treat the violence like any other contextual variable, gradually adjusting their lives around it and aspiring to follow the same paths out of poverty as their counterparts in more peaceful states. However, the high proportion of those stuck in abject, chronic poverty in Assam—nearly 90 percent—suggests that very few are successful in using these mechanisms to escape poverty. We can only speculate on whether this may reflect the indirect adverse effects of conflict.

The next section presents some basic descriptive statistics on the mover households and the chronic poor as a means to explore whether the two groups differed in any basic dimension. We present data on both the community and household levels.

Profile of communities

We start with a broad description of the economic, social, and political characteristics of the communities visited for the study.

Trajectory and intensity of conflict. More than one-third of the communities visited for the study had experienced high conflict that was still going on in 2005. Another 36 percent were in conflict in the late 1990s but had moved to a peaceful state by 2005. Our sample also included a slightly smaller group of communities that had remained relatively peaceful over the 10-year study period, as well as one village that went from peace to conflict (table 7.5).[19]

The sample villages also varied in the intensity of conflict, that is, whether conflict resulted in deaths, physical injuries, or property damage or only led to an atmosphere of fear and harassment. A careful rating of the 50 communities along these dimensions (with more weight attached to physical injuries and deaths, and somewhat less to loss of property) showed that nearly 24 percent of the communities surveyed were still experiencing high-intensity conflict in 2005. Nearly twice as many (46 percent), however, had shifted to low-intensity conflict that did not result in deaths or injuries after the year 2000.[20] The remaining 30 percent of the sample were classified as no-conflict villages, with no reports of deaths or injuries over the study period (table 7.6).

TABLE 7.5
Trajectory of conflict in communities visited in Assam, 1995–2005

Conflict trajectory over 10 years	Frequency	%
Conflict to conflict	17	34
Peace to conflict	1	2
Conflict to peace	18	36
Peace to peace	14	28
Total	50	100

TABLE 7.6
Conflict intensity in communities visited in Assam, 2005

Conflict intensity in 2005	Frequency	%
High conflict	12	24
Low conflict	23	46
No conflict	15	30
Total	50	100

Conflict trajectory and community-level mobility. The central question in our study is the nature of the relationship between conflict and escaping poverty. To address this issue we analyzed the distribution of MOP rates at the community level in relation to the three main conflict trajectories (table 7.7).

We find no significant difference in poverty escape rates between peaceful communities and those affected by persistent conflict. Overall, more of the conflict-affected communities (41 percent) than peaceful communities (28 percent) fell in the middle range of MOP. Overall, 29 percent of conflict-affected communities experienced high mobility rates compared to 36 percent of the peaceful communities. Our point is simply that mobility out of poverty in conflict-affected communities was not zero. In terms of averages, there is no difference in mobility rates between peaceful and conflict-affected communities: both are 11 percent.

TABLE 7.7

Distribution of Assam study communities by conflict trajectory and community MOP terciles

| | Rate of community MOP (%) | | | Community |
Conflict trajectory	Bottom third	Middle third	Top third	MOP (mean)
Peace to peace	36	28	36	11
Conflict to peace	39	28	33	10
Conflict to conflict	29	41	29	11
Total	35	33	33	11

Note: There is no statistically significant variation in the two-way tables. The one community that went from peace to conflict has been dropped.

TABLE 7.8

Strength of local economy in Assam study communities, 1995 and 2005

| | 1995 | | 2005 | |
Strength of local economy	Frequency	%	Frequency	%
Very strong	1	2	0	0
Strong	1	2	4	8
Medium	10	20	31	62
Weak	32	64	12	24
Very weak	6	12	3	6
Total	50	100	50	100

Local economic strength. The poor economic conditions in the villages we visited confirm that conflict in Assam has taken place in the context of a weak economy. Informants in 76 percent of the communities in the sample reported that their village had a weak to very weak local economy at the start of the study period—the time when conflict was at its peak. The decade between 1995 and 2005 witnessed some improvement, with only 30 percent of the sample villages in 2005 calling their local economy weak or very weak (table 7.8). Private employment, though, became more difficult to access, with 56 percent of communities finding it difficult or very difficult to get jobs now compared to 36 percent in 1995 (table 7.9). This is consistent with the adverse dynamics in overall and youth unemployment based on NSS data observed earlier. Moreover, floods afflicted nearly half of the communities visited for the study, severely affecting prospects for agriculture. We found no significant differences along this dimension between no-conflict, low-con-

TABLE 7.9
Access to private jobs in Assam study communities, 1995 and 2005

	1995		2005	
Access to private jobs	Frequency	%	Frequency	%
Very easy	5	10	3	6
Fairly easy	13	26	9	18
Not so hard if help is available from relatives/friends	9	18	8	16
Not so hard if help is available from a paid agent/middleman	5	10	2	4
Somewhat difficult	13	26	17	34
Very difficult	5	10	11	22
Total	50	100	50	100

flict, and high-conflict communities or between villages that had ongoing conflict and those that had made the transition to peace.

Security/law and order. There are striking differences between the perceptions of officials and those of ordinary villagers with respect to peace and security. According to key informants, who were usually local officials, a decline in the intensity of conflict and a shift to peace in some communities has led to a decrease in crime and violence and a dramatic improvement in public safety. Key informants in more than 80 percent of the villages surveyed believe that their communities have become moderately peaceful or very peaceful places. Discussions with groups of men and women in the same villages, however, revealed a different picture. When asked directly about safety, community discussion groups in both peaceful and conflict-affected communities reported an overall decline in safety and an increase in danger over the last 10 years. In fact, the decline was more marked in peaceful communities since conflict-affected communities were already unsafe 10 years ago (table 7.10; see also annex table 7.C for change over time).

Corruption. Corruption in local government offices took a turn for the worse. Respondents in more than 65 percent of the communities surveyed agreed that most or almost all government officials in their village or neighborhood are corrupt. This was a clear deterioration from 1995, when only 28 percent of communities were identified as having corrupt officials (annex table 7.D).

TABLE 7.10
Peace and safety in Assam study communities: Perceptions of key informants and community groups, by conflict trajectory

Conflict trajectory	Key informants: % reporting community is very or moderately peaceful		
	1995	2005	Change (%)
Peace to peace	71	93	+30
Conflict to peace	28	89	+220
Conflict to conflict	24	88	+275
Total	39	90	+132

1995: Pearson chi2(6) = 14.65 Pr = 0.023
2005: Pearson chi2(6) = 9.18 Pr = 0.164

Conflict trajectory	Community groups: % reporting community is very safe or safe		
	1995	2005	Change (%)
Peace to peace	36	14	–60
Conflict to peace	44	17	–62
Conflict to conflict	18	12	–33
Total	33	14	–56

1995: Pearson chi2(8) = 4.87 Pr = 0.772
2005: Pearson chi2(8) = 10.50 Pr = 0.232

TABLE 7.11
Perceived corruption among local officials in Assam study communities, by conflict trajectory

Conflict trajectory	% of communities reporting most or all local officials take bribes		
	1995	2005	Change (%)
Peace to peace	29	100	+250
Conflict to peace	22	44	+100
Conflict to conflict	29	59	+100
Total	27	65	+146

1995: Pearson chi2(6) = 13.61 Pr = 0.034
2005: Pearson chi2(6) = 6.16 Pr = 0.406

The increase in perceived corruption is higher in the peaceful communities than in the conflict-affected communities. All the peaceful communities reported high levels of corruption among local officials, while only 59 percent of the conflict communities did (table 7.11).

Social capital. On the social side, it seemed that conflict did not affect or even had a positive effect on community cohesion and relations within the village. More than 90 percent of the communities visited for the study responded in the affirmative for both time periods when asked, "Do people cooperate to solve common problems like access to water and help each other in case of accidents like fire?" It is interesting to note that both in 1995 and 2005, communities that remained in conflict scored higher than (or at least as high as) peaceful communities or the communities becoming peaceful (table 7.12)

More communities reported the presence of people's own groups and organizations in 2005 than in 1995. Nearly 40 percent of the communities visited had 10 or more groups operational in 2005. This was in sharp contrast to the situation 10 years earlier, when only one village was reported to have 10 groups. The increase in the number of groups in these villages was confirmed by the increase in the average or mean number of groups per community, from nearly three groups to eight groups per village. In conflict communities, the increase in the number of groups was almost double the increase in peaceful areas, with a mean of nine groups compared to seven in peaceful areas (table 7.13).

Finally, a majority of communities (nearly 60 percent) reported that there was no division in their village along lines of caste, ethnicity, or religion. We also found evidence that inequality based on both gender and ethnicity has eased among children in schools. A majority of the communities reported an improvement in the treatment of girls (compared to boys) and children of lower-caste groups over 10 years (annex table 7.E). There were no significant differences across communities, whether peaceful or conflict-affected, in this trend; overall 65 percent reported improvement on both counts (annex table 7.F).

TABLE 7.12

Propensity for collective action in Assam study communities, by conflict trajectory

| Conflict trajectory | % of communities reporting people cooperate to solve water shortages | | |
	1995	2005	Change (%)
Peace to peace	71	93	+30
Conflict to peace	89	94	+6
Conflict to conflict	94	94	0
Total	86	94	+10

1995: Pearson chi2(6) = 8.84 Pr = 0.183
2005: Pearson chi2(6) = 3.62 Pr = 0.728

TABLE 7.13
Number of local groups in Assam study communities, by conflict trajectory

	Number of local groups per community (mean)		
Conflict trajectory	1995	2005	Change (%)
Peace to peace	4	7	+110
Conflict to peace	3	9	+185
Conflict to conflict	3	9	+192
Total	3	8	+163

Profile of households: Movers versus chronic poor

Most poverty analysis until recently has focused on individual assets and capabilities in determining who is and who is not able to move out of poverty. Poor people are usually defined as lacking assets like land and as deficient in the skills, education, and training needed for a climb out of poverty. Their bodies are their sole resource and are used for backbreaking labor under harsh conditions, leading to frequent health problems. We would argue, however, that households differ not only in terms of their assets and skills but also along social and political dimensions that are important to moving out of poverty.[21]

Responsiveness of local democracy. Movers, on average, have more positive perceptions of their local democratic structures than those who remain stuck in poverty. More than 40 percent of movers but only 29 percent of the chronic poor reported satisfaction with the way local democracy works in their village (table 7.14). Initial conditions also seemed to play a role. Those who escaped poverty by the end of the study period reported having had a higher level of trust in their local government officials in 1995 compared with those who remained poor (25 vs. 18 percent). There were no striking differences across conflict contexts.

Fairness in access. Those who escaped poverty were slightly more likely to receive fair prices when they went to sell their goods in the market. Fifty-two percent of the movers said that their ability to get fair prices for their produce had increased over 10 years, compared to 45 percent of the chronic poor (annex table 7.G). Households in persistent conflict communities, across mobility groups, reported much lower levels of improvements than the peaceful areas (annex table 7.H).

TABLE 7.14
Satisfaction with local democracy, by mobility group, 2005, Assam

Satisfaction with local democracy	Movers		Chronic poor		Fallers		Never poor		Total	
	Freq.	%	Freq.	%	Freq.	%	Freq.	%	Freq.	%
Very satisfied	9	5	6	2	2	3	14	6	31	4
Somewhat satisfied	67	37	73	27	13	20	97	43	250	34
Somewhat dissatisfied	63	34	99	37	21	32	74	33	257	34
Very dissatisfied	44	24	93	34	29	45	42	19	208	28
Total	183	100	271	100	65	100	227	100	746	100

Aspirations and psychological well-being. Opportunities offered by the local democracy or the market may not result in mobility unless the individual believes that he or she can use them to advantage and move out of poverty. Aspirations for a better future can be a strong trigger for mobility. The importance of such aspirations is reflected in our quantitative data as well. The mover households, for instance, spoke passionately about their dreams for themselves and for their children, with more than 80 percent expecting themselves and their children to be better off in the future. By contrast, only half of the chronically poor had such expectations (table 7.15). These differences gain significance in light of the fact that mobility status is not self-reported but decided by the wider focus group in the community. This minimizes the risk that a mover household will retrospectively report higher aspirations because it rates itself as having moved out of poverty. There were no differences across conflict settings.

Empowerment. In community after community, poor men and women cite empowerment—proxied by their control over everyday decisions and their sense of their power and rights—as crucial in escaping poverty. The significance of empowerment is reflected in the quantitative data as well. While 34 percent of those who escaped poverty reported an increase in control over their everyday decisions between 1995 and 2005, only 13 percent of the chronic poor did (table 7.16). The mover households also placed themselves higher on average on a 10-step ladder of power and rights, both in 1995 and 10 years later, compared with the chronic poor. Once again there were very few differences across conflict settings.

TABLE 7.15
Aspirations for self and for next generation, by mobility group, Assam

Aspirations for self	Movers		Chronic poor		Fallers		Never poor		Total	
	Freq.	%	Freq.	%	Freq.	%	Freq.	%	Freq.	%
Better off	151	83	126	46	33	51	170	75	480	64
About the same	26	14	97	36	19	29	45	20	187	25
Worse off	6	3	48	18	13	20	12	5	79	11
Total	183	100	271	100	65	100	227	100	746	100

Aspirations for next generation	Movers		Chronic poor		Fallers		Never poor		Total	
	Freq.	%	Freq.	%	Freq.	%	Freq.	%	Freq.	%
Better off	158	86	149	55	40	62	194	85	541	73
About the same	18	10	79	29	14	22	25	11	136	18
Worse off	7	4	43	16	11	17	8	4	69	9
Total	183	100	271	100	65	100	227	100	746	100

TABLE 7.16
Change in control over everyday decisions, 1995–2005, by mobility group, Assam

Change in control over everyday decisions	Movers		Chronic poor		Fallers		Never poor		Total	
	Freq.	%	Freq.	%	Freq.	%	Freq.	%	Freq.	%
More	63	34	36	13	14	22	59	26	172	23
About the same	113	62	186	69	32	49	159	70	490	66
Less	7	4	49	18	19	29	9	4	84	11
Total	183	100	271	100	65	100	227	100	746	100

How did conflict affect the mental distress felt by members of households? Clashes and violence are known to leave deep psychological scars. We find evidence of such trauma in our sample, but there are differences between households depending on mobility category. Those who escaped poverty were less psychologically affected by conflict than those who had remained poor. When people were asked whether they were bothered by nervousness or shakiness, 79 percent of movers said they were not bothered at all, compared to only 35 percent of the chronic poor (table 7.17). Over-

TABLE 7.17
Psychological well-being, by mobility group, Assam

Bothered by distress, nervousness, shakiness	Movers		Chronic poor		Fallers		Never poor		Total	
	Freq.	%	Freq.	%	Freq.	%	Freq.	%	Freq	%
Not at all	144	79	94	35	19	29	172	76	429	58
A little	28	15	119	44	35	54	42	19	224	30
Quite a bit	7	4	34	13	7	11	13	6	61	8
Extremely	4	2	24	9	4	6	0	0	32	4
Total	183	100	271	100	65	100	227	100	746	100

all, more households from peaceful communities and communities moving from conflict to peace reported mental distress (14 percent), compared to households from conflict-affected communities (10 percent).

Those stuck in chronic poverty also reported more feelings of restlessness, low energy, worthlessness, and apathy. We think this is because the livelihoods of the chronic poor, who generally work as daily wage labor or do odd jobs, are usually the worst affected when conflict strikes. Intense fighting and a climate of fear restricts those at the bottom from stepping out of their homes, leading to a loss of their daily bread. This may create a vicious cycle of poverty, fear, and low expectations for the future (box 7.1).

Ability to come together for collective action. In addition to their own efforts, poor men and women often cited the importance of their social networks and groups in helping them cope with shocks and move out of poverty. Of all the social formations cited, the family emerged as the most important. Households often used monetary support from children, for example, to expand their business or upgrade their farming, in some cases enabling them to escape poverty. Financial support from children working in cities was particularly crucial to mobility. A mover from Konwar Gaon village said, "In 1998 I bought a water pump set. The money was given by my younger son. He is a soldier in the Border Security Force. Now I can give water in my fields even during the dry season. My production has increased." A mover from Thengal Gaon related, "In 1996, after my elder son got a teaching job, our family condition became smooth. In 1999 my son built a pucca house. Before that we had a thatched roof. In 2003 he bought 11 bighas [about 4 acres] of land. The produce from the land covers our entire year's food requirements and we are also able to sell a portion."

BOX 7.1
Living in fear: The story of Sibpur

Sibpur is a scenic village in the district of Jorhat, surrounded by tea gardens. Most people work as laborers on the tea estate, farm small tracts of land, run market stalls, or do odd jobs. The village has been through an intense period of conflict over the past 10 or 12 years. Though it is more peaceful now, the villagers recount with much fear the days when the conflict was at its peak.

The origins of the conflict lie in the Bodo insurgency. The hills around town provide shelter to Bodo insurgents from surrounding states that include Manipur, Mizoram, and Meghalaya. The insurgents have been operating in the village since 1991. While they started as an extortion group, making claims on both poor and rich people in the area, villagers say they became increasingly violent as time went on. "In 1993 they attacked the temporary army outpost and looted the weapons. We were terrified as we had no security to protect us then," recalled a discussion group of men in the village. Armed with weaponry, the insurgents mounted attacks with increasing frequency and intensity. A year later they burned down the forest office near the village along with a number of houses. A few people were killed in the fires and several lost their belongings. In 1995 the rebels kidnapped the manager of the tea estate, leading to widespread fear in the village. "We were not able to sleep in peace. We ensured that our children were back to home before the night fell. Till date, we pay money to them. Nobody opens their doors during the night. At times, we even put locks on our own doors and sleep elsewhere," said the men.

Conflict had an adverse effect on livelihoods within the community. The most severely affected were the bottom poor, who usually worked for daily wages on the tea estate or sold small quantities of firewood that they gathered in the Bhuban hills. The kidnapping of the tea estate manager led to a temporary closure of the gardens and loss of livelihood for many villagers. Furthermore, with insurgents hiding out in the hills, there were reports that villagers were assaulted or went missing when they ventured out to collect wood. The men explained: "These people used to live by selling firewood or making things of bamboo and cane. They have now stopped going to the hills after hearing reports of people getting lost. They are very frightened."

Insurgent activities have decreased in recent years. The decline in violence is attributed to the setting up of a permanent army post and the formation of a village defense party in the village. "Now we recognize that if we stay united, nobody can do anything to us," the men say. But they say they still live under a "shadow of terror."

While family is paramount, the movers also engaged more in groups outside of their households. On average, a mover household belonged to 0.9 groups versus 0.6 for those remaining in poverty. Moreover, nearly 28 percent of the groups that movers belonged to frequently interacted with other groups outside the village, compared to 18 percent of the groups to which the chronic poor belonged. In other words, the level of *linking* social capital seemed to be higher for groups of which movers were members. The movers were more trusting of others than the chronic poor: only 30 percent of movers said that someone in their village could take advantage of them if they were not careful, whereas 38 percent of the chronic poor believed this.

Education and assets. There were differences in two of the usual correlates of mobility. On average, those who moved out of poverty had completed at least primary education or education until the lower secondary grade. In contrast, the chronic poor in our sample found it difficult even to complete primary education. The mover households also seemed to do marginally better on initial assets owned, including land: on average, movers owned 2.7 units of land in 1995, while the chronic poor owned 2.4 units.

The effect of shocks. The sharpest contrast between the two sets of households, however, emerged in the reporting of health shocks faced between 1995 and 2005. Nearly 62 percent of the chronic poor reported facing a health shock, compared to only 45 percent of the movers. While idiosyncratic, recovery depended on the nature and frequency of the shocks and on the individual's ability to finance recovery or obtain loans to do so. Several times, the chronic poor spoke of a series of illnesses, some long-term, whose treatment they struggled to pay for. More often than not, they had no choice but to sell their assets or take a high-interest private loan. This pushed many households into destitution (box 7.2).

The speed of recovery from health shocks is also contingent on the availability of health facilities, and these were generally weak in all communities. Nearly half the communities visited for the study reported their health facilities to be bad or very bad. A teacher in the conflict-affected village of Leteku Gaon reported, "A health subcenter lies near the border of our village, but there is no doctor. Long back there was a doctor and a nurse. But as the village is at the border and as the Naga insurgents demand money, the doctors have gone away. Government officials fear to come here. As a result

BOX 7.2
"Shocked" into poverty

Multiple and closely spaced shocks often featured in the life histories of those stuck in chronic poverty and those that fell into poverty during the study period. The life story of 53-year-old Jatin is a case in point. Born into poverty in Choudhuri Pum, a village in Kamrup district, he migrated to Guwahati at age 13 to work as a salesman. But he returned to his native village after six years because of a conflict with the store owner, and he has been working as a farm laborer since. In 1995 his wife died in childbirth. "I was stunned. My condition was extremely pathetic." Three years later his son became ill with malaria. He just managed to save him, with the help of other villagers. As a final shock, in 2001 he broke his hand and could no longer work. His son now works and feeds him. "I feel very sorry about that [his son supporting him]. I could not buy any property in my life so far and have not made any major profit. I have not made any deposit too. I have to spend more than I earn because of illness," he said.

Joy Chandra in Bilpar village, Nalbari district, has a history of illness in his family. Born in 1965 into a prosperous family (his father had 20 bighas of land, about 7 acres), he started farming at the age of 20 and then expanded into other activities, including a grocery business. However, ill health in the family has been a constant bane. The Rs 85,000 loan he took to open the grocery was spent on the illnesses of his father and mother. Eventually he had to sell part of the land to repay the loan. His elder brother is mentally handicapped because of the torture inflicted by the army during the conflict period. Finally, floods in 2005 damaged almost 10 bighas of his land. He says "I don't think my life is dynamic. It has become static. I feel demoralized."

The life of Biren in Leteku Gaon village, Jorhat district, is yet another example of how the cumulative impact of shocks can cause a fall. The son of rich parents, 40-year-old Biren has "had many problems," as he put it. When he was 25, he and his brothers divided their parents' property. Left with a meager share, Biren was forced to take up work as a laborer. Five years later both his parents died, and another two years later he discovered that his wife suffered from a mental illness. His prospects improved temporarily when his elder son received a scholarship and Biren himself was offered a reader's post in the local prayer hall. But soon thereafter, shocks struck again. In 2002 the roof of his house collapsed in a storm, and three years later a thief entered his house and took everything. Over the years he has been forced to give his land on contract, instead of tilling it himself, and sell his wife's jewelry. He does not find work regularly and now lives in near destitution.

the public is deprived of getting better health service. In 2004 our village was severely affected by malaria and cerebral malaria. About 12 people died. Before cremating one [body] we had to prepare for another. [Disease] will continue since we do not get good quality water. We drink boiled water all the time, winter or summer."

Factors influencing upward mobility: Regression analysis

We consider a range of factors in our study of mobility in the conflict context of Assam.[22] The first group of variables relates to local economic vibrancy. Two indicators considered here are the initial strength of the economy (a proxy for initial level of income) and change in economic prosperity (a proxy for growth). In the standard growth literature, the first indicator is expected to be associated with a negative sign (sign for convergence). In the conflict scenario, however, the opposite possibility also exists, as the richer areas are likely to be less affected, allowing greater chances for escape from poverty. That is why the expected sign appears to us quite indeterminate on an a priori basis. Growth is expected to be positively associated with mobility, but given the low-growth context in Assam, one would not expect a strong association.[23]

The second group of indicators captures various dimensions of the local state. We consider two indicators: the level of corruption in the local government and the strength of local democracy. Again, in the context of conflict, the effect of corruption is uncertain: more corruption opportunities may actually mean more transfer of resources from the state to the area, indirectly aiding mobility of the poor. The strength of local democracy is a statistical index that takes into consideration several dimensions of the "supply" and "demand" sides of democracy, such as community trust in local government officials, ability to contact local government and influence their actions, level of responsiveness of local government to local problems, and overall level of satisfaction with the way democracy works in the local government. It must be mentioned, however, that local government elections could not be held in many areas of Assam because of conflict, and hence the very existence of local government needs to be seen as an indicator of stronger local democratic aspiration.

The third group of variables captures a broad measure of fairness. The latter is empirically constructed based on three aspects of accessibility: rural producers' ability to get fair prices for their produce, the degree of fair treatment by law, and access to credit. The last two dimensions are especially important for mobility of the poor and are likely to be even more important for asset recovery and growth in a conflict-afflicted context.

The fourth group of variables pertains to personal empowerment, rights, and aspiration. Individuals or households that were initially located higher on the ladder of power and rights are expected to be better prepared to take advantage of the available opportunities to improve their life situation, livelihood, and prospects for upward mobility. The precise channels through which personal empowerment can have an independent effect on income growth and mobility are somewhat debated. Does it work through better connectivity with the existing power structure—in which case empowerment of a few movers may contribute to disempowerment of the rest of the poor? Does it imply improved networking capacity or bargaining power in the marketplace? Perhaps an empowered individual is a person "with a plan" even under the most adverse circumstances. Or does being empowered simply indicate freedom from extra-economic coercion? We were able to answer some of these questions.

The last argument may actually mean that empowered individuals represent distinct economic actors who do not depend on the landlord or moneylenders for their livelihood. They may be working in occupations that are more formal, perhaps in salaried jobs or self-employed trading, or they may be members of some self-help group with a measure of independence from the traditional rural middlemen and landlords. In this view, empowerment is a derivative of initial occupational choice, with few extra effects. In order to explore this issue we included several indicators of empowerment: (a) an initial-status indicator such as "position on the ladder of life 10 years ago" (as self-perceived by the household); (b) a change-status indicator that rates whether control over everyday decisions has increased in the last 10 years; and (c) an "aspiration" indicator that rates the person's degree of optimistic expectation about the future. The economic impact of positive aspiration is well known: it has an important bearing on savings and investment behavior. Does it also work through better personal initiatives on the work front? It is quite possible that the so-called culture of poverty has important effect on mobility outcomes through the aspiration channel.[24] While poverty of aspiration may be one of the crucial aspects of poverty in general, it is not altogether clear whether it is conditioned by more deep-seated factors such as family and inheritance.[25] What we need to test is whether empowerment picks up some independent effects even when the level of aspiration is significant.

The fifth group of factors captures the presence of social capital, while the sixth group focuses on the theme of discrimination based on ethnicity/

caste, gender, and class-based distinction (as in the case of unequal treatment of students in public schools). In Assam, especially in the ethno-linguistic Assamese community, caste-based discrimination is unheard of. However, there are social divisions based on ethnicity in some places, and these may be advantageous for some social groups of movers in the context of conflict.

The seventh and eighth groups of variables draw attention to the conventional factors of importance such as human capital (both educational and health capital, the latter represented negatively as health shocks) and other land and nonland assets. It should be noted, however, that these assets may bring very low return in the slow-growth context of Assam. Thus, only about 15 percent of the state's cultivated land is presently irrigated, although the potential for introducing a winter-season crop is very high in the plains. This may partly explain why often just owning or cultivating land does not provide a basis for upward mobility.

Finally, we have the target variable of interest: the nature of the conflict regime. In this chapter we have opted for the indicator of "conflict trajectory," which is a continuous variable. Areas that were peaceful during the last 10 years receive a value of 1, areas where the situation has graduated from conflict to peace a value of 2, areas where peace has given way to conflict a value of 3, and areas where conflict has become more intense a value of 4. The conventional expectation is that higher mobility will be associated with peace. However, as discussed above, there may be an alternative possibility: the rate of progress in poverty reduction may actually increase in the presence of durable conflict as the government makes more public resources available to the conflict-ridden area in an effort to buy peace. Again, this may not work for all classes of the poor; the urban areas may claim a disproportionate share of this resource flow, followed by the rural top echelons, leaving very little for the poorest. We test some of these hypotheses in a multivariate framework and for different economic groups that have experienced upward mobility.

The test for public-private interest congruence is of added utility in the context of conflict where the possibility of such divergence cannot be excluded. From this angle, a statistical clarification of the community-level variables created by aggregating the household responses through calculation of the leave-out mean (LOM) is in order.[26] This relates to five factors: strength of local democracy, fairness in access, level of initial empowerment, personal aspiration, and violence against women. For each of these variables, both the household rating and the average rating for the rest of the community minus the household have been included. The idea is to statistically test whether some of these factors function as a public good (benefiting all residents of the community) or a private good (benefiting the fortunate few). In the case of local democracy, for example, if the individual household rating is higher than the average community rating, then local democracy would seem to be working for the movers only (who may be a select few), but not necessarily for the entire community.

Regression results

We focus here on two groups of the upwardly mobile poor: (a) the narrow set of "mover" households that escaped poverty during 1995–2005 (represented by the MOP index); and (b) the broad set of initially poor households that moved up some degree during this period, irrespective of whether or not they escaped poverty (represented by the MPI index). As discussed earlier, the first group is a subset of the second group. A linear probability model is estimated to perform multivariate analysis of factors that influence upward movement for the two groups separately.[27] The characteristics of these two groups are compared with those observed for the chronic poor. The detailed results are presented in annex tables 7.I and 7.J. Several variants (model specifications) were implemented; we focus on the results of the extended model (column 9 in each case). Here we shall mainly discuss the results for the first group, those who moved out of poverty, in comparison to the chronic poor (table 7.18).

Local democracy helps movers, but not everyone. First, the presence of vigorous and responsive local democracy appears to be a strong predictor of escape from poverty as well as for upward mobility of the poor in general. This is in line with our findings regarding the differential impact of local democracy on movers and the chronic poor. However, the leave-out mean community rating of local democracy is significant and negative for both models. Statistically, it suggests that distribution of benefits through the channel of local democracy is benefiting the movers but not the rest of the community.[28] This is not to downplay the value of local government as an institution. In the case of Assam, local government is of recent origin and rationing of its benefits may reflect its early stage of development. The fact that local government emerged as an important factor for mobility of the poor indicates its future potential, provided the structure of governance is further democratized and empowered fiscally, politically, and administratively.

Fair access matters. Second, fairness in terms of accessibility is an important determinant of upward mobility. Unequal and low access to credit is frequently cited in the community focus group discussions as a major constraint

TABLE 7.18
Factors influencing escape from poverty (MOP) during conflict, Assam

Variable		Variable	
Initial strength of economy	0.043	Index collective action (PCA rc412b rc413b with current weights)	0.009
	[1.77]*		[0.43]
Change in economic prosperity	0.008	Access to networks and associations	−0.031
	[0.51]		[0.75]
Corruption	0.04	Social divisions	0.013
	[1.50]		[0.59]
Responsiveness of local democracy	0.036	Violence against women	0.089
	[2.07]**		[3.35]***
LOM of responsiveness of local democracy	−0.092	LOM of violence against women	−0.153
	[2.19]**		[2.99]***
Conflict trajectory	0.037	School inequality	0.009
	[1.83]*		[0.44]
Fairness index	0.034	Education of head of household	0.043
	[1.91]*		[3.12]***
LOM of fairness index	−0.009	Health shocks	−0.079
	[0.16]		[1.76]*
Step on the ladder of power and rights	0.017	Initial landholding	−0.005
	[0.81]		[0.84]
LOM of step on the ladder of power and rights	0.122	Ownership of house	0.115
	[2.00]*		[0.79]
Control over everyday decisions	0.138	Assets index	0.06
	[3.55]***		[1.26]
LOM of control over everyday decisions	−0.137	Livestock index	−0.029
	[0.92]		[0.98]
Household aspirations	0.088	Constant	−0.167
	[4.98]***		[0.33]
LOM of household aspirations	−0.077	Observations	452
	[1.32]	R^2	0.31

Note: Robust t-statistics in brackets.

*p < .10   **p < .05   ***p < .01

to household recovery and mobility. Lack of access to fair prices (largely reflective of the prevailing poor infrastructural conditions) is also a matter of common concern for those stuck in poverty. Unequal treatment before law in Assam may have an important ethnic dimension.

Empowerment and aspirations are both important. Third, both empowerment (proxied by control over everyday decisions) and aspiration matter statistically. The average attainment (score) of the "rest of the community" (as measured by the leave-out mean method) with respect to position on the ladder of power and rights shows similar directionality, implying that empowering community life, livelihood, and institutions is likely to favor the process of escape from poverty. Control over decisions is a significant determinant of mobility even when personal aspiration is accounted for separately. This means there is more to empowerment than the element of aspiration as such: each of these aspects of greater power and freedom should be accorded individual importance. Perhaps the movers are characterized by higher *internal* empowerment before *external* (such as economic and political) empowerment takes place; perhaps both take place simultaneously. Case studies show that movers almost invariably have better family relationships, greater determination to educate their children even in extremely adverse circumstances, and a core of will to succeed incrementally through saving, hard work, and grabbing whatever fleeting chances come their way. Part of the route to achieving power and freedom surely lies in personally empowering measures such as credit access, greater women's agency, and lesser ethnic, class, gender discrimination in the public sphere. But there is also a need to strengthen pro-poor institutions, that is, institutions that protect the poor from coercion and shocks, help them access new technology, credit, and land, and increase their participation in the local political process.

Living in communities with high levels of violence against women slows mobility. Fourth, inequality and unfairness toward women (proxied by an indicator on violence against women within households) is strikingly significant for mobility. The negative and significant coefficient on the leave-out mean for this variable suggests that communities where such violence is practiced are also those that experience lower movement out of poverty.

Human development indicators, especially education and health, matter. Fifth, expansion of human development is expected to have further favorable influence on escape from poverty. This is anticipated by the positive and significant sign for the household head's education and the negative though weakly significant sign for health shocks.

The insignificant variables. Finally, a number of variables emerged as statistically insignificant, including local growth (indicated by changes in community prosperity), corruption, inequality, social capital, and accumulation of physical assets, including land, livestock and other assets. One can see these factors as interconnected with the broader context of sluggish macro growth. Many of the village economies are actually passing through phases of low or stagnant growth or are at best recovering from such stagnation. With large-scale rural unemployment, low diversification of the rural economy, and slow expansion of irrigation technology, there is very little statistical variation in the community growth variable in the first place (or at least the people cannot see any resurgent growth beyond these structural signs). With modest local growth, the return on rural assets must have been very low to have any independent effect.

Similarly, one of the two variables used for capturing social capital is "access to networks and organizations." The supply of such organizations is also likely to be limited by slow growth and durable conflict. The other indicator of social capital, "collective action," shows little intercommunity variation, largely because collective action for mutual survival is common in times of conflict: youth committees were formed in almost every conflict-prone village. The insignificance of corruption needs to be weighed against the clientelist practices of local government, but it is quite possible that the scope for extensive corruption at the village level is limited by the low overall vibrancy of the economy.

It must be noted, however, that there is some evidence for "divergence": the stronger the economy 10 years ago, the higher the chances of mobility on the part of the poor (although weakly significant at the 10 percent level). This would mean that redistributive transfers on the part of the state government could not moderate the regional differences in well-being between richer and poorer areas afflicted by the conflict.

Validity of the statistical results under alternative methods and assumptions

Annex table 7.K presents the statistical results of the multivariate analysis of the factors explaining escape from poverty for weighted and unweighted models, as well as for ordinary least squares (OLS) and probit specifications. Although there are some expected differences, the results for the key correlates for escape from poverty are broadly similar across specifications. These results point to the importance of local democracy, fair access, empowerment, aspiration, and human capital (education of household head). The relative disadvantage of nonmovers in relation to movers in accessing the benefits of local democracy (the leave-out mean result) is also upheld across the methods of estimation. The same is true of the negative influence of dysfunctional households in terms of intrahousehold gender relations, as captured by the indicator of low or absent violence against women (the expected sign is positive, as higher value means lower violence). Corruption appears to be positively correlated with escape from poverty in all variants, suggestive of the role of rent-seeking and patronage distribution in moving out of poverty in the adverse governance context of Assam.

Association with conflict. With respect to conflict and its association with escape from poverty, however, the analysis gives a very different picture across unweighted and weighted as well as across methods of estimation. In the unweighted OLS version of the model, we find evidence that long-duration, low-intensity conflict tends to create conditions for greater escape from poverty. This leads us to speculate that the more conflict-prone areas become the target of greater resource allocation at the margin.

However, other methods of estimation do not support this regression result. This does not mean that the overall argument that redistributive policy mitigates the effects of conflict is lost in the statistical wilderness. Such a policy must have been working for Assam to some extent, given that the conflict-ridden state managed to reduce poverty considerably during the slow-growth decade of 1995–2005. However, the lack of robustness of the link between conflict and poverty escape shows that at the margin the aggravation of conflict hurts some poor people but *still benefits others.* Perhaps it is only a segment of the poor population, connected to political and other influential networks, that moves out of poverty in the conflict context.

What our results do establish is that *there is no significant negative relationship between conflict and moving out of poverty.* Clearly, supporting conflict is not a policy choice for poverty reduction, but when low-intensity conflict does happen, not all is lost. Even in such tough environments many poor people manage to escape poverty. Among our sample communities experiencing prolonged conflict over a decade or more, at least 29 percent experienced high levels of movement out of poverty, only slightly lower than the percentage in communities experiencing peace (table 7.7). Conventional wisdom would predict no movement out of poverty in contexts of prolonged conflict, but this is not what we observed.

Understanding the Association between Conflict and Local Democracy

As we have seen, local democracies can play a positive role in influencing mobility in conflict-affected contexts. This effect, however, may be compromised by exclusionary redistributive practices that lead to elite capture of resources. The Assam study also examined the association between conflict and local democracy.

Local democracy as a factor in upward mobility

The positive and significant coefficient on the local democracy variable in the regressions suggests that the responsiveness of local democratic structures can go a long way toward helping people move out of poverty, even in the context of conflict. Our qualitative data reveal that local governments usually facilitate mobility when they serve as effective conduits for transfer of projects and funds from the state to the local level. People in village after village mentioned construction of public infrastructure such as roads and markets using state finances as opening up opportunities for all, including the poor. Often community members identified the presence of a strong and cooperative leader as the most important factor leading to such investments. The comparative stories from Raja Pukhuri and Gobordia illustrate this point.

Raja Pukhuri and Gobordia are located near the Brahmaputra River in Assam's Kamrup district. The two villages have a lot in common: similar livelihoods, a history of conflict between the ULFA and the army, the presence of self-help groups, and high unemployment. Yet their stories are very different. Despite continuing conflict in Raja Pukhuri, its people feel that their village has become more prosperous over 10 years and estimate that nearly 16 percent of the villagers have moved out of poverty. In contrast, in Gobordia, where peace has been restored, only 5 percent of the residents moved out of poverty over the same period. Residents of that village also say they have fewer economic opportunities, despite the transition to peace.

The most important factor in Raja Pukhuri's increased prosperity is its strong and proactive local government. Both men and women agree that their ability to contact the local government and influence its decisions has increased over the past 10 years. People also seem generally satisfied with the performance of the local government, which is credited with effective implementation of state schemes to build new roads, expand markets, and provide education and health facilities in the village. In particular, the opening of a large market in Raja Pukhuri has led to high demand for products produced locally, and people have started getting fair prices for their produce. A group of key informants in Raja Pukhuri said, "The government set up a market at Raja Pukhuri near M.E. school in 1983. The market is big. Many people come to this market because the market is only 7 kilometers far from Guwahati [the state capital]. The market is held two times a week. From this market, the businessmen buy many things at a wholesale rate."

Better roads translate into reduced transportation costs and improved access to markets, schools, and hospitals. The government's initiative to set up self-help groups, which began 10 years ago, has also facilitated access to credit and helped people start new businesses. Today Raja Pukhuri has several well-functioning self-help groups that have helped women increase their savings and start new livelihoods such as poultry farming and livestock rearing. The establishment of a wine factory in the village has opened up employment opportunities to many young women who are now able to contribute to the family income. According to a female focus group, "If we compare between the last 10 years and the present we see that the people are getting more profits . . . The local government brings plans for the development of the people. The local government sends the public's appeals to the state government."

Another significant factor in Raja Pukhuri is community unity. The village has a diverse population of Hindus, Muslims, and Christians, and people from West Bengal and Bihar also live there. Respondents in the group discussions proudly call their village a "mini India" and agree that the greatest strength of the community is the high degree of solidarity and unity among its members. This enables people from these different groups to live together in peace and harmony, even though they are surrounded by conflict.

Gobordia presents a different picture. The village is composed almost entirely of Assamese Hindus belonging to different caste groups. The village is about 40 kilometers from Guwahati, but it is only 3 kilometers away from the town of Bijoynagartam. Like Raja Pukhuri, the village has experienced high conflict, and men and women in the community have faced torture and harassment by the ULFA and the army. Over the past 10 years the conflict has subsided and peace has been restored. Yet the community has become less prosperous during this time, with fewer economic opportunities. Today Gobordia is characterized by poor roads, lack of access to markets, and a high rate of unemployment; soil erosion has cut down severely on the availability of cultivable land.

Poor governance has hindered community development in Gobordia. Both men and women agree that over the past 10 years their ability to contact the local government has decreased. Decisions affecting the community are made by a few influential people. As a result, only the rich and those with links to political parties get the benefits of government programs. People in the community clearly express their disappointment with local democracy. Members of a male focus group said, "In the last 10 years, the quality of democracy has deteriorated to a much lower level. Democracy has been replaced by *dhanatantra* [a system where only money matters]. The [state] parliament has taken the form of piggery. The members of the parliament make a hue and cry in the parliament only to satisfy their own interests rather than the interest of the public."

The degradation of democracy in the village manifests itself in the form of poor access to roads and drinking water, lack of new economic opportunities, and increasing unemployment. Poor roads make transportation to nearby cities difficult and severely hinder the livelihoods of people engaged in business and trade. Village men in a focus group pointed out, "Despite being so near to Guwahati city, the roads of our village are very bad for commuting. Car and vehicles cannot run on this road. As a result it has become difficult for the local people to do shopping and marketing or for the people who are earning their livelihood say by running pan shop and vegetable shop to go to the market. If it rains these people remain indoors as they cannot travel on that road. For those days, they find it difficult to even feed their families."

On the whole, access to economic opportunities in Gobordia has dwindled, and respondents attribute this to a highly corrupt and inefficient local government. A male focus group said, "Our people got very few economic opportunities such as government aid, houses, tin sheet, etc., even 10 years ago, and still today they are getting fewer economic opportunities and facilities. The reason behind this is political interest according to party lines. The people do not get government aid if they are not supported by a certain party."

Exclusionary practices of local democracy

The literature on India's political economy suggests that while central government transfers help, the actual distributive mechanism adopted at the local level may be discretionary along lines of ethnicity or between rural and urban areas. As a result, everyone may not benefit equally. A negative sign on the leave-out mean variable of local democracy in our regressions supports this conclusion at the community level. (The negative sign suggests that *within* communities, only a few people benefit from local projects initiated by the democratic structure in the village, and they do so at other people's expense.)

Nearly 80 percent of the households reported that the local government worked for its own self-interest, with no differences across groups.

The case of Gobordia provides some indication of how the elite or the rich capture resources and how political connections matter for accessing government aid. The qualitative data yielded many similar examples (box 7.3).

Relationship between conflict and local democracy

It is possible that poor local democratic structures increase the probability of conflict or serve to perpetuate it. Elbadawi and Sambanis (2002) and Gurr (2000) find that a low level of democracy is associated with a higher risk of conflict, while Sambanis (2003) presents robust evidence that a functional democracy reduces the risk of civil war.

We tested this association in our sample of communities by running simple linear regressions. We used our variable of interest, that is, conflict trajectory, as the dependent variable. The latter is a continuous variable: areas with endemic conflict get the highest score, followed by areas of recent conflict, followed by areas of peace. We take elite capture, corruption, and responsiveness as measures of efficacy of the local panchayat. The results are reported in annex table 7.L.[29]

The results point to three key findings. First, higher corruption and elite capture have a very significant, positive association with ongoing conflict. In other words, communities with high levels of persistent conflict are also the ones where discretionary resources are likely to be captured, resulting in high levels of corruption. The evidence is in line with Collier's theory of the "inextricable fusion" of greed with grievance in the lead-up to civil conflict (Collier, Hoeffler, and Sambanis 2005). The large transfer of resources to a region (as has been the case in Assam) combines with low and stagnant levels of per capita income to make the prolongation of conflict in the best interests of all parties—for the elite who influence the local government as well as for the insurgents.[30]

Second, we observe a positive and significant association between the conflict trajectory variable and the law and order index within the community. Though counterintuitive at first glance, this result is mostly explained by the strong military presence we found in high-conflict zones in our sample.

Finally, we find that the ability of citizens to influence local democracy is lower in areas of higher conflict. This is indirectly confirmed by the indicator of "household political activism," which measures initiatives taken by households themselves to contact politicians or to influence their panchayat. The results show an inverse association between the level of household political activism and the degree of conflict (annex table 7.M).

BOX 7.3
Evidence of elite capture: village voices

The local government takes all decisions on its own. It doesn't pay importance to public opinions. There is nothing like a good or a bad decision. They do everything for their own profit. They distribute the government aids [looms, thread, houses, and tin] as they like. The needy people don't get these resources. They are distributed among the supporters of the political party.

—Discussion with a group of young girls, Bogar Gaon

Those from the richer classes get preferential treatment whenever opportunities like loans or government projects come to the village. As everywhere, the main thing that matters is *monirami* [money]. They can pour money so they get the preference.

—Discussion with a group of women, Bogar Gaon

Their [the panchayat's] decisions don't have any influence on the society because they don't give importance to matters of public interest. They are more eager to fulfill their own self-interests. They distribute government facilities among their near and dear ones and to those who have links with them. Other people don't get these facilities.

—Discussion with a group of male youths, Langpuria

In our village the panchayat is like a *vekovaona* [a useless spectacle]. There is not a single person in the village who believes in the panchayat. They take all decisions among themselves. They keep themselves busy by thinking how can they rob the seeds or plunder the government grants. *Bortukulai gita di Khai pelaise*, that is, they gulp them [all facilities and grants] like a crane. If any supply contract comes, they give it to their son, cousin, etc., secretly and spend only [5 percent of allocated amount] on actual development work; [the remaining 95 percent] enters into their pockets. The common people do not get even the skin of the banana. The villagers cannot affect the decisions of the panchayat. Actually the panchayat does not give us a chance to speak about any decision. Every decision is taken in meetings in the village leader's house or in the drawing room of the president.

—Discussion with a group of men, Upper Deuri

They [the panchayat] have done one or two works. But most have made their pockets hot. It is like throwing sand in the eyes of the people.

—Discussion with a group of women, Leteku Gaon

The panchayat does not distribute the government grants, fertilizers, seeds, etc., among the people who should be the actual beneficiaries of these schemes. They are pocketing the money meant for us. The members of the panchayat sanction the contracts to repair the roads and bridges of the village from the government but do not sanction the contract to other contractors. They take the contracts but do not do the works properly. They even construct bamboo bridges in place of [all-weather paved] roads.

—Discussion with a group of women, Langpuria

Concluding Remarks

We have argued that democracies are not likely to take the same approach to civil conflicts as dictatorships, which depend primarily on military might. The Indian experience bears this out: the central government deploys the army for counterinsurgency, but it also transfers public resources to the embattled areas to weaken insurgents, undermine their base, and build alliances with regional politicians. Some of this transfer helps the poor.

It is striking to note that conflict does not have a predominantly negative relationship with moving out of poverty. In fact, there are few large differences between mobility rates in conflict-affected areas and more peaceful areas of Assam, and it is important to consider factors that may enable mobility of the poor in such difficult circumstances. Nonetheless, the overall rates of poverty escapes are low in Assam compared to other states. This fact, along with the continuing conflict, points to an urgent need for greater investment in Assam to improve roads, create more local economic opportunities, promote fairness in the marketplace, and strengthen functioning of local democracy. Only then will educated but unemployed youth, who provide the recruits to fuel the insurgency, have alternatives. Only then will poor people' initiatives, ingenuity, persistence, and aspirations translate into improved well-being, security, and peace.

Conflicts destroy. In this environment, resource transfers from outside—in the case of Assam, from the central government—become very important in rebuilding destroyed infrastructure and enabling people to begin life over. Without hope for better lives, people have few incentives to stop fighting or supporting the insurgents. Substantial central transfers could, in principle, jump-start the process of economic recovery in a region. However, in Assam, the nature and magnitude of central transfers have not been sufficient to generate a favorable investment climate and dynamic economic growth, despite the fact that Assam has much higher literacy rates than other low-income states and education rates higher than the all-India average.

Responsive local democratic structures can go a long way toward helping people move out of poverty, even in the context of conflict, and they can have an economic healing effect. In Assam, local democracy was found to have a positive influence on the likelihood of moving out of poverty. We asked, however, whether the movers are a select category, as the actual distributive mechanism adopted at the local level may be discretionary along lines of ethnicity or political affiliation and consequently everyone may not benefit equally from robust local democracy. A negative sign on the leave-out mean variable of local democracy in our regressions bears out this hypothesis at the community level. This suggests that the practice of local democracy needs to be deepened and broadened and made more inclusive to have greater poverty-reducing impact.

Our results also show a strong association of higher corruption and elite capture with ongoing conflict. While some poor household's have escaped poverty despite persistent conflict, the overall magnitude of escape in Assam is much less than in the other states included in the study, especially West Bengal. We also find some indication of "poverty divergence": that is, the likelihood of escape from poverty is higher for initially richer areas than for initially poorer areas.

The policy response of the central, state, and local governments to the conflict was clearly important in providing connectivity, electricity, local market access, schools, and health centers. It also enabled the rapid expansion of self-employment opportunities after 2000 through support to self-help groups. And the structure of local governance, however imperfect, provided a mechanism for interaction between villagers and the local state.

However, gains in upward mobility of the poor in Assam cannot be explained just by referring to development initiatives from "above." The qualitative evidence culled from the case studies, even in the villages marked by high conflict, shows that people also drew on their own internal resources, resilience, and initiatives. In village after village, we found instances of social empathy and unity amid diversity; of collective action for local peace maintenance, often through youth clubs; of increasing demand for higher education, especially among youth; of adoption of new agricultural practices; of diversification for job creation at the local level; and of migration within the state to find opportunities. Perhaps most striking was the widespread persistence of optimism and aspiration. Even in communities plagued by long-lasting conflict, 50 percent of the chronic poor and 80 percent of the movers hope for a better future in either this generation or the next, through their own upward mobility or that of their children. All these findings suggest that the silent activism of development initiatives from "below" are critical for inclusive growth. When individual and collective agency meet economic opportunity, where people are no longer afraid to go out for work or play, lives will improve and communities will heal.

Annex 7.1 Supplementary Tables

ANNEX TABLE 7.A
State revenues and expenditures, India, 2000/01

State	Per capita state domestic product (Rs)	Poverty ratio, 1999–2000 (%)	Per capita revenue (Rs)	Own revenue as % of state domestic product	Per capita transfers (Rs)	Per capita current spending (Rs)	Per capita transfers as % of current spending	Own revenue as % of current spending
High-income states	22,461	17.8	2,932	13.1	500	4,387	11.4	66.8
Goa	44,613	4.4	14,310	15.8	588	11,905	4.9	120.2
Gujarat	18,685	14.1	2,685	13.2	863	5,168	16.7	52.0
Haryana	21,551	8.7	3,210	12.1	502	4,108	12.2	78.1
Maharashtra	22,604	25.0	2,741	11.1	448	3,853	11.6	71.2
Punjab	23,254	6.2	3,333	10.2	494	4,713	10.5	70.7
Middle-income states	17,635	20.3	1,869	10.6	658	3,400	19.4	55.0
Andhra Pradesh	14,878	15.8	1,930	10.7	713	3,320	21.5	58.1
Karnataka	16,654	20.4	2,148	11.3	686	3,581	19.2	60.0
Kerala	17,709	12.7	2,296	10.2	690	3,689	18.7	62.2
Tamil Nadu	18,623	21.1	2,343	11.3	658	3,594	18.3	65.2
West Bengal	4,874	27.0	1,091	5.5	576	3,093	18.6	35.3
Low-income states	9,013	34.3	847	9.4	673	2,243	29.9	37.7
Bihar	4,813	42.6	338	8.9	724	1,516	47.8	22.3
Chhattisgarh	10,405	—	1,264	4.9	—	2,455	—	51.5
Jharkhand	9,223	—	1,128	9.0	—	2,229	—	50.6

Madhya Pradesh	11,626	37.4	1,062	11.5	624	2,696	23.1	39.4
Orissa	8,733	47.2	901	9.3	969	2,785	34.8	32.3
Rajasthan	13,046	15.3	1,297	10.4	693	2,864	24.2	45.3
Uttaranchal	—	—	1,296	—	—	4,913	—	26.4
Uttar Pradesh	9,323	31.2	791	8.1	598	2,136	28.0	37.0
General category states	14,476	26.0	1,594	11.0	660	3,045	21.7	52.3
Special category states	12,339	—	1,156	9.4	2,896	5,715	50.7	20.2
Arunachal Pradesh	13,352	33.5	1,068	5.3	7,985	9,992	79.9	10.7
Assam	9,720	36.1	799	7.2	1,216	3,317	36.7	24.1
Himachal Pradesh	17,786	7.6	1,661	7.8	3,070	7,421	41.4	22.4
Jammu and Kashmir	12,373	3.5	1,150	7.9	4,602	6,080	75.7	18.9
Manipur	12,721	28.5	406	3.1	3,971	6,032	65.8	6.7
Meghalaya	12,063	33.9	1,067	6.3	3,149	5,878	53.6	18.1
Mizoram	14,909	19.5	679	3.8	9,602	12,846	74.7	5.3
Nagaland	12,594	32.7	507	3.7	6,332	7,291	86.8	7.0
Sikkim	14,751	36.6	5,998	15.9	7,945	12,201	65.1	49.2
Tripura	13,195	34.4	730	4.8	3,376	5,839	57.8	12.5
All states	14,359	26.1	1,570	10.9	768	3,191	24.1	49.2

Source: Rao and Singh 2004.

— Not available.

ANNEX TABLE 7.B
Unemployment among youth ages 15–29 in Assam and other states

percent

State	1983/84	1993/94	State	1983/84	1993/94
Andhra Pradesh	2.5	3.5	Maharashtra	2.8	6.6
Assam	3.0	19.3	Orissa	2.5	7.4
Bihar	2.8	7.4	Punjab	4.2	5.3
Gujarat	2.2	4.1	Rajasthan	1.3	1.8
Haryana	3.3	6.2	Tamil Nadu	5.9	8.0
Karnataka	2.6	5.0	Uttar Pradesh	2.0	3.8
Kerala	13.5	25.6	West Bengal	5.7	11.5
Madhya Pradesh	0.9	4.4	All India	3.3	6.5

Source: Aggarwal and Goyal 2000, cited in GoI 2002, 64.

ANNEX TABLE 7.C
Peace and safety in Assam study communities, 1995 and 2005:
Perceptions of key informants and community groups

	1995		2005	
Safety rating of own community	*Frequency*	*%*	*Frequency*	*%*
Key informants				
Very peaceful	7	14	21	42
Moderately peaceful	13	26	23	46
Moderately violent	20	40	5	10
Very violent	10	20	1	2
Total	50	100	50	100
Community focus groups				
No response	1	2	0	0
Very safe with no crime	2	4	1	2
Safe with only minor crimes	13	26	6	12
Neither dangerous nor safe	10	20	26	52
Dangerous with theft and assault	17	34	15	30
Very dangerous	7	14	2	4
Total	50	100	50	100

ANNEX TABLE 7.D
Community perceptions of corruption among local government officials, 1995 and 2005, Assam

	1995		2005	
Corrupt officials	Frequency	%	Frequency	%
Almost none	14	28	5	10
A few	22	44	12	24
Most	10	20	21	42
Almost all	4	8	12	24
Total	50	100	50	100

ANNEX TABLE 7.E
Trends in school inequality, 1995–2005, Assam

Equal treatment of boys and girls in schools	Frequency	%
Improved	32	64
Stayed about the same	12	24
Deteriorated	6	12
Total	50	100
Equal treatment of different ethnic/religious groups in schools	Frequency	%
Improved	33	66
Stayed about the same	13	26
Deteriorated	4	8
Total	50	100

ANNEX TABLE 7.F

Trends in school inequality by conflict trajectory, 1995–2005, Assam

	% reporting equal treatment in schools has improved	
Conflict trajectory	Treatment of boys and girls	Treatment of different ethnic/religious groups
Peace to peace	64	71
Conflict to peace	67	61
Conflict to conflict	65	65
Total	65	65

Pearson chi2(4) = 2.29 Pr = 0.683

	% reporting equal treatment in schools has improved or stayed same	
Conflict trajectory	Treatment of boys and girls	Treatment of different ethnic/religious groups
Peace to peace	79	93
Conflict to peace	94	94
Conflict to conflict	88	88
Total	88	92

Pearson chi2(4) = 1.08 Pr = 0.898

ANNEX TABLE 7.G

Trend in ability to get fair prices, 1995–2005, by mobility group, Assam

Trend in ability to get fair prices	Movers		Chronic poor		Fallers		Never poor		Total	
	Freq.	%	Freq.	%	Freq.	%	Freq.	%	Freq.	%
Improved	96	52	121	45	22	34	126	56	365	49
Same	65	36	110	41	24	37	77	34	276	37
Deteriorated	22	12	40	15	19	29	24	11	105	14
Total	183	100	271	100	65	100	227	100	746	100

ANNEX TABLE 7.H

Trend in ability to get fair prices, 1995–2005, by mobility group and conflict trajectory, Assam

Trend in ability to get fair prices	Movers	Chronic poor	Fallers	Never poor	Total
Peace to peace					
Improved	62	55	65	61	59
Same	38	42	29	39	39
Deteriorated	0	3	6	0	2
Total	100	100	100	100	100
Conflict to peace					
Improved	47	39	25	47	42
Same	33	46	50	42	42
Deteriorated	21	15	25	10	16
Total	100	100	100	100	100
Conflict to conflict					
Improved	48	37	20	57	46
Same	38	34	25	26	32
Deteriorated	14	29	55	16	23
Total	100	100	100	100	100

ANNEX TABLE 7.1

Factors influencing escape from poverty (MOP) during conflict, Assam

Variable	Model 1	Model 2	Model 3	Model 4	Model 5	Model 6	Model 7	Model 8	Model 9
Initial strength of economy	0.023	0.034	0.036	0.032	0.031	0.031	0.039	0.035	0.043
	[0.76]	[1.12]	[1.22]	[1.12]	[1.11]	[1.21]	[1.51]	[1.37]	[1.77]*
Change in economic prosperity	−0.003	−0.001	0.012	0.015	0.014	0.014	0.021	0.016	0.008
	[0.15]	[0.07]	[0.64]	[0.80]	[0.75]	[0.79]	[1.15]	[0.93]	[0.51]
Corruption		0.01	0.01	0.013	0.031	0.032	0.035	0.036	0.04
		[0.36]	[0.44]	[0.55]	[1.46]	[1.45]	[1.48]	[1.36]	[1.50]
Responsiveness of local democracy		0.106	0.107	0.096	0.053	0.03	0.031	0.035	0.036
		[5.63]***	[5.72]***	[4.96]***	[2.83]***	[1.72]*	[1.75]*	[1.99]*	[2.07]**
LOM of responsiveness of local democracy		−0.155	−0.156	−0.149	−0.112	−0.083	−0.083	−0.101	−0.092
		[4.08]***	[4.26]***	[3.80]***	[2.66]**	[1.93]*	[1.91]*	[2.12]**	[2.19]**
Conflict trajectory			0.049	0.051	0.047	0.048	0.038	0.041	0.037
			[2.13]**	[2.18]**	[2.15]*	[2.24]**	[1.71]*	[2.00]*	[1.83]*
Fairness index				0.046	0.052	0.046	0.045	0.038	0.034
				[2.52]**	[2.92]***	[2.71]***	[2.65]**	[2.12]**	[1.91]*
LOM of fairness index				−0.012	0.029	0.036	0.018	0.009	−0.009
				[0.17]	[0.49]	[0.60]	[0.30]	[0.17]	[0.16]
Step on the ladder of power and rights					0.045	0.031	0.031	0.031	0.017
					[2.57]**	[1.66]*	[1.65]*	[1.67]*	[0.81]

LOM of step on the ladder of power and rights	0.112	0.134	0.124	0.135	0.122
	[1.77]	[2.02]**	[1.84]*	[2.16]**	[2.00]*
Control over everyday decisions	0.216	0.169	0.17	0.176	0.138
	[4.62]***	[3.97]***	[4.01]***	[4.14]***	[3.55]***
LOM of control over everyday decisions	-0.217	-0.204	-0.198	-0.166	-0.137
	[1.45]	[1.27]	[1.30]	[1.05]	[0.92]
Household aspirations		0.094	0.093	0.101	0.088
		[5.45]***	[5.33]***	[5.92]***	[4.98]***
LOM of household aspirations		-0.078	-0.088	-0.082	-0.077
		[1.20]	[1.36]	[1.39]	[1.32]
Index collective action (PCA rc412b rc413b with current weights)			0.005	0.011	0.009
			[0.24]	[0.53]	[0.43]
Access to networks and associations			-0.047	-0.039	-0.031
			[1.21]	[0.95]	[0.75]
Social divisiveness				0.013	0.013
				[0.60]	[0.59]
Violence against women				0.087	0.089
				[3.10]***	[3.35]***
LOM of violence against women				-0.128	-0.153
				[2.56]**	[2.99]***
School inequality				0.006	0.009
				[0.25]	[0.44]

continued

ANNEX TABLE 7.1 (continued)

Variable	Model 1	Model 2	Model 3	Model 4	Model 5	Model 6	Model 7	Model 8	Model 9
Education of head of household									0.043 [3.12]***
Health shocks									-0.079 [1.76]*
Initial landholding									-0.005 [0.84]
Ownership of house									0.115 [0.79]
Assets index									0.06 [1.26]
Livestock index									-0.029 [0.98]
Constant	0.404 [14.15]***	0.418 [14.22]***	0.303 [5.06]***	0.302 [4.98]***	-0.225 [0.78]	-0.193 [0.60]	0.035 [0.09]	-0.071 [0.15]	-0.167 [0.33]
Observations	454	454	454	454	454	454	454	454	452
R^2	0	0.08	0.09	0.10	0.19	0.25	0.25	0.27	0.31

Note: Robust t-statistics in brackets.

*p < .10 **p < .05 ***p < .01

Factors influencing upward mobility of all poor (MPI) during conflict, Assam

Variable	Model 1	Model 2	Model 3	Model 4	Model 5	Model 6	Model 7	Model 8	Model 9
Initial strength of economy	0.045	0.059	0.06	0.059	0.063	0.066	0.069	0.067	0.073
	[1.65]*	[2.14]**	[2.24]**	[2.15]**	[2.54]**	[3.03]***	[3.14]***	[3.00]***	[3.54]***
Change in economic prosperity	0.002	0.005	0.013	0.015	0.012	0.013	0.016	0.009	0.003
	[0.10]	[0.29]	[0.84]	[0.98]	[0.72]	[0.80]	[0.94]	[0.60]	[0.17]
Corruption		0.006	0.006	0.006	0.014	0.014	0.002	0.007	0.008
		[0.44]	[0.44]	[0.39]	[0.83]	[0.86]	[0.12]	[0.40]	[0.41]
Responsiveness of local democracy		0.114	0.114	0.099	0.06	0.032	0.033	0.036	0.037
		[5.62]***	[5.68]***	[4.76]***	[3.08]***	[1.82]*	[1.88]*	[2.04]**	[2.14]**
LOM of responsiveness of local democracy		-0.174	-0.175	-0.159	-0.124	-0.088	-0.082	-0.098	-0.092
		[6.19]***	[6.23]***	[5.06]***	[3.65]***	[2.61]**	[2.39]**	[2.62]**	[2.60]**
Conflict trajectory			0.031	0.031	0.027	0.029	0.029	0.031	0.029
			[1.47]	[1.51]	[1.39]	[1.51]	[1.40]	[1.64]*	[1.58]
Fairness index				0.06	0.063	0.056	0.055	0.049	0.043
				[3.37]***	[3.72]***	[3.35]***	[3.32]***	[2.85]***	[2.54]**
LOM of fairness index				-0.071	-0.054	-0.043	-0.058	-0.07	-0.088
				[1.05]	[0.89]	[0.68]	[0.92]	[1.14]	[1.43]
Step on the ladder of power and rights					0.026	0.01	0.008	0.008	-0.004
					[1.62]	[0.54]	[0.44]	[0.49]	[0.18]

continued

ANNEX TABLE 7.J *(continued)*

Variable	Model 1	Model 2	Model 3	Model 4	Model 5	Model 6	Model 7	Model 8	Model 9
LOM of step on the ladder of power and rights					0.035 [0.68]	0.065 [1.11]	0.042 [0.76]	0.054 [1.07]	0.038 [0.77]
Control over everyday decisions					0.237 [4.99]***	0.179 [4.18]***	0.179 [4.15]***	0.182 [4.26]***	0.151 [3.64]***
LOM of control over everyday decisions					-0.202 [1.37]	-0.193 [1.19]	-0.191 [1.25]	-0.18 [1.12]	-0.15 [0.97]
Household aspirations						0.118 [7.07]***	0.118 [7.01]***	0.125 [7.74]***	0.113 [6.60]***
LOM of household aspirations						-0.084 [1.34]	-0.094 [1.50]	-0.081 [1.35]	-0.076 [1.27]
Index collective action (PCA with current weights)							-0.033 [1.34]	-0.025 [1.10]	-0.028 [1.29]
Access to networks and associations, 10 years ago							-0.041 [1.06]	-0.042 [1.06]	-0.034 [0.82]
Social divisiveness								0.003 [0.21]	0.004 [0.26]
Violence against women								0.07 [2.58]**	0.069 [2.71]***

	(1)	(2)	(3)	(4)	(5)	(6)	(7)	(8)	(9)
LOM of violence against women								-0.134	-0.153
								[2.84]***	[3.24]***
School inequality								0.009	0.013
								[0.48]	[0.66]
Education of head of household									0.035
									[2.41]**
Health shocks									-0.069
									[1.67]*
Initial landholding									-0.002
									[0.32]
Ownership of house									0.161
									[1.05]
Assets index									0.066
									[1.50]
Livestock index									-0.057
									[2.03]**
Constant	0.497	0.512	0.441	0.445	0.175	0.224	0.464	0.501	0.352
	[21.33]***	[21.72]***	[10.25]***	[10.25]***	[0.69]	[0.83]	[1.33]	[1.19]	[0.79]
Observations	454	454	454	454	454	454	454	454	452
R^2	0.01	0.09	0.1	0.12	0.2	0.29	0.29	0.3	0.33

Note: Robust *t*-statistics in brackets.

*p < .10 **p < .05 ***p < .01

ANNEX TABLE 7.K
Factors explaining movement out of poverty in Assam: Household-level regressions under alternative methods of estimation (movers vs. chronic poor within initial poor set)

Variable	OLS weighted	OLS unweighted	Probit weighted	Probit unweighted
Initial strength of economy	0.01	0.042	−0.237	0.017
	[0.48]	[1.72]*	[0.85]	[0.08]
Change in economic prosperity	0.007	0.008	−0.809	−0.563
	[0.45]	[0.50]	[1.53]	[1.26]
Responsiveness of local democracy	0.004	0.036	1.116	0.747
	[0.41]	[2.02]**	[4.24]***	[4.25]***
LOM of responsiveness of local democracy	−0.001	−0.088	−0.16	−0.124
	[1.27]	[2.09]**	[3.69]***	[3.87]***
Corruption	0.031	0.042	0.984	0.744
	[1.69]*	[1.62]	[2.61]**	[2.26]**
Conflict trajectory	0.002	0.035	−0.085	−0.077
	[0.17]	[1.67]*	[0.70]	[0.53]
Fairness index	0.019	0.036	0.265	0.242
	[2.91]***	[1.97]*	[1.94]*	[1.87]*
LOM of fairness index	−0.004	−0.008	−0.239	−0.187
	[3.44]***	[0.16]	[4.81]***	[4.68]***
Initial position on 10-step ladder of power and rights	0.007	0.016	−0.171	−0.062
	[0.77]	[0.77]	[0.97]	[0.42]
LOM of initial position on 10-step ladder of power and rights	−0.004	0.126	−0.286	−0.222
	[3.93]***	[2.08]**	[5.52]***	[7.81]***
Change in control over everyday decisions	0.052	0.137	1.894	1.221
	[2.41]**	[3.48]***	[3.90]***	[3.16]***
LOM of change in control over everyday decisions	0.006	−0.138	0.513	0.423
	[2.45]**	[0.91]	[5.78]***	[7.00]***
Household aspirations	0.03	0.088	0.901	0.702
	[4.14]***	[5.10]***	[5.04]***	[4.85]***

Variable	OLS weighted	OLS unweighted	Probit weighted	Probit unweighted
LOM of household aspirations	−0.006	−0.079	−0.449	−0.352
	[4.02]***	[1.34]	[3.55]***	[3.84]***
Index of collective action	−0.016	0.009	−0.178	0.083
	[0.63]	[0.43]	[0.32]	[0.15]
Trend in access to networks and associations	0.026	−0.031	1.138	0.58
	[0.93]	[0.74]	[1.84]*	[1.11]
Social divisions	−0.003	0.012	1.172	0.76
	[0.14]	[0.55]	[2.88]***	[2.49]**
Trend in school inequality	−0.011	0.008	0.773	0.463
	[0.87]	[0.38]	[2.06]**	[1.80]*
Violence against women in households	0.025	0.093	0.694	0.551
	[1.89]*	[3.45]***	[1.87]*	[2.13]**
LOM of violence against women in households	0.002	−0.156	0.101	0.049
	[0.90]	[3.07]***	[1.87]*	[1.16]
Education status of head of household	0.024	0.043	0.636	0.541
	[3.62]***	[3.16]***	[5.85]***	[7.77]***
Health shocks	−0.001	−0.079	−0.674	−0.306
	[0.06]	[1.75]*	[1.56]	[0.84]
Initial landholding	−0.003	−0.006	−0.356	−0.267
	[0.89]	[0.99]	[3.52]***	[4.00]***
Ownership of house	0.016	0.11		
	[0.29]	[0.74]		
Assets index	0.019	0.056	0.29	−0.094
	[0.99]	[1.19]	[0.48]	[0.21]
Livestock index	0.006	0.002	1.144	0.787
	[0.84]	[0.16]	[3.50]***	[3.30]***
Constant	−0.143	−0.158	−13.932	−8.866
	[0.87]	[0.30]	[4.25]***	[4.01]***
Observations	452	452	452	447
R^2	0.40	0.31		

Note: t-statistics for OLS and z-statistics for probit are in brackets.

*p < .10   **p < .05   ***p < .01

ANNEX TABLE 7.L
Association between conflict trajectory and functioning of local democracy, Assam

Variable	Model 1	Model 2	Model 3	Model 4	Model 5
Index of responsiveness	−0.109	−0.056	−0.056	0.095	0.057
	[0.43]	[0.29]	[0.29]	[0.50]	[0.32]
Index of corruption		0.189	0.189	0.207	0.267
		[1.00]	[1.00]	[1.58]	[2.16]**
Index of law and order		0.463	0.463	0.445	0.435
		[2.45]**	[2.45]**	[2.51]**	[2.61]**
Elite capture				5.03	5.323
				[3.57]***	[4.12]***
Household political activism					−0.582
					[1.52]
Constant	2.397	2.408	2.408	−7.219	−7.929
	[13.18]***	[14.35]***	[14.35]***	[2.70]***	[3.24]***
Observations	50	50	50	50	50
R^2	0.01	0.14	0.14	0.28	0.33

Note: Robust t-statistics in brackets.

*p < .10   **p < .05   ***p < .01

ANNEX TABLE 7.M
Association between conflict intensity and functioning of local democracy, Assam

Variable	Model 1	Model 2	Model 3	Model 4	Model 5
Index of responsiveness	−0.09	−0.029	−0.029	0.024	0
	[0.57]	[0.25]	[0.25]	[0.21]	[0.00]
Index of corruption		0.097	0.097	0.103	0.143
		[0.92]	[0.92]	[1.24]	[1.98]*
Index of law and order		0.36	0.36	0.354	0.347
		[3.53]***	[3.53]***	[3.51]***	[3.59]***
Elite capture				1.79	1.982
				[1.88]*	[2.26]**
Household political activism					−0.381
					[2.09]**
Constant	1.921	1.934	1.934	−1.492	−1.956
	[18.04]***	[20.49]***	[20.49]***	[0.80]	[1.14]
Observations	50	50	50	50	50
R^2	0.01	0.22	0.22	0.27	0.32

Note: Robust t-statistics in brackets.

*p < .10   **p < .05   ***p < .01

References

Aggarwal, S. C., and J. K. Goyal. 2000. "Trends in Youth Unemployment in India: An Empirical Analysis." *Indian Journal of Labour Economics* 43 (4).

Baruah, S. 2005. *Durable Disorder: Understanding the Politics of Northeast India.* Delhi: Oxford University Press.

Bowles, S., H. Gintis, and M. Osborne Groves, eds. 2005. *Unequal Chances: Family Background and Economic Success.* Princeton, NJ: Princeton University Press.

Carbonnier, G. 1998. "Conflict, Post-war Rebuilding and the Economy: A Critical Review of the Literature." War-torn Societies Project, *UNRISD Occasional Paper 2.* Geneva, Switzerland: United Nations Research Institute for Social Development.

CMIE (Centre for Monitoring Indian Economy). 2000. *Profiles of Districts.* Mumbai: CMIE.

Collier, P. 1999a. "Doing Well Out of War." Paper presented at Conference on Economic Agendas in Civil Wars, London, April 26–27.

Collier, P. 1999b. "On the Economic Consequences of Civil War." *Oxford Economic Papers* 51: 168–83.

Collier, P. 2007. *The Bottom Billion: Why the Poorest Countries Are Failing and What Can Be Done about It.* New York: Oxford University Press.

Collier, P., and A. Hoeffler. 2004. "Greed and Grievance in Civil War." *Oxford Economic Papers* 56: 563–95.

———. 2006. "Military Expenditure in Post-Conflict Societies." *Economics of Governance* 7: 89–107.

Collier, P., A. Hoeffler, and N. Sambanis. 2005. "The Collier-Hoeffler Model of Civil War Onset and the Case Study Research Design." In *Understanding Civil War: Evidence and Analysis,* ed. P. Collier and N. Sambanis, 1–34. Washington DC: World Bank.

Deaton, A. 2003. "Regional Poverty Estimates for India, 1999–2000." Research Program in Development Studies, Princeton University.

Deaton, A., and V. Kozel, eds. 2005. *The Great Indian Poverty Debate.* Delhi: Macmillan India.

Deolalikar, A. 2005. *Attaining the Millennium Development Goals in India.* New York: Oxford University Press.

Dev, S. M., and C. Ravi. 2007. "Poverty and Inequality: All-India and States, 1983–2005." *Economic and Political Weekly,* February 10–26, 509–22.

Elbadawi, I., and N. Sambanis. 2002. "How Much War Will We See? Explaining the Prevalence of Civil War." *Journal of Conflict Resolution* 46 (3): 307–34.

Gleditsch, N. P., P. Wallensteen, M. Eriksson, M. Sollenberg, and H. Strand. 2002. "Armed Conflict 1946–2001: A New Dataset." *Journal of Peace Research* 39: 615–37.

GoA (Government of Assam). 2002. *Economic Survey Assam, 2001–2002.* Guwahati, India.

———. 2004. *Economic Survey Assam, 2003–2004.* Guwahati, India.

GoI (Government of India). 2002. *Assam Development Report.* State Plan Division, Planning Commission, New Delhi.

Gurr, T. R. 2000. "Ethnic Warfare on the Wane." *Foreign Affairs* 79 (3): 52–54.

Himanshu. 2007. "Recent Trends in Poverty and Inequality: Some Preliminary Results." *Economic and Political Weekly*, February 10–26, 497–508.

Kijima, Y., and P. Lanjouw. 2004. "Agricultural Wages, Non-farm Employment and Poverty in Rural India." World Bank, Washington, DC.

Lewis, O. 1969. *On Understanding Poverty: Perspectives from the Social Sciences.* New York: Basic Books.

Public Affairs Centre. 2002. *The State of India's Public Services: Benchmarks for the New Millennium.* Bangalore: Public Affairs Centre.

Rao, M. G. 2000. "Fiscal Decentralization in Indian Federalism." ISEC Working Paper 98. Institute for Social and Economic Change, Bangalore.

Rao, M. G., and N. Singh. 2004. "Asymmetric Federalism in India." UC Santa Cruz International Economics Working Paper 04-08, University of California, Santa Cruz. http://ssrn.com/abstract=537782.

Sambanis, N. 2003. "Using Case Studies to Expand the Theory of Civil War." Conflict Prevention and Reconstruction Working Paper 5, World Bank, Washington, DC.

Stewart, F., F. P. Humphreys, and N. Lea. 1997. "Civil Conflict in Developing Countries over the Last Quarter Century: An Emprical Overview of Economic and Social Consequences." *Oxford Development Studies* 25(1): 11–41.

Stewart, F., ed. 2008. *Horizontal Inequality and Conflict: Understanding Group Violence in Multiethnic Societies.* Hampshire: Palgrave Macmillan.

Weiner, M. 1978. *Sons of the Soil.* Delhi: Oxford University Press.

World Bank. 2005. *State Fiscal Reforms in India: Progress and Prospects.* Delhi: Macmillan India.

Notes

1. In Assam, normal processes of democracy and development coexist with the brutalities of a civil conflict, resulting in what Baruah (2005) calls "durable disorder."

2. For an analytic account of the role of migration in Assamese politics, see Weiner (1978).

3. The central government followed a similar two-pronged strategy in Punjab during the civil conflict there (1984–93), as well as in Kashmir, Mizoram, and Nagaland. The civil conflicts in these states have varied in their intensity and duration, but the central government's strategy, in essence, has been the same.

4. See Collier and Hoeffler (2004, 2006) and Collier (1999a, 1999b, 2007). There is an extensive literature on the causes and consequences of conflict. See Stewart et al (1997), Carbonnier (1998), Sambanis (2003), and Stewart (2008), among others.

5. This can take the form of additional fiscal transfers to some states within the same nation if conflict takes place within a federal polity.

6. There is a negative correlation between per capita state gross state domestic product and the amount of central government transfer received by the state (coefficient of correlation is –0.78). Central transfers to the poor states as a proportion of total transfers increased between 1985/86 and 1989/90, dropped between 1991/92 and 1997/98 under fiscal stress, and rose thereafter (World

Bank 2005). These trends, of course, are based on transfers occurring through the formal system and do not take into account the so-called hidden transfers. There are three forms of formal transfer from center to state: (a) Finance Commission transfers, accounting for two-thirds of total transfers; (b) block plan grants that are linked to plan loans, making up about 20 percent of total transfers; and (c) specific-purpose grants for centrally sponsored projects. Unfortunately, the World Bank report on state fiscal reforms in India (2005) does not include any of the northeastern states. In general, the broader issue of intergovernmental fiscal transfer to the conflict-prone northeastern states, including Assam, represents a serious gap in the literature.

7. The number of fatalities came closest to reaching this level during 1983, the year of the Nelie massacre. In that incident, about 900 Muslim inhabitants of a single village perished in an antimigration backlash.

8. Both these propositions can be tested by quantifying the rate of upward movement of the poor (MPI index) and the rate of downward movement of the non-poor (FRI and FRIP indexes) as used throughout the study.

9. Intertemporal comparison based on indirect evidence seems to show increasing dependence on the central transfers over the period between 1993/94 (the year for the earliest estimate presently available) and 2000/01 (the year for the latest estimate available). Thus, in 1993/94, 33 percent of current spending in Assam was accounted for by own revenue; in 2000/01 it dropped to 24 percent (Rao and Singh 2004). However, the issue of intertemporal comparison needs to be probed further.

10. Poverty numbers are based on Planning Commission estimates using expert group methodology. The drop will be greater if one uses the seven-day recall method.

11. The same applies to maternal mortality, where Assam's position in 1997 was slightly better than the all-India average (401 versus 408 deaths per 100,000 live births). Its performance was also better than that of some low-income states such as Bihar, Madhya Pradesh, and Uttar Pradesh, but worse than Orissa and Andhra Pradesh (see GoA 2002, table 10.10).

12. The highest youth unemployment rate is in Kerala, a special case where widespread education is combined with relatively limited economic opportunities.

13. The most conflict-affected districts include Barpeta, Bongaigaon, Dhubri, Goalpara, Golaghat, Karbi Anglong, Kokrajhar, Nagaon, North Cachar Hills, and Tinsukia. Flood-prone districts include Cachar, Dhemaji, Hailakandi, Karimganj, Lakhimpur, and Morigaon.

14. Pulling such information across communities, of course, assumes some degree of homogeneity in the way "poor" is defined, but this homogeneity should be less of a problem in the within-state context, given shared norms and experiences.

15. There is a yet a fifth group that could be considered, consisting of initially *nonpoor* households that experienced upward mobility. They are significant for two reasons: first, many of the nonpoor households are located not much above the poverty line and can slip into poverty following unforeseen shocks. Second, communities where nonpoor households can increase their income and assets are likely to have higher growth prospects, which affects poor aspirants positively as

well. In the conflict context, however, there is also a different relational possibility: winning for some may mean losing for others. The nonpoor may move up at the expense of the poor, or vice versa, if the initial nonpoor and initial poor belong to two contending ethnic groups whose political fortunes are changing because of the conflict. However, we have decided against including the group of initially non-poor households that experienced mobility in our subsequent statistical exercises for Assam because of very small number of observations in this group.

16. It is also interesting to note that of the set of initially poor households, fully 20 percent experienced some degree of upward mobility (although they may or may not have escaped poverty). This is more than double the 8.6 percent of initially nonpoor households that moved up-a pattern uniformly observed across the four Moving Out of Poverty study states.

17. These two self-reported reasons for escape each comprised several types of responses. "Job" combines (a) steady job/increase in wages; (b) got a job/got a better job; and (c) increase in work opportunities. "Individual initiative (agricul-tural)" combines (a) crop diversification; (b) increased crop production because of improved agricultural technology/irrigation/high-yielding varieties of seeds.

18. The various self-reported reasons for downfall were grouped as follows. "Decreasing national/local prosperity" combines (a) vulnerability to market price fluctuations; (b) economy got worse; (c) high inflation/increase in price of basic necessities; (d) inconsistent work opportunities; (e) increased restric-tions on business/increased taxes. "Failure in agriculture" combines (a) low agricultural yield/bad harvest; (b) death of animal (cow, goat, etc.). "Health/death shocks" combines (a) health problems/accidents/high health expenses; (b) death of earning member; (c) aging.

19. While the relatively peaceful communities also experienced conflict, it was not of the separatist or ethnic kind that we consider in this chapter. Rather, conflicts in these villages revolved around land, local crimes including theft and robbery, and alcoholism.

20. This may reflect the army crackdown on the ULFA and other militant outfits in the late 1990s, as well as the ULFA's integration into local and mainstream poli-tics in the state.

21. There are, of course, potentially worrying problems of the direction of causality (e.g., the problem of endogeneity) in some of the associational links that may arise with respect to some indicators discussed in this and subsequent sections. This is because we are drawing our conclusions on the basis of a one-shot survey rather than a panel survey. For instance, greater trust in local government on the part of movers may reflect their optimistic frame of mind after they have escaped poverty, rather than proving that local government played an important role in their ascent from poverty. We tried to address this issue of endogeneity as much as possible by considering the respondent's rating of the state of local government and other such social and political institutional indicators pertain-ing to the initial period (1995). Nevertheless, given the nature of data, we do not claim any causal role of local democracy and other institutional factors here and merely indicate their associations with movement out of poverty.

22. The discussion of the choice of explanatory factors here closely follows the basic conceptual framework discussed in chapter 1 as well as in other chapters of this volume.

23. The strength of association will differ by the exact choice of the growth variable from the qualitative data. For example, the indicator of whether it is "easier or harder for people to make a living and get ahead than it used to be" is positively related to mobility, though only weakly significant at 10 percent.

24. The term "culture of poverty" was popularized decades ago by anthropologist Oscar Lewis in his studies of poor families in Mexico, San Juan, and New York. Lewis maintained that poor people display certain characteristics and values that are not held by the nonpoor in the same societies and that these attitudes and social isolation from the cultural mainstream are major barriers to economic mobility. According to this theory, poverty is not a short-lived financial predicament but a way of life transmitted across generations, underpinned by the perceived hopelessness of accomplishing even minor economic goals (Lewis 1969).

25. The family/inheritance line of reasoning-as opposed to the culture of poverty argument-has been developed by Samuel Bowles and others (see Bowles, Gintis, and Osborne Groves 2005).

26. For a detailed discussion of the leave-out mean variables, see chapter 1 and appendix 1 of this volume.

27. The dependent variable takes the value of 1 if the household is identified by the community as a mover, 0 otherwise. The model explaining escape from poverty (as in annex table 7.I) or mobility within poverty (as in annex table 7.J) is estimated for the sample of the *initial poor* only.

28. This is consistent with the picture of patronage through local government. The fortunate few who are well connected with local government officials through political and other collusive mechanisms are able to use these connections to their advantage.

29. Since the conflict trajectory is a community-level variable, most indicators used as explanatory factors are also community-level variables. These include the index of corruption and law and order, using the same questions as used for the descriptive statistics outlined above. All household-level variables used, such as index of responsiveness, elite capture, and political activism, were appropriately weighted, using weights from community-wide rankings. This was done to correct for the distributional bias of the household sample toward the movers.

30. Collier (2007) calls this "the conflict trap," made possible by "lootable resources."

Appendix 1: Technical Note on Household Regressions

This note addresses technical issues pertaining to the use of data from the household survey carried out as part of the Moving Out of Poverty study. In particular, it discusses the use of the household responses in a multivariate regression to examine the correlates at the individual and village levels of moving out of poverty. It looks at the sampling frame, the construction of the dependent and independent variables, and the multivariate regression functional form and weights. The India study is a part of a larger global study.[1]

Description of the Study

The Moving Out of Poverty study is a large, complex research program carried out in 21 diverse study regions in 15 countries around the world. The study combines both qualitative and quantitative work in an attempt to unpack from below the processes, interactions, and sequencings associated with household transitions out of poverty. The focus is on learning from men and women who have managed to move out of poverty over the last decade about the factors and processes that came together for their asset accumulation and the role of broader community institutions, if any, in supporting or obstructing their mobility.

Choosing the study regions

In selecting countries and regions within countries to participate in the study, an effort was made to ensure that a variety of contexts would be covered. As shown in table A.1, the 15 countries differ in terms of their income levels, national growth rates, and governance environments. Not surprisingly, while there is considerable variation along the dimensions, some cells of the table are empty: for example, there are no low-income/high-governance countries in the study.

Selection of regions also took into account the availability of local research institutes with the interest and capacity to carry out the multidisciplinary study, as well as interest on the part of national governments and World Bank country teams.

Sampling for communities (villages, neighborhoods)

In addition to a broad set of hypotheses, the study addressed specific policy questions that are of current concern in each study region. The focus was

TABLE A.1
Countries in the Moving Out of Poverty study stratified by income, growth, and governance

Economy	High governance	Low governance	Very low governance
Low income ($825 or less)			
High growth		India, Malawi, Senegal	Bangladesh, Cambodia, Tanzania, Uganda
Low growth			Afghanistan
Lower middle income ($826–$3,255)			
High growth	Philippines, Thailand	Indonesia, Morocco, Sri Lanka	
Low growth		Colombia	
Upper middle income ($3,256–$10,065)			
High growth		Mexico	
Low growth			

Note: Income figures are per capita gross national income. Growth and governance classifications reflect the growth rate in 2004 and the average governance rating for 1996–2004. A growth rate <= 3 indicates a low-growth country. High governance rating refers to a governance average > 0 and < 2.5; low governance rating, a governance average < 0 and > –0.5; very low governance rating, a governance average < –0.5 and > –2.5. Governance average is the simple average of six components (voice and accountability, political stability, rule of law, government effectiveness, regulatory quality, and control of corruption) of the governance dataset in "Governance Matters IV: Governance Indicators for 1996–2004."

on one or two variables that are central to understanding growth and poverty reduction in the local context. These variables were identified through an iterative process based on data availability and discussion with different actors familiar with the growth and poverty debate in the region, including national and state-level policy actors and poverty and growth experts within government, research institutes, civil society, and donor agencies. In the state of Uttar Pradesh, India, for example, the study examines the role of caste in facilitating or hindering people's movements out of poverty. The Malawi study explores the impact on mobility of access to social and economic infrastructure. The Indonesia study seeks to understand how local-level conflicts in different growth contexts affects people's ability to move out of poverty. The focus in Thailand is on growth and inequality.

Three different sampling strategies were employed for districts/blocks/villages to identify study sites within the 21 regions, which were grouped in three categories (table A.2):

- *Study regions with a preexisting panel data set.* In regions where panel data were available, the communities that had been in the previous panel were revisited. This was the method used in five regions: Cambodia; the Bukidnon region of the Philippines; the Kagera region of Tanzania; Uganda; and the state of Andhra Pradesh, India.
- *Study regions with a particular focus.* Where the focus was on a specific theme, this theme informed sampling. The desire was to select provinces/districts, blocks, and communities that differed substantially in the thematically relevant dimensions. This was the method used in 10 regions.
- *Study regions with conflict.* The Moving Out of Poverty study included a separate substudy with an emphasis on conflict. It was carried out in six regions: Afghanistan, Colombia (with an emphasis on the displaced population), Indonesia, Sri Lanka, the Philippines, and the state of Assam in India. In these regions the spatial sampling was devoted to finding communities within the broader region with higher and lower levels of conflict.

All local-level communities in the study are identified by pseudonyms in the Moving Out of Poverty book series. Higher-level entities (blocks, mandals, districts, states) are identified by their real names.

Sampling for household questionnaires: The community mobility matrix

The study consists of several different instruments, one of which is the household quantitative questionnaire (see appendix 2 for a list of data collection methods). For studies that used panel data, the questionnaires were conducted by revisiting panel households and interviewing the same person that was interviewed for the panel before. Where panel data were unavailable, the selection of informants for the household questionnaire was based on a household sorting exercise undertaken during a focus group discussion called the "ladder of life." The discussion, conducted in each study community, proceeded in four steps:

1. The focus group first discussed events and factors that had affected their community's prosperity over the past 10 years.

2. The group then constructed a figurative ladder of life for their community. Each step of the ladder corresponded to a category of household well-being that the group defined in terms of specific household characteristics (land ownership, assets, occupation, living conditions, and social prestige, among others). The process did not force a set number of ladder steps, and the focus groups varied in the number of steps they defined for their communities.

3. As part of this discussion, each group developed its own definition of a poverty line, called the community poverty line (CPL). The CPL marked the step on the ladder above which people were considered no longer poor in their community.

4. Once it had created the ladder in the abstract, the focus group did a household sorting activity. Every household on a list of up to 150 households residing in the community (developed prior to the discussion) was mapped onto the ladder to denote its status both 10 years ago (1995) and today (at the time of the survey, 2005). Based on these rankings, a community mobility matrix was developed (see chapter 3 for examples). The matrix showed which households had moved up or down the ladder or stayed at the same step over the 10-year study period. This study's community mobility matrixes are similar in many ways to standard transition matrixes based on measured income or consumption, except that they are based on community-defined categories (not constructed categories like quintiles of income) and on community recall.

Since the matrix was based on the sorting of 100–150 individual households in a community, it provided a useful source for selecting respondents for the household survey. Four mobility groups were considered:

- *Movers*: households that were poor in 1995 but had moved out of poverty by 2005
- *Chronic poor*: households that were poor in 1995 and remained poor in 2005
- *Fallers*: households that were not poor in 1995 but fell into poverty by 2005
- *Never poor*: households that were not poor in 1995 and remained not poor in 2005

In each case, "poor" means below the locally defined community poverty line and "not poor" means above it.

TABLE A.2
Choosing locations within study regions

Study region	Provinces/districts	Selection criteria			No. of communities	No. of household surveys
		Blocks	Communities			
India sample						
Uttar Pradesh	Growth	Irrigation and caste	Random		110	1,635
Andhra Pradesh	Panel study				60	839
West Bengal	Purposive using government survey	% of land reform beneficiaries	Random		80	1,200
Assam	Growth and conflict	Conflict			50	746
India subtotal					300	4,420
Rest of the sample						
Cambodia	Panel study				9	—
Philippines: Bukidnon	Panel study				10	259
Uganda	Panel study				18	724
Tanzania: Kagera	Panel study				8	—
Bangladesh	Poverty headcount	Average landholding and literacy rates	Women's empowerment, food security, and growth in agricultural wages		16	862
Sri Lanka: tea and rubber estates	Crop type, geographic spread, poverty headcount	Ownership of estate (private/state), population size, remoteness, labor supply (resident/nonresident)			20	—

Thailand	Growth and income inequality	Growth and income inequality	40	600
Mexico	Yucatán and Oaxaca	Communities with high % of indigenous population, varying in growth	12	346
Morocco	Growth and migration	3 communities (2 rural, 1 urban) selected in each of 3 provinces	9	—
Tanzania: Ruvuma	Growth	Distance to district headquarters, population size	8	332
Malawi	Access to infrastructure and markets		15	139
Senegal	Access to infrastructure		15	301
Sri Lanka: conflict	Growth and conflict	Conflict	9	—
Afghanistan: conflict	Conflict, proximity to city or borders, cultivation and trade of poppy, degree of exposure to international aid		6	91
Indonesia: conflict	Type of conflict (ethnic, religious, local)	Growth	Conflict and ethnic/ religious composition	10	372
Colombia: conflict	Growth, conflict, and whether communities were receiving displaced populations or were themselves displaced		8	252
Philippines: conflict	Study conducted only in the Mindanao region	Growth	Conflict	10	300
Total			*523*	*8,998*

Note: In all conflict regions, districts with a very high level of active conflict at the time of the survey were not chosen for reasons of safety of the field team.

Once households in the matrix were stratified into these groups, a minimum of 15 households in each community were selected for the survey. We deliberately oversampled movers and the never poor because of the study's interest in learning from those who had moved out of poverty and those who had been able to maintain their wealth. Table A.3 shows the approximate desired distribution for sampling the household questionnaires in each community.

Adherence to this distribution depended on availability of sufficient numbers of households in each of the four mobility groups. Sometimes it was not possible to match the target percentages: in very poor communities, for instance, the number of movers was limited and therefore fewer movers were interviewed. The study in Andhra Pradesh was a clear exception to the distribution rule, as it used panel data. The questionnaires were conducted by revisiting panel households and interviewing the same person that was interviewed for the panel before.

The questionnaires were conducted mainly with adults between 30 and 60 years of age. The aim was to identify and understand the range of factors that helped or hindered the mobility of individuals within the larger context of their households and communities. The multimodule questionnaires were innovative in that they collected information on the individual respondent's social capital, personal aspirations, and perceptions of local governance, freedom, crime, insecurity, and violence, in addition to the usual demographic and economic information on assets, expenditure, health, and education. While many of the questions on expenditure and assets related to the household, the subjective questions were about the individual. The far-right column table A.2 summarizes the number of household surveys collected in the different study regions. These varied from only 91 in Afghanistan to over 1,600 in Uttar Pradesh, for a total of 4,420 household surveys in India and 8,998 household surveys in the entire study.

Two points are worth noting. First, the study made no attempt to create a nationally representative sample. In the discussion, country names are used merely as a shorthand way of identifying data from the study regions within

TABLE A.3

Desired distribution of households across mobility groups

	Now	
10 years ago	*Poor or worse off*	*Nonpoor or better off*
Poor or worse off	Chronic poor: 20%	Movers: 40%
Nonpoor or better off	Fallers: 10%	Never poor: 30%

those countries. Thus, by "India" it should be clear that we mean "the communities/households sampled for our study within the selected regions in the four states of India." As noted above, we try to provide in our acronyms both a country and a study focus in order to remind the reader that the unit is the study region, not the country.

Second, the household surveys were not used to estimate numbers of poor or nonpoor or movers. Those are estimated in the community mobility matrix. The household surveys had two main uses. One was to reveal difference in reported characteristics, attitudes, behaviors, and outcomes between the movers out of poverty and other groups. The second was to run multivariate regressions using the household's mobility status, as ascribed by the focus group, to establish associations between household mobility and characteristics of the household and locality. We made no attempt to establish causality or make causal claims based on these regressions, though that is one possible way to interpret the associations.

Background to the Regressions: Dependent and Independent Variables

To construct the regressions, we first specify (a) a measure for the dependent variable, i.e., "movement out of poverty" or "mobility of the poor"; (b) measures for each of the conceptual variables; (c) the way we propose to distinguish between private and community impacts of some of the conceptual variables (particularly the local democracy and agency measures); and (d) the control variables included in the regressions.

Measures for movement out of poverty (MOP) and mobility of the poor (MPI)

Since the study is about the mobility of poor people, only those households that were poor 10 years ago, at the beginning of the study period, were included for purposes of regression analysis. Within this "initial poor set," the objective was to differentiate between those who moved up from poverty over the 10 years and those who did not. Two dependent variables were used for the regression analysis:

- *MOP:* households that were initially poor and moved up and out of poverty over 10 years, crossing the community poverty line
- *MPI:* households that were initially poor and moved up any distance over 10 years, irrespective of whether or not they crossed the community poverty line

The data offered two measures that could be used to calculate the dependent variables. The first was status of and change in the household's rank on the ladder of life, now compared to 10 years ago, as identified by the ladder of life focus group discussion. The second was status of and change in the household's self-assessed rank on the ladder of life, now compared to 10 years ago, as identified by respondent himself/herself in the household questionnaire.

Both dependent variables were constructed using the first measure—community perceptions of the household's mobility on the ladder of life. It is important that the mobility ratings were *not self-assessed*. This was to avoid endogeneity biases or "halo effects" that might arise in regressing a household's own perception of movement against its perception of variables measuring the conceptual categories. For instance, it may well be that people who subjectively *feel* they have more control of decision making also subjectively *feel* they are moving up—even if others perceive them as economically stagnant. By using the *community's* perception of mobility as the dependent variable and the *individual's* responses about the household as measures of the right-hand-side variables, this particular problem is attenuated, if not eliminated.

Construction of MOP score. The ladder of life discussion group developed mobility rankings of each household that received the survey. Focus group members recalled the household's placement on the well-being ladder 10 years ago and then determined its current step on the ladder. Based on these mobility ranks and the community poverty line, the MOP score was constructed as a binary variable (yes/no) using the following formula:

$$MOP^{h,j} = \begin{cases} 1 & if \quad step_{t-n}^{h,j} < CPL^j, \ step_t^{h,j} \geq CPL^j \\ 0 & otherwise \end{cases}$$

where *step* is the step on the ladder of life constructed by the focus group and CPL is the community poverty line set by the group and *n* is the (roughly 10-year) recall period.

Construction of MPI score. Any score constructed for movement out of poverty is subject to the placement of a threshold line that can vary across communities and contexts. Given problems that relative lines like the CPL pose, a broader score of upward movement of the poor (MPI) was also used as the dependent variable using the following formula:

$$MPI^{h,j} = \begin{cases} 1 & if \quad step_t^{h,j} > step_{t-n}^{h,j} \\ 0 & otherwise \end{cases}$$

Measures for conceptual categories of independent variables

The MOP and MPI dependent variables were regressed against various independent variables to produce the partial associations (no attribution of causality is expressed or implied). These included both household variables and community variables. A list of all of the variables, their sources, and coding is presented in appendix 3.

Household-level standard control variables. In estimating the regressions, we control for variables that may influence household mobility but that are not a major focus of the study. These are mainly well-known correlates of mobility and are included mainly to distinguish the influence of various other variables that may be correlated. For instance, more educated households may feel more empowered or may have more influence over their local governments. In each multivariate regression the household demographic and economic characteristics included a proxy for the household's initial wealth. Ownership at the beginning of the study period was included for (a) house, (b) collection of household assets, (c) livestock, and (d) farmland. The education level of the respondent and reported health shocks experienced by the household over 10 years were also included as variables in each regression.

Household variables unique to the study. In addition to the usual covariates, there are several variables from the household questionnaire that are of special interest to this study (see appendix 3):

- *Aspirations.* Respondents were asked two questions, one about aspirations for the respondent herself/himself and one about aspirations for future generations. These were combined into a single index.
- *Personal agency.* Respondents were asked two questions about their level of agency, one about control over everyday decisions and one about their position on a ladder of power and rights. Again the two questions were combined into a single index with principal components analysis.
- *Responsiveness of the local government.* Respondents were asked four questions about (a) their trust in local government officials, (b) their satisfaction with local democracy, (c) the extent to which local government takes into account people's concerns, and (d) their ability to influence the actions of the local government. These were combined into an index using principal components analysis (see below for more detail on PCA).

- *Fairness of the economy.* Respondents were asked four questions about (a) farmers getting fair prices, (b) fairness in treatment by the law, (c) whether the respondent had been denied credit, and (d) whether he or she expected to be denied credit. Again, these were combined into a single index of fairness for each respondent based on weights from PCA.
- *Violence against women.* Respondents were asked about their perception of the prevalence of violence against women in their community.

We also included a policy focus variable for each of the study regions. In Uttar Pradesh, for example, proxies are included for the caste of each household.

For the household-level variables we used the respondent's recollection of conditions 10 years ago rather than current levels. This is an attempt to mitigate the endogeneity bias of using current perceptions, as current conditions are certainly affected by changes over the last 10 years. One can easily imagine that households that moved out of poverty would be likely to report more positive aspirations because of that move. Of course, given that our only option was to use recall data, there is no guarantee that currently reported perceptions of the past are not also affected by events.

In addition to the household variables, there are community-level variables of two types. One set comes from the community instruments, such as the focus group. The other comes from using the household responses and computing leave-out means.

Community variables from community instruments. There were seven community-level variables used in the regressions that were drawn either from the community-level information provided by key informants or from the focus group discussions.

- *Corruption.* Three questions were combined into an index using PCA. The key informant questionnaire included two questions about corruption, one about officials at the national level and one about officials at the local/community level. In addition, the focus group discussion produced an estimate of corruption among government officials in the community.
- *Initial strength of the economy.* Key informants were asked about the strength of the local economy, the presence of private employers, and the difficulty of finding a job 10 years ago.
- *Change in economic prosperity over 10 years.* The focus group discussions were asked about trend in community prosperity, trend in available

economic opportunities, trend in access to such opportunities, and whether it was easier or harder to make a living.

- *Collective action.* Key informants were asked two questions, one about the likelihood of the community coming together to solve water problems and one about community members coming together to assist each other.
- *Social stratification.* Key informants were asked one question about the divisions among people based on locally relevant social categories (e.g., ethnicity, caste).
- *School inequality.* Key informants were asked about trends over 10 years in the extent of discrimination in schools based on (a) ethnic or religious factors and (b) gender.
- *Access to networks or associations.* Focus groups were asked to estimate whether access to networks and associations within the village had increased or decreased (or had remained the same) over 10 years.

Community variables constructed from household survey instrument. The household questionnaire contains several questions about household perceptions, including perceptions of the responsiveness of the local democratic structure and perceptions of the household's own empowerment and aspirations. An average of household responses for these questions cannot be treated as an indicator of a responsive local democracy or of an empowered community. At best, the responses are indicators of the "perception of democracy" or "perception of empowerment" based on the sample surveyed within a community.

Furthermore, it could well be that some households answered that their local democracy is responsive because they have had an opportunity to participate in it or derive benefits from it. However, one household's participation can have a strong "chilling" or "crowding out" effect on other households in the same community. The association of the average or net perception therefore may not necessarily be the sum of individual perceptions (Alatas, Pritchett, and Wetterberg 2007).

In order to distinguish between private effects (association of the own household's perceptions with outcomes) and social effects (impact of one household on other households), we use the fact that our sampling is by communities. We can therefore calculate for each community both the perception of each household (private effect) and perceptions of all *other* households in the community (social effect). Consider as an example the response to the following question: "Compared to 10 years ago, does the local government now pay more, less, or about the same attention to what people like you think when it decides what to do?" The leave-out mean for a given individual is simply the perception of local government responsiveness of all other individuals in their community, leaving out that one person.

The use of leave-out means is an attempt to disentangle social effects from private effects or pure household perceptions by aggregating all individual responses in community j, except for household i. Suppose there were a linear, causal relationship between the mobility of poor household i in village j and whether it reports higher local government responsiveness and the perceptions of government responsiveness of all other households in the community.

$$\text{MPI}^{i,j} = \alpha + \beta_{HH}(\text{LG}^{i,j}) + \beta_{LOM}(\text{LG}^{-i,j})$$

The *private* impact of the ith household's perceptions of the local government on the likelihood that it moves up is the coefficient β_{HH}.

The impact of the ith household's perceptions of the local government on all other households in the community is to raise the "community less household" average by $1/N^j$ for each household. The *social* impact of the ith household's perceptions of the local government is then β_{LOM}/N^j on each other household in the community. This could be zero if there is no interaction at all. However, if the ith household's positive perceptions of responsiveness are influenced by the benefits it derives from a zero-sum public good, say a local public works program from which the ith household benefits by excluding others, the social impact on others could be negative (in fact, it would have to be negative). In this case the net impact on mobility of the poor associated with the ith household's perceptions of local government responsiveness is just the sum of the private and social impacts—but it cannot be assumed to be the sum of the individual coefficients alone.

Using principal components to combine conceptually related variables

For many of the phenomena that the analyst might wish to elicit and examine, it is impossible to know with any precision which question will produce the most reliable responses. Hence questionnaires often include questions on closely related concepts. When data are to be used in multivariate regressions this leaves the analyst with four options. We chose to combine conceptually similar questions into a single index using principal components.

A word about the three options rejected. One is "profligacy," simply including in the regressions all of the possible variables. This has the advantage of "letting the data decide," but it has the disadvantages of creating regressions with 50 or more individual variables and of producing massive multicollinearity if the variables are in fact closely related conceptually. A second option is to choose the "best" indicator for each conceptual category. This can be done a priori, which runs the risk of choosing the empirically least successful (e.g., most subject to measurement error), or it can be done based on "horse races" of available candidates, which is the very definition of data mining. The third option is to use some index based on a weighted average of the questions. This has the advantage of reducing the numbers of variables and avoids data mining, but the weights are arbitrary. A common practice of using "equal" weights has nothing in particular to recommend it.

The technique of principal components is a commonly used data reduction technique that reduces a set of variables to a single variable. Principal components analyzes the correlations between a set of variables and produces a set of weighted averages of the underlying variables such that (a) each captures the maximum common variation among the set of variables, and (b) each additional factor after the first is orthogonal to the previous factor. So the first factor is a linear weighted average of the set of N variables with weights chosen so as to maximize the overall common variance of all the variables.

While in many ways the index produced is arbitrary, this does have three advantages. First, it is not data mining, as it does not use any information about the dependent variable in choosing the specification. Second, it chooses weights that, if the set of N variables are truly conceptually related, statistically best capture the common variation. Third, since it is a linear index it is relative easy to map back from the underlying variable through the regression coefficient to the association with the dependent variable.

We did the principal components analysis study region by study region, rather than imposing common weights across all study regions. The results for each study region for each PCA-constructed variable are presented in appendix 4. First, whenever there are only two variables, PCA just produced equal weights. Second, the results are mostly in accord with expectations. All variables are recoded so that movements in the same direction numerically represent movement in the same conceptual direction (this is not necessarily true in the raw questions). We see that most of the PCA therefore produce, as expected, indexes with all positive weights, often nearly equal. But third, there is considerable variation across countries in the weights, including some negative values. Rather than attempt to choose the "best" fit for each study region, we just implemented the data reduction technique for each and used the weights produced.

The only way in which this process differed from the perfectly garden-variety PCA was that we wanted an index of conditions 10 years ago. But rather than using the PCA weights from 10 years ago, we did PCA on the current variables and then used those weights to construct an index for 10 years ago, based on the values of the underlying variables from that time.

Once we had the PCA scores we could infer the estimated associated with each individual component variable in that index with the dependent variable (MOP or MPI). To do so, we proceeded in two steps. First, we used the PCA weights to calculate how much a change in an individual component of the index would change the index (which involved the variance of the component because PCA norms the raw variables) would produce in the PCA score. Next, we multiplied this value with the ordinary least squares (OLS) regression coefficient for the PCA score to estimate the concomitant associated change in MOP/MPI.

Here is an example of going from raw component to estimated association when PCA has been used. Take the case of the study region in Uttar Pradesh, where aspirations had a significant positive association with an initially poor household's ability to move out of poverty over 10 years. Considering the individual components of the aspirations index, we find that a 2-unit increase in beliefs about one's own future (1 = worse off, 3 = better off) is associated with a change of nearly 2 units in the aspirations index using the following formula:

Change in PCA index = (loading on individual component × range
of individual component)/standard error of
individual component

(for aspirations in Uttar Pradesh) = $(0.7071 \times 2)/0.708$

The subsequent change of 2 units in the PCA index for aspirations when multiplied with the OLS regression coefficient for household aspirations in Uttar Pradesh (0.1405) is associated with an increase of nearly 28 percent in the likelihood of escaping poverty.

Functional Form and Weights

Functional form

An OLS model was used for running regressions. Since the dependent variable is a binary outcome (0/1), this is sometimes referred to as the linear probability model (LPM). It is well known that with a limited dependent variable, there are estimation techniques (such as probit and logit) that are more statistically efficient. This is because by imposing in estimation the constraint (which must be true) that the predictions of outcomes by the regression techniques have to be strictly between zero and one, these techniques produce lower standard errors than OLS.

We did not do this, however, for three reasons. First, the loss from not using a logit or probit estimator is only efficiency (a second-order property of estimators), not consistency, and we suspect that in this case the gains to precision are not particularly meaningful. Second, the LPM has ease of interpretation, particularly when moving from the underlying PCA-constructed indexes to the reporting of outcome associations. Third, with nonlinear functional forms like logit and probit, the use of the leave-out means is much more complicated.

All of the standard errors used the standard adjustment to be consistent with cluster-based sampling using the cluster techniques available in Stata data analysis software.

While a complete specification was run for the study regions in India, a relatively parsimonious model was used for the non-India study regions, where sample sizes were much smaller. The sparse specification excluded the PCA index on fairness, the PCA index for social inequality in schools, and ownership of land. Leave-out means were only included for the responsiveness of local democracy and personal agency PCAs.

Weighted versus unweighted regressions

The structure of the sampling of those who were interviewed for the household instrument produces four issues about weights, even though in this appendix we are focused on the regressions.

Let us use a simple example to illustrate these issues. Suppose in a given country 25 percent of the population consists of red people and 75 percent of blue people. Red people are taller on average than blue people. Suppose an instrument contains observations on height and weight. Finally, assume the sample was chosen to have equal numbers of red and blue people (so red people were oversampled).

First, since sampling was not random, the overall averages from the household surveys of any characteristic are not consistent estimates of the sampled population. The unweighted average height would be wrong about the average height of the population, as red people are taller and are oversampled. In the present study, this means that since the movers were oversampled, if they are different, the overall averages of characteristics from household surveys are not estimates of the overall average of the population characteristics.

Second, as long as the individuals *within* the groups are chosen randomly, then summary statistics of the *differences* across the groups on an unweighted basis are consistent. In the example, comparing red people's average height to blue people's average height is a consistent estimate of the subpopulation heights.

Third, all of the regression results reported are unweighted in the global study. For the regressions themselves, since we assume a linear functional form, the issue of weighted versus unweighted regressions is an issue of estimator efficiency (in that the weighted estimates might produce lower standard errors), but not one of consistency.

Returning to the example, suppose that there is a linear relationship between height and weight and that linear relationship is the same for red and blue people. In this case an unweighted regression would produce a consistent estimate of the relationship between height and weight, even though red people are oversampled.

It is possible that using sampling weights would produce a more efficient (lower standard errors) estimator, but our view is that these gains are likely to be small and we don't want to give ourselves over to *t*-statistic fetishism in any case. That is, if the difference between "statistical significance" (usually taken as rejecting the null hypothesis at some standard significance level such as 5 percent or 1 percent) is whether estimates are weighted or unweighted, it would be questionable to make much of the relationship in any case. This is a general point about reported empirical work, not about our report, as in most instances there are large deviations of the actually applied statistical procedures and the conditions under which the classic theory of hypothesis testing are valid.

Moreover, if the weighted and unweighted partial association estimates were to differ—which they do not, for the most part, in the cases where this has been explored—this would not be an indication that the weighted results are to be preferred. In fact, heuristically, the differences between unweighted and weighted results can be thought of as a Hausman-like (1978) test for model specification. Since under the maintained null used in estimating an OLS regression the unweighted and weighted are both consistent for the "true" coefficient, this implies that they should also converge (in large samples) to be "near" one another. Hence, a large difference (where "large" would be normed for statistical tests by the appropriate variance-covariance matrix of the difference between the two estimators) between weighted and unweighted results suggests model misspecification. But as this type of test is an omnibus specification test (that is, it has power against many forms of misspecification), a difference between weighted and unweighted to first order is difficult to interpret and cannot be taken to mean the weighted result is "better."

Fourth, there is a tricky final issue, not about the weighting of the regressions in general but about leave-out means. These are used, in some sense, as "community characteristics," and thus although they are not reported they might seem to fall under the first category of not using the unweighted results to estimate summary statistics of characteristics. But there are two points. One, this does maintain the assumption of the linearity of the effect, so we assume that in the leave-out mean the impact on a mover of a having a higher value of the variable of a faller or never poor person is the same, so in that case the same issue of linearity discussed above applies. Second, as long as the sampling was done consistently across villages, the bias as community variables of the sample should be (roughly, on average) constant across villages.

However, in this volume on the study in India, the authors of individual chapters and several reviewers wanted us to report both weighted and unweighted regressions. We still give primacy to unweighted results, except in Andhra Pradesh.

Notes

1. This technical note replicates appendix 2 of the second volume in the Moving Out of Poverty series (*Success from the Bottom Up;* Narayan, Pritchett, and Kapoor 2009), with minor modifications reflecting the Indian case studies.

Appendix 2:
Data Collection Methods

Activity	Data collection method	Purpose	Sources of information
1	Selective literature review	• Provide background to the key growth and poverty puzzles in the country • Help design the study	Secondary sources
2	Key informant interview or workshop: national timeline	• Identify policy questions to be addressed by the study • Develop a national timeline of key events and policies that have helped or hindered people's movements out of poverty	Policy experts from government, civil society, and private sector
3	Community profile	• Identify community-level factors that have helped or hindered movement out of poverty and the overall prosperity of the community over the past 10 years • Quantify and code data emerging from focus discussions based on their ratings of issues ranging from community prosperity to freedom and inequality	Key informants Focus group discussions
4	Key informant interview: community timeline	• Understand community-level events or factors that have helped or hindered movement out of poverty and the overall prosperity of the community • Gain an understanding of the local context	2–4 key informants in a group or individually

5	Focus group discussion: ladder of life	• Identify the range of factors that help or hinder movement out of poverty or prosperity over time at the community level	1 focus group of adult men 1 focus group of adult women
		• Identify the range of factors that help or hinder movement out of poverty or prosperity over time at the household level, and the reasons for movement at the different levels	
		• Identify the sequencing and interaction among factors at the household level that enable movement between different steps of the ladder of life	
		• Identify the mobility status of specific households in the community	
6	Focus group discussion: livelihoods, freedom, power, democracy, and local governance	• Understand trends in economic opportunities for the community	1 focus group of adult men 1 focus group of adult women
		• Understand the impact of government rules and regulations and other factors on access to economic opportunities	Depending on the local context, this activity can be conducted as one discussion or there can be 2 sections discussing (a) sources of economic opportunities and the role of governance, and (b) freedom, power, inequality, and democracy. If there are 2 sections, a total of 4 focus group discussions per community will be needed for this activity.
		• Explore people's understanding of the concepts of freedom, power, and inequality, and how these concepts relate to economic mobility and well-being	
		• Explore people's understanding of democracy and how democracy is working at the local level	

Activity	Data collection method	Purpose	Sources of information
7	Focus group discussion: aspirations of youth	• Explore youths' aspirations for earning a living and steps they are taking to prepare for their future • Explore youths' understandings of the concepts of freedom, power, inequality, and democracy, and how these concepts relate to economic mobility and well-being	1 focus group of male youths 1 focus group of female youths
8	Two mini–case studies: community-wide events and factors affecting mobility	• Provide in-depth analysis from a range of perspectives on two important events or factors affecting the overall economic prosperity of the community over the past 10 years	Key informants and focus group discussions
9	Household questionnaire	• Identify the range of factors that help or hinder mobility of individuals within the larger context of their households	For countries with panel data: Depending on panel sample size and sampling strategy chosen, the team should revisit panel households and interview an adult member of the household (30–60 years of age). If it is not possible to identify a large enough sample from the panel, individuals may be randomly selected from households identified by the ladder of life focus group discussion as belonging to a particular mobility category. For countries without panel data: Select informants based on the household sorting exercise undertaken during the ladder of life focus group discussion.

| 10 | Open-ended interviews: individual life stories | • Understand how and why some individuals escaped poverty, and the factors and processes that led to their escape

• Understand how and why some individuals managed to stay out of poverty, and the factors and processes that helped them maintain their wealth

• Understand how and why some individuals remained trapped in chronic poverty, and the factors and processes that kept them in poverty

• Understand how and why some individuals fell into poverty, and the factors and processes that led to their decline

• Understand the factors and processes that come together for accumulation or depletion of assets and savings | Adults (men or women) 30–60 years of age. It is important that a household questionnaire be completed with each informant who provides an individual life story. Identification of informants follows a process similar to selection of informants for the questionnaire. |

Appendix 3: List of Variables for Household Regressions

Explanatory variable	Source	Coding/directionality
Economic opportunity		
Initial strength of economy (PCA index[a])		
Strength of local economy 10 years ago (rc205b)	KI	very weak = 1, very strong = 5
Presence of private employers 10 years ago (rc208b)	KI	yes = 1, no = 0
Difficulty of finding a job 10 years ago (rc209b)	KI	very difficult = 1, very easy = 6
Changes in economic prosperity (PCA index)		
Whether easier or harder to make a living (rc904)	FGD	harder = 1, easier = 2
Trend in community prosperity (rc903)	FGD	less prosperous = 1, more prosperous = 3
Trend in available economic opportunities (rc912)	FGD	fewer = 1, more = 3
Trend in access to economic opportunities (rc917)	FGD	fewer have access = 1, more have access = 3
Local democracy		
Responsiveness of local democracy (PCA index)		
Trust in local government officials (rh415bi)	HH	not at all = 1, to a very great extent = 5
Satisfaction with democracy in local government (rh511)	HH	very dissatisfied = 1, very satisfied = 4
Extent to which local government takes into account concerns (rh502b)	HH	less = 1, more = 3
Ability to influence actions of local government (rh504)	HH	decreased = 1, increased = 3
Corruption (PCA index)		
Corruption in government officials at the country level (c505b)	KI	almost none = 1, almost all = 4
Corruption in government officials in village (c506b)	KI	almost none = 1, almost all = 4
Corruption in government officials in community (c924)	FGD	almost none = 1, almost all = 4

Fairness

Fairness index (PCA index)

Farmers getting fair prices (rh240b)	HH	deteriorated = 1, improved = 3
Fairness in treatment by law in community (rh606b)	HH	yes = 1, no = 0
Denied credit (h234)	HH	yes = 1, no = 2
Expectation of denial of credit (h236)	HH	yes = 1, no = 2

Violence against women

Violence against women in households 10 years ago (h609b)	HH	none at all = 1, very much = 4

Individual agency

Initial position on 10-step ladder of power and rights (h708)	HH	scale from 1 to 10
Control over everyday decisions (trend) (rh501b)	HH	less = 1, more = 3

Household aspirations (PCA index)

Aspirations for self (rh716)	HH	worse off = 1, better off = 3
Aspirations for future generation (rh717)	HH	worse off = 1, better off = 3

Collective agency

Index of collective action (PCA index[a])

Coming together to solve water problems 10 years ago (rc412b)	KI	very unlikely = 1, very likely = 4
Coming together to assist each other 10 years ago (rc413b)	KI	very unlikely = 1, very likely = 4

Access to networks and associations

Change in access to networks and associations within the community (rc919)	FGD	less access = 1, more access = 3

Explanatory variable	Source	Coding/directionality
Social stratification		
Extent of social divisions in the village 10 years ago		
Differences between people based on ethnicity, caste, etc., 10 years ago (c414b)	KI	no division = 1, to a very great extent = 5
Change in school inequality		
Ethnic/religious discrimination in schools (c305b)	KI	improved = 1, deteriorated = 3
Gender discrimination in schools (c304b)	KI	improved = 1, deteriorated = 3
Control variables		
Present education status of household head[b] (h106)	HH	no schooling = 1, university = 8
Health shocks over 10 years (rh305)	HH	yes = 1, no = 0
Initial landholding (h204 i+ii+iii+iv)b[c]	HH	number of hectares owned
Ownership of house 10 years ago (rh206b)	HH	whether owned (yes = 1, no = 0)
Initial assets index (PCA index[a] of assets owned 10 years ago) (rh201 i-xiii)b	HH	whether owned (yes = 1, no = 0)
Initial livestock index (PCA index[a] of assets owned 10 years ago) (rh203 i-x)b	HH	whether owned (yes = 1, no = 0)
State-specific control variables		
Uttar Pradesh		
Change in access to irrigation over 10 years (rc219iii)	KI	deteriorated substantially = 1, improved substantially = 5
SC dummy (compared to the general caste category)	HH	
OBC dummy (compared to the general caste category)	HH	

West Bengal

SC dummy (compared to the general caste category)	HH	
ST dummy (compared to the general caste category)	HH	
District dummies (five sample districts)		
Source of income 10 years ago (rh208b)	HH	multiple sources = 1, single source = 0
Religion of head of household (h025)	HH	Muslim = 1, others = 0
Sex of head of household (rh102)	HH	male = 1, female = 0
Age of head of household (h104)	HH	age in years
Membership in groups 10 years ago (h401+h402+h403+h404+h405+h406)b	HH	number of groups household belonged to 10 years ago
Political activism (PCA index of political activism over 10 years) (rh503 i-ix)d	HH	yes = 1, no = 0

Assam

Conflict trajectory	FGD: conflict timeline	peace to peace = 1, peace to conflict = 2, conflict to peace = 3, conflict to conflict = 4

Note: Reference questions in the community questionnaire are indicated by *c* and in the household questionnaire by *h*. Prefix *r* means variable was recoded. Suffix *a* means current (at time of the study); *b* means initial (approximately 10 years ago). KI = key informant; FGD = focus group discussion; HH = household.

a. A PCA was first done on current conditions, and weights were applied to initial conditions 10 years ago. A weighted average of initial conditions (with current weights) was then used as an explanatory variable.

b. In the survey, the education level of the household head is measured in 2005, but it is unlikely to have changed significantly over the previous 10 years for an adult head of household.

c. The symbols i, ii, iii, and iv signify irrigated land, unirrigated temporary crop land, unirrigated permanent crop land, and grazing land/wasteland respectively.

d. Question asks whether household has done any of the following in the past 10 years: attended an organized meeting of residents to discuss community issues, met a local politician, met a national politician, participated in protest or information campaign, and notified police or media about a local problem.

Appendix 4: Weights for the PCA-Constructed Indexes, by State

	Uttar Pradesh	Andhra Pradesh	West Bengal	Assam
Initial strength of local economy				
Strength of local economy, 10 years ago (rc205b)	0.47	0.57	0.72	−0.05
Presence of private employers, 10 years ago (rc208b)	0.6	0.54	0.17	0.71
Difficulty in finding a job, 10 years ago (rc209b)	0.65	0.62	0.68	0.7
	1.72	*1.73*	*1.56*	*1.36*
Changes in economic prosperity				
Trend in community prosperity (rc903)	0.58	n.a. (rc903 used directly)	0.55	0.5
Whether easier or harder to make a living (rc904)	0.42		0.66	0.44
Trend in available economic opportunities (rc912)	0.54		0.41	0.49
Trend in access to economic opportunities (rc917)	0.45		0.3	0.56
	1.98		*1.92*	*1.99*
Responsiveness of local democracy				
Trust in local government officials (rh415bi)	0.39	0.47	0.51	0.36
Satisfaction with democracy in local government (rh511)	0.53	0.47	0.57	0.57
Extent to which local government takes into account concerns (rh502b)	0.58	0.56	0.22	0.51
Ability to influence actions of local government (rh504)	0.49	0.49	0.61	0.54
	1.98	*1.99*	*1.9*	*1.98*
Corruption				
Corruption in government officials at the country level (c505b)	0.67	0.71	0.7	0.68
Corruption in government officials in village (c506b)	0.69	0.71	0.71	0.73
Corruption in government officials in community (c924)	0.28	n.a.	0.09	0.06
	1.64	*1.41*	*1.5*	*1.47*
Fairness				
Farmers getting fair prices (rh240b)	0.13	n.a. (rh606b used directly)	0.32	0.23

	Uttar Pradesh	Andhra Pradesh	West Bengal	Assam
Fairness in treatment by law within community (rh606b)	0.23		0.5	0.08
Denied credit (h234)	0.67		0.69	0.7
Expectation of denial of credit (h236)	0.7		0.41	0.68
	1.72		*1.92*	*1.68*
Household aspirations				
Aspirations for self (rh716)	0.71	0.71	0.71	0.71
Aspirations for future generation (rh717)	0.71	0.71	0.71	0.71
	1.41	*1.41*	*1.41*	*1.41*
Collective action				
Coming together to solve water problems, 10 years ago (rc412b)	0.71	0.71	0.71	0.71
Coming together to assist each other 10 years ago (rc413b)	0.71	0.71	0.71	0.71
	1.41	*1.41*	*1.41*	*1.41*
School inequality				
Ethnic/religious discrimination in schools (c305b)	0.71	0.71	0.71	0.71
Gender discrimination in schools (c304b)	0.71	0.71	0.71	0.71
	1.41	*1.41*	*1.41*	*1.41*
Political Activism				
Attended organized meeting of residents to discuss community issues (h503i)	n.a.	n.a.	0.31	n.a.
Attended neighborhood council meeting, public hearing/discussion (h503ii)			0.43	
Met with local politician, called him/her, or sent letter (h503iii)			0.35	
Met with national politician, called him/her, or sent letter (h503iv)			0.27	
Signed petition to make demand from local/national government (h503v)			0.26	
Participated in protest or demonstration (h503vi)			0.36	
Participated in information or election campaign (h503vii)			0.42	
Alerted newspaper, radio, or TV to a local problem (h503viii)			0.22	
Notified police or court about local problem (h503ix)			0.31	
			2.94	

Index

NA →

Boxes, figures, notes, and tables are indicated by b, f, n, and t following the page number.

453

ECO-AUDIT
Environmental Benefits Statement

The World Bank is committed to preserving endangered forests and natural resources. We have chosen to print *Moving Out of Poverty (vol. 3): The Promise of Empowerment and Democracy in India* on 60-pound Roland Opaque, a recycled paper with 30% post-consumer waste. The Office of the Publisher has agreed to follow the recommended standards for paper usage set by the Green Press Initiative, a nonprofit program supporting publishers in using fiber that is not sourced from endangered forests. For more information, visit www.greenpressinitiative.org.

Saved:

- **18** trees
- **13 million** BTUs of total energy
- **1,587** pounds of net greenhouse gases
- **6,589** gallons of waste water
- **846** pounds of solid waste

green
press
INITIATIVE